NON-GOVERNMENTAL ORGANIZATIONS AND
RURAL POVERTY ALLEVIATION

Non-Governmental Organizations and Rural Poverty Alleviation

ROGER C. RIDDELL
MARK ROBINSON

WITH
JOHN DE CONINCK, ANN MUIR, *AND*
SARAH WHITE

Overseas Development Institute · London

CLARENDON PRESS · OXFORD
1995

Oxford University Press, Walton Street, Oxford OX2 6DP

Oxford New York
Athens Auckland Bangkok Bombay
Calcutta Cape Town Dar es Salaam Delhi
Florence Hong Kong Istanbul Karachi
Kuala Lumpur Madras Madrid Melbourne
Mexico City Nairobi Paris Singapore
Taipei Tokyo Toronto
and associated companies in
Berlin Ibadan

Oxford is a trade mark of Oxford University Press

Published in the United States
by Oxford University Press Inc., New York

British Library Cataloguing in Publication Data
Data available

Library of Congress Cataloging in Publication Data
Riddell, Roger.
Non-governmental organizations and rural poverty alleviation /
Roger C. Riddell, Mark Robinson ; with John de Coninck, Ann Muir,
and Sarah White.
Published in association with Overseas Development Institute,
London.
Includes bibliographical references.
1. Non-governmental organizations—Developing countries. 2. Non-
governmental organizations—Developing countries—Case studies.
3. Rural poor—Developing countries. 4. Rural poor—Developing
countries—Case studies. I. Robinson, Mark, 1951- . II. Title.
HC59.7.R493 1995 338.9'1'091724—dc20 95-20181
ISBN 0–19–823330–2

1 3 5 7 9 10 8 6 4 2

Typeset by Graphicraft Typesetters Ltd., Hong Kong

Printed in Great Britain
on acid-free paper by
Biddles Ltd., Guildford & King's Lynn

CONTENTS

FOREWORD

The greatest single challenge to aid agencies and governments in developing countries is poverty in rural areas. Virtually all the major social and environmental problems of developing countries arise directly or indirectly from the persistence of rural poverty and the consequent movement of the rural poor into urban areas where, usually, there is neither the work nor the services to provide support. In the West, the most powerful images of third world poverty are of rural people, impoverished by war, natural disasters or economic exploitation.

This developmental, and ethical, challenge of rural poverty has dominated development policies from the 1960s, when the World Bank, in particular, made this the central component of its purpose and strategy. Yet political will, even large amounts of aid directed towards 'integrated rural development'—a proxy for rural poverty— have not substantially altered the prospects for the poorest people in rural areas.

In more recent times, improved economic incentives have not had much effect on subsistence producers poorly connected to markets. The widespread provision of capital, especially through subsidized credit, has not produced long-term changes in productive assets. Technology to improve productivity of land and labour has often been ill-suited to those unwilling to risk changes to existing patterns of technology. Many poor people still cling to social relationships with local landlords, farmers, and merchants, and distrust efforts to challenge the power of the existing order.

However, after several decades of relative failure in rural poverty programmes a new consensus has emerged on what may be needed to assist the poorest to escape from the conditions of poverty. This revolves around four propositions: the first is that the identification of opportunities for change comes most frequently from within the communities of the poor and the way forward can only be found by working with the poor and obtaining their 'participation'. The second proposition is that this, in turn, requires external agencies to become more flexible and innovative as large project bureaucracies or government ministries cannot easily devise local approaches to assisting the poor. The third proposition is that commitment and patience, and willingness to listen are essential to effective poverty work. The fourth is that the purely economic and technical approach to poverty lacks a social and political dimension and, in particular, fails to recognize the need to encourage the poor to assert their rights, particularly through group action. As an NGO leader interviewed for this study has claimed, 'The poverty of the mind is our greatest challenge'. Others talk of 'empowerment', especially in stratified South Asian societies where relative poverty is seen as a natural condition, and dependence and subservience are a requirement of maintaining social and economic order.

All these concerns together—participation, flexibility, commitment, and a social dimension—have led to a re-examination of the non-governmental sector which, on the face of it, has considerable advantages over governments and official agencies in addressing poverty. The sector has a tradition of selectively working with the poor (and has the ability to exclude the non-poor in ways that governments—with more universal responsibilities—cannot); it has a relative emphasis upon small-scale projects; and it has a tradition of voluntarism and ethics as a basis for its activities. Thus NGOs have come to be seen as the natural partners of the rural poor.

For official donors there have been several trends in response to this changing consensus on assisting the poor: first, to channel more of their own aid through NGOs; second, to involve NGOs in implementing parts of their own programmes; and, third, to try to incorporate NGO best practice into official programmes. The emphasis on the NGO approach has been strengthened by NGOs' own advocacy: their supporters have been constantly reminded of successful work with the poor, and this has formed the basis of much of the fundraising effort by NGOs.

This change in policy towards NGOs provided the background to the major ODI study which forms the basis of this book. Our initial question was 'Are NGOs better at reaching the poor than governments and official donors?' It is possible to reach judgements on this, especially in specific countries, but this was not, in the event, the question we set ourselves. Instead, we decided to ask whether the record of achievement of NGOs could justify claims for their effectiveness in assisting the poor, and if so, what special characteristics of NGOs could explain their impact on rural poverty.

We recognize that NGOs are not solely concerned with rural poverty and that their effectiveness should not be judged by rural poverty alleviation alone. Similarly, NGOs should not be judged solely by criteria of economic benefits to the poor, such as rises in living standards or acquisition of assets. Several NGOs in this study, for example, regard their effectiveness in terms of the human spirit and political action as much as by economic status.

None the less, the level of incomes and assets of the rural poor are an important measure because this is a key barometer for development assistance as a whole. If NGOs are making a significant impact, this would be encouraging to all of those involved in development. If NGOs have made less impact than some of their supporters claim, this is also important to ascertain as, ultimately, only the evidence of well-informed empirical research will sustain public support for NGOs in their most formidable task. This book provides such evidence on the impact and effectiveness of NGOs and, while its results may not always read comfortably, it marks a major step in placing the NGO contribution to rural poverty in its proper perspective.

John Howell
Director, Overseas Development Institute

ACKNOWLEDGEMENTS

Numerous people contributed to the production of this book, both in the UK and in the four countries in which the research was undertaken. John Howell, the Director of ODI, played an instrumental role in providing intellectual support and encouragement throughout. Special thanks are also due to our research advisory committee, in providing advice on the scope and purpose of the research and in commenting on drafts of the research findings as they emerged. In this respect we would like to thank the following people: Jane Cocking, Cathy Corcoran, Mike Edwards, Hugh Goyder, Eric Hanley, Rip Hodson, Shakeeb Khan, Stephen King, John Morris, Paul Robson, Frances Rubin, Paul Spray, and David Wright.

We would also like to acknowledge the contributions made by our research collaborators, as well as the NGOs that took part in the study. In India, the former include Anitha Kumari Amma, Koshy Cherail, Rajani Kumar, and Sampath Kumar. Within the individual NGOs, we would like to thank Vincent and Anne Ferrer, Damodaram, Lalitha, Sampath, Sanjivi and Ignatius Sunder Raj at the Rural Development Trust, J. K. Michael, S. Devadas, Eric D'Souza, Jayant Kumar, Poonaswamy and John Victor at Church's Auxiliary for Social Action, Veeraiah and Vijaya Mohan at Arthik Samata Mandal, and Lucas, Maria Dhas, and Xavier at the Kanyakumari District Fishermen Sangams Federation.

In Bangladesh, special thanks are due to the staff of the four NGOs which participated in the study: Stuart Rutherford and Md. Mukhlesur Rahman of ActionAid Bangladesh; Md. Shafiuddin and Dhirendro Kumar Ray of the Gono Kallyan Trust; Md. Ataur Rahman, Ali Reza, Md. Ali Reja Raj, S. A. Emadaduk Pattu, and Ajit Kumar Biswas of Gono Ullayan Prochesta; and Alo D'Rozario, Bernard Corraya, and Sri Birendronath Roy of Caritas Bangladesh. The assistance of Farid Hasan, Enamul Kabir, Ruksana Samad, and Farmeeda Zaman in conducting the field research is also gratefully acknowledged.

In Uganda, special thanks are due to Mary Nannono, Sam Kayabwe, and Alan Tulip who worked on the case-studies, and to the staff of the four NGOs which participated in the study: Sarah Mangali at the Uganda Women's Finance and Credit Trust; Margaret and colleagues at the Multi-Sectoral Rural Development Programme; various staff at the West Acholi Cooperative Union and ACORD; and Christopher Muyingo and Faustine Vuningoma in ActionAid Uganda.

For the Zimbabwe case-study, we would like to acknowledge the support of the staff and officials of Silveira House, especially Fr. Roland Von Nidda and Brian MacGarry; Christian Care; Mr S. Matandike and the National Organisation of Non-Governmental Organisations in Zimbabwe; Dr Rob Munro and staff at the Zimbabwe Trust both in Zimbabwe and in the United Kingdom; the Collective Self-Financing Scheme; Ms Judy Acton and Mr Paul Nyathi of the Zimbabwe Project; the Simukai Collective Farming Cooperative, and especially Mr Andrew Nyathi; Professor Marshall

Murphree and staff at the Centre for Applied Social Studies at the University of Zimbabwe; Sister Veronica Brand and Ms Frances Chinemasa.

At the ODI in London various people contributed at different stages from initial research to final production, and their combined assistance played a significant part in raising the quality of the work undertaken. Particular thanks go to Kate Cumberland, Geraldine Healy, Peter Gee, Jane Kennan, Pippa Leask, Moira Reddick, and last, but by no means least, to Margaret Cornell for her much appreciated editorial and indexing skills.

Finally, acknowledgement needs to be made to those organizations which assisted financially. These were the Economic and Social Committee on Overseas Research and the Evaluations Department of the Overseas Development Administration; the Leverhulme Trust; Barclays Bank and five British NGOs: ActionAid, CAFOD, Christian Aid, OXFAM, and the Save the Children Fund. However, none of these organizations are in any way responsible for the comments and conclusions contained in this book, which remain our own.

R.C.R.
M.R.

LIST OF ABBREVIATIONS

ACORD	Agency for Co-operation and Research in Development
ADAB	Association for Development Agencies in Bangladesh
AFC	Agricultural Finance Corporation (Zimbabwe)
AMP	ActionAid Mityana Programme
ARDA	Agricultural and Rural Development Authority
ASM	Arthik Samata Mandal
BRAC	Bangladesh Rural Advancement Committee
BRDB	Bangladesh Rural Development Board
CAFOD	Catholic Fund for Overseas Development
CAMPFIRE	Communal Areas Management Programme
CAPART	Council for the Advancement of People's Action and Rural Technology
CARE	Co-operative Agency for Relief Everywhere
CASA	Churches' Auxiliary for Social Action
CASS	Centre of Applied Social Science (University of Zimbabwe)
CBA	Cost-Benefit Analysis
CCF	Community Credit Fund
CDO	Community Development Officer
CEBEMO	Centrale voor de Bemmiddeling bij Medfinanciering van Ontwikkelingsprogramm's (Netherlands)
CHS	Community Health Services
CIDA	Canadian International Development Agency
CITES	Convention on International Trade in Endangered Species
CMB	Cotton Marketing Board
COP	Community Organizaton Programme
COTA	le Collectif d'Echanges pour la Technologie Apropriée (Belgium)
CSFS	Collective Self-Financing Scheme
DCSO	district council safari operation
DAC	Development Assistance Committee
DDF	District Development Fund
DEEDS	Development Extension Education Services
DENIVA	Development Network of Indigenous Voluntary Associations
DNPWLM	Department of National Parks and Wildlife Management
DTW	deep tube-well
EZE	Evangelische Zentralstelle für Entwicklungshilfe
FAO	Food and Agriculture Organization

FCR	fibro-cement roofing
FCRA	Foreign Contributions Regulation Act (India)
FOS	Fonds voor Ontwikkelingssamenwerkingoperation (Belgium)
GDCWC	Guruve District Council Wildlife Committee (Zimbabwe)
GDP	Gross Domestic Product
GKT	Gono Kallyan Trust
GMB	Grain Marketing Board
GNP	Gross National Product
GSO	Grass-roots Support Organization
GUP	Gono Unnayan Prochesta
HDI	Human Development Index
HDR	Human Development Report
HIVOS	Humanist Institute for Co-operation with Developing Countries (Netherlands)
IAF	Inter-American Foundation
ICCO	Interkerklijke Coördinatie Commissie voor Ontwikkelingsprojekten
IDA	International Development Association
IFAD	International Fund for Agricultural Development
IGP	Income-Generating Project
ILO	International Labour Office
IRDP	Integrated Rural Development Programme
ITDG	Intermediate Technology Development Group
KDFSF	Kanyakumari District Fisherman Sangams Federation
LDC	Less Developed Country
MSO	Membership Support Organization
MSRDP	Multi-Sectoral Rural Development Programme
NANGO	National Association of Non-Governmental Organizations (Zimbabwe)
NCVSS	National Council for Voluntary Social Services
NGDO	Non-Governmental Development Organization
NGO	Non-Governmental Organization
NOVIB	Netherlands Organisatie voor Internationale Ontwikkelingssamenwerking
NRM	National Resistance Movement (Uganda)
OBM	out-board motor
OCCZIM	Organization for Collective Co-operatives in Zimbabwe
ODA	Overseas Development Administration
oda	official development assistance
ODI	Overseas Development Institute (London)
OECD	Organization for Economic Co-operation and Development

OJ	Operation Joseph
ORAP	Organization of Rural Associations for Progress (Zimbabwe)
PPRLF	Pump-Priming Revolving Loan Fund
PVO	Private Voluntary Organization (USA)
RC	Resistance Committee
RDT	Rural Development Trust
RLF	Revolving Loan Fund
SCF	Save the Children Fund
SCFC	Simukai Collective Farming Co-operative
STW	shallow tube-well
TSTU	Technical Skills Training Unit
UNDP	United Nations' Development Programme
UNIDO	United Nations' Industrial Development Organization
USAID	United States Agency for International Development
UWFCT	Uganda Women's Finance and Credit Trust
VANI	Voluntary Action Network India
VOICE	Voluntary Organizations in Community Enterprise (Zimbabwe)
WACU	West Acholi Co-operative Engineering Union
WID	Women in Development
WWB	Women's World Banking
WWC	ward wildlife committee
WWF	Worldwide Fund for Nature
ZIMFEP	Zimbabwe Foundation for Education with Production

1

Introduction

Until recently, the activities of non-governmental organizations (NGOs) in developing countries were widely considered to be peripheral to the mainstream efforts of governments and official aid agencies to resolve the problems of world poverty. Studies at universities and development centres rarely examined the role and impact of NGOs in the development process, and few development journals carried articles about NGOs. The development profession viewed NGO projects as, at best, interesting oddities, but more widespread was the view that they were largely irrelevant to what were considered the more fundamental issues of development.

By the early 1990s, all this had changed. Together with issues such as women and the environment, NGOs have become 'fashionable' in more orthodox development circles. The universities now run courses and seminars on NGOs for students and government officials, as well as for the staff of NGOs themselves. Long-standing development journals are publishing more articles about NGOs, occasionally devoting whole issues to the subject, the NGO community has established its own (international) development journals, and funding agencies are providing money for research on what has now become a mini-growth industry. These developments have occurred because, in many respects, NGOs have grown to become significant, if not major, actors in the broader efforts to reduce poverty. Global statistics recording trends in NGO income flows are acknowledged (not least by their compilers, the OECD) to be extremely inaccurate. None the less, they record that by 1991 funds channelled through NGOs to the developing world amounted to about $6bn. This was almost equivalent to the total amount of official aid provided to the developing world by Western governments and international institutions as recently as 1970. More recent official figures, for 1993, record that NGOs transferred some $6.3bn. to developing countries, a 5 per cent rise in real terms (OECD, 1995: 126–7). Though there is great variation from country to country, at least one-third of such funds come from grants from official aid agencies, most of which now channel 10 per cent or more of government aid through and to NGOs. Indeed, in some countries, such as Sweden, government funds now constitute 80 per cent or more of the annual income of some of the larger NGOs, while in other European countries, such as Germany and the Netherlands, special NGO agencies have been established almost exclusively to dispense government development funds to the voluntary sector.[1] For its part, the World Bank now has a formal mechanism for liaising with NGOs and is involved in 'a major effort to promote the involvement of NGOs in its projects in different countries' (Paul and Israel, 1991: x).[2] As for the poor themselves, it is likely that today NGOs assist in some way one in eight of those living in poverty in the developing countries (Schneider, 1988: 222). The 1993 *Human Development Report* judged that some 250 million people were being touched by NGOs, and that the numbers would rise considerably in the years ahead (UNDP, 1993: 93).

There are various reasons for the increasing importance of NGOs in development. One has been the growth in the number of such NGOs, due partly to the increase in official funding, but also to the changing, and increasingly positive, perceptions of the public at large, who have significantly increased their contributions to the NGO movement. According to estimates from the OECD's Development Assistance Committee (DAC)—widely thought to be too low—by 1988 there were over 2,500 NGOs in the leading Western industrialized countries engaged in international assistance, compared with only 1,700 in 1981 (OECD, 1990*a*: 29). The numbers of NGOs located in the developing world itself must now be closer to 50,000 (UNDP, 1993: 86), rising to many hundreds of thousands when one includes not just larger and often intermediary NGOs but reaches down to different types of grass-roots organizations (see Carroll, 1992). No one has ever tried to count much beyond the country level.[3]

Partly, too, the growth of NGOs has occurred as a result of the failure of official aid programmes to reach down and assist the poor, and partly because of donor pressure on recipient governments to reduce their direct involvement in development programmes. Moreover, the 1990s are likely to see a further rise in their importance, as the World Bank and bilateral agencies continue to expand their funding of NGO projects, as locally based NGOs expand their activities, and as NGOs are increasingly brought in to the mainstream of the development debate—both official donors and NGOs are now working directly (and often together) in efforts to strengthen civil society (see Riddell and Bebbington, 1995).

What is remarkable is that this phenomenal growth in the number of NGOs, in the funds at their disposal, and in their influence, has been accompanied by a dearth of independent information on the impact of NGO aid. NGOs working in developing countries assert that the projects and programmes they fund and promote play a positive and usually important role in helping to alleviate the poverty of the millions of people who live in misery. It is on this basis that they appeal for funds. Yet beyond the walls of particular NGOs, very little is known about individual project performance or, more generally, the extent to which NGOs succeed in their task of promoting development and reducing poverty. Until very recently, much of the independent information that is available is little more than anecdotal and impressionistic 'development tourism', and based on little more than short visits to particular projects. As a recently published World Bank study observes (Paul and Israel, 1991: 12, 11): 'a review of the NGO literature reveals our extremely limited knowledge of this (NGO) sector . . . There is . . . little hard evidence on their impact, costs, and other measures of performance.' In the last two years, especially, more and more official donors have commissioned independent assessments of the impact of NGO projects which they fund (see Riddell *et al.*, 1994, and Riddell *et al.*, 1995). While the growing data and evidence of these studies are certainly helping to fill crucial gaps in our knowledge, these official-sponsored studies differ from the present study in at least two respects. First, they tend to be undertaken more hurriedly, usually providing insufficient time to carry out more than a quick, cursory assessment. Second, and relatedly, they are only rarely able to assess impact from the vantage-point of the community.

One of the aims of the present book is to contribute to filling this important gap in our knowledge. It is based on one of the largest and most systematic assessments ever carried out of the impact of NGO poverty alleviation projects in the developing world, presenting the first cross-country analysis of projects funded by British NGOs. It was undertaken by the Overseas Development Institute in London with the co-operation and assistance of some of Britain's largest and most well-known NGOs—ActionAid, the Catholic Fund for Overseas Development (CAFOD), Christian Aid, the Save the Children Fund, and Oxfam—and a dozen or more NGOs in developing countries, many of whom have the direct responsibility for executing the projects funded, or part funded, with British NGO money.

Even so, the scope of the study is limited and thus its conclusions need to be placed in perspective. The book presents the findings of sixteen case-studies undertaken by a team of evaluators in four countries in Asia and Africa—four studies each in Bangladesh, (south) India, Uganda, and Zimbabwe. Each evaluation took a month or more of detailed fieldwork to complete, supplemented by country analyses which placed the results of the case-studies in their broader perspective. The results of the evaluations are presented in Part II of the book, which contains separate chapters for each of the four countries. Although some of the comments contained in these pages are critical of some of the NGOs and some aspects of the projects examined, it needs to be highlighted that none of the NGOs asked for anonymity with regard to their own involvement or the projects discussed. Thus none of the findings presented here have been subject to any degree of censorship.

However, the discussion is not confined to the details of the case-studies. The first part of the book attempts to place the results of this particular investigation into a wider context by discussing the manner in which the evidence throws light on the more general question of the effectiveness of NGOs in contributing to poverty reduction.

Chapter 2, 'Rural Poverty and Approaches to Poverty Alleviation', provides an overview of the extent of poverty in the developing world and of the more orthodox attempts to solve the problems, especially of rural poverty. It begins with an overview of poverty trends, the concepts used to analyse the nature of poverty, and the key characteristics of poverty in different parts of the developing world. It then moves on to examine the various approaches to rural poverty alleviation adopted by govern-ments, official aid donors, and international institutions since the mid-1960s, drawing on examples from the four countries examined in Part II of the book, with a view to understanding better the characteristics which NGOs frequently claim are unique to their particular approach to poverty alleviation and reduction.

Chapter 3, 'The Characteristics of NGOs: Is There a Comparative Advantage?', discusses the particular features which distinguish NGOs from other agencies in-volved in promoting and assisting development. It describes the growth of NGOs, and highlights the differences between the various types of NGOs involved in devel-opment, paying particular attention to the evolving and differing roles played by NGOs based in the industrialized world and those more operational agencies located in the developing countries. It also includes a brief review of the emerging literature on NGOs, focusing particularly on the apparent comparative advantage of NGOs, and assesses the claims made by and on behalf of NGOs in the light of the (sparse) evidence available. The chapter concludes that it is by no means easy to come to any firm overall conclusions about either the factors which characterize the uniqueness of NGO interventions or the degree to which NGOs have succeeded in their task of helping to reduce poverty.

Chapter 4, 'Evaluating NGO Performance', focuses on the general topic of impact assessment, and considers three main issues. It begins by drawing attention to the problems associated with the evaluation of NGO projects and discusses why so little attention has been paid by NGOs to the assessment of their impact in alleviating poverty. This is followed by a discussion of the approaches to assessment being adopted by NGOs, highlighting in particular participatory approaches to impact evaluation. The chapter ends by describing the common evaluation method which was used in the sixteen case-studies, which tried to steer a middle course between having too loose a framework, where individual judgement could unduly influence the analysis, and too rigid a structure, which might lead to the underplaying of important local characteristics. As one research objective was to find out what worked (or did not) and why, the approach used placed major emphasis on assessing and synthesizing the judgements of different actors—beneficiaries, the project sponsors, non-beneficiaries, and other local people—about the project's performance and impact, and trying to weigh the merits of judgements which differed. It involved a broad assessment of costs and benefits, embracing relevant non-economic as well as economic and financial indicators, the exact selection of which varied from project to project.

Chapter 5, 'The Impact of NGO Poverty Alleviation Projects: Overview of the Results of the Case-Studies', provides a summary of the conclusions of the sixteen evaluations, while Chapter 6, 'NGOs and Poverty Alleviation: Some Policy Implications', draws out some of the implications of the results for the remainder of the decade in which the role and importance of NGOs in poverty reduction are set to increase.

The book finds much to commend in the activities of both NGOs in general and British NGOs in particular. They work at the cutting edge of development in a world where mere survival often involves a fight against the enemies of extreme poverty, fundamental injustice, and glaring exploitation. What is remarkable is that, in spite of these handicaps, most of the projects examined in the study appear to have performed reasonably well: people's lives, especially those of the poor, have improved, sometimes quite significantly, as a result of the NGO intervention.

At the same time, some unexpected characteristics, problems, and weaknesses of NGO intervention to help the poor are highlighted in the book. In general, while NGO projects reach poor people, they tend not to reach down to the very poorest. Furthermore, as NGO projects tend to be small scale, the total numbers assisted are also small. It is also rare for NGO projects to be financially self-sufficient. At times, too, the NGO's concern to keep costs down to the minimum has meant that the level and quality of the benefits have been adversely affected. It would also appear that, although they execute a number of very imaginative projects, many appear unwilling to innovate in certain areas or activities.

Overall, therefore, while the book concludes that NGOs can, and many probably do, make a contribution to alleviating poverty and making the lives of the poor a little more tolerable, it stresses that this contribution is limited, both in terms of the increases in income which can be achieved in a typical NGO project, and in terms of the impact that the NGO contribution to development can have in relation to the vast, complex, and structural problems of poverty. There is little reason for NGOs to be hesitant in acknowledging that their contribution is frequently limited, and that in each country the impact of the overall NGO effort is usually still marginal to solving the wider problems of poverty. Greater transparency on the part of NGOs in respect of the problems that they face in project implementation and the often major problems involved in trying to overcome poverty would not only help to undercut the hollowness of criticisms made against them; it would also reinforce the moral basis of public support for the important work which they are trying to accomplish.

NOTES

1. Examples would be the Interkerkerlijke Coördinatie Commissie voor Ontwikkelingsprojekten (ICCO) and the Evangelische Zentralstelle für Entwicklungshilfe (EZE).
2. 'Of the 228 projects approved by the Bank in 1990, 50 have involved NGOs—in contrast to an annual average of 16 projects during the preceding 17 years.' (Paul and Israel, 1991).
3. See the discussion in Schneider (1988: 78–80), where some estimates are attempted.

Part I

ASSESSING THE SUCCESS OF NGOs

2

Rural Poverty and Approaches to Poverty Alleviation

INTRODUCTION

Poverty alleviation, and its eventual elimination, are central objectives of development. But there remains considerable doubt about how these objectives can be achieved in practice. In the 1990s poverty remains a pervasive problem in many developing countries, and—although by no means exclusively so—it is predominantly a rural phenomenon. In the early 1970s it was widely assumed that the benefits of sustained economic growth would gradually percolate down to the poor; particular programmes targeted on the poor therefore received scant attention. However, during the decade it was increasingly acknowledged that growth in itself may not produce a significant reduction in poverty in the absence of direct programmes of assistance, especially when there is an unequal distribution of land and other assets. Then in the 1980s in many parts of the developing world, the motor of economic growth slowed, exposing still further the extent of poverty and raising with more urgency the question of how best to address and resolve its problems.

The design and implementation of appropriate measures to enhance the economic status of the poor have largely been the prerogative of national governments, though influenced to an increasing extent by the large international agencies and individual official aid donors. Both the slowdown in growth and the problems encountered in devising programmes aimed at transferring resources to the poor have focused attention on the limitations of government and official aid agencies in reducing poverty. In the 1980s, especially, this led to a growing interest in the potential of NGOs to alleviate poverty, as they claim, and are widely perceived, to be more effective than governments in reaching the poorest.

POVERTY TRENDS AND CHARACTERISTICS

Global and Regional Trends

It is by no means easy to quantify either the absolute numbers of poor people in the world today, or trends in the extent of world poverty. However, in 1990 it was estimated that over one billion people were living in poverty, roughly one-third of the total population in the developing world. Two-thirds of the poor live in Asia, a quarter in sub-Saharan Africa, and the remainder in Latin America and the

Caribbean (World Bank, 1992: 30). Although between 1970 and 1990 there was an apparent reduction in the percentage of people living in poverty, the absolute number of poor in the developing world increased possibly by up to one-third, largely as a result of population growth. Most of this increase took place in Africa, as both the absolute number and the percentage of people living in poverty declined in Asia over this period. None the less, it is important to note that today there are more poor people living in India and Bangladesh than the entire population of sub-Saharan Africa.

In 1990 it was estimated that the number of people living in poverty in Africa amounted to 290 million, roughly half the total population. On current trends, it is predicted that the figure will have risen to 400 million by 1995. By the year 2000, nearly 30 per cent of the developing world's poor will be living in sub-Saharan Africa, up from 18 per cent in 1985. By comparison, the number of poor in South Asia is expected to decline from 530 million in 1985 to about 510 million, and in East Asia, from the current level of about 280 million to just 70 million, compared with 126 million in Latin America and the Caribbean (World Bank, 1992: 30).

Although the overall incidence of poverty remains high, developing countries as a whole have registered some major achievements over the past three decades, especially in the areas of health, nutrition, and literacy. Four out of five people living in developing countries are now living longer and are better educated than was the case thirty years ago. The under-fives mortality rate fell from 232 deaths per 1,000 live births in 1960, to 100 in 1992, and three-quarters of all one-year-olds are now inoculated against childhood diseases. Per capita calorific intakes increased by almost 20 per cent in the period 1965–88. Life expectancy at birth rose from an average of 46 years in 1960 to 63 in 1992; and adult literacy rates rose from 46 per cent to 69 per cent in the period 1970 to 1992. Although income per capita in developing countries amounted to only 17 per cent of that in the industrialized countries in 1992, life expectancy was 84 per cent and adult literacy 71 per cent of that achieved in the North (UNDP, 1994).

Against the background of this catalogue of achievements for the developing world as a whole, there is still great cause for concern over the increasing incidence of poverty, especially in Africa and, to a lesser extent, Latin America. While there has been continuing progress in reducing the under-fives mortality and increasing the primary-school enrolment rates in much of the developing world in the 1980s, these regions have experienced reversals. Whereas per capita incomes grew by an average of 1.6 per cent per annum in sub-Saharan Africa in the period 1965–80, for the decade of the 1980s average SSA incomes fell by almost 15 per cent, with average living standards falling more rapidly in the second half of the decade than in the first. With the rise in the number of people living in poverty in sub-Saharan Africa, malnutrition has been increasing, with a substantial rise in the number of underweight children: during the 1980s sixteen African countries experienced a decline in per capita calorific intakes. Sub-Saharan Africa now has the lowest life expectancies, the highest infant mortality rates, and the lowest literacy rates in the developing world. Many SSA and Latin American countries registered a significant decline in spending on health and education, largely as a result of public expenditure cutbacks introduced under structural adjustment programmes.

These aggregate trends, however, disguise considerable variations in individual country performance. Equally, a ranking of countries on the basis of per capita GNP does not take into account disparities in purchasing power in different countries. The UNDP *Human Development Report* uses a composite Human Development Index (HDI) which is designed to capture these dimensions by combining indicators of life expectancy and adult literacy with purchasing-power-adjusted estimates of GDP. At the bottom end of this scale, some countries with very low per capita GNP improve their performance (Mozambique rises from bottom to fifteenth from bottom place, Ethiopia from third to twenty-third), but the overall performance of African countries remains uniformly poor, with a high proportion classed as having 'low human development'.

The four countries examined in this book are ranked as follows in the *Human Development Report 1994* (UNDP, 1994): Bangladesh, with average GNP per capita of $220 in 1992, is ranked tenth poorest in the World Bank tables (World Bank, 1994: 162), but is listed as 28th poorest (rank 146 out of 173) on the UNDP scale; Uganda, with per capita income of $170, rises from 6 to 20; India, with per capita income of $310, rises from 18 to 39; while Zimbabwe, with a 1992 per capita income of $570, goes up from the 33rd position (World Bank) to the 53rd lowest position (UNDP). Yet neither the World Bank nor the UNDP indices shed light on changes in the economic and social status of the poor, or on the distribution of income between different groups.[1]

Characteristics of Poverty

To try to understand better the nature of poverty, the poor are sometimes classified into three sub-groups: the chronically poor, the borderline poor, and the new poor. The chronically poor are those whose income levels remain continually below a given poverty-line, defined by minimum consumption standards: they suffer from acute deprivation. The borderline poor move in and out of poverty, often on a seasonal basis, according to the availability of food and work. A third group, who have been termed the new poor (World Bank, 1990c: 91), are those who were previously above the poverty-line but have since joined the ranks of the poor as a result of economic recession or structural adjustment programmes. Sometimes a further distinction is made between the poor and the ultra-poor, illustrating people's differing capacity to satisfy their daily consumption needs (Lipton, 1985). The ultra-poor are those who are always deficient in terms of minimum food requirements, whereas the poor are disadvantaged in relation to the consumption standards prevailing in the wider society.[2] In Bangladesh, for example, 80 per cent of the population is poor, while more than half the rural population subsists below the minimum calorific intake necessary to lead an active working life—ultra-poor.

In this book we make a quite sharp distinction between the 'poor' and the 'poorest' in line with the terminology favoured by most NGOs. These categories broadly correspond to those used by Lipton—the poor and the ultra-poor—in so far as they relate to nutritional requirements. In South Asia and sub-Saharan Africa, a significant proportion of the poorest are physically disabled, elderly, or chronically sick. However, the poor and the poorest are also differentiated in other ways, which are often regionally specific.

In South Asia, the incidence of rural poverty is strongly correlated with lack of access to land. In much of Bangladesh and India, government policies (colonial and post-Independence), caste discrimination, and population pressure have resulted in unequal structures of land ownership, with a large number of people possessing no land at all. The poor generally own or lease some land, largely in order to grow food crops, but do not produce enough to meet their subsistence needs. Most small farmers have to find additional work to feed their families, or else they have to lease out the small amount of land they might have to others to generate additional income. The poor can generally make ends meet, although some may experience periods of seasonal deprivation. The poorest households possess few fixed assets and generally depend on casual wage-labour as their major source of income; but for many months of the year they are unable to secure employment. Such households find it difficult to meet their subsistence needs and experience periods of under-nutrition (Robinson, 1991*a*; White, 1991). In rural Bangladesh, as White (1991: 5) observes, it is usually obvious who the poor are:

[T]hey live in a makeshift single roomed house; they have few and poor quality clothes; they have little in the house but a few cooking pots, plates and dishes; they may have no bed but sleep on bamboo mats; they have at best a few ducks and chickens, sheep or goats; they eat at most twice a day and may go without food all day at the lean times of the year . . . the poor quality of their diet means that they commonly suffer from illnesses such as diarrhoea and eye problems.

In sub-Saharan Africa, the rural poor are mostly the families of small farmers, artisans, and pastoralists, who are just about able to produce or sell enough to fulfil their basic consumption needs (O'Connor, 1991: 23–30). In Uganda and Zimbabwe, the poorest generally have access to small plots of land but lack the means to cultivate it productively and, as a result, have to supplement their meagre agricultural incomes with earnings from casual labour, or else go without the food they need. In Uganda, there are marked differences between urban and rural areas: a large proportion of rural households, especially in the remoter northern region, are clustered in the lowest expenditure groupings, and two-thirds are classed as poor peasants. Although landlessness is generally not a problem in Uganda, the poorest households do not possess land in sufficient quantity or quality to provide an income to raise them above the poverty-line. In some areas, food and livestock are in short supply, largely due to protracted civil and political instability, and in others land concentration and alienation have resulted in large-scale out-migration (De Coninck with Riddell, 1992).

In Zimbabwe more than half of all rural households are poor. Rural poverty is concentrated in the most densely populated communal areas, although the families of commercial farm employees (over one million people) are also extremely poor. In the communal areas, inadequate land, poor soil, shortage of livestock, and isolation from markets are the major causes of poverty. But even in the communal areas, there are marked variations in living standards, with the top 10 per cent of households accounting for over 40 per cent of total communal-area household income. There are a growing number of landless households who depend on casual wage-labour or migrate elsewhere in search of work (Muir with Riddell, 1992).

Men and women experience poverty in different ways. Women tend to be more restricted in their ability to secure employment and in many cases receive inferior rates of pay for the same work. Besides low-paid casual labour, poor women also perform a wide variety of domestic tasks which greatly extend the length of their working day: in rural India, for example, women work up to 15 hours more a week than men. There is a preponderance of women working in informal sector employment, especially in urban areas, where the rates of pay are lower (UNDP, 1990: 32). In developing countries, literacy rates tend to be far lower for women than for men, reflecting lower rates of school attendance and cultural attitudes towards women's education. For all developing countries the male literacy rate in 1992 was 79 per cent, compared to only 58 per cent for women. Disparities are even greater in the least developed countries, where the literacy rate among men was 58 per cent compared to only 34 per cent for women. Although the gap in enrolment rates has declined since 1960, a significant disparity remains.[3] It is only in relation to life expectancy rates that women achieve higher scores than men. Although women generally live longer, they suffer from very high maternal mortality rates. The maternal mortality rate in 1988 for all developing countries was 420 per 100,000 live births. In India and Bangladesh the figures were 550 and 650 respectively, compared to 700 in Uganda and 330 in Zimbabwe. For sub-Saharan Africa as a whole, the average was 690. These figures compare with an average maternal mortality rate in industrial countries of 24 per 100,000 births (UNDP, 1994).

Poverty also affects children disproportionately. Thus children in poor households are especially at risk from malnutrition and disease, due to both inadequate diet and poor sanitation. Despite improvements in infant mortality and primary-school enrolment rates in many developing countries, these have not been evenly spread between rich and poor households, or between urban and rural areas. According to UNDP (1991), 14 million children under the age of 5 die each year and 35 per cent are malnourished. Bangladesh, India, and Uganda all have infant mortality rates in excess of 98 per 1,000 live births; Zimbabwe is slightly better with 59 per 1,000 live births, but this still compares unfavourably with an average rate of just 13 for industrialized countries.[4] There are similar disparities with regard to the percentage of one-year-olds receiving immunization: in East Asia 94 per cent of all children are immunized compared to only 49 per cent in sub-Saharan Africa and 84 per cent in South Asia (UNDP, 1994: 209).

While poverty is predominantly a rural phenomenon, urban poverty is pervasive in many countries, especially in those with high rates of urbanization. Although services are more readily accessible in urban areas, the urban poor, who are often crowded into slums and squatter settlements, suffer from problems of overcrowding, poor sanitation, and lack of safe drinking water. While incomes are generally higher in urban areas, so too is the poverty-line. For example, most of those in formal-sector employment in urban Zimbabwe receive sub-poverty wages. In Uganda at least 60 per cent of urban households are living in a serious state of poverty and are unable to meet their basic consumption needs, despite the fact that the average urban household spends more than twice as much as the average rural household.

APPROACHES TO POVERTY ALLEVIATION

Conventional models of development prominent in the 1950s and much of the 1960s were principally models of economic growth: it was assumed that over time economic growth would 'trickle down' and thereby benefit all sections of society. Present-day proponents of a growth–centred approach to development argue that economic growth remains of fundamental importance for three reasons. First, growth is a prerequisite for raising per capita incomes in society as a whole, and for expanding the economic opportunities of which the poor are able to take advantage. Second, economic growth is needed to provide the resources required to support increased social expenditure. Third, growth is essential for investment which is necessary to sustain improvements in living standards in the longer term.

But in many countries the evidence, sparse though it is, suggests that growth alone has not been able to reduce poverty to any great extent in the absence of more direct policy initiatives. In particular, in countries with a marked inequality of income, an increase in per capita incomes tends to have a very limited impact on lower-income groups. Conversely, where a government intervenes to reduce inequality in the context of economic growth, a more even distribution of gains will result. It is note-worthy that the most consistent and durable declines in poverty have taken place in countries where economic growth has occurred in the context of a reasonably equita-ble distribution of income and assets, as the examples of countries such as Costa Rica, South Korea, and Indonesia indicate. For this reason, many governments in develop-ing countries have sought to complement growth strategies with some attempt at income redistribution and programmes targeted at the poor.[5]

In its 1990 *World Development Report*, and its subsequent Policy Paper, *Assistance Strategies to Reduce Poverty* (1991*b*), the World Bank advocates a two-part strategy for achieving sustainable improvements in the quality of life for the poor. The first component is premissed on economic growth, which provides opportunities for pro-ductive employment and the resources to fund government development expendi-ture. The second is focused on an expansion of basic social services, in particular primary education, health care, and family planning, mainly for the benefit of the poor. It is also argued that safety-nets in the form of subsidies and employment-generation measures are required to provide support for the most vulnerable sections of the population and to protect the poor during periods of economic adjustment.

The UNDP put forward a similar approach in its 1990 *Human Development Report*, arguing in favour of a combination of policies designed to increase incomes and to provide the poor with a decent standard of living and the potential to lead full and creative lives, through economic growth, targeted anti-poverty programmes, and enhanced social expenditure. Both approaches are based on an implicit assumption that the state should provide an enabling policy environment for efficient production and equitable distribution. The state has an important role to play in the design and implementation of programmes aimed at alleviating poverty which, by their very nature, imply an interventionist approach.

Although these are a major advance on growth-only approaches to development and poverty reduction, experience has shown that it is extremely difficult to reach and benefit the poor even through direct programmes of assistance. As a result, there has been a great deal of experimentation in using alternative approaches to poverty alleviation, and much of the current interest in the role of NGOs in this respect derives from the perceived inadequacies of official programmes and the possible use of such alternative approaches. But first we consider the range of direct assistance programmes in the wider policy context.

Types of Programmes

Present-day attempts to alleviate poverty fall into three broad categories. The first are macroeconomic policies, designed to promote and accelerate growth, combined with fiscal policies aimed at reducing inequality. A second set centre on public investments in physical infrastructure and expenditure on health and educational provision to promote human resource development, which may involve targeting for vulnerable social groups. Third are a range of programmes which directly aim to contribute to rural poverty alleviation. These operate at three different levels: national, local, and individual.

At the national level some programmes entail attempts at a physical redistribution of assets from the rich to the poor, of which land reform is perhaps the most obvious example. A further set of programmes target the poor by providing credit and technological inputs for poor farmers or workers engaged in non-farm activities. These often exclude wealthier groups either by designing burglar-proofing innovations which prioritize research in low-value food crops, or by means of special programmes centred on the provision of credit, subsidized inputs, and extension services. Special employment programmes and targeted subsidies (in the form of credit, food, etc.) aim to increase the entitlements of the poor to enable them to purchase and consume more. Such programmes may be national or regional. In India, for instance, they would include the Tjawahar Rozgar Yojana, which operate on a national scale, while the Employment Guarantee Programme of the Maharashtra State government is an example of a programme which has been regional in its focus. Then there are programmes which focus on institution-building, either by encouraging participation through group formation at the grass-roots, or through measures designed to render public-sector institutions accountable and effective in delivering services to the poor, which tend to be more localized.

Universal Versus Targeted Programmes

There has been some debate about the merits of universal programmes—which benefit all sections of the population regardless of their economic situation—as against programmes tailored specifically to cater to the particular needs of the poor. The more universal approach, with its concern for the overall provision of health and education services and the fulfilment of certain standards of nutrition, underpinned the basic-needs approach popular with many aid donors in the 1970s and early 1980s. Targeted programmes are designed to concentrate resources on low-income people and other disadvantaged groups: they thus lead to a proportionate reduction in the volume of resources which accrue to the non-poor through universal provision. However, targeting presupposes that the careful identification of eligible groups is both administratively and politically feasible, which is by no means the case: the process can also be time-consuming and costly (Besley and Kanbur, 1990).[6]

Some programmes are designed with the aim of encouraging self-selection, as for example in employment-generation schemes, where the value of the benefits has to exceed the opportunity cost of alternative sources of income for people to want to participate. Since schemes of this nature are designed to provide employment to vulnerable groups during the slack season when little work is available, the opportunity costs to the poor are minimal whereas the non-poor will have alternative sources of income to tide them over.[7]

Development Agencies

Three groups of agencies are involved in the design and implementation of programmes aimed at reducing poverty: governments, official donors, and NGOs. Macroeconomic policies are largely determined by governments but, with the spread of policy-based reforms in the 1980s, especially in sub-Saharan Africa, the IMF and the World Bank have come to play an increasingly important role in determining policy content. Indeed, stabilization policies and structural adjustment programmes usually entail extensive reform, not only in fiscal and monetary policy, but also in terms of rationalizing public-sector expenditures and cutting back on resource transfers such as food subsidies. The structural adjustment era of the 1980s has meant that governments are under growing pressure to reduce 'excessive' public-sector expenditures. Such pressure has encouraged a more selective approach to social expenditure in general, and to services and programmes targeted on more vulnerable groups in particular. At the same time, there is a growing need to protect the poor from the effects of structural adjustment through special programmes of assistance (such as the Programme for the Alleviation of Poverty and the Social Costs of Adjustment—PAPSCA—in Uganda), many of which remain inadequately funded.

Official development assistance (oda) in the form of concessional loans and outright grants currently provides a significant share of the government development budget, particularly in the least developed countries. In Bangladesh, for example, more than 80 per cent of the government's development budget is financed in this way, whereas in India it is less than 10 per cent. In the period 1992–3 the ratio of oda to GNP amounted to 15 per cent on average for the countries of sub-Saharan Africa, amounting to an astonishing 111 per cent in the case of Mozambique (OECD, 1995: 118). Direct donor support for poverty-reduction programmes usually takes the form of grant support for government projects, or training programmes for improving the calibre of technical or field staff engaged in service provision. However, during the 1980s there was a general shift away from project aid to quick-disbursing balance-of-payments assistance. The unwillingness of donors to fund the recurrent costs of development projects for a protracted period can pose budgetary difficulties for governments with limited access to resources over the longer term, although there usually remains a ready supply of funds available from donors for poverty-focused projects.

The third group of agencies involved in poverty-alleviation programmes are the non-governmental organizations (NGOs). Most NGOs are explicitly involved in programmes drawn up to meet the needs of the poorest, and attach particular importance to the role of effective grass-roots organizations (see Chapter 3). They tend to fund discrete development projects covering a range of sectors, such as health, education, shelter, food production, and small-scale infrastructural investments.

RURAL DEVELOPMENT PROGRAMMES

Land Reforms

Land is a fundamental determinant of economic well-being in rural areas in developing countries. Governments committed to agrarian reform have attempted to redress the unequal distribution of land by introducing legislation to limit the amount that can be owned by any one individual. Surplus land is then purchased or confiscated by the state and redistributed to landless cultivators. Tenurial legislation has sought to enhance the security of leaseholders, curb usurious rents, and raise the share of net output accruing to the sharecropper.

In general, implementing land-reform programmes has proved to be extremely difficult. An ILO study of six Asian countries (India, Bangladesh, Pakistan, Nepal, Sri Lanka, and the Philippines) concluded:

It is . . . evident that the history of land reforms in most Asian countries is characterised by high ceilings compared to average farm size, lack of will, and opposition from landlords. The result has been very little redistribution of land among the landless and the land-poor and a meagre impact on the condition of living of the rural poor. Attempts at tenancy reform have also faced a number of problems regarding implementation, and consequently contributed very little towards improving the levels of productivity and income of the tenant farmers (quoted in Getubig and Ledesma, 1988).

In India, the land available for redistribution is often of very poor quality and poor farmers lack the resources to cultivate the land productively. Moreover, landlords pre-empt legislation by ejecting tenants from their lands and disguise the real extent of their landholdings, or find loopholes which render the legislation inoperative.[8] This does not negate the principles underlying land reform, but problems in securing their implementation limit the scope of legislation to effect a significant shift in assets from rich to poor farmers. It is for this reason (and because of the political sensitivity of land reforms) that successive governments, in India and elsewhere, have focused their attention on enhancing the productivity of assets already in the possession of small farmers, through a strategy of integrated rural development programmes and intensive agricultural development.

In Zimbabwe, land-resettlement schemes have been central to the government's overall approach to promoting labour absorption through increased self-employment in agriculture. Although only one-third of the 160,000 farming households scheduled to benefit from the programmes had actually received land by mid-1990, a significant number achieved improvements in production levels. Resettled farmers have been drawn from among the poorest households, and prior to the 1991/2 drought, most were able to grow enough food to meet their own requirements.

Integrated Rural Development Programmes

The impetus for an approach to rural development which gave priority to poverty alleviation came from governments committed to progressive reforms on the one hand, and from changes in donor policies towards the agricultural sector on the other. From the early 1970s the World Bank played an influential role, with an overt commitment to rural poverty alleviation in its project lending, in order to offset the bias towards large-scale agricultural production which had a very marginal impact on poverty reduction.[9] The key element of this strategy was to enhance the productivity of smallholders in order to increase incomes and the availability of food. In most cases these programmes also involved an expansion in rural services (especially health and education), as well as measures to stimulate agricultural employment and to promote a more equitable distribution of the benefits arising out of increases in output, in an integrated approach (World Bank, 1988).

During the 1970s, integrated rural development projects (IRDPs) were promoted by aid donors in conjunction with recipient governments in many parts of the developing world, and particularly in Africa. IRDPs were usually donor-funded interventions, located in resource-poor environments and with smallholders as the main target group. They aimed to increase agricultural productivity through targeted investments in irrigation and the provision of fertilizer and modern seed varieties, and to raise the level of social service provision. The operational goals of the large-scale multi-sectoral projects supported by the World Bank have been summed up in the following manner: 'improved productivity, increased employment and thus higher incomes for target groups, as well as minimum acceptable levels of food, shelter, education and health' (World Bank, 1988: 2). Additional objectives were to influence government policy in favour of prioritizing rural development and to strengthen the capacity of public institutions to implement and finance complex development projects (Launonen and Ojanpera, 1985; Howell, 1990).

By the early 1980s there was a growing realization that many of the original objectives of projects supported by the World Bank in Africa were not being met, although performance varied by sector and region.[10] Many projects either failed to generate any significant improvements, or the benefits accrued to the non-poor. Nevertheless, although the record was generally disappointing, the poorest did benefit from improved services and infrastructure. Several reasons have been advanced for the poor performance of IRDPs in sub-Saharan Africa. These include weak co-ordination between government agencies, inadequate project research capacity, difficulties in introducing effective training to ensure skills transfer, unviable technical packages and insufficient expertise on the part of donor agencies (World Bank, 1988: 27–36).[11] Furthermore, projects were often poorly designed, over-ambitious, and difficult to monitor (Howell, 1990).

Governments in India and Bangladesh have experimented with approaches to rural poverty alleviation centred on the integrated approach, which were subsequently expanded into national programmes with donor assistance. An influential model was the Comilla approach to rural development which evolved in Bangladesh in the late 1960s. The programme was principally designed to benefit small and marginal farmers (i.e. those owning or cultivating less than two hectares) and the landless, who were organized into a two-tier system of co-operatives. It formed the basis for what subsequently became the Intensive Rural Development Programme (IRDP), which by 1980 covered more than half the country (Jones and Hossain, 1983). In 1982 this was replaced in turn by the Bangladesh Rural Development Board. Although more than 3 million rural people had been organized into co-operatives by 1988, the evidence suggests that their impact has been patchy. Many lack an active membership, while others are poorly managed. More fundamentally, most members of the co-operatives are not poor, and wealthier members monopolize the available resources. The result is that wealthier households register increased crop production with a gradual decline in the assets and landholdings of the poor (World Bank, 1990*b*).

A similar experience occurred in India. In the Community Development Programme, which was first introduced in the early 1950s, the emphasis was on increasing agricultural production by means of improved farming practices and infrastructural development. Farmers were organized into co-operatives to achieve these objectives, but these were dominated by the wealthier farmers, and the benefits were slight. The failure of the programme laid the basis for the Green Revolution approach promulgated by the Indian Government in the more developed parts of the country in the 1960s and early 1970s. This was an example of an approach which concentrated resources on high-potential areas and more enterprising farmers in the expectation that the benefits would trickle down to smaller farmers. The intensive application of subsidized agricultural inputs (such as hybrid seed varieties, fertilizer, and small-scale irrigation) on a selective area basis led to sustained increases in production in areas well endowed with irrigation, but did not bring about any significant reduction in poverty nationally (Dasgupta, 1977). Although small farmers did secure access to subsidized inputs, larger farmers were in a better position to invest in the new technology by virtue of their superior asset-holdings. A similar pattern emerged in other countries where the Green Revolution strategy was introduced (Griffin, 1974).

More recently, some NGOs have also adopted an integrated multi-sectoral approach which combines technical inputs and physical investments for small-scale agriculture with social services such as health care, education, safe drinking water, and family planning. Despite their similarity in terms of content, integrated projects implemented by NGOs have differed from government interventions in several key respects. First, NGO projects tend to be smaller and more localized. Secondly, their concern is more narrowly focused on the needs of the poorest (i.e. assetless labourers as well as smallholders). Thirdly, and perhaps most importantly, IRDPs implemented by NGOs lay particular emphasis on working through grass-roots organizations to further community participation; this was considered integral to the success and sustainability of projects because people could influence their design and implementation, although this has not been a feature of NGO programmes exclusively.

Poverty-Focused Interventions

The failure of both integrated development programmes and the intensive Green Revolution approach comprehensively to address the needs of poor farmers gave rise to a consideration of approaches targeted at more particular, and narrower, objectives. These include programmes designed to improve their asset position and productivity through credit provision and the improved supply of productive inputs and training. In the process, greater attention was given to participation, community development, and institution-building as means of improving programme implementation and sustainability.

The poor performance of integrated development programmes was often attributed to a lack of community participation in planning and designing different sectoral components (Uphoff, 1985). The programmes tended to emphasize a top-down approach in which programme content was determined by government officials and outside experts without consulting local people on their priorities. While, as a result, some integrated rural development programmes were redesigned to facilitate greater community involvement, there were not always adequate institutional mechanisms put in place to further participation.[12] As Cernea observed, there was a tendency for rural development projects to 'simply proclaim participation as a goal, assume that once proclaimed it will happen, but lamentably fail to take the processual steps for translating this goal into practice' (1983: 9).

Problems of putting participation into practice generated interest in local grass-roots organizations to further community involvement in project design and implementation (Uphoff, 1985). These include functional organizations, such as water users' associations and credit groups, where a particular activity or programme provides the focus for group formation. Others, such as farmer co-operative societies, have multiple roles in bringing together individuals on the basis of a shared economic identity, as well as providing a mechanism for channelling information and resources (Esman and Uphoff, 1984). The notion of participation has also informed approaches to farming-systems research and technology transfer.

Problems encountered in finding technologies which were acceptable and of use to small farmers in traditional IRDPs gave rise to a concern with on-farm research which drew on existing technical knowledge (Farrington and Martin, 1988). This entailed a shift away from standardized packages of technical inputs disseminated by government research and extension agencies, in favour of localized innovations tailored to local circumstances and farmers' specific requirements (Chambers *et al.*, 1989). In some cases this extended to building the research agenda around crops grown by small farmers for consumption rather than export, in order to burglar-proof certain types of technologies.

SAFETY-NET MEASURES

Developing country governments have also favoured different forms of safety-net measures as the most appropriate means of reaching the poorest. Most popular have been the provision of guaranteed employment through food-for-work schemes, and food-subsidy schemes. Increased expenditure on social services, perhaps with targeted programmes for the poor, also constitute an important element of safety-net provision.

Employment Programmes

In countries where part of the problem of poverty is linked to seasonal unemployment, and where opportunities for paid agricultural work are minimal, governments have devised schemes to provide temporary employment to landless labourers and marginal farmers. These schemes have been introduced for the most part in South Asia, where such problems are especially acute. Food-for-work programmes in India and Bangladesh provide short-term employment on public works, in particular developing the physical infrastructure in the form of roads, irrigation facilities, land levelling, etc., in return for food rations, the value of which is usually below the prevailing market rate for agricultural labour. Besides problems related to the poor quality of public works constructed under these programmes, most provide only very limited periods of employment, and the benefits tend to be marginal. In their favour, it is argued that food-for-work schemes contribute to food security during the most difficult period of the year and have the advantage of targeting those most in need (World Bank, 1989: 99–103).

Food Subsidies

Food subsidies have been a popular method of controlling (limiting the rise in) the prices of basic food commodities and raising the nutritional status of the poor. In most cases they focus on essential food commodities, such as rice and wheat in South Asia and maize or millet in sub-Saharan Africa. Subsidized food is usually rationed as a proportion of normal household requirements to prevent hoarding and leakages. Some governments have restricted the eligibility of such programmes to low-income groups, or have subsidized foods which are primarily consumed by the poor in order to target them more finely to vulnerable groups, and to reduce costs. Two different examples of food-subsidy schemes from India illustrate the distinction. All state governments in India distribute subsidized basic foodstuffs through the public food-procurement system. The Andhra Pradesh government has extended the scheme to enable all those below a certain income level to purchase rice at a heavily subsidized price from public ration shops. The Tamil Nadu government has taken a different approach, focusing its attention on universal feeding programmes for children, and special feeding programmes for lactating mothers and infants from poor households. It is acknowledged that both schemes have benefited low-income groups by improving their food security, but at great expense in terms of state government resources (Murthy *et al.*, 1990; World Bank, 1989).

In recent years food subsidies have been the focus of substantial criticism for their alleged bias towards urban consumers, their excessive cost, their inefficiency as a mechanism for resource allocation, and their potential to provide a disincentive to even small-farmer production, especially when producer prices are thereby held down. Nevertheless, food subsidies have been found effective in highly unequal societies in transferring income to the poor, and in creating safety-nets to protect the poor during periods of economic recession. There is evidence that they have succeeded in raising the consumption standards and purchasing power of the poor. In Bangladesh, for example, food subsidies increased the consumption of the poorest 15 per cent of the population by 15–25 per cent in 1973–4, while in the Indian state of Kerala in the late 1970s they contributed about half the income of poor families (UNDP, 1990: 63).

Budgetary constraints resulting from economic recession have encouraged a shift in favour of targeted subsidies in many developing countries and a consequent abandonment of universal provision in order to reduce public expenditure. But reductions in the level of direct subsidy or increases in the price of essential foodstuffs (as in Egypt and Zambia) have triggered off violent reactions, illustrating the difficulty of moving from universal to targeted provision. They have also resulted in a marked worsening in the health and nutritional status of the poor. For instance, the effects of a shift from a universal to a poorly-targeted food-subsidy scheme in Sri Lanka were reflected in a 9 per cent reduction in the average per capita calorie consumption of the poorest 20 per cent of the population in the period 1979–82 (UNDP, 1990: 49; Edirisinghe, 1987).

Social Services

An important element in public-sector efforts to alleviate poverty has been in the area of social-sector expenditure, encompassing health-care, education, drinking-water supply, etc. Evidence from as far apart as Cuba and Sri Lanka suggests that high investment in universal health and education services does bring about rapid improvements in social welfare and thereby alleviates some of the symptoms of poverty (UNDP, 1990).[13] Sustained investment in public-health services in the Indian state of Kerala, combined with a determined effort to promote universal literacy, is associated with the highest levels of life expectancy in the country: 66 years compared to a national average of 52 in 1976–80.

In marked contrast, many low-income countries in sub-Saharan Africa, such as Sierra Leone, Malawi, Somalia, Chad, and Sudan, continue to record poor social development indicators largely because they have been unable to sustain recurrent expenditure on health and education. Uganda, for example, experienced a marked deterioration in infant-mortality rates, primary-school enrolment, and safe drinking-water provision from the mid-1970s as a result of the devastating effect of protracted civil war, reinforced by reduced state spending on health and education. In 1988–9 financing of the government health budget was only 17 per cent in real terms of the level achieved in 1970–1. Similarly, state expenditure on education in the mid-1980s was only one-third of that reached in the late 1970s (De Coninck with Riddell, 1992: 2). However, the experience of Zimbabwe since Independence in 1980 stands in marked contrast to Uganda's dismal record. Increased expenditure in real terms on health and education has resulted in better health provision and improved primary-school enrolment, especially in the less advantaged communal areas (Muir with Riddell, 1992: 11–12). But then Zimbabwe had the resources to embark on these programmes, whereas in the case of Uganda, the funds were simply not available in spite of massive injections of aid.

NGOs have long had an active involvement in social-welfare provision, especially in health and education. In the health field, NGOs tend to concentrate on providing basic medical facilities, establishing dispensaries and clinics in areas where public services are either inadequate or totally absent. In addition to formal health-care provision, where they perform a small but effective gap-filling role, preventive measures centring on education and community involvement form a distinctive thrust of NGO programmes. The success of NGOs in encouraging a greater awareness of health, contraception, and sanitation has been widely acknowledged, and they have influenced the design of official programmes with a view to making them more effective and responsive to people's needs (see Salmen and Eaves, 1991; Beckmann, 1991). NGOs have long been involved in education, initially through the construction of schools and offering schooling to children. They have also pioneered a range of informal education techniques, and cater for the needs of adults through literacy classes and skills training.

Evidence on the impact of minimum needs programmes indicates that it is possible to raise the health, educational, and nutritional status of the poor by concentrating resources on social-service provision and food subsidies. Although the level of re-sources required for such a programme inevitably implies a central role for govern-ment with official donor assistance, NGOs can play a significant role where government services are weak and by focusing attention on preventive health measures and community participation, as the example of Uganda clearly suggests (see Chapter 9).

CONCLUSION

This overview of rural poverty and approaches to its alleviation points to two main conclusions. The first is that widespread poverty still persists and that in some regions, most vividly in sub-Saharan Africa, it is clearly on the increase. The second is that neither the broad nor the more narrowly focused programmes to reduce poverty have been able to make a major dent in the problem, even if specific, carefully designed and executed programmes manage to make people's lives a little more tolerable, and even if economic growth has played an important role in particular countries. It is in this context that the efforts and the role of NGOs in poverty alleviation need to be viewed. And it is this topic that the remainder of this book seeks to address. The next chapter examines the broad characteristics of NGOs and assesses the assumptions commonly made about their comparative advantage in development and poverty alleviation.

NOTES

1. The most widely used indicator of income inequality is the Gini coefficient, which measures the share of income between different quintiles of the population in relation to the average per capita income. Unfortunately the available data do not permit comparisons of this sort between countries, since this type of information has been gathered in less than one-quarter of all developing countries.
2. The terms absolute and relative poverty are also used in relation to these two groups, with the use of a poverty-line to distinguish them from each other and from the non-poor (Scott, 1985).
3. Data taken from various tables in UNDP, 1994. The links between female literacy and poverty are examined at some length in Bown, 1990.
4. Of course, wide disparities exist within different industrialized countries. For instance, infant mortality rates in parts of New York and Chicago are higher than 100 per 1,000 live births.
5. Fiscal policies have a relatively limited potential for effecting transfers between rich and poor in developing countries. Taxation is usually regressive, in that governments raise the bulk of their revenues from indirect taxes (such as sales taxes and excise duties) which fall disproportionately on the poor, who tend to spend a higher proportion of their incomes on commodities.
6. There are provisions in the Indian constitution for reserving places in higher education and government employment for the scheduled castes and tribes. In September 1990 the government decided to extend reservations to the backward castes who were selected on the basis of a combination of social and economic criteria, and ultimately caste affiliation.
7. One potential drawback is the social stigma attached to participation in such programmes, although it is questionable how far this acts as a disincentive to non-poor groups when the potential benefits are significant in financial terms.
8. Land-reform legislation introduced in India after Independence succeeded in weakening the power of the traditional rural élite (the *zamindars*) and strengthened the position of

tenants, but had the effect of consolidating a rural middle class which has proved highly resilient in the face of any further reduction in land ceilings (Joshi, 1974).

9. The UK government outlined its own approach to poverty-focused aid in the 1975 White Paper, *The Changing Emphasis in British Aid Policies: More Help for the Poorest.* However, since it proved difficult for the Overseas Development Administration to initiate Integrated Rural Development Programmes independently, UK aid in practice 'often meant either conventional projects which fitted poverty-focus requirements or support for area-based programmes already identified by governments or other donors such as the World Bank' (Howell, 1990: 274).

10. In East Africa only 45% of projects yielded an acceptable rate of return, compared to 61% in West Africa and between 68% and 83% in other parts of the world (World Bank, 1988: xvi).

11. Lack of confidence in the contribution that the aid programme could make and limitations in the scale of support that it provided have been identified as contributory factors in the case of projects assisted by the ODA (Howell, 1990: 275–82).

12. The experience of the PIDER programme in Mexico is illustrative of the problems encountered in attempting to introduce participatory mechanisms in a traditionally top-down project (Cernea, 1983; Uphoff, 1985; World Bank, 1988: 63–6).

13. The Sri Lankan Government sharply increased public-health provision and expenditure on education at Independence. Together with increased food security resulting from universal rice subsidies, this policy contributed to a significant reduction in mortality rates, from 20.6 deaths per 1,000 population in 1940 to 8.6 in 1960 and 6.1 in 1980 (Drèze and Sen, 1989: 227–9).

3

The Characteristics of NGOs:
Is There a Comparative Advantage?

INTRODUCTION

Non-governmental organizations (NGOs) embrace a wide array of agencies within and across different countries of the world. At their broadest, NGOs are simply agencies or groups which are different from government bodies. However, NGOs are distinctive in containing a voluntary component and because they do not operate for profit. Development NGOs are thus a category of NGOs defined by their purpose of providing development assistance. But even in development parlance, the term NGO is used to encompass a whole range of organizations which differ in size, function, and geographical location. Thus the term can be used to describe small, locally based, and loosely established voluntary and largely grass-roots types of associations, as well as large, national, and even transnational voluntary associations with formal constitutions, employing hundreds of staff. They may be engaged in relief, emergency, or longer-term development work or a mixture of all three.

The term NGDO—non-governmental development organization—is frequently used to describe the growing numbers of associations whose work is exclusively concerned with broader development concerns. A distinction is also commonly made between NGOs which originated in and have their home-base in the industrial countries, which are referred to as 'northern' or 'international' NGOs, and those which originate in and operate within developing countries, which are termed 'southern' NGOs.

Over the past quarter-century, and especially during the past two decades, there has been a rapid growth in the numbers of NGOs involved in development, in the numbers of people working for NGOs, and in the amount of money which flows into voluntary agencies working in relief and development. Perhaps the greatest growth has been in the thousands of new grass-roots organizations (sometimes referred to simply as 'groups', sometimes as 'people's organizations', as in the *Human Development Report 1993*) which have grown up locally—some extending no further than one or two villages. However, there has also been a rapid growth in larger indigenous NGOs in the south, as well as in the numbers of northern NGOs. During this period, a number of the older NGOs have changed their role, the most common change being a shift from an exclusive concern with relief and emergency work to a focus which embraces, or sometimes is exclusively concerned with, broader development issues (Korten, 1990*b*). These trends, and closer examination of the characteristics of different groups, have led to a distinction that is now commonly made between intermediary, or secondary, and primary organizations. Indeed Carroll (1992), whose work in this field has been particularly influential, distinguishes further between grass-roots support organizations (GSOs) and membership support organizations (MSOs).

On occasion this growth has led to a blurring of the differences between governmental and non-governmental, and even between non-profit and for-profit organizations. Thus, in an increasing number of developing countries, it has now become common for government and state agencies or for politicians to set up their own 'non-governmental' organizations, while in industrial countries it is now common practice for governments to channel some of their aid funds to and through NGOs. Similarly, concern with longer-term survival has encouraged some NGOs to raise funds by establishing commercial-type ventures such as shops, stores, and mail-order facilities, while in Italy 'business NGOs' have been formed for the specific purpose of securing aid contracts from the Italian Government. In some countries, NGOs have been established which are little more than advisory or consulting agencies to service the growing voluntary sector.

NORTHERN NGOS

The number of northern development NGOs has increased rapidly in the 1980s. At the same time, there has been growing diversification and specialization within the NGO community, reflecting the wide range of activities in which they are now engaged. As a result, it has become increasingly difficult to make generalizations about what northern NGOs do and about the particular role that they see for themselves in development.

Within individual industrialized countries, NGOs operate within different legal systems and with different public expectation of their role. However, in most countries there is a strong church-based link to at least one, and often more, of the major NGOs. Indeed, agencies affiliated to the Protestant and Catholic churches dominate the NGO sector in Denmark and Germany (where they account for two-thirds of private contributions), although most maintain a strict separation between pastoral and development work. The Dutch movement is dominated by four large NGO groupings, two of which are church-based. They receive significant funding from the government, most of which is channelled to indigenous NGOs in the south. In Britain, most development NGOs are registered as charities, which means that they have to adhere to quite strict legally defined guidelines, in common with all other registered charities. In Germany, in addition to the large church-based NGOs, there are also the four political foundations which constitute an important element of the NGO community, promoting development within their explicit and different political objectives.

Some important non-denominational NGOs whose interests include work on development were founded in the nineteenth and early twentieth centuries. The British Anti-Slavery Society was established as far back as 1823 and Save the Children Fund in 1919. Others were formed during and after World War II, initially with a focus on relief: Oxfam was founded in 1942 (Black, 1992), CARE (Co-operative Agency for

Relief Everywhere) in 1945, War on Want in 1953, NOVIB in 1956, and Misereor in 1958. In the 1960s there was a major expansion in the number of development-focused NGOs, both secular and denominational. In the 1970s and on into the 1980s, new organizations were formed which had a more specific sectoral, technical, or geographical focus. One such in Britain, the Intermediate Technology Development Group, was founded as early as 1965.

Northern NGOs are principally engaged in funding development projects and providing food and other materials for disasters and emergencies. An important distinction is whether they are operational or not: operational agencies implement projects directly in developing countries using their own staff and resources, whereas non-operational agencies finance projects from their headquarters or regional office, often channelling funds through partner organizations with whom special relationships are frequently developed. Large US-based NGOs like CARE, Plan International, and World Vision are all operational, as are ActionAid and Save the Children Fund in the UK. The trend, however, is away from hands-on involvement and towards working directly with indigenous NGOs. In Britain this is now common practice for agencies such as CAFOD (Catholic Fund for Overseas Development) and Christian Aid.

Many NGOs tailor their approach to the situation in particular countries; thus, the non-operational approach is favoured more in South Asia and Latin America, whereas in many parts of Africa northern NGOs continue to be strongly interventionist. Some northern NGOs, such as Oxfam, Save the Children Fund, Misereor, and NOVIB, have in-country offices which liaise with and offer support to indigenous NGOs in the form of training and exchange visits. Others, such as Christian Aid, have made a deliberate decision not to do so (Riddell, 1993), though recent changes have occurred in this policy.

In addition to providing financial support for development projects, many NGOs are involved in development education and advocacy work in their own countries. Indeed, distinct NGOs, like the Centre for World Development Education in England and Wales, have been set up in order to concentrate on such activities. However, emphasis on work in this area varies, and in a number of European countries, where a large share of funds come from the state, advocacy work receives a low priority.

While the statistics are known to be incomplete, OECD data suggest that there were 2,542 NGOs in the twenty-four OECD countries in 1990, compared with 1,603 in 1980 (OECD, 1990a). In addition, almost all NGOs grew in terms of funds and personnel during this period. Between 1980 and 1990, the total flow of private funds sent by northern NGOs to developing countries rose from $2.4bn. to $5.1bn., rising eventually to $6.3bn. (for recent figures see OECD, 1995: 58). However, a relatively small group of large organizations predominate: some 200 NGOs (less than 10 per cent of the total) account for some three-quarters of the volume of grants to developing countries (*The Courier*, 1987). Absolute numbers and growth trends also conceal significant variation among countries: there are hundreds of NGOs in Canada, the USA, and northern European countries where NGOs have strong historical traditions and thrive on public philanthropy, and comparatively few in Mediterranean countries such as Greece and Portugal.[1]

In Britain, the sector is dominated by a small group of large agencies: out of some 300 development NGOs, twelve account for over 80 per cent of total voluntary income, and seven of these had incomes in excess of £10m. in 1990. Oxfam is the largest in terms of turnover, followed by Save the Children Fund, Christian Aid, the World Wide Fund for Nature, ActionAid, Tear Fund, and CAFOD. Another fairly recent development has been the creation of a number of specialist NGOs, which focus on specific constituencies, approaches to development, and sectors of activity. These include Water Aid, Health Unlimited, and the Intermediate Technology Development Group, while increased interest in the environment has raised the profile of the World Wide Fund for Nature.

Growth in the number and incomes of development NGOs in the industrialized countries has tended to raise their significance in relation to the total voluntary sector. Thus, in Britain, development NGOs account for approximately one-sixth of the total volume of funds raised by charities in the form of private contributions. There are two main reasons for this growth in size and numbers of northern NGOs. The first has been the increase in media exposure of famine and disasters, together with the more professional manner in which these issues have been presented. Not only has the role of NGOs been highlighted, the NGO BandAid owed its origins to public interest aroused by media coverage of the Ethiopian famine of the mid-1980s. This provided a major stimulus for increased levels of private contributions,[2] which appears to have been sustained into the early 1990s in spite of worries expressed within the NGO movement that a combination of 'aid fatigue' and the media dominance of problems in eastern Europe and the former Soviet Union would lead to a drop in public donations. More recently, however, contributions have begun to fall.

A second set of factors contributing to NGO growth is related more to events outside the world of NGOs. One has been growing disillusion among official aid organizations about their own ability to alleviate poverty through their often large-scale rural development programmes. This has led, in part, to a switch in focus away from small and localized development projects to larger macro-political issues in official aid provision. Another factor has been the increasing prominence given to private initiatives in development. These influences have not only combined to raise the profile and status of the voluntary-sector NGOs in development, but have also led to significant increases in the quantity of public money which government ministries and aid agencies have channelled to and through NGOs. Government funding grew at a faster rate than private contributions during the 1980s. In the period 1980–8, official contributions increased in real terms by 55 per cent, as compared with 25 per cent for private contributions. By 1988 NGOs in the eighteen DAC member states raised $4.2bn. from private contributions but received $2.3bn. from official sources, giving a total of $6.3bn. (see Table 3.1). By 1992 the total had risen to $8.8bn., though still equivalent to around 15 per cent of total official aid.

In the period from 1970 to 1993, the total non-government funds of NGOs channelled to developing countries rose from $860m. to $6.3bn. Yet as a share of total official aid there was a slight decline over this period—from 12.3 per cent in 1970 to 11 per cent in 1993. The most significant change over the past quarter of a century

TABLE 3.1. *Resources for development and relief activities of Non-Governmental Organizations, from OECD development assistance committee members, 1974–1993*

Year	Private grants extended by NGOs		Official contributions to NGOs[a]	
	US$ m. equivalent	1987 US$ equivalent[b]	US$ m.[c] equivalent	1987 US$ equivalent[b]
1974–6 average	1,320	2,866	239	519
1977–9 average	1,720	2,777	(808)	(1,305)
1980	2,386	3,150	1,045	1,380
1981	2,005	2,754	1,253	1,719
1982	2,317	3,257	1,159	1,630
1983	2,318	3,268	1,183	1,668
1984	2,598	3,744	1,324	1,908
1985	2,884	4,109	1,473	2,099
1986	3,338	3,840	1,951	2,244
1987	3,525	3,525	(1,899)	(1,899)
1988	4,224	3,943	(2,287)	(2,134)
1989	4,042	4,041	—[d]	—
1990	5,077	4,719	—	—
1991	5,403	4,392	—	—
1992	6,005	4,605	—	—
1993	5,634	4,408	—	—

Notes: [a] Excludes contributions to international voluntary agencies.
[b] Current year.
[c] In most cases, contributions for private volunteer schemes are included, as are contracts with NGOs for the official projects.
[d] This series of data was discontinued after 1988.
Figures in brackets are estimates by the DAC Secretariat.

Source: OECD, 1990*a*: 17; OECD 1995: Statistical Annex, Table 20.

has been the growth of total NGO income coming from official aid sources. According to the World Bank (World Bank, 1995: 23), in 1970 official donors only provided about 1.5 per cent of total NGO income. But by 1992 the figure had risen to $2.5bn., and to account for some 30 per cent of total NGO income.

The exact proportions vary markedly between individual countries. Though, in some cases, the data are known (by the OECD) to be little more than crude estimates, and it has not been possible for some years to provide comprehensive data for eleven OECD donors, the best available country by country data are shown in Table 3.2. For at least four donors, over 20 per cent of all official aid is now channelled to or through NGOs. Of importance, too, the data show that in the case of at least six countries, over 40 per cent of total NGO income comes from official aid sources. However, the figures quoted in Table 3.2 need to be treated with some caution, for other sources indicate that the ratio of official aid going to NGOs in 1993–4 for some of the leading donors was as follows: Australia, 4.5 per cent; Canada, 13.7 per cent; Germany, 10 per cent; the Netherlands, 10 per cent; Norway, 23 per cent; Sweden, over 25 per cent;

TABLE 3.2. *Resources for development and relief activities of Non-Governmental Organizations, 1993*

	Private Grants by NGOs			Official Contributions to NGOs		
	$ m. equivalent	% of total NGO equivalent	$ per capita	$ m. equivalent	% of total NGO aid flows	Total NGO aid flows as % of total oda
Australia	92	84.4	5.2	17	15.6	11.4
Austria	69	93.2	8.6	5	6.8	13.6
Belgium	130	(99.2)	12.9	(1)	(0.8)	(16.2)
Canada	284	57.5	9.9	210	42.5	20.8
Denmark	45	88.2	8.8	6	11.8	3.8
Finland	5	41.7	1.0	7	58.0	3.9
France	190	90.0	3.3	21	10.0	2.7
Germany	801	80.4	9.9	195	19.6	14.3
Ireland	25	92.6	7.0	2	7.4	33.3
Italy	50	—	0.9	—	—	—
Japan	159	54.6	1.3	132	45.4	2.6
Luxembourg	5	100.0	12.9	0	0	10.0
Netherlands	272	56.7	17.8	208	43.3	19.0
New Zealand	14	93.3	4.0	1	6.7	15.3
Norway	130	—	30.1	—	—	—
Portugal	0	0	0	0	0	0
Spain	71	—	1.8	—	—	—
Sweden	130	(48.7)	14.9	(137)	51.3	(15.1)
Switzerland	144	58.3	20.8	103	41.7	31.1
United Kingdom	451	90.4	7.8	48	9.6	17.2
United States	2567	—	9.9	—	—	—

Note: Figures in brackets are repeated from 1992.

Source: OECD, 1995; Table 12.

the United Kingdom, 6.6 per cent; and the United States around 10 per cent (see Smillie and Helmich, 1993; Riddell *et al.*, 1995).

A major cause of this rise in official funds to NGOs has been the rapid expansion of emergency aid and a rising share of this which now passes through NGOs. Thus, whereas less than $1bn. of total official aid went to emergencies and distress relief in the late 1980s, it amounted to over $3bn. by 1993. By the early 1990s, almost 30 per cent of Britain's total official aid allocated by the Overseas Development Administration's (ODA) Disaster and Refugee Units was funnelled through NGOs, compared with less than 1 per cent ten years earlier. For the aid from the European Union the trend has been even greater, with the share of emergency aid chanelled through NGOs rising from less than 1 per cent in the mid-1970s to 40 per cent by the early 1990s (Borton, 1993). In 1993–4, 30 per cent of official Swedish aid going to NGOs was solely for disaster relief (Riddell *et al.*, 1995: 11). Funds are provided to NGOs through five major mechanisms: block grants for which no detailed accounting requirements are stipulated; matching grants for development projects (co-financing);

food aid and disaster relief; support for volunteer programmes; and grants for development education. Project co-financing has grown to be the most important of these, with matching grants providing NGOs with from 50 to 100 per cent of total project costs of co-financed projects. Not only do official aid agencies use NGOs to distribute food aid and emergency aid, but some donors now sub-contract specific elements of bilateral aid projects to NGOs for implementation. USAID has relied on this mechanism for some years. Thus in CARE's food-for-work programme in Bangladesh, the NGO assumed responsibility for food distribution and supervision of public works under contract from USAID. Some other donors have since followed suit. For instance, in its 'country-focus' approach, the Canadian Government involves NGOs in the execution, and in some cases the design, of CIDA-financed projects in the main recipient countries.

Besides these different forms of financial support to northern NGOs, some donors provide funds directly to southern NGOs, either bilaterally to individual organizations from aid headquarters or through diplomatic missions. Canada has progressed furthest down this path. In 1987 it provided some $16m. to indigenous NGOs through aid missions in 115 countries. In a variant of this approach, USAID provides umbrella grants through its aid missions for use by US PVOs as well as indigenous NGOs (OECD, 1988: 91–3). The British Government has also started to fund local NGO activities, initially by supporting indigenous NGOs involved in family planning as part of a larger bilateral aid programme in Bangladesh. In 1994 a further new initiative began in east Africa, when ODA began a programme to fund the work of local NGOs directly with an initial budget of £1.5m. (Riddell and Bebbington, 1995). On the multilateral front, a significant channel for indigenous NGO funding is through the European Community's micro-project schemes, which in many Lomé Convention countries are administered by an official paid for by the Community. Overall, however, this channel covers only a minor proportion of official aid allocated to NGOs. Both resistance on the part of some northern NGOs and the limited capacity of most aid missions to monitor small project grants have worked against any major shift in favour of direct funding.

SOUTHERN NGOS AND GRASS-ROOTS ORGANIZATIONS

While there has been a steady growth in the number and size of northern NGOs in the 1980s, there has been an explosion in the number of southern NGOs.[3] For instance, there are now several thousand NGOs in India engaged in rural development, 550 in Bangladesh, and over 200 in Zimbabwe. In Kenya the number of NGOs active in development doubled from 70 in 1970 to 140 by 1980, with a further increase to some 250 by the late 1980s; the number would expand to many thousands if local women's and other grass-roots organizations were included (see Ng'ethe *et al.*, 1990: 129 ff.).

This rapid growth has been spurred by the more positive attitude on the part of donors and many host governments towards the NGO sector, and by the increased availability of funds from foreign donors, both NGOs and governments. It has also been facilitated by the retreat of government provision in many developing countries, manifest in a much reduced role in welfare services as a result of public expenditure cutbacks and a weakening of its legitimacy in the face of pressures for democratization, which have in turn widened the potential for non-state initiatives (Robinson, 1995).

Some southern NGOs now reach very large numbers of poor people: the Grameen Bank in Bangladesh has over 160,000 borrowers, the Working Women's Forum of Madras 38,000 members, and the Self-Employed Women's Association in Ahmedabad 15,000 members (Tendler, 1987: 6). It has been estimated that in the early 1980s NGO activities reached some 100 million people in developing countries: 60 million in Asia, 25 million in Latin America, but only 12 million in Africa, although, with a rapid expansion in NGOs in the 1980s, this figure has probably increased dramatically (Schneider, 1988). By then (and if it were assumed that NGOs work primarily with the poor), NGOs would have reached approximately one in eight of those living in poverty in developing countries. More recently the 1993 *Human Development Report* judged that some 250 million people were being touched by NGOs and that the numbers would rise considerably in the years ahead (UNDP, 1993: 93).

Southern NGOs vary enormously in their approach and orientation, in their size and location of operation, in the physical, financial, and technical resources they have available, in the scale of their interventions, in the degree of support they receive from government, and, last but by no means least, in the socio-political context in which their interventions are located. They range from small localized NGOs working in a handful of villages in a single locality, to large NGOs working at a regional or national level, for the most part with funds from external sources. In addition to these local NGOs, there are also large international NGOs (often working with local representation) providing funding and support to indigenous NGOs.

A typical southern NGO is a small agency with a handful of staff working in a cluster of villages in a particular locality. Relatively few NGOs possess the staff or financial resources to work intensively at regional or national level, although it is these organizations which are the best known in government and donor circles. Most of these NGOs are engaged in promoting self-help activities, service provision, community organization, and poverty alleviation with funding from foreign NGOs and, in some cases, government sources. In vulnerable areas, it is still far from rare for development projects to be interrupted by the need to address emergency problems, at times resulting in emergency and development programmes running alongside each other.

A common characteristic of most NGO interventions is working through groups, although some interventions, most notably emergency-type projects, work with the poor on a one-to-one basis. NGO groups range from informal community-based organizations to formal membership bodies established, for instance, for the purpose of the project, often facilitating credit or service schemes provided by the government, or else initiated by the NGOs themselves. They are bound together by voluntary contributions of time and resources and function for mutual benefit. These traits distinguish them from NGOs which act as service providers or facilitators (Fowler, 1988: 3–5; Verhagen, 1987: 21–4). In Africa these organizations 'draw cohesion and legitimacy by building on existing forms of social organisation and adapting their procedures to traditional norms of reciprocity' (Bratton, 1990: 92). In Latin America, and more recently in parts of Asia, it is common for NGOs to promote and work with grass-roots organizations in order to create popular movements which can use their growing power to attempt to modify government legislation in the interests of the poor, and to strengthen democratic participation in the wider society (Korten, 1990*a*: 123–8; Clark, 1991; Stephen, 1990; Carroll, 1992; Bebbington and Kopp, 1995).

There are other differences between NGO approaches, notably between the approaches frequently used in Africa and Asia, reflecting differing historical traditions and political environments. In Bangladesh, NGOs pursue remarkably similar approaches to poverty alleviation, centred on the setting up of savings and credit groups which provide the focal point not only for revolving loan schemes, but also for a range of other sectoral activities in the fields of health, education, income generation, social forestry, irrigation, etc. In this they are strongly influenced by the models promoted by the Bangladesh Rural Advancement Committee (BRAC) and the Grameen Bank (see the introduction to Chapter 7).

Yet Indian NGOs generally exhibit a greater diversity of approach. Two main approaches prevail: small-scale integrated rural development on the one hand and social action on the other. The former is premissed on support for specific programmes and projects organized sectorally and implemented through grass-roots organizations (known as *sangams* in southern India). In contrast, social action groups concentrate on mobilizing the poor to demand better services from government, and work for improved working conditions, higher wages, tenurial reform, etc. While the approaches are very different, there has been some convergence in recent years, with the growing belief among some NGOs that material improvements and empowerment are complementary and can reinforce each other.

In many countries in Africa, the churches play a major role in NGO development activities, many having shifted from relief to development work in the past 10 to 15 years. For instance, in Uganda most dioceses have development arms responsible for channelling funds from northern churches and NGOs to grass-roots organizations in rural areas. Similarly, foreign NGOs tend to be operational more in Africa than in Asia, in part because of the relative weakness of indigenous NGOs and the lack of suitably qualified personnel, and in part because of the many areas which government services simply do not reach and where, as a result, any intervention tends to be relatively expensive.

TRENDS IN NGO ACTIVITIES

Health care and education were prominent among the initial concerns of many NGOs in the 1950s and 1960s. Increasingly, however, NGOs have moved into projects directly targeted at alleviating poverty and attempting to raise the incomes of the poor. Thus, projects aimed at increasing poor farmers' incomes became fashionable in the 1970s, manifest in a growing concern with income generation, the supply of credit, and crop production. These were often accompanied by measures designed to improve the rural infrastructure in the shape of minor irrigation schemes, the construction of schools and community buildings, local roads, etc.

A rather different trend also emerged in the 1970s, where the emphasis was not so much on service delivery or development programmes, but on organizing the poor with a view to enabling them to exercise greater influence over decisions affecting their lives. This 'empowerment' approach has its roots in the view that literacy can often become a means by which the poor can reflect on the causes of their poverty and find ways of tackling them, usually by forming activist groups which put pressure on governments to reassess their policies or persuade the rich to redistribute power and resources in favour of the poor.[4]

New concerns came to the fore in the 1980s, such as gender and the environment, with social forestry and soil conservation prominent among environmental concerns. These reflect an increasing concern about how projects affect the wider setting in which the poor live. Part of the reason for this extension of interests comes from another characteristic which NGOs emphasize: innovation. NGOs pride themselves on being innovative, in the sense of introducing new techniques as well as in fostering novel forms of social organization. As regards the former this has centred on the development of appropriate, low-cost, technologies, which are accessible to the poor. Similarly, as noted above, some NGOs claim to be innovative in their organizational approach, by promoting participation and forging new co-operative alliances among the poor through the formation of grass-roots organizations.

The 1990s have witnessed yet more changes in the nature of NGO activities. Work in the areas of gender and the environment has been widened, deepened, and in many ways integrated under the umbrella of 'sustainable development'. Additionally, some NGOs have focused their efforts in initiatives aimed at strengthening the power and influence of different (poorer) groups in civil society and in a range of projects and programmes striving to build up the capacity of local organizations.

Cutting across these concerns has been a growing interest in sustainability. There are two reasons for this. One stems from a concern with cost recovery, and the desire among NGOs (especially northern NGOs) to transfer the recurrent costs of project management to the community following the withdrawal of the support agency. This is based on the belief that development interventions can be sustained over the longer term only if the community assumes ownership of the project or programme. A second reason for the interest in sustainability is bound up with the desire to avoid promoting dependence on an external agency. This is based in part on NGOs' not wishing to be perceived as benevolent patrons, especially when external dependence simply replaces the influence of locally dominant élites without addressing the structural reasons for such dominance.

NGO COMPARATIVE ADVANTAGE: ASSUMPTIONS AND EVIDENCE

So much for the development of the different characteristics and modes of operation of both northern and southern NGOs. In this section we focus more specifically on the advantages which NGOs are said to bring to bear on the issue of trying to solve the basic problems of development and poverty. At one time, there was widespread scepticism outside NGO circles about the potential of NGOs in development. This has now diminished, although as Cernea (1988: 17) notes, 'there are many contradictory views about the comparative advantages and weaknesses of NGOs. These views range from quasi-denial of NGO effectiveness to hyperbolic exaggeration.'

It is common (and understandable) that northern NGOs tend to project a positive image of their work and the projects that they support in developing countries. This is partly because the public has high expectations of what they can achieve, fuelled by media attention in the 1980s. As Clark astutely observes (1991: 51): 'The media project Northern NGOs as virtuous Davids fighting the Goliaths of famine, climate, government inequity, slavery and oppression. Their staff make such great sacrifices . . . their projects allow crops to grow abundantly where previously there was desert.' It is also in part a function of the literature produced by the NGOs themselves, especially that which is directed to fund-raising. There is a pervasive belief among NGOs in the superior quality of their interventions compared with those supported and executed by official donors and governments. But, to quote Clark again (1991: 53):

there is surprisingly little objective reporting of NGO projects. Northern NGOs' own writing generally concentrates on the success stories and, being aimed largely at their supporting publics, serve a propaganda purpose . . . Most contributors have an implicit faith in the 'NGO approach' which they don't want rocked. After all, one doesn't scrutinize magic too closely, otherwise it loses its charm.

One way of assessing the impact and effectiveness of NGO interventions is to attempt to isolate those features of NGOs which, it is argued, place them in a comparatively advantageous position to work with and assist the poor. In an important early analysis, Tendler (1982: 2 ff.) lists some seven 'articles of faith' about the positive nature of private voluntary organisations. These include:

• that PVOs succeed in reaching the poor;
• that the poor participate in their projects;
• that emphasis is laid more on the process through which people learn to gain control over their lives rather than in the execution of particular tasks;
• that interventions are characterized by flexibility and experimentation in large measure because they tend to be small-scale;
• and that the costs of intervention tend to be lower than more traditional official agency as well as host government interventions.

A similar sort of listing of NGO attributes is given by van der Heijden (1986: 6–7), who argues that the unique features of NGOs, or their 'comparative advantages', are:

their ability to deliver emergency relief or development services at low cost, to many people, in remote areas; their rapid, innovative and flexible responses to emerging financial and technical assistance needs at the grass roots level; their long-standing familiarity with social sector development and poverty alleviation; their experience with small-scale development projects as well as with those requiring a high degree of involvement by, and familiarity with, the concerned target groups.

These attributes have been confirmed in some of the more recent literature which continues to make similar claims about the role and often the uniqueness of NGOs. Thus, from the World Bank, Williams (1990: 32) writes that 'international NGOs have been effective in their ability to work at the grassroots level, and to operate in remote areas or those sectors that did not have efficient development activity'.

Not surprisingly, given their growing involvement in the funding of NGOs, official aid donors have tended to confirm the claims made by the NGOs themselves. Thus, according to a review of NGO projects supported by official aid agencies, Cameron and Cocking state that Canadian NGOs meet their project objectives; Danish NGOs are believed to supplement and complement official aid work; Irish NGOs are effective in meeting their objectives; British NGOs effectively complement official aid; and New Zealand NGOs contribute to the alleviation of poverty in the poorer regions of the world (1991: 18–19). And in the words of a recent overview of NGOs, undertaken by the OECD (1988: 114–15): 'In general, evaluations conducted so far by the official aid agencies of DAC members, many of them relating to rural development and social services, conclude that NGOs have a good record in rural development.' Such a view is likely to have been strongly influenced by a 1986 Canadian International Development Agency study, based on a review of 420 projects sponsored by CIDA and Canadian NGOs. This concluded not only that the vast majority of such interventions were very successful, but that a full one-third of projects appeared to have achieved financial autonomy. Overall, it is argued that the projects showed a strong rural emphasis and a 'clear focus on the poor' (OECD, 1988: 103).

This viewpoint has, however, been increasingly challenged. Indeed, more common are contributions which refine these rather bold assertions, which challenge outright one or more elements of the conventional wisdom, or which highlight what are seen as weaknesses in NGO interventions. These writings are based on a mix of personal experience, surveys of already completed evaluations, and the results of specially commissioned assessments of particular interventions in one or more countries. Among the most serious problems pinpointed are that the management of projects tends to be weak and, in part relatedly, that sustainability is very difficult to achieve (Brown and Korten, 1989). A third problem is that there is little sign of replicability of particular interventions either by the same or by other NGOs. This clearly weakens the overall impact of NGO intervention. A typical critical assessment of the sustainability problem would be the following comment by USAID quoted by Dichter (1988: 1): 'A review of ongoing and completed AID projects in small-scale enterprise credit indicates that most never become self-sustaining even in their pure credit functions. Even more rarely does any project totally cover the costs of its non-financial components.' Indeed, detailed studies tend to suggest that NGO projects invariably founder once outside support is terminated (Cernea, 1988: 19), unless inputs are locally available, beneficiaries are strongly motivated, and the project is compatible with existing social and economic structures (de Crombrugghe *et al.*, 1985).

On the management issue, Korten (1990*a*: 12) reflects an increasingly shared view that NGOs are 'characteristically weak on management and planning'. To which Clark adds (1991: 66):

NGOs are prone to slow response resulting from cumbersome decision making, are susceptible to paralysis arising from power struggles between competing factions, and can evolve conflicting aims as different departments perceive a freedom to interpret their own role without reference to a strongly defined overall mission.

Similarly on the government/NGO contrast, with experience in East Africa, Fowler (1988) maintains that NGOs do not possess an innate comparative advantage over government institutions: rather, they have a potential comparative advantage which can be realized only if they consciously adopt management tools that are appropriate to small-scale development projects in an uncertain external environment.

In some cases, however, it is apparent that management *per se* is sometimes not such a problem, but that, especially in smaller projects, leadership can often be crucial to NGO impact. Indeed, a new article of faith is simply that 'good leadership is essential to project success' (Commonwealth Secretariat, 1987: 10). Conyers and Kaul (1990: 131) even go so far as to maintain that 'local leadership is one of the most important factors contributing to the success of most of the development projects'. Such a view has been confirmed by Tendler who, writing in 1987, drew attention to the significance of charismatic leadership in successful projects, noting that good political connections and a technocratic outlook were instrumental in their success (1987: 21–2). More detailed analysis also suggests that organizations can stagnate when leaders are away for long periods, that they are prone to decay, and that they have little potential for replication and limited capacity for absorbing new ideas. These observations lead Clark to conclude (1991: 66): 'Though leadership is critical to the success of NGOs usually little attention is paid to the development of leadership potential or to management training. And, once in post, leadership skills are rarely fostered because most NGOs are poor at delegation.'

Management and leadership questions lead naturally to the competence of NGO staff to undertake and execute projects and programmes. Although the issue does not feature widely in the published literature, it has been raised in particular by those with experience in the field. Thus Edwards (1989) maintains that he knows of no project in Zambia or Malawi in which inadequate training did not feature as a problem in project implementation (see also Edwards and Hulme, 1992). Highly committed staff are seen as an important element in NGO comparative advantage, although it is also recognized that this may create inflexibility and resistance to new ideas (Clark, 1991: 62).

Moving to the issue of replication, Brodhead and Herbert-Copley (1988: 110) argue that this is the key factor in evaluating success, but that 'the available evidence suggests that NGOs have had at best limited success in ensuring the replication of their work'. For Tendler (1987: v), there is an inherent conflict between small scale and replicability: smallness and social homogeneity often get lost when NGOs expand. She also links the issue of replicability to the leadership question, arguing that, unless the project is replicated by its founder, the chances of success in replication are thin (ibid: 21). Similarly, Cernea (1988: 18) argues that staff intensity and motivation are essential to successful replication.

While one component of the literature highlights these weaknesses of NGO intervention, another goes on to challenge some other articles of faith. Thus, Annis
comments (1987: 129): 'In the face of pervasive poverty, for example, "small-scale"
can merely be "insignificant"—"Politically-independent" can mean "powerless" or
"disconnected"—"Low-cost" can mean "underfinanced" or "poor quality"—And 'innovative' can mean simply "temporary" or "unsustainable."' What is more, Tendler
(1982) contends that in practice many NGO interventions do not reach the lowest 40
per cent of the poor, and that they are neither participatory nor low-cost, although she
goes on to argue that projects are not necessarily failures as a result of being burdened
with these particular characteristics. Similarly, from a study of NGO projects in two
villages in the Indian state of Gujarat, Griffiths (1987: 43) concludes that, despite a
systematic attempt at proper identification and targeting, 'the poorest were by and
large not identified whatever the circumstances'. Nevertheless, in contrast, Avina
(1990) reports that, in his experience, the beneficiaries are among the poorest sectors
of society, even if some of the not-so-poor also benefit.

On the cost issue, a series of USAID-sponsored studies on the effectiveness of
NGO projects in health, nutrition, water supply, and sanitation, found that the
'largely voluntary nature of NGO activities, their commitment to use low cost
technologies and streamlined services, and low staff costs, enable them to operate
efficiently on low budgets' (Cernea, 1988: 18). In contrast, Bowden (1990) maintains
that NGO interventions are not low-cost, Brodhead and Herbert-Copley (1988: 100)
that low cost is no guarantee of cost-effectiveness, and Korten (1990a: 12) that the
projects are not as cost-effective as the NGOs themselves think.[5] Brodhead hints at
an underlying tension between simultaneously achieving the twin goals of reaching
the poorest and executing low-cost projects. He draws on work by Chambers (1983)
to suggest that projects which effectively reach the poor require a high degree of
administrative skill and capability, which means higher costs per beneficiary.

On the question of the innovative nature of NGO activities, Kottack's analysis
leads him to conclude that the projects promoted are anything but innovatory (1985:
323). In contrast, USAID (1986) asserts that NGOs are adaptive and innovative in
their approach.[6] As Tendler is often seen as a critic of the conventional wisdom, her
contrasting views on innovation are particularly noteworthy. In 1982 (1982: 114), she
wrote that PVOs seem to be exceptionally innovative in relation to credit to small
business, but five years later she maintained (1987: vi) that NGOs often claim they are
pioneering a new approach when they are merely reinventing the wheel.

There has been considerable discussion in the literature on the issue of participation and its importance to project impact. The assumption, as Brodhead and Herbert-
Copley (1988: 123) point out, is that participation increases the likelihood of attaining
the project's objectives and its sustainability, as well as promoting a more equal
distribution of project benefits. Their own view is that participation is important but
by no means a sufficient condition for project success. This contrasts with the 1986
CIDA study which argued that community participation was one of three factors
leading to project success. In strong contrast, Tendler (1982, 1987) maintains that
projects which are not participatory but which are top-down and authoritarian can be

very successful. Similarly, de Crombrugghe *et al.* (1985: 80) argue that projects may sometimes succeed without the beneficiaries being involved in the identification of needs, even if their evidence also leads them to the view that projects 'almost always fail' if the beneficiaries are excluded in the planning phase.

Moving from the particular to the general issue of the overall impact of NGO interventions, what is noteworthy is that, with only rare exceptions, most substantive analyses based on commissioned studies come to fairly gloomy conclusions about the performance of NGO projects, even though there is considerable reluctance on the part of analysts to be drawn into making overall or general statements about impact— even in cases where opinions are based on the examination of only a limited number of interventions.

The main reasons put forward for this high degree of diffidence are: the lack of data with which assessments can confidently be made, the differing quality of evaluations which have found their way into the public domain, and a reluctance to make broader generalizations from limited evidence. These points are made strongly, for instance, in the writings of Brodhead and Herbert-Copley (1988) and de Crombrugghe *et al.* (1985). A typical comment reflecting this sense of unease would be the following (Smith quoted in Gorman, 1984: 146, 155): 'the unevenness of evaluations of pvo projects does not help to prove pvo claims that they are more effective than governmental agencies in certain areas of development . . . there is insufficient evidence to substantiate these claims solidly . . . The rhetoric is at times great but adequate information is sparse.'

In spite of the reservations, some overall judgements have been made. They usually share the viewpoint that, while the projects selected are frequently those which the NGOs themselves believe are among their better ones, independent assessments frequently come to far less favourable judgements about performance and impact. Not surprisingly, therefore, the overall view of the impact of NGOs in poverty-alleviating and/or income-generating projects is one ranging from, say, mediocre to poor, rather than, say, from acceptable to good. A typical selection illustrates this particular cluster of viewpoints and conclusions.

eight of the self-selected 17 projects failed to return benefits equivalent to the costs expended. Another study of 19 projects found 40 per cent to be borderline or unsatisfactory (Ellis quoted in Gorman, 1984: 202).

Both Netherlands and FINNIDA evaluations point to a lack of success with income-generating projects (OECD, 1988: 19).

Ford's experience after 10 years examination of income generating projects is that there are very few successes to talk about, especially if you look at post-intervention sustainability (Fowler, personal communication, 1989).

Projects which were initially selected on the grounds that they were successful in fact turned out not to satisfy the evaluation criteria outlined in a surprisingly large number of cases . . . Of the seven micro-projects visited, six exhibited quite serious problems (de Crombrugghe *et al.*, 1985: 18, 48).

These and similar comments from this critical school lead on to the highlighting of a fourth problem, which, it is argued, plays a major contributory role in the low success rate of their projects.[7] This is the vagueness of many of the objectives of NGO projects, leading to the charge that imprecise objectives are bound to be difficult to monitor and evaluate. In this vein, de Crombrugghe *et al.* argued in the mid-1980s that steps needed to be taken to improve the way that projects were identified, prepared, and initially appraised (1985: 36). Nevertheless, towards the end of the decade, there was still 'a widespread need for better project planning' (OECD, 1988: 115).

A number of more recent studies have placed increased emphasis on yet more factors said to influence project performance. Particular emphasis is placed on the importance of the wider environment—the large number of factors external to the project—which, it is argued, not only need to be analysed when initiating and executing particular projects, but which also help to explain what appears to be the relatively poor performance of NGO projects. For instance, Tendler (1987: 102) maintains that the success of NGO operations depends upon a complex set of factors including macroeconomic and socio-political environmental factors, many of which are often beyond the control of the NGOs.

Similarly, Carr *et al.* (1984: 1) contend that a *sine qua non* of any evaluation of performance is a full understanding of the environment in which the project is located; only when this is achieved can one begin to understand the changes which are taking place, and among them the ones which are applicable to project intervention. More dynamic and historical factors are also highlighted. Thus, Brown (1990) and Korten (1990*b*) write about the role and importance of institutions and organizations for achieving sustainable development, and draw on an even wider literature to illustrate their concerns in these areas.[8]

A discussion of the importance of power, power relations, and empowerment processes in understanding current impact and future prospects is also relevant in this context (see, for example, Marsden and Oakley, 1990). Debate on these issues can be highly specific, relating to élites and interest-group interests that directly impinge upon the project, or it can be very broad and general, focusing on the nature of the state and the manner in which it is possible for agents external to central power structures to meet the objectives of their very different agendas. Usually, however, when discussion of impact takes place within these wider parameters it also tends to veer towards pessimism. Thus, Schneider (1988: 139, 202) writes that:

Although NGOs often work diligently to eliminate the symptoms of poverty, they are not always conscious of its true dimensions and are frequently unaware of the spiralling effect of these factors of impoverishment . . .

In the light of the findings of our study, it is obvious that rural development remains essentially a prerogative of government . . .

When discussion is broadened to external factors it usually emphasizes the complexity of factors affecting project performance. Some authors have argued that, because the communities with which NGOs work are always changing, if not the objectives then at least the means to achieve these objectives need continually to be re-assessed and altered as circumstances, both internal and external to the project, change. Conyers and Kaul (1990: 132) suggest that this inevitably brings conflict. Yet another layer of complexity is added when it is argued that project success in one time-period could well be the cause of problems in another. This is well illustrated by a recent review of a World Lutheran Federation water project in West Nile Uganda, where clear success in easing the plight of thousands of people whose lives were threatened, contributed to the build-up of future problems. Thus, according to Brett (1989):

The field director said they had made three errors: of efficiency, of kindness and of expatriate methods. Efficiency had both created widespread dependency and let it be possible for the government to ignore the area. Providing services that were subsidised had created a false sense of values among the people; using foreign methods meant it would be more difficult for others to follow. While all this is very true, there were in fact no alternatives (at the time).

This chapter suggests that it is by no means easy to come to any firm overall conclusions about either the factors which characterize the uniqueness of NGO interventions or the degree to which NGOs have succeeded in their task of helping to alleviate poverty. It is clearly far from simple to judge whether the views of the optimists or the pessimists better reflect reality.

There are four main reasons for this. The first is simply a lack of data. For all the claims and counter-claims made and for all the evidence provided, the extent of reliable evidence upon which judgements have been and are made still remains minute in comparison with both the absolute numbers of NGO interventions and the very different types of project embarked upon. The second is that there still seems to be confusion in the eyes of both the general public and the agencies over claims and assertions about the comparative advantage of NGOs and the evidence which is available. The third is the growing realization that a range of both complex and external factors play a powerful role in influencing the outcome of NGO intervention in very different social, economic, and political contexts. Finally, judging impact is handicapped by the lack of an agreed method of assessing the performance of NGO projects and programmes. It is to the question of impact assessment that we now turn: the next chapter examines the problems underlying the evaluation of NGO project performance and existing approaches to NGO evaluation, and ends by setting out the approach used in the case-studies contained in this book.

NOTES

1. For example, there are 290 in France, 300 in the UK, 320 in Canada, and some 200 in Sweden. In Japan the number of NGOs has grown rapidly in recent years, and by 1990 there were a reported 157 development NGOs in the country. The paucity of NGOs in Greece and Portugal is a reflection of the relative poverty of the two countries and history of domination by dictatorial regimes (and with it the suppression of an independent voluntary

sector). However, recent accession to the European Community has provided an important source of funding and contact with other European NGOs. For details on individual countries see Robinson (1991*b*).

2. US PVOs (Private Voluntary Organizations), for example, increased their aid to Africa by two-thirds in the period 1984–6 (from $486m. to nearly $800m.) following media coverage of the Ethiopian famine (Smith, 1990: 3).

3. In an unpublished OECD paper, van der Heijden (1986) estimated that the number of southern NGOs ranged between 10,000 and 20,000.

4. It should be noted that many of the ideas that have proved influential among NGOs worldwide originated in southern NGOs and with grass-roots activists, especially the importance now accorded to participation and empowerment. The concepts of empowerment and conscientization were developed in Brazil by Paulo Freire, and were rapidly taken up by NGOs elsewhere in Latin America, and in countries like India and the Philippines. Participatory approaches to development had their origins among NGOs in India, leading to techniques of participatory appraisal and evaluation. These themes were subsequently taken up by NGOs in the North, many of whom now see them as integral to their own approach and have encouraged counterparts in other countries to adopt them. It is important to recognize that ideas and resources do not simply flow from northern to southern NGOs, and to highlight that there is a two-way exchange which is not always openly acknowledged.

5. Put simply, cost-effectiveness is the cost per unit of output, which could be adapted to the net income and/or wealth generated by the project divided by the direct and indirect costs of the project. In some of the US literature, the cost-effectiveness (C-E) ratio is defined as the present value of benefits divided by the present value of costs, and defined as follows (Bowman *et al.*, 1989: 10): 'The C-E Ratio equals NET BENEFITS (income of the project less an estimate of what the income would have been without the NGO input) DIVIDED BY direct and indirect costs less any fees paid by the project for services provided by the NGO.'

6. Confirming the general assumption, a USAID-sponsored assessment found that: 'NGOs have a comparative advantage in identifying needs and building upon existing resources. More flexibly than government they can transfer technologies developed elsewhere and adapt them to local conditions, as well as work out innovative responses to these local needs.' (Cernea, 1988: 18).

7. The three other weaknesses, discussed above, are management problems, lack of sustainability, and low replicability rates.

8. Brown (1990: 26–7) talks about three paradigms which guide development action. He expresses concern about both the 'market' and the 'planning' paradigms: 'in neither do resources trickle down very fast, in spite of much rhetoric to the contrary'. He proposes an alternative 'multisectoral' paradigm, drawing on a range of sectors and processes, and which would permit a variety of institutional paths to accomplish objectives rather than relying on a single sector or approach.

4

Evaluating NGO Performance

INTRODUCTION

Any organization dependent upon voluntary contributions attempts to assess the extent to which its goals are being achieved, and to do so as efficiently and openly as possible. Development NGOs are no exception. In fact, both they and their supporters would rate them highly in all these respects, but the benefits of assessment are both broader and deeper than this. To the extent that goals are not being achieved or performance is sub-optimal, the practical lessons can be fed into current decision-making, thereby enhancing future performance. Furthermore, if voluntary organizations are able to show that the funds made available to them are well spent, support will tend to be strengthened and funding based on a firmer footing, while, at the same time, criticisms of poor performance can be more substantially met.

Evaluation is the term most commonly used to describe the process of assessing performance against objectives. At their best, evaluation techniques should be able to assess performance results against objectives, and benefits against costs, and in so doing identify strengths and weaknesses in a way which can have a positive impact on the effectiveness of projects and programmes. Evaluation can also be used to highlight weaknesses in current monitoring practices, as well as to provide a wider perspective on different types or clusters of projects or programmes—in the case of NGOs, in relation to either particular countries or to different types of intervention.

If this was all that had to be said about evaluation and assessment, and about monitoring the performance of projects under way, evaluation would by now have become widespread across the NGO movement. This, however, is far from the case. For most European NGOs working in the development field, evaluation is still very new and, if used at all, tends to be more of a one-off affair, most often embarked upon either because things have gone very wrong—the fire-brigade approach—or when a particular project has been completed but there is a request for further funding, or when a second or third phase of a particular project is to be launched. Indeed, the vast majority of projects and programmes funded by British NGOs in developing countries are not subject to any sort of formal evaluation nor bound to specified cycles of expenditure for committed support, as is common with official aid projects.[1] Most NGOs do not carry out any assessment of the impact of the projects and programmes they fund beyond simple project report-back and financial audit.[2]

Evaluation is probably most advanced within Oxfam, the biggest British NGO, which has a separate unit for research and evaluation, and in Christian Aid. But even here, no common framework, guidelines, or procedures have yet been adopted.[3] The same is broadly true of current practice among even the largest NGOs in the Netherlands and Germany and among other northern European NGOs, such as those in Finland and Sweden. What is more, while most of the larger NGOs have carried out or commissioned evaluations of particular projects, there has been no uniformity of approach, and in most cases the results have remained confidential to the organization.[4] In short, evaluation has tended to be discrete and mostly marginal to the cycle of project identification and implementation. As a result, agencies have not devised any method of absorbing the lessons or recommendations of evaluations into the normal rhythm of the project cycle; neither have they devised—or in many cases even discussed—procedures for accepting, rejecting, or acting upon the recommendations made and the conclusions drawn (Robinson, 1992).

There are understandable (even if not compelling) reasons for this state of affairs. At the best of times, and in the best of circumstances, evaluation is a delicate and difficult enterprise. This is not simply because evaluations attempt to assess the worth of things done (or not done), and to suggest ways in which they might be done either better or differently, but because the conclusions drawn and the recommendations made invariably have a bearing on the work undertaken by particular individuals and/or the organizations for which they work. What is more, the very nature of evaluation can frequently create tension between the evaluator, those who made the decision to fund a particular project, and the project itself. Indeed, even if sympathetically executed, evaluations are often of greatest benefit or interest when they indicate how processes, methods, or objectives should or might differ from present practice. Yet such conclusions are precisely those which raise questions about the performance of people and/or institutions responsible for what has been or is currently being done.

Institutional concern with (or, sometimes, fear of) the evaluation process is significantly reduced when the decision to evaluate is taken internally and is supported by staff from top to bottom; when evaluations are undertaken by people either from within the organization or employed by it; when there is an agreed system for taking action on the results and conclusions drawn; and when individuals responsible for the projects under evaluation do not feel that their jobs, institutions, or public image will be threatened.

The rest of this chapter is divided into two parts. The first discusses some of the broader issues of—and difficulties associated with—NGO evaluations. The second outlines the approach to evaluation used in the ODI study and upon which the case-study evidence—summarized in Chapter 5 and described for each of the four selected countries in Chapters 7 to 10—is based.

CONCERNS ABOUT EVALUATION

The increase in public funding of NGO activities has raised the prominence of evaluation within NGOs, increased the pressure to undertake more evaluations, and encouraged the examination of more rigorous methods of evaluation. But herein lies the first concern: NGOs remain to be convinced that they should adopt the evaluation techniques familiar to official aid agencies—for three main reasons. First, there is no agreed methodology of evaluation either across different sectors or of particular types of aid interventions, and NGO projects and programmes are characterized by a much greater variety of purpose and process than are those of official agencies.[5] They are also much smaller in terms of cost, size, and numbers of beneficiaries. More fundamentally, NGOs believe that through their interventions they are addressing a different set of concerns from those of official donors, particularly in relation to social development.

Almost all NGOs share a perception of the development process which is far wider than simply the provision or acquisition of goods, services, or the means of production. Most subscribe to the view that raising the living standards of the poor in a sustainable manner necessitates the poor acquiring more power, for example through promoting community organization and encouraging non-formal education, with some NGOs going so far as to equate 'development' totally with 'empowerment' (Marsden and Oakley, 1990). More recently, a cluster of NGOs in Britain (the British Overseas Aid Group) has focused on the notion of '*inclusion*', linking the idea that success in achieving greater inclusion of the poorest in the mainstream of development should help to make the world more secure. Even if NGOs believe that development is achieved only in part by promoting self-reliance,[6] many feel the compulsion to dismiss as largely irrelevant mainstream techniques, with their apparent bias towards quantitative measurement and their perceived under-playing of the role of non-quantifiable and non-economic elements. These factors tend to reinforce a view that each intervention is unique, or nearly so, thereby down-playing any potential lessons that might be learnt for future interventions.

Furthermore, NGOs pride themselves on being particularly sensitive to the needs of the poor in developing countries and on responding quickly to them. This, together with extreme pressures on staff time to shorten the pre-project assessment or feasibility period and to keep costs down, means that objectives are frequently couched in terms which are rather general, or which are altered, often substantially, during the life of the project or programme. The more imprecise the objectives, the harder it is to provide an evaluation with clear-cut conclusions. Indeed, because it is not uncommon in aid interventions for the initial objectives to be altered, there is often an even less firm foundation for deriving durable conclusions. These concerns have been influential in introducing what is termed a process approach, which is now beginning to inform evaluation methods employed by some official aid agencies. The process approach gives explicit recognition to the fact that many projects, especially those with a poverty focus, often do not have firm, fixed, and durable objectives against which performance may be judged.

Secondly, official aid evaluations tend to be dominated by methods that encompass some sort of cost–benefit analysis, with benefit 'streams' being identified and made subject to some form of measurement. But there is doubt about both the appropriateness and the reliability of NGOs adopting such approaches. One reason is simply that, for most NGO projects, no base-line study has been carried out, and there is therefore no objective base from which to compare subsequent performance. Another is that many NGO interventions have multiple objectives, and most include objectives for which no, or minimal, quantifiable data can be obtained. Yet there is no agreed or reliable method of judging how non-quantifiable benefits can be accurately ascertained, or how their influence ought to be integrated with more quantitative data on benefits. Furthermore, it is argued that cost–benefit analysis has played a limited role in bringing about improvements in official aid agency practice, and this questions the practical benefits of such a technique and its usefulness to decision-makers.[7]

Thirdly, to date it has not been possible to use the results of evaluations of official aid to prove either that this aid helps the development process and the relief of poverty, or that it does not. In part, this arises because only a fraction of all official aid—probably less than 15 per cent (Riddell, 1987: 185 ff.)—has ever been evaluated; in part, this is due to the fact that official aid performance is significantly influenced by a range of other external factors, and in part it is because official aid cannot be usefully isolated from the larger recipient government public spending to which it contributes.

There are, however, other reasons why so little advance has been made by NGOs, at least until recently, in evaluating their development effort, and why there is some reluctance to adopt evaluation techniques and methods in a more systematic manner. One reason is that there has been little demand for evaluation among those who support the work of the development NGOs, or, at least until quite recently, from the more vocal opponents of aid. From the late 1970s major criticisms of official aid, especially those made by free-market critics,[8] spurred official agencies to pay more attention to the impact of their projects and programmes and put pressure on them to convince their legislatures that these public funds had been well spent. Yet similar questions were not widely raised about the aid provided by voluntary organizations until the second half of the 1980s; indeed, because the free-market critics of official aid supported the private sector, they tended (at least implicitly) to favour NGO initiatives. If donations are an indication of approval of methods, then the 1980s could be judged a period when the public reaffirmed its faith in the ability of NGOs to achieve their objectives.[9]

There have, too, been fewer pressures from the NGO movement as a whole, or from within individual NGOs, to adopt a more formal approach to, or a more general advocacy of, evaluation. One reason is that the staff of NGOs, from their directors downwards, are typically fully stretched, so that there is no spare capacity to devote to such activities; if additional staff are taken on, this is usually in response to an expansion of project work.[10] Continued pressure to keep down costs discourages all but the major four or five NGOs from either employing staff to work on evaluation or incurring significant additional costs in employing outside evaluators. Another important factor is that in the recent past, and even today, a vigorous debate has been taking place within NGOs about the precise role they should be playing in development. As a result, the little time which NGOs devote to reflection has been taken up predominantly with incorporating new ideas into what they should do. This has tended to eclipse consideration of how well they might have achieved the often outdated objectives they strove to achieve some years previously.

It is certainly true that as NGOs grow, accounting procedures tend to be tightened and become more institutionalized; yet generally this has not led to a more formalized system of evaluating how well the money is being spent in relation to either the broad objectives of the NGOs or the more immediate objectives of the particular projects or programmes supported.[11] There are a number of important reasons for this.

One is that it is becoming less and less common for northern NGOs to manage and execute their own projects and programmes in developing countries: it is most common for NGOs to provide resources to selected southern NGOs to assist them in promoting projects or programmes which they or other southern NGOs have drawn up and wish to execute. Thus, Christian Aid and CAFOD channel most of their funds to their overseas partners rather than promoting their own projects from Britain, while Oxfam, too, has minimized its direct intervention in a number of countries. This development throws at least some doubt on the appropriateness of British NGOs evaluating projects and programmes which are not theirs and for which they do not have direct responsibility—even if it raises the question of the extent to which these partners have been, or ought to be, evaluated when significant funds are given to them.

A related issue is the question: evaluation for whom? Insights from participatory evaluation methods indicate that the perception of the intervention by the intended beneficiaries can and often does differ significantly from that of the donor (Feuerstein, 1986). Thus, to the extent that evaluations are initiated by the northern donor in a manner which attempts to provide a framework whose constituency is donor-based, the likelihood of the process of evaluation missing its target is increased.

Finally (although it is often not aired so publicly), there is also a fear that more evaluations will provide evidence that a number—and possibly quite a significant proportion—of NGO interventions fail to meet the objectives of alleviating the poverty of the beneficiaries, or that in some the intended beneficiaries are not the poorest. More evidence increases the risks both that knowledge of such failures will become more widespread and that such knowledge could be used malevolently. The more immediate concern is that this might lead to voluntary income from supporters being adversely affected. More subtly, there would be the fear that those supporting development NGOs will be more selective and donate to those NGOs having what they believe to be a more tangible record of success.

Even without a representative sample of evaluations of NGO projects, what we already know about aid interventions would tend to suggest that the failure rate of NGO projects is likely to be far from insignificant. Two factors are of relevance here. First, overall evidence from official projects indicates that at least 10 per cent could be deemed a 'failure' (Cassen *et al.*, 1986: 11–12), while more detailed country-based analysis gives figures of upwards of 15 per cent (Federal Republic of Germany, 1986). Second, the points already made about pressures to keep costs low and to respond quickly to requests, and the often rather general objectives of projects would tend to suggest that the environment in which NGOs operate is probably less favourable than it is for official interventions. Far more NGO than official aid projects and programmes tend to be targeted directly to the poor, and it is difficult to achieve sustainable improvements in living standards in short periods of time, while poverty-targeted projects of official agencies have a far lower success rate than do their other projects (see Cassen *et al.*, 1986: 11). In other words, one would not expect NGO projects to achieve their objectives as easily as most official aid projects.

PRESSURES FOR CHANGE

The more significant the allocations of public funds to NGOs, the greater the pressure for northern governments to be able to justify them. Evidence of the success of former publicly funded projects could be expected to be a condition at least of further funding. However, as public money is also provided on a block-grant basis, there are pressures for NGOs to provide more general evidence of overall achievement.

Greater amounts of public money channelled to development NGOs, growing incomes from individual sources, and a greater public attention given to development NGOs (derived in Britain in part from increased resources going to development education and in part from the public response to famines in Africa) have all combined to raise the profile of NGOs as agencies which work to alleviate poverty by aiming for long-term development. Thus not only is government putting pressure on NGOs to prove their effectiveness, but the public is becoming increasingly concerned to know that NGOs are effectively and efficiently achieving their objectives. Thus as the British Minister for Overseas Development, Baroness Chalker, has argued (1989):

Honesty about the standard of all aid work is essential. Not all NGOs are in fact good at grassroots development. Not all NGOs are cost-effective. Some spend a great deal on glossy public relations and awards which have little to do with the needs of the poor. And there are, I fear, rather too many who are readier to be unhelpfully critical of each other or of our ODA programme than to look honestly at their own failings.

But there are other, perhaps stronger, factors involved. Many NGOs now feel that they are being pulled into having to answer questions about their involvement in longer-term, more substantive and integrated development projects and programmes rather than short-term and discrete projects, and, more generally still, about the appropriateness of their involvement in particular countries. As these questions are raised within different organizations, it is increasingly recognized that development work is complex and difficult and that it needs a more systematic approach which includes assessment of ongoing forms of intervention.

It would appear, therefore, that the main worry is increasingly likely to be not so much about the theoretical merits of introducing a system of assessment to help achieve objectives more effectively and efficiently, but rather about the likelihood of these objectives being attained in practice, especially when judged against both the costs and adverse consequences (internally and externally) which might also result. This perspective is also borne out by the fact that some of the larger NGOs are evaluating their projects and have begun to assess the wider impact of their interventions.

That NGOs have contracted external evaluators to examine some of their (larger) projects and are continuing to do so suggests, at minimum, that these exercises are deemed useful to them. The more pressing question is therefore the extent to which they should expand these efforts, especially by using a more systematic approach, and whether more of the smaller NGOs should follow their lead.[12]

This raises other, more detailed, questions. Should evaluations continue to be one-off affairs related to particular questions or problems, or could the process be incorporated more permanently into the project cycle and country strategy? Is it possible for larger organizations to extend, and for smaller NGOs to initiate, an approach to evaluation which can provide reasonably clear indications not only of success or failure but of reasons for varying performance? Can such an approach be adopted without excessive expense in terms of money or human resources and, relatedly, could it be undertaken without employing external experts? Finally, to what extent can evaluation contribute towards a learning process within NGOs, whereby the insights derived from the experience of discrete project evaluations inform the overall perspective and approach of the implementing agency?

THE ART OF JUDGING NGO PERFORMANCE

Once it is agreed that evaluations should be undertaken by NGOs in a more systematic way, the next question is the approach which should be adopted. The overriding problem is that there neither are—nor can there be—firm rules for judging the effectiveness either of NGO projects and programmes in particular or of poverty alleviation projects in general. Why is this?

First, there are difficulties in measuring achievement. Social and political objectives are involved as well as economic: there is no satisfactory way of objectively evaluating qualitative achievements (Marsden and Oakley, 1990). Second, there is no correct time when an assessment should be made. If projects fail five years after the NGO has withdrawn, what sort of success is the project measuring in comparison, say, with projects that fail when the NGO is still providing assistance, or with those that never even started? If failure is due largely to circumstances external to the project, then the evaluator's view of the project (and the NGO) will be different from projects failing because of internal weaknesses, such as faulty project design, poor management, and lack of skills in execution. Thirdly, not only is the society in which an NGO project is being executed constantly changing, but also what could be the right thing to do in one period may well turn out to be wrong in another.

More technical difficulties also need to be acknowledged. There are no satisfactory ways of evaluating changes in economic status and of determining what changes have been due to the project if there are no base-line data against which to judge the current situation and there is no accurate control group against which to assess what has been happening. Yet it appears that the absence of these critical data is more the rule than the exception in the vast majority of projects undertaken and funded by northern NGOs. In relation to the control group, numerous economic studies of

Africa during the 1980s (for example) inform us of an important and quite widespread generalization: that the continent has suffered from a significant fall in living standards. In this context a project which succeeded merely in maintaining living standards would probably be judged successful.

Similarly, a judgement of the performance of a project needs to consider not only what has been achieved (the benefits) but also its costs. The problem of benefits has been discussed above; for most projects funded by British NGOs the cost data tend to range from sketchy to almost non-existent. While there is usually some idea of the direct and running costs of the project, there is usually no attempt to estimate all the costs. Mostly lacking are the indirect home-originating costs, as well as the start-up costs. In addition, NGOs rarely make any allowance for the opportunity costs of participation, in terms of the time input of the intended beneficiaries.

Having made a judgement about the success of a particular project, there remains the question of whether the venture was worthwhile. Could the resources (financial and human) utilized have been spent more efficiently in a different way, or used more productively for the benefit of other groups of equally needy people? Did the NGO intervention have any effect on the ability of the host government to promote its own development projects?[13]

Given these difficulties, what is the scope for evaluating NGO programmes? The first point to make is that there are many possible types and styles of NGO evaluation, which have different information requirements and operate at different levels: that of the donor agency (northern NGO or funding agency), that of the implementing agency (local NGO), and that of the beneficiaries themselves (Marsden and Oakley, 1990: 12–13). For each of these levels, three corresponding types of evaluation can be distinguished: external evaluation (where the evaluators are not involved directly in project implementation), joint evaluation (involving both external evaluators and project staff), and self-evaluation (beneficiaries and project staff, perhaps with the assistance of an outside facilitator).[14]

In practice, there has tended to be some cross-over among these various types of evaluation, reflected in a growing measure of agreement on the desirability of beneficiary-oriented or participatory approaches, where 'the actual indicators for evaluating social development in any specific project or programme must be developed in the concrete context of the project or programme's specific objectives, its socio-economic context and the people's culture' (Rahman, 1990: 40). In other words, it is argued that 'people's self-assessment of progress' should form the starting-point for evaluation and not externally determined performance criteria (ibid. 43; Feuerstein, 1986).

A further point which emerges from the literature on social development is that evaluation is a continuous process which can promote organizational learning, and not a discrete exercise which excludes the intended beneficiaries (Marsden and Oakley, 1990: 7):

In line with an approach that is process-oriented rather than product-oriented, evaluations should not be seen as separate discrete activities; they should pervade the process of development itself and become an integral part of the continuous reorientation and internal examination of objectives required of process projects. As such, the chronological distinctions that have traditionally separated evaluations from appraisals and from monitoring exercises are necessarily blurred.

While such a perspective is relevant for most NGO interventions, this should not be interpreted as being incompatible with a search for indicators of impact and effectiveness that allow conclusions to be derived about the strengths and weaknesses of NGOs in different sectors of activity.

Methods of data collection can range from quick and dirty techniques of visual inspection and informal discussions through to more detailed techniques drawing on interviews with the intended beneficiaries, project staff, and key informants (knowledgeable local people), project records, and relevant secondary materials (see Chambers, 1985; 1994). For the most part, however, the 'two-week blitz' model predominates, where 'one or two consultants are sent out to the field for two weeks to evaluate an operating project, using judgemental assessments, qualitative data and a minimal search through administrative records' (Barclay *et al.*, 1979: 5).

Two more specific aspects of NGO project interventions have also received attention in the evaluation literature. One is the recognition of the wider context of NGO interventions as a critical determinant in project outcomes (Carr *et al.*, 1984: 1–2):

The *sine qua non* of evaluation 'as if people mattered', is that far more attention than usual should be paid to understanding the context within which development projects take place. Only when a reasonably comprehensive impression has been formed of the environment and of the networks of economic, social and political relationships in which people are involved, does it become possible to determine the types of changes which have been taking place in their lives; and to differentiate those which derive from the project under investigation, from those which find their origin elsewhere.

This emphasis on the external environment counters a tendency among some NGOs to assume that the project constitutes the principal universe of those being assisted. Clearly, however, NGO interventions represent only one among a number of influences on the lives of the poor. A further advantage in examining the contribution of 'external' influences on project outcomes is that an understanding of the immediate environment of the project can help in assessing the prospects that exist for the replication of successful interventions.

The second aspect concerns the identification of suitable indicators to measure the impact of projects with social development objectives which, by their very nature, tend to be qualitative. As yet, however, there is no agreement on what constitute appropriate indicators for measuring participation, empowerment, and other aspects of social development,[15] nor on the most appropriate methodology to be used for this purpose (Marsden and Oakley, 1990). Indeed, a major problem with NGO evaluations which focus predominantly or exclusively on qualitative indicators, is their susceptibility to subjective evaluator bias, since there are no clearly specified means of verifying the findings of such evaluations.

THE ODI APPROACH

This final section outlines the major elements of the approach developed in the present study to help judge the effectiveness, impact, and potential sustainability of NGOs in sixteen poverty-alleviating projects in Bangladesh, India, Uganda, and Zimbabwe.[16] The need to incorporate qualitative indicators and to place the impact of particular interventions within the broader external environment were key considerations in devising this approach.

The aim was to formulate an approach for assessing not all projects and programmes but, more narrowly, those whose purpose was to alleviate the poverty and/or improve the living conditions of the beneficiaries, principally of people living in rural areas. Thus, projects and programmes focused on emergencies were excluded, as were those aimed principally at welfare-enhancing objectives, namely health, education, and care of the elderly and the infirm. These were set aside not because they were judged unimportant but because it was felt that a common sectoral focus would offer a firmer basis for making comparisons. Previous evaluations of NGO projects across and between countries found it difficult to draw useful conclusions about impact and effectiveness largely because they were trying to compare very different types of interventions (Crombrugghe *et al.*, 1985).[17]

There is, of course, nothing original in this attempt. With few restrictions on time, resources, and specialist skills, it would not be difficult (although not always easy) to undertake evaluations of these sorts of projects and programmes (big or small). One reason for looking for a different approach is that almost no NGO has the resources, time, and skills to undertake these sorts of evaluations on a regular basis. In addition (as noted above), most NGOs remain resistant to adopting wholesale an approach close to that used by official agencies, and one which they see as dominated by quantitative statistical techniques. Perhaps of more importance, the complexity of rural societies and the difficulties of alleviating poverty point to the need to approach the evaluation of these particular projects from the viewpoint of the socio-economic (and ideally the historical) context of the communities into which the particular project is inserted.

The challenge, therefore, was to design a method of evaluating the impact of what are complex NGO projects and programmes on the basis of limited time, financial resources, and skills, and in a manner which is able to incorporate qualitative indicators of performance into the assessment. But it was even more demanding than this because of the paucity of quantitative data available: most British-funded and British-run NGO projects and programmes typically have no, or at best limited, quantitative base-line data against which to judge effects and outcome, while the data on project effects, costs, and benefits also tend to be far from comprehensive.

These circumstances provide an inauspicious context for serious evaluation. In particular, professionals trained in economic techniques and evaluators skilled in cost–benefit analysis and in constructing quantitative rates of return and net present value estimates for projects might well argue that there is little here to inspire confidence. How, it can be asked, can firm conclusions be made when there is not enough time or skill to gather the data, nor enough data to be gathered, and therefore when assessment is so dominated by subjectivity? These ingredients would appear to be a recipe for sloppiness of approach and inconclusiveness of outcome.

But, equally, it has to be asked whether it is necessary to make use of these sophisticated, time-consuming, and expensive tools of analysis. Gaps in resources, technique, and data become a serious problem only if the conclusions drawn are controversial, and need to be defended against opposing views and conclusions; it is only then that the struggle for objectivity and the elimination of personal bias becomes paramount. Similarly, there is no point in spending time and resources gathering very detailed quantitative data to show that income levels have risen from, say, $4.30 a month to $6.50 at fixed prices, if the purpose of the evaluation is merely to discover if incomes have risen significantly and to list, in order of importance (rather than put an accurate figure on), the factors contributing to the increase in income. If the conclusions derived from evaluations are clear and are accepted by the different interested groups as a reflection of reality, then techniques used to arrive at these judgements become less important.

In short, it is unnecessary to concentrate time, effort, and resources on project or programme evaluation if firm conclusions can be drawn without using sophisticated techniques. Similarly, if judgements made about qualitative aspects of projects are not substantially challenged by the relevant actors or groups (the beneficiaries, the NGO donor, and the recipient government), or if the differences can be sufficiently understood or explained by interest-group bias, then purist worries about objectively assessing these factors tend to become largely irrelevant.

This perspective provides the entry-point for the approach to NGO evaluation outlined here, and utilized in the case-studies described in the second part of the book. The primary objective—in common with conventional evaluations—was to make judgements about the project or programme under investigation: whether, overall, it could be deemed successful, and whether it had made an appreciable impact on alleviating the poverty of a particular community or group of people.

The first step was to devise a common methodology to be used for each of the case-study evaluations.[18] It was important to try to steer a middle course between too loose a framework, where individual judgement could unduly influence the analysis, and too rigid a structure, which might lead to the under-playing of important local characteristics. The overriding issue was to assess the extent to which project objectives had been met, the reasons for the outcome achieved, and the extent to which this was related to the influence of the project itself, or to some other (external) factors. More specifically, the assessments set out to discover the extent to which the project had been able to assist in poverty alleviation, how the benefits were distributed, what the costs were, the prospects for sustainability, and the potential for replication.

The approach involved a broad assessment of costs and benefits, but this embraced relevant non-economic as well as economic and financial indicators, the exact selection of which varied from project to project. For none of the projects was it possible to undertake any sort of rigorous cost–benefit analysis, as a common feature was the lack of any base-line data with which to compare present-day living standards. This, however, proved no major drawback, as the main purpose of the assessments was not to provide detailed statistical analysis of changes in economic status but rather to understand better what factors were important in contributing to the (more generally assessed) alleviation of poverty or what factors were preventing people becoming less poor. Because a key objective was to find out what worked (or did not) and why, the approach placed major emphasis on assessing and synthesizing the judgements of different 'actors'—beneficiaries, the project sponsors, non-beneficiaries, and other local people—about the project's performance and impact, and trying to weigh the merits of judgements which differed.

The approach was also participatory in that the criteria used to determine the impact and effectiveness of the project were assessed in relation to the beneficiaries' own perceptions of change, and the importance that they attached to different factors (Rahman, 1990; Robinson, 1991c). In some instances, the particular factors selected differed from those of the project staff and the evaluators. In most cases, too, the fieldwork (approximately five weeks for each project) was carried out as a joint evaluation with members of the project staff, or other selected locally based personnel.

In practice, the evaluators systematically gathered primary data only if it was felt that further data would be helpful in clarifying differing views on project results, and if it was judged that the data required could be obtained relatively quickly and easily. In most cases, the data were predominantly based on field investigations, with a principal primary source being interviews with the intended beneficiaries (in groups and as individuals) and project staff. This was complemented by review and analysis of relevant secondary materials and discussions with local officials.

Methods of evaluation can stimulate interest only when they answer specific questions. In this approach to assessing discrete NGO projects, the purpose was to attempt to provide answers to a series of interrelated categories of questions, the first of which, although the most fundamental, is likely to be answered last. The seven categories of questions are:

(1) Has the project been successful in achieving its objectives: what were the project objectives, when were the results expected, what assumptions were made about the project and the wider environment, what lessons from elsewhere were incorporated into the project?[19]

(2) Has the overall economic status of the intended beneficiaries been enhanced following the NGO intervention; that is, has the project had an impact in addressing the problems of poverty? What are the different factors which led to the impact achieved and which specific factors are judged to be more and which less important?

(3) Have the benefits of the project been distributed equitably between different groups of people—richer and poorer, men and women, landed and landless?

(4) Has the change in economic status of the beneficiaries been due more to the impact of the project than to the influence of other non-project factors, or vice versa?

(5) Has the project been executed efficiently—that is, were the costs appropriate to the range, level, and distribution of benefits?

(6) Do the results of the project provide grounds for believing that this type of intervention can be replicated so that the benefits can be spread more widely?
(7) If the NGO is still involved in the project, is a date set for withdrawal and is withdrawal likely to lead to any particular problems? If the NGO has already withdrawn, did this lead to any particular problems? In general, what are the prospects for project sustainability?

Answers to these questions do not simply appear through following a prescribed method of approach. In particular, they are vulnerable to bias. Answers and an increase in knowledge emerge from a process of further questioning based on judgements evolving from the interaction of the evaluator with the world of the project—the world of people and their opinions as well as the material world. Thus evaluations consist of more than merely gathering information and, in the case of projects which have complex social and other non-economic components, more than collecting and organizing quantitative data.

The nature of evaluating NGO projects aimed at alleviating poverty leads to two further considerations. The first relates to the perspective of the poor. To be sensitive to the complexity of issues surrounding not only the project but, more importantly, the society into which the project has been inserted, requires special skills. These include a sensitivity to the community, gained most probably through past experience of undertaking these sorts of evaluation. Academic skills helpful in this context are clearly far broader than technical training in economics and quantitative cost–benefit techniques. They would probably embrace other fields of development, not least anthropological skills.[20]

This leads on to the second consideration: the blending of technical skills in evaluation methods and approaches with specific knowledge of particular projects or particular communities. Two extremes need to be noted. On the one hand, it is difficult to undertake a sound evaluation of a project with no knowledge of the language and culture of the beneficiaries. On the other hand, giving a prominent role in evaluations to someone with knowledge of the language and culture but who in addition might be either one of the beneficiaries or a member of the NGO sponsoring the project is likely to colour the process of gaining knowledge about the project and answering the key questions.

One way of addressing this range of problems is to make use of an evaluation team or a joint evaluation approach, which maximizes the talents and skills required and minimizes the potential biases of particular individuals. For most of the case-study projects this was the approach adopted. In some cases, the ODI evaluator was joined by a local researcher with the requisite skills but without any knowledge or known view on the project. In other cases, however, and especially if the project being evaluated was under the care of a small southern NGO with few or no skills in evaluation, the national partner on the team was often a person selected from the NGO, although ideally not directly involved in the project and therefore not known to the beneficiaries or with responsibilities within the organization for that particular locality.

NOTES

1. In this respect British NGOs differ from many of their counterparts in the US, for whom evaluation is now an integral element of their management information systems.
2. Not all British NGOs have formalized even these procedures for all of their interventions in developing countries.
3. Save the Children Fund and CAFOD have also set up separate evaluation departments and are in the process of developing their own approaches and policies. Guidelines on evaluation have been prepared for the use of British NGOs, following a three-day workshop hosted by the co-financing arm of the Overseas Development Administration in July 1992.
4. In Germany a handbook on evaluation and impact assessment entitled *Evaluation in the Churches' Development Cooperation* was published in 1991 by a joint editorial team of the leading Catholic and Protestant NGOs for (voluntary) use by the member agencies and their partners in developing countries. A variety of approaches to evaluation is described in the handbook.
5. However, most bilateral agencies now use some version of the logical framework.
6. Rahman (1990: 46), for example, defines self-reliance in the following manner: 'Self-reliance is not the same as self-sufficiency, but a combination of material and mental strength by which one can deal with others as an equal, and assert one's self-determination'.
7. A recent assessment concludes: 'At best *ex ante* CBA is performing a useful ceremonial function in justifying projects selected on other grounds. Similarly *ex post* CBA may help convince policy makers and the general public of the merits of development aid. But CBA is almost never used in a systematic way to guide *ex ante* project selection.' (Renard and Berlage, 1990: 28).
8. Particularly influential were Peter (now Lord) Bauer in Britain, and Milton Friedman and Melvyn Krauss in the United States.
9. At the end of 1991 Oxfam, Christian Aid, and CAFOD all reported record levels of voluntary income.
10. Although in the larger agencies, as noted above, it has also been related in Britain to the felt need to direct more resources to campaigning and development education work.
11. This was borne out in a study of thirty-two projects co-financed by the European Community which found that a lack of attention to monitoring and evaluation was a weakness in all but one of the projects studied (de Crombrugghe *et al.*, 1985).
12. Some of the smaller NGOs have already started to adopt a more systematic approach to monitoring and evaluation, with base-line surveys and regular evaluations.
13. In a recent study of NGOs in Mozambique, Hanlon (1991) puts forward the thesis that the growth of NGOs undermined both the immediate and longer-term impact of government agencies.
14. Uphoff (1991) provides a useful outline of a methodology of participatory self-evaluation developed for the People's Participation Programme of the FAO. Sometimes self-evaluation is used to refer to evaluations undertaken by the staff of the NGO responsible for implementing the project or programme: see, for example, Sen (1987).
15. For an attempt to measure the contribution of participation to project success in a series of USAID-funded projects see Finsterbusch and Van Wicklin (1987).
16. Effectiveness is used to refer to the extent to which an NGO project or programme's objectives are being achieved, as a measure of performance. Impact is associated with the broader consequences of the intervention, rather than simply the immediate benefits

(outputs). It extends beyond income improvements and related material benefits to incorporate social changes brought about by the project. Sustainability or viability, refers to the longer-term continuation of project benefits following the withdrawal of external NGO support.

17. While such studies can convey the breadth and diversity of NGO interventions, they inevitably lack depth and do not provide a sufficiently detailed basis from which firm conclusions can be derived about NGO effectiveness and impact in specific sectors of activity. In a recent Canadian study, fifty-one projects were visited by the research team, ranging from teacher training in Zimbabwe through to cocoa production in Haiti (Brodhead *et al.*, 1988). A study sponsored by the Club of Rome in the mid-1980s surveyed ninety-three projects in nineteen countries, covering a wide range of sectoral activities (Schneider, 1988).

18. For details see Riddell, 1990.

19. Initially performance may be judged against original objectives, but in some cases it is judged against evolving or changed objectives.

20. As Widstrand has commented (1990: 6): 'What anthropology has to offer, uniquely, is a range of models and theories dealing with the most important issues in development work: the interplay of social, economic and technical factors in human communities undergoing change. Anthropology has made a speciality of the pragmatic study of change in small-scale societies.'

5

The Impact of NGO Poverty-Alleviation Projects: Overview of the Results of the Case-Studies

OVERVIEW AND SUMMARY

It is widely assumed that NGOs are able to reach and improve the well-being of the poorest who are the subject of NGO assistance. Overall, the sixteen evaluations of NGO projects paint an encouraging picture. Twelve of the sixteen broadly achieved their objectives, and had a positive impact in alleviating poverty, even if only one was clearly successful in achieving all its objectives. In contrast, only two can be said to have failed both to meet their overall objectives and to make headway in reducing poverty. The final two achieved some of their objectives, but fell short in others, with the result that it was not possible to derive a firm assessment of their overall contribution to poverty alleviation.

This overall judgement of project success, while subject to a number of qualifications, appears to be consistent with the findings of other comparative studies: three-quarters of the sample appeared to meet objectives set, and had an impact in alleviating poverty. In the successful projects there was evidence that incomes had increased, in some cases quite substantially, consumption had improved, and there were ongoing investments in land, livestock, and assets. In addition, the social status and self-confidence of the poor were found to have been enhanced in the process, increasing their capacity to make use of locally available opportunities.

Successful project interventions were found to be related to a number of different factors, none of which in isolation was sufficient to achieve project objectives. Three, in particular, stand out: beneficiary participation, effective management, and skilled and committed staff. In addition to these factors, a favourable external environment was found to be conducive to project success: it was far easier for projects to succeed in their objectives when the local economy was expanding (or at least not contracting), resources were plentiful, and local élites were broadly supportive of their objectives. The evidence also suggested that those projects which had been prepared and designed more carefully were among the more successful performers.

The sixteen case-studies confirmed the importance of beneficiary participation in the planning, design, and implementation of projects. Projects were more likely to succeed where their objectives corresponded to the priorities of the poor, and where the intended beneficiaries were regularly consulted and involved in decision-making at all stages of the project cycle. Although there was some evidence of success in projects lacking in participation, the benefits derived were unlikely to be sustained over the longer term without more direct involvement. Most of the NGOs placed a high premium on the formation of new groups or the strengthening of existing groups as a means of raising awareness, fostering participation, and empowering the poor, although these were not always integral to successful interventions.

The sixteen projects highlighted the importance of a strong and competent leadership, skilled in management and possessing an overall vision of project goals. Strong leaders were able to maintain channels of communication with government officials, enabling them to lever additional resources or circumvent potential problems. At the same time, excessive centralization of decision-making in some projects undermined staff commitment and limited the potential impact of the intervention.

A third factor underlying project success was staffing. The calibre of project staff, their commitment to overall project objectives, and their degree of empathy with the intended beneficiaries all contributed to the more successful projects. Well-trained and educated staff motivated by a reasonable level of remuneration and decent working conditions played a critical role in this regard.

Not unexpectedly, while the overall judgement of project performance was favourable, the projects exhibited weaknesses in certain key respects.

1. *Reaching the poorest.* First, and most importantly, many of the projects failed to reach the very poorest, and even in cases where poverty alleviation occurred, improvement in economic status was modest. There was little evidence to suggest that many beneficiaries had managed to escape from poverty on a permanent basis. However, these results need to be seen within the wider context. Thus what appear to be marginal improvements to an outsider (even for those closely associated with the project) can be of major importance for the poorest themselves, especially when considered in a broader environment of marked economic decline. Equally, it would be unrealistic to expect rapid change to occur in a relatively short space of time. Some of those assisted are what are sometimes called 'borderline' poor—people who experience spells of seasonal poverty. For them, even small increases in income during the peak agricultural season can be enough to tide them over a lean patch. Similarly, the creation of new or, more commonly, additional periods of employment during the off-peak months was found to play an important role in reducing vulnerability to the fairly hostile external environment in which most poor people have to live.

2. *Cost-effectiveness.* Second, most of the studies revealed that these types of interventions are costly to implement and the benefits take time to mature. In five of the projects, the benefits clearly exceeded the costs of achieving them. In five others the objectives were achieved, but at a high cost in terms of staffing and resources. In the two projects which failed to meet their objectives the costs far exceeded the benefits. For the remaining four projects, it was difficult to make precise judgements, either because the project was relatively new or because the data were insufficient. In addition, the studies confirmed that cost–benefit analysis appears novel to some NGOs, and that overall costs are usually higher than NGOs believe them to be.

3. *Sustainability.* On the question of sustainability, relatively few of the projects

demonstrated the potential to continue once the NGO ceased operating in the area. Some were heavily constrained in this respect by an adverse physical environment. In others, insufficient attention on the part of the NGO to cultivating the capacity of grass-roots organizations to manage economic programmes undermined their potential for self-reliance over the longer term.

BACKGROUND TO THE STUDY

At the core of this study are case-study evaluations of sixteen poverty-alleviating projects executed or funded by some of Britain's leading NGOs, utilizing the approach outlined in the previous chapter and in the methodology framework paper (Riddell, 1990). This chapter summarizes the main conclusions of these evaluations. It begins by outlining the reasons for the choice of countries and the case-study projects, providing a brief description of each. It then summarizes the main findings from the evaluations, followed by a discussion of a number of specific issues arising from them.

Choice of Countries

Poverty-alleviating projects were selected for analysis in four countries: two in South Asia (Bangladesh and India) and two in sub-Saharan Africa (Uganda and Zimbabwe). The choice of these particular countries was based on a broad range of factors: a significant level of indigenous NGO activity in the country, a substantial British NGO involvement, and a comparatively large official British aid programme. Another consideration was the differing nature of poverty in each country. Within the overall context of poor countries, the attempt was made to select countries characterized by variations in the incidence, extent, and causes of poverty, and different approaches of government, as it was anticipated that this would be likely to give rise to different types of NGO project intervention and to differing approaches to poverty alleviation.

Bangladesh is ranked among the six poorest countries in the world in terms of per capita GNP ($220 in 1992), placing it in the category of least-developed countries. It has a population of 114 million (1992), growing at the rate of 2.3 per cent per annum. Over two-thirds of the population is classed as poor, and in the rural areas more than half the people do not earn or produce enough to meet their basic food requirements. Foreign aid plays an important role, accounting for 87 per cent of government development expenditure and more than 50 per cent of the value of imports. There are estimated to be over 500 local NGOs involved in development work, which together receive external aid of $85–100m. per year, equivalent to 6 per cent of official aid commitments. British NGOs annually transfer in excess of $20m. to their local counterparts. Bangladesh is the second most important country after India in terms of its receipt of UK NGO funds.

India is the second-largest developing country in the world. In 1992 it had a population of 884 million, growing at an annual rate of 2.3 per cent. GNP per capita was $310, with one-third of the population below the official poverty-line, most of whom live in the rural areas, but are distributed unevenly across the country. In sharp contrast with Bangladesh, in 1991 foreign aid represented 12 per cent of the value of total imports. There are more than 10,000 NGOs engaged in development activities in India, spending between them an estimated $500m. per year, 90 per cent of which comes from foreign contributions, equivalent to 25 per cent of official development assistance. British NGOs account for about 10 per cent of total NGO expenditure, equivalent to some $30m. annually.

Uganda has a population of around 18 million, growing annually at a rate of 2.6 per cent. GNP per capita stood at $170 in 1992. The changes in Uganda's per capita income for the period 1965–88 are the worst recorded for all developing countries, having contracted by an average of 3 per cent a year over the period, and reflecting the cumulative effects of war and political turmoil. Poverty is most acute in the rural areas, where two-thirds of the population are classified as poor, although foreign aid contributed more than 50 per cent to total government expenditure and represented more than 60 per cent of the value of imports. There are approximately 300 NGOs active in Uganda; at least eighteen of these are British. British NGOs provide in the region of £10m. annually for development projects and disaster relief, but there are no accurate figures on the total volume of NGO aid to the country.

Zimbabwe has a population of just over 10 million, growing at the rate of 2.9 per cent per year. With a GNP per capita of $570 in 1992, it is now classified as a low-income economy, with significant disparities of wealth between classes and regions.[1] Poverty is concentrated in the rural areas, especially in the communal areas where more than half the population live, the majority of them smallholders. Foreign aid flows account for just 2.6 per cent of total government expenditure, and represent about 25 per cent of the total value of imports. NGOs number around 400, and spend well in excess of £20m. a year, equivalent to 20 per cent of official aid flows. British NGOs have stepped up their involvement since Independence in 1980, and play a prominent role in funding the activities of a range of Zimbabwean counterparts.

Case-Study Selection

Clearly, given the range of projects funded by and/or implemented by British NGOs across even these four countries, there is considerable variation in relation to size, duration, objectives, level of funding, and approach.[2] The sixteen projects selected for the study share two common characteristics: all are located in or involve major activities in rural areas; and, more importantly, all are explicitly concerned with poverty alleviation through income generation, even if the particular approach used differs from project to project. Thus projects with an exclusive single focus on social services (education, health, and shelter), or on relief were excluded from the study, even though it is recognized that such projects may mitigate some of the most pernicious effects of poverty.[3]

The term 'poverty alleviation' is shorthand for an intervention aimed at a sustained improvement in the economic status of the poor, by raising incomes and creating new opportunities for employment, which in turn bring about increased consumption, savings, and investment. Within these parameters, an attempt was made to strike a balance between projects concerned with off-farm employment and those with a focus on small-scale agriculture. Finally, most of the projects selected had among their objectives increasing the participation of poor people in development activities, improving self-reliance, or enhancing social mobility.

There are a number of reasons for focusing on projects stressing the raising of incomes and the enhancing of economic status. First, it was considered easier to compare interventions within and between different countries by focusing on more narrowly defined projects. Second, it was assumed that it would be easier to come to firmer, and less impressionistic, judgements about changes in economic status than, for example, in assessing the achievement of less tangible goals such as 'raising the awareness of the poor' or 'increasing their empowerment'. Third, the type of approach adopted here reflects the growing realization on the part of NGOs that any long-lasting attempt to redress the causes of poverty, as opposed to its symptoms, has to include a focus on improving the economic well-being of the poor.

Two further considerations underpinned the selection of the sixteen projects. As a primary objective of the study was to assess impact, it was necessary to select reasonably sized projects, to try to choose those that had been running for some time (at least two, and preferably five, years), and to pick those which exhibited a level of continuity of both objectives and methods of approach. In the event, only one of the sixteen projects had started less than two years prior to the evaluation; five were less than five years old; and eight (half) had been in operation for ten or more years. One project had ended over five years prior to the evaluation, and in others, particular areas or groups assisted no longer received direct NGO support. Another criterion for selection was that the projects should have some direct link with a UK NGO, although only two of the sixteen are implemented by British NGOs—in this case by ActionAid.

In Bangladesh, the four projects selected highlight different NGO approaches to poverty alleviation, and the types of problems that have been encountered in the course of their implementation. The four are: the ActionAid Development Centre Programme, which focuses on savings and credit for off-farm income generation; the horticulture and agriculture programmes of the Gono Kallyan Trust, which provide technical support to enable small groups of the poor to farm land on lease; the fisheries programme of Gono Unnayan Prochesta, which helps the landless to develop disused ponds for fish cultivation; and the Caritas social forestry programme, where the aim is to motivate people to grow more trees around their homesteads and on public land.

The four projects chosen in India also reflect a range of approaches common to many NGOs in the south of the country, as well as embracing different types of local NGO organizations. These are: the Community Organisation Programme of Rural Development Trust, which focuses on a crop loans scheme; the CASA Phase III programme, which is concerned with accessing subsidized bank credit supported by government grants for off-farm income generation; the Arthik Samata Mandal agricultural development programmes, whose main thrust is the provision of crop loans from institutional sources, grants for small-scale irrigation, and land improvement schemes; and the Kanyakumari District Fishermen Sangams Federation, which aims at improving the marketing of fish caught by Federation members. Similarities between most of the projects in both India and Bangladesh include: a concentration on group formation; an emphasis on the poor, the landless, and women; and the provision of credit.

The four projects in Uganda are the Uganda Women's Finance and Credit Trust, which provides credit for employment and income generation to rural women; an engineering workshop under the West Acholi Co-operative Union, which produces agricultural equipment for local farmers; the health component of the Multi-Sectoral Rural Development Programme, which attempts to fund its activities through user fees and income-generating projects; and the technical skills training unit of the ActionAid Mityana rural development programme. They highlight different aspects of NGO interventions: three focus on relatively well-established agencies, two of the local NGOs promoting the projects have had a long involvement with British NGOs, and one is implemented by the Anglican church which, with its Catholic counterpart, plays a major role in NGO development activities in the country.

In Zimbabwe, while all four case-study projects focus on rural enterprise and group work, three have adopted very different approaches to poverty alleviation. The Catholic Church's Silveira House is one of the oldest NGOs in the country, and pioneered group approaches to credit for communal farmers in the pre-Independence period; the Mzarabani farmer credit project provides an example of an NGO attempting to move away from a primary focus on relief to promoting development; the Campfire project, supported by the Zimbabwe Trust, represents an innovative approach to sustainable wildlife resource management; finally, the Simukai collective co-operative focuses on joint productive enterprises, consistent with the government's desire to promote rural development along more equitable lines.

Expectations of the Results

In common with the experience in other leading donor countries, British NGOs fund many hundreds of different types of projects, of differing size, in differing environments, and in very different types of developing countries: sixteen projects thus represent a minute sample. It is clearly not possible to derive general conclusions about the impact of British NGO projects as a whole, although some more specific conclusions emerge about the sorts of economic interventions favoured by NGOs.

It is therefore important to stress a number of points. First, only a few NGO evaluations reach the public domain each year and, of these, very few attempt a comprehensive cross-country evaluation of NGO projects. Hence there is little evidence against which to judge the results of this particular initiative: indeed, one of its purposes was substantially to increase the amount of information available about NGO project impact. What is more, we know that the sixteen selected constitute a biased sample of projects, for two reasons. In the first place, and as mentioned already, certain specific selection criteria were used, although they do include important and representative types of NGO interventions. But secondly, there has been an additional bias, towards what could be termed less contentious projects: the selection was made in consultation with the UK NGOs, who suggested a range of projects which fitted the selection criteria for possible inclusion.[4]

This raises the question of why the selection was not random. The objective of the study was not to try to answer the question of whether NGO projects in general are any good, or not: there was insufficient evidence prior to the study to be able to come to a firm conclusion on this point. The explicit objectives of the exercise were:

- to try and see the extent to which a narrow representative group of poverty-alleviating projects have been successful in achieving their objectives;
- to isolate those factors for particular projects which have contributed to or frustrated project success; and, if the data merit,
- to isolate those factors across projects which seem to have contributed to or frustrated project success; and, again, if the data merit,
- to make some tentative wider generalizations about the types of projects selected.

RESULTS OF THE EVALUATIONS

The remainder of this chapter discusses NGO project interventions in relation to nine themes, drawing on the evidence from the sixteen evaluations to highlight similarities and differences between projects and across countries.

1. Reaching the Poorest

Conventional wisdom asserts that NGOs are particularly good at reaching the poorest: the assertion that they are better at this than government and official aid agencies suggests both that they may be better at involving poorer or the poorest groups, and that they may be better at improving their lives. Thus an important aspect of project impact is the distribution of gains accruing to different groups of beneficiaries. The evidence from the sixteen evaluations shows—positively—that the projects were not set up for the rich, and that few direct and exclusive benefits were obtained by the non-poor. Equally, however, no projects were both set up for and exclusively benefited the poorest. Almost without exception, the poor benefited to a greater extent than the poorest, and men to a greater degree than women, by virtue of having prior access to land and other assets. In only four of the sixteen projects evaluated were the incomes of the poorest raised significantly; in eight they were either bypassed or the benefits that they received were limited in comparison to individuals who were less poor. These results lead to the important question of the characteristics of projects which did reach the poorest, and why even NGOs find it difficult to reach down to and improve the lives of the poorest.

One sub-group of the poorest are the chronically poor who lack the means to satisfy their basic food requirements. These include the sick, the elderly, and others who are not generally economically active, together with a small number of people who will be reluctant or unable to participate in projects due to suspicion, lack of motivation, or pressure from dominant social groups. Such people tend to constitute a minority of the rural population; they are usually beyond the reach of most economic interventions and stand to benefit more from improved social services, rather than through development projects designed to promote self-reliance.

But another—and larger—sub-group include landless labourers, marginal farmers, those with few durable assets and little or no education, and a high proportion of households headed by women. Part of the reason for NGOs failing to reach these people in larger numbers lies in the constraints of human and financial resources. Almost by definition the poorest tend to be scattered, disorganized, and living in resource-poor areas, or are heavily dependent on the non-poorest groups for employment and credit requirements. When NGOs attempt to design projects exclusively for these people they form functional groups to encourage their participation. Alternatively, they try to implement projects on the basis of direct contact. But even if NGOs follow the latter course of action, they are constrained in this: it is no easy task to devise programmes aimed at raising the incomes of individuals without land or other assets: unskilled workers with little capital tend to produce products that sophisticated consumers do not want to buy, while the poorest have no money to buy such goods. These problems were encountered both by the ActionAid Mityana Programme (AMP) in western Uganda and ActionAid Bangladesh.

However, four of the sixteen projects where the poorest did benefit directly offer some insights into the types of NGO interventions which stand a higher chance of success: the CASA Phase III programme in coastal Andhra Pradesh, the ActionAid credit programme in southern Bangladesh, the Simukai collective farming co-operative and the Campfire project in Zimbabwe. The CASA and ActionAid Bangladesh projects both used rigorous targeting of beneficiaries, and worked hard to ensure that the poorest were well represented in beneficiary groups. Beyond that, a concentration on the disbursement of small loans directed towards activities selected by the beneficiaries in consultation with, and subject to careful monitoring by, project staff helped to ensure both that the poorest could cope with the (small amount of) assistance provided and that the money loaned was likely to go into productive uses of value to the poorest even though the loans were not always sufficient to meet their needs. In Zimbabwe, the Simukai co-operative benefited the poorest, as co-operative members were largely young unskilled, uneducated, and assetless ex-combatants, but the numbers involved were very small (less than forty). In the case of the Campfire project, the poorest gained because the project embraced everyone living in the designated area. In both instances, however, the administrative costs were high in relation to the numbers of people benefiting and the extent to which positive benefits were generated.

In some of the other projects, the poorest clearly gained as the benefits trickled down to them even though they were not actively participating. Small farmers assisted by crop loans provided by RDT in India expanded the area they cultivated, increased their share of cash-crops, and in some cases started to cultivate several crops a year: all these activities led to expanded employment opportunities for the poorest.

Similar employment expansion is evident from the UWFCT and ActionAid projects in Uganda generated by small businesses set up by individuals who received credit and skills training. However, few of the NGOs participating in the study realized the extent to which some types of intervention had a multiplier effect manifest in increased local demand for goods and services and employment.

Alleviating poverty is, of course, concerned with far more than raising income levels or attempting to increase short-term financial security (although it is often linked with these): a point recognized in the usually broad set of objectives of the projects examined. These include a range of social benefits which are less amenable to quantification but can be of great significance to the poor, especially in the South Asian context: for example, reduced dependence on money-lenders and local political élites, greater independence in decision-making, lower seasonal out-migration, improved ability to cope with contingencies such as illness and natural disasters, greater political participation and awareness, reduced social discrimination, and increased self-respect and mobility for women. Thus in Uganda, the Women's Finance and Credit Trust not only provides examples of increasing income, for instance from developing a small business, but in addition the income gains enhanced the status of the poor (especially those previously without land or assets) within the wider community, providing the conditions for a widening of opportunities for subsequent gain in the medium term. Or again, people from the scheduled-caste community in coastal Andhra Pradesh report that the practice of untouchability has declined as a result of their being able to sell goods and provide services valued by higher castes, as a result of the NGO intervention.

Most of the evaluations revealed few major, new social tensions arising from successfully enhancing the social and economic status of the poor, either with local (male) élites or other poor non-beneficiaries. This is a notable achievement for, as the evaluations make clear, attempts to raise the incomes of the poor usually take place in a social and political environment which is at best difficult, and often hostile to the objectives of the projects. However, it could also signify that the projects failed to challenge the prevailing balance of power or existing patterns of gender discrimination.

The relative absence of tension between rich and poor was usually related to the type of projects executed. Four factors appeared to play a role here: the economic benefits were perceived by the rich to be too insignificant to be of interest to them, or the project was completely self-contained (ActionAid, Bangladesh; CASA, India; and the Simukai co-operative, Zimbabwe); the particular technological innovation (homestead-based tree planting) introduced primarily benefited only the poor (e.g. Caritas Bangladesh); the rich also gained as the benefits accrued to the entire community (natural-resource management or investments in the village infrastructure as in India and Bangladesh and under the Zimbabwe Trust); and the NGO was able to persuade the rich to co-operate because the increased income for the poor also led to increased income for the rich (e.g. the fisheries programme in Bangladesh). In some projects, the NGO was able to exploit differences between rival dominant groups and successfully avoid polarization, or else to eliminate the exploitation of politically weak middlemen (CASA and fishermen's federations in India). But the lack of tension in most of the projects reflects the fact that they focused less on mobilizing the poor to challenge the structural causes of poverty (unequal landholdings, low wages, etc.) and more on enhancing their incomes and material status.

However, social tensions did arise in some projects, sometimes spilling over into violence, especially when richer groups felt that their interests were under potential or actual threat. In India especially, dominant social groups (landlords, money-lenders, and high castes) sometimes reacted violently to a loss of patronage and income (from high-interest loans for example) by resorting to coercion, smear campaigns, exploiting factional divisions, and physical attacks on project participants or staff members. In the Zimbabwe Trust project, the comparatively powerful district council appeared to try to control the significant income gains acquired from wildlife management which ought to have been channelled down to the ward participants.

2. The Involvement of Women

Since the early 1980s, NGOs have been highlighting discrimination against women and the relative disadvantages that women suffer in many societies in the developing world. This is probably why their interventions are believed to be effective in reaching poor rural women. While this study's selection of projects indicated a commitment to gender issues, their involvement and impact upon poor women was generally limited. With the notable exception of the Uganda Women's Finance and Credit Trust, set up exclusively for women, there was little evidence to suggest that the projects selected effectively challenged prevailing patterns of gender discrimination. Men dominated the agricultural credit schemes studied—Christian Care in Zimbabwe, RDT in India—even if these included special programmes for women. Women were also usually under-represented both in committees of beneficiaries set up to liaise with the NGO and among the project staff of the NGO, unless there was a positive attempt to expand their involvement.

In only six of the sixteen projects did women benefit to any significant extent, either through their direct participation and involvement, or in terms of a perceptible improvement in their economic and social status. Equally, however, it needs to be said that improving the economic status of women in male-dominated societies is both a complex and delicate issue and one which is bound up with the wider problem of poverty. In the face of women's difficulties, it is highly unlikely that significant advances can be made in a short space of time; indeed, it would be naive to expect NGO projects, especially over a short period, to transform their role and status. In some projects, pressure from the men forbidding their wives to take on new income-enhancing activities was often outweighed by the extent of family poverty, and the chance to obtain more cash or food.

This was evident in the GKT horticulture and agriculture programme and the ActionAid credit programme in Bangladesh. In both cases, the rise in income contributed towards increasing women's confidence in the prospects of an improved quality of life. As the UWFCT project in Uganda and the CASA project in India demonstrate, in the short term at least, increased self-respect and even limited financial independence can be very important for poor women in a male-dominated society. Nevertheless, there are frequently limits to the extent that disadvantaged women can gain increased independence from such interventions. For example, the ActionAid credit programme in Bangladesh indicated that male family members used loans secured by women to finance their own economic activities.

Where efforts were made to involve women and promote their economic well-being, the projects revealed a tendency to emphasize more traditional occupations for women, characterized by relatively low economic return and market potential. The reason is understandable: it reflects existing economic and domestic commitments which place severe restrictions, especially time restrictions, on the ability of women to take on new tasks. The result, however, is that gender divisions tend to be reinforced rather than resolved by such interventions. Yet there were examples of projects where NGOs were able to help women identify opportunities for deriving new sources of income include tree cultivation and backyard nurseries on household plots, in the Caritas social forestry programme in Bangladesh, and tailoring, poultry-raising, and dairying, in the CASA Phase III programme in India. In such cases it was apparent that increased income for women brought wider benefits in the form of improved food intake for children and higher expenditure on health and education.

3. The Role of Groups

The sixteen case-studies broadly confirm the view that most NGOs place a high premium on the formation of new groups, or the strengthening of existing groups, as a means of raising awareness, empowering the poor, and promoting self-reliance. However, not all the NGOs operated through fully fledged groups. In Uganda, for instance, in two of the four projects (UWFCT and the Busoga diocese health programme) beneficiaries interacted with NGO personnel largely on an individual basis. For the remainder, groups have differed in their origins, size, and function. In some instances, groups were already in existence prior to the NGO intervention; these included self-help groups (such as the farmers' groups in Christian Care and Silveira House) and membership organizations (the ASM farmer's co-operatives and the fishermen's associations in India). For the most part, groups were established by the NGO at the outset of the project.

In some of the projects, the groups functioned little differently from groups set up or utilized in non-NGO projects. Their main function was to facilitate the distribution and collection of credit, or to provide a mechanism to channel inputs to the beneficiaries. In others, however, the groups performed a rather different, or at least additional, role, best captured in the notion of 'empowerment'. In Uganda the NGOs usually worked with groups formed prior to project commencement, or with very loosely structured associations. In Zimbabwe individuals with similar backgrounds, especially common church membership, were brought together to facilitate the allocation of small-scale credit and agricultural inputs to farmers. But in neither country was there much evidence of NGOs spending time forming new groups, or explicitly attempting to involve the poorest. To some extent, this appeared to reflect a wish to reduce risk and to maximize the anticipated impact of particular interventions.

In contrast, in Bangladesh and India seven of the eight projects began with the explicit task of forming groups which were established with the objective of bringing together the poor, on the basis of class, gender, and locality.[5] Here groups were formed for two purposes: first, to promote participation in the design and organization of economic programmes, and to provide a channel through which credit and other inputs could be directed; and secondly, in order to achieve a range of specific social and political objectives. In India, in particular, the case-studies provide evidence of the groups formed playing an effective role in empowering their members. The results are manifested in various ways. In some cases, groups provide the basis for collective social action, enabling communities to seek redress over legal wrangles, to mediate in conflicts over land rights, or to challenge government legislation. The fishermen's associations in Tamil Nadu illustrate not only the way in which the exploitative mark-ups of middlemen and money-lenders were successfully circum-vented, but also how substantial political leverage was acquired by the associations, which enabled them to influence government policy on fishing rights. Likewise, the CASA project provided the structure for poor people not only to gain confidence to approach officials, and to interact with people from outside their own community, but also to secure access to resources from government institutions and banks.

The positive gains from NGOs working with and through groups, however, needs to be put into broader perspective. Five of the sixteen projects lacked community participation but were, none the less, clearly successful in raising incomes. Groups only appeared to play a significant role when they genuinely represented the interests of the poor (rather than acting as a front for élite groups) and where they provided effective channels of communication with the NGO. In projects where groups were characterized by unstable membership or internal conflicts, performance was adversely affected. Equally, even with projects which resulted in higher incomes or increased status for the beneficiaries, fear of losing the gains achieved often pushed group members towards exclusivity and a reluctance to open up membership to the poorest. Thus, in some projects where members were self-selected (such as the Silveira House farmers' groups in Zimbabwe or the fishermen's associations in India), the beneficiaries introduced stringent entry requirements: membership became con-ditional on the ownership of land and assets, which resulted in the poorest automatically being excluded.

Projects are often designed so that, if individual members perform poorly, the project as a whole suffers. For example, some credit projects operate in such a way that when one member defaults it adversely affects the credit standing of the others. Default or an inability to meet repayment obligations was the most common cause of group break-up in ActionAid Bangladesh and Silveira House in Zimbabwe (although an underlying factor was the vulnerability of the poor to domestic and environmental calamities). Furthermore, group pressure to repay loans to the project can result (as in the case of RDT) in some members of the credit scheme returning to the village money-lenders to borrow funds simply in order to remain in good standing with the NGO.

Another problem with functional groups is that, while they may be conducive to effective project management in the short term, longer-term sustainability can be more difficult to achieve. Certainly the small-scale credit programme of ActionAid Bangladesh, the crop loan programme of Arthik Samata Mandal and RDT in India, and the Silveira House credit programmes in Zimbabwe all appeared to have similar problems with the capacity of project members to take over administrative responsibility from project staff.

Another frequent objective in the NGO group approach is to try to develop effective leadership among the poor. Again, a number of the case-studies provide evidence of successes here, notably in the CASA project and the fishermen's associations in India, although strong leadership can adversely affect the nurturing of group democracy and in the long term heighten the risk of non-sustainability, since other group members can lose interest and fail to take an active part in group affairs, as the ASM case-study illustrates.

Clearly, therefore, the issue of groups and their role in NGO projects is more complicated than might initially be thought. Groups may not be a *sine qua non* for successful NGO interventions. During the life of the project, performance is related to a range of factors, only one of which is the way in which the beneficiaries are organized and their input into decision-making structured.

4. Management and Staffing

The quality and effectiveness of management and project staff constitute one of the key clusters of factors identified as playing a major role in project impact. The term 'management' encompasses a wide range of factors. It begins with project selection and ends with the process of disengagement; in between comes the constant monitoring of the project against objectives, perhaps the altering of objectives, but certainly their continual adaptation as internal and external factors change, as well as the training and competence of the different employees. It also includes matters such as record-keeping and accounting. Moreover, project management entails close and continual interchange with the beneficiaries, sensitivity to their changing needs and priorities, and the ability to sense when and how the project is helping, and when it is hindering, their lives.

The case-studies throw light on the varying importance of each of these issues. The calibre of NGO project staff, their commitment to its philosophy and overall objectives, and their degree of empathy with the participants all appear to play an important part in meeting project objectives. Well-trained field staff, motivated by a reasonable level of remuneration and committed to the goals of the organization, clearly play a critical role in successful interventions. Poorly paid staff have cause to be less committed to the projects they are managing or executing, and will be tempted to spend more project time engaged in moonlighting activities. It is therefore no surprise to find that weak projects such as the Mzarabani project in Zimbabwe are often characterized by high rates of staff turnover, leading to project disruption, even if there is little evidence among these NGO projects of the petty corruption which plagues many government programmes, especially in South Asia. There also appears to be a link between the degree of staff commitment and project outcome: locally recruited staff tend to have closer affinity with and understanding of the needs and desires of the intended beneficiaries, because of a similarity of background and education.

Religious affiliation also appears to be important. Thus, commitment to helping the rural poor in some cases had a religious basis, which tended to heighten commitment to the project. This was true, for example, of the CASA project in India. But in addition, common religious affiliation between project promoters and beneficiaries provided an extra level of binding which proved especially useful as projects went through times of strain or crisis. In Zimbabwe, this is illustrated in both the Silveira House and Mzarabani projects.

Commitment, of course, is by no means a sufficient condition for success. Pre-project design and preparation are critical, while training in technical and financial expertise is also an important factor. The case-studies suggest that it is far from uncommon for NGOs to try to promote a project which staff are not qualified to initiate, or which is too large for them to manage efficiently, to the detriment of the achievement of its goals. This problem tends to be most visible when NGOs attempt to switch from promoting relief to trying to promote and nurture development. Both the Mzarabani and Simukai case-studies in Zimbabwe illustrate different types of problem within this perspective. Sometimes, too, poor staff training and expertise can be associated with an unjustifiably poor (perhaps patronizing) attitude to the intended beneficiaries, which inhibits the important process of feedback as the project evolves.

Some of the case-studies, most notably the Asian ones, show that excessive centralization of decision-making in the hands of the project leadership, especially if bound up with family ties and patronage, tends to undermine staff commitment and limit the potential of a programme. Yet in both Africa and Asia, strong leadership gave almost all projects a powerful momentum, sometimes overriding other staffing weaknesses, especially when project leaders were able to influence government officials. But strong leadership also brings its own dangers. Thus to the extent that more fundamental management and decision-making problems are concealed, the NGO appears to become over-dependent on the leadership of particular individuals and therefore vulnerable to changes in management.

5. Innovation and Replication

As the role and place of NGOs in development has gained prominence, so the issue of project replicability and NGO influence has become of increasing importance (Edwards and Hulme, 1992). The Zimbabwe case-studies provide good examples of both project replicability and NGO innovation. Thus, the Silveira House group-loan scheme was taken over by the government and replicated almost throughout the country: poor subsequent performance was in large measure due to the fact that some of the core benefits of smallness and group cohesion were lost in the process of scaling up. For its part, the Campfire project of the Zimbabwe Trust provides an example of a project which, although still in its infancy, is already being used as model for a completely new way of marrying income-generation and wildlife-management objectives, both by official aid agencies (the USA and Canada) and by other NGOs.

However, few of the case-study projects were introduced with the intention of being replicated; the majority were started simply in the hope that the direct project members would benefit from the intervention. Indeed, the studies confirm the view of Korten (1980) that where lessons are learnt, they tend to play a larger role in influencing the organizational capacity of the implementing NGO rather than leading to a redesign of the project approach. None the less, NGO poverty-alleviation projects in rural areas tend to share many broad characteristics, especially those which involve the provision of credit and other forms of material assistance. Thus, the most common form of replication is for an NGO to repeat in one area what it, or sometimes another NGO, has done in another, with modifications in line with local circumstances.

NGO projects are frequently believed to be innovatory in their approach, involving some degree of experimentation in methods and technology. It was found that nine of the sixteen case-study projects contained some element which could be termed innovatory, ranging from those which introduced a new technology or production process, to those which devised a novel approach to a familiar problem. New fibrocement roofing tiles were introduced by the ActionAid Mityana programme in Uganda, and the engineering workshop set up initially by Acord produced specially designed ox-ploughs, thus revealing both innovation and flexibility. In south India, new boat technology has been developed by the Intermediate Technology Development Group in association with artisanal fishermen.

However, the more common form of innovation lay in the specific approach adopted in different socio-economic and political contexts: half the projects appeared to use a new type of approach to help address the problems of rural poverty, including all four projects in Uganda. Besides the ActionAid and Acord projects, the UWFCT pioneered credit for poor rural women, and the health programme of the Busoga diocese devised cost-recovery mechanisms for its curative health services—methods and approaches which were certainly new to Uganda. In contrast, there was little especially innovatory about the ActionAid Bangladesh programme: it was largely the successful reproduction of a well-tried approach to group credit which had originally been pioneered by the Grameen Bank, in the same country.

6. NGOs and Credit

Credit-focused initiatives constitute a major proportion of NGO projects across both Africa and Asia, and the present selection of case-studies reflects this. Credit was a central element in seven of the sixteen projects, and a subsidiary component in several others, although only one (UWFCT in Uganda) focused exclusively on credit. In four projects (Silveira House and Christian Care in Zimbabwe, and the Rural Development Trust and Arthik Samata Mandal in India), credit took the form of crop loans to peasant farmers, which enabled them to purchase agricultural inputs (seed, fertilizers, pesticide, and implements) and/or to cover the costs of ploughing. In three other projects (UWFCT in Uganda, ActionAid in Bangladesh, and CASA in India), credit was primarily used to promote off-farm employment by helping beneficiaries to invest in income-generating assets. Of these seven schemes, five consisted of revolving funds directly administered by the NGO, and two (CASA and ASM in India) drew on credit available from the formal banking sector.

The first thing to say about the credit schemes is that they were popular initiatives: the demand for credit tended to exceed the ability of NGOs to provide it. The NGOs were able to reach the poor (though not necessarily the poorest) with targeted small-scale loans, for three main reasons. First, the credit provided by them was invariably cheaper (because of subsidized interest rates) than loans provided by traditional money-lenders, and/or more easily accessible than normal bank credit. Second, the volume of credit was large enough to meet borrowers' most immediate needs, but small enough to ensure relatively high levels of repayment, even if the amount lent usually fell well short of total requirements. In the case of RDT in India, this was deliberate policy in order to encourage less-poor beneficiaries to supplement NGO funds with credit from other sources. It was, however, popular for a third reason— it was perceived to be less risky than other forms of credit: members of NGO credit schemes usually believe that they will be treated less harshly if they fail to repay on time.

The evaluations also indicate that rates of repayment to NGO credit schemes have often been better than those to comparable state credit agencies. In addition, as the CASA example shows, where the role of the NGO has been to assist the poor to borrow from institutional sources, repayment rates to these non-NGO institutions have also increased. In part, this could be attributed to the lower rates of interest charged in the NGO schemes. But, in all cases, it appears that the different forms of group membership characteristic of the NGO schemes, combined with a more personal face-to-face relationship between the implementing agency and the credit recipient, were important factors leading to better NGO performance. This was certainly true of the Silveira House schemes in Zimbabwe: in the first five years of the Silveira House pump-priming scheme, repayment rates were 97 per cent, declining to an average 73 per cent over the following five years, largely as a result of disruption caused by the pre-Independence war. In the case of ActionAid Bangladesh, too, registered repayment rates in excess of 95 per cent occurred, largely as a result of its insistence on regularity and strict monitoring.

The CASA, RDT, ActionAid Bangladesh, Silveira House, and UWFCT credit schemes all helped to raise incomes from new sources of off-farm employment or from increased agricultural production. The loans provided were used productively (following consultation with project staff or discussion within a group) and responded to farmers' needs. In the cases of Silveira House in Zimbabwe and the RDT scheme in India, small farmers increased cash-crop production by purchasing inputs which were otherwise difficult to obtain. However, not all the schemes were successful: the Mzarabani credit scheme did not lead to any significant rise in the incomes of participants, largely because of administrative and technical problems experienced by the NGO.

It is also evident that unless they are carefully monitored, and unless sufficient funds are provided, NGO credit schemes often fall well short of their intended objectives. In part, the problem lies with the insufficient attention paid to the practicalities of administering a credit programme once it is up and running: both the demand and need for credit clearly encourage NGOs to establish programmes quickly. In the case of the Mzarabani project, even the promoters of the programme appeared to be confused about the method, timing, and amounts of repayment which should be made. More common is confusion at the level of the borrower. There is often a real tension between, on the one hand, providing sufficient credit to make a significant difference to people's incomes, and, on the other, providing amounts too large for people to be able easily to repay the money borrowed, often because insufficient attention has been focused on the income-generating schemes for which the money is to be used.

The issue, however, is more complex than this. In practice, poor people do not always want access to credit for investment purposes, as they have far more pressing demands: immediate consumption needs or family emergencies are frequently the uses to which the loan is put, whatever the ostensible reason for granting it. Thus, credit can have an immediate and beneficial effect on individual borrowers (and may be repaid in due course), but it may not have positive longer-run effects on incomes and living standards.

There are also longer-term issues which are often not sufficiently addressed. For instance, even if the money provided is channelled predominantly into income-generating activities, the Silveira House, Mzarabani, and RDT evaluations reveal considerable differences in incomes across different years—the fluctuations arising largely as a result of varying rainfall. In drought years, defaults increase dramatically. Loans are invariably repaid on stop-orders for market output from the current season, and there is no cushion to stretch repayments over a number of years. Thus, these credit schemes often fail to lead to any reduction in the vulnerability of rain-fed farms to risk; indeed, with loans in place and drought far from uncommon, farmers ironically could often face even higher risks when they take on loans than when they do not.

The case-studies also reveal that NGO credit schemes are costly to administer. Without doubt, it is expensive to process and monitor large numbers of small loans. Silveira House had administrative costs of 12 per cent excluding the costs of group formation and extension work, and for Christian Care the comparable figure was 14 per cent. For RDT and the UWFCT, the total cost of administering the crop loans scheme reached 30 per cent, although in the former this also included time spent on non-credit activities such as group motivation and non-formal education. In projects such as CASA, where the NGO facilitated loans from commercial lending institutions, the administrative costs were lower since the beneficiaries dealt directly with bank and government officials.

This problem leads on to the question of sustainability. Most NGO revolving credit funds are designed to become self-sustaining. Yet those examined show few signs of either sustainability or self-administration in their present form. None demonstrated the ability or the potential to become self-sufficient following the withdrawal of the NGO, for two main reasons. First, administrative costs remained too high to be borne by the poor, and training beneficiaries to run their own schemes has always been a low priority for NGO credit schemes. Second, recurrent drought or disasters quickly erode any (small) capital base that an NGO credit scheme is able to build up over the good years. A third factor is that it is difficult for revolving credit schemes to shift from subsidized interest rates (sometimes well below the rate of inflation) to charging full market rates.

In common with a number of state-financed credit schemes for the rural poor, all the schemes examined were subsidized by the donors, either through below-market interest rates (sometimes well below the rate of inflation) or matching grants. However, NGOs do not wish to continue to provide subsidized credit *ad infinitum*, and they are faced with the options of either trying to make the scheme self-financing, or transferring the group assisted to a government or commercially based scheme. Particular difficulties arise if a government scheme charges higher interest rates than the NGO scheme— a common phenomenon in Africa. When the Silveira House scheme was transferred to a government agency after Independence, and the group system of repayment was abandoned, default levels rose markedly, although falling repayment rates were also associated with the incidence of drought and a rapid expansion in loan size.

In summary, while the case-studies provide powerful evidence of a short-term impact on the poor in NGO credit schemes, credit interventions do not provide much encouragement in terms of a durable and more widespread answer to enhancing the income opportunities of the rural poor.

7. Sustainability and Self-Reliance

Sustainability is a far broader issue than credit programmes. To be financially sustainable, a project must be able to cover its costs and generate sufficient funds to make it worth while for the poor to take it over. Institutional sustainability is essentially a function of the capacity of groups and individuals to organize and manage all project activities. NGO withdrawal is therefore premissed on the existence of some organizational structure to which it can hand over responsibility for project management.

Most of the projects examined were still functioning under the auspices of the NGO promoters of the project; thus the issue of sustainability was a matter more of speculation than of analysis. None the less, the evaluations provided some useful insights into the broad issues. Few projects could be termed financially self-sustaining over the longer term: at least five were clearly not sustainable in their existing form, while seven exhibited limited potential for sustainability. Scarcely any could be expected to stand on their own feet financially without continued donor support or the continuation of some sort of subsidy.

Nevertheless, there is a strong expectation that the Campfire project in Zimbabwe, the Multi-Sectoral Rural Development Programme in Uganda, the Caritas social forestry programme in Bangladesh, and the fisheries and CASA Phase III programme in India could be financially self-sustaining in the medium term. These projects share several features: the participants are strongly committed to the objectives and have been involved in project management; there are a range of identifiable and tangible benefits; and, perhaps of major importance, the NGO has been able to find ways of covering recurrent costs. The attempt of the Busoga diocese in its Multi-Sectoral Rural Development Programme to fund services through user fees and community income-generation schemes has proved moderately successful, although reducing subsidies remains a significant obstacle. These findings suggest that where NGOs take an active role in promoting self-help initiatives, the problems of over-dependence are lessened and withdrawal becomes easier to attain over the longer term.

Conversely, the projects which have little potential for sustainability or are clearly not sustainable (the majority) shared the following features: a rather low level of commitment on the part of the beneficiaries; high administrative costs; and little chance of the project becoming economically viable in terms of generating an adequate level of income.

Relationships with host governments also play a role. For instance, the CASA and ASM programmes were strengthened by the availability of credit subsidized by the government which could be tapped for use by beneficiary groups. In contrast, RDT concentrated on providing credit and other inputs from its own resources with the result that it had rather tenuous links with the government. Projects developed in conjunction with government stood a higher chance of being sustained following the withdrawal of the NGO, as a more enduring relationship had been created with the local community: in many ways Zimbabwe's Campfire project was designed to be and is being executed hand in hand with the Department of National Parks.

In contrast, the virtual absence of systematic government efforts to alleviate poverty in many parts of Uganda has meant that NGOs are often the sole source of external assistance. This has often resulted in their playing a gap-filling role where government services are weak or ineffective. The implication for NGOs in Uganda is of a long-term involvement until such time as the government is able to rebuild local services or communities are able to maintain services established with their assistance.

Finally, it should be noted that sustainability and dependence are issues of more concern to NGOs than they are for the people assisted. In general, and from their viewpoint quite understandably, those in receipt of NGO assistance remain quite content to continue to receive external inputs for the foreseeable future.

8. NGO Impact and the External Environment

The question of sustainability leads naturally to the contribution of the external (i.e. non-project) environment to project outcomes. For each of the sixteen projects, impact was usually contingent on local and, to some extent, on national and international factors. Yet most of the evaluations indicate that the NGOs underestimated or failed to take into account the wider environmental context in which they were operating: they repeatedly underplayed the significance of economic and social factors outside the immediate parameters of individual projects. In particular, any positive changes in the lives of the poor are primarily attributed to the development projects initiated by NGOs, even though they might result from external factors.

The West Acholi Engineering Workshop in Uganda provides the clearest example of this. The workshop was initially set up to produce ox-ploughs to service the needs of small farmers in the area. But demand dwindled due to a rapid depletion of cattle brought about by continuous bandit raids in the context of political insecurity. The workshop attempted to diversify production, but the quality of the products was poor and its economic viability was threatened. While it may not have been possible to anticipate a drastic fall-off in demand when the project was being initiated, there was clearly a need to build in an element of flexibility to allow a range of products to be manufactured in the face of market uncertainties.

Crop prices and demand for products are clearly important determinants of success in projects which attempt to raise the income of farmers through cash cropping. In Zimbabwe, the case of Silveira House illustrates that the economic viability of maize production by small farmers supported by crop loans was conditional on the attractive prices set by the official Grain Marketing Board, while the Mzarabani case-study illustrates the weakness of the marketing system which the project simply failed to address. In India the Rural Development Trust provided credit to help farmers invest in crop inputs, which in turn encouraged a shift towards groundnut production. This was feasible in economic terms because increased national demand for groundnut oil had pushed up prices. Yet in both the Silveira House and the RDT projects, crop output was itself conditional on climatic variations: recurrent drought reduced yields, and farmers defaulted on their loans.

A rather different illustration is provided by the CASA project in India, where prawn cultivation was introduced by the NGO to provide new sources of income generation for the poor. The initiative succeeded despite the fact that it was located in a remote and relatively inaccessible area, because Japanese demand for prawns had escalated over the previous decade, driving up prices, creating a profitable activity, and making it worth while for private traders to arrange transportation and marketing. Similarly, sericulture in both the CASA and the ASM projects succeeded in part because national demand for silk was buoyant, and grants and subsidized credit were made available by the government. There is no guarantee, however, that favourable prices will continue to prevail, particularly if local production reaches saturation point as a result of competition from private investors, and this highlights the risk element in such ventures.

In other cases, however, the NGOs proved insensitive to the pattern of local demand and potential competition from the private sector when identifying opportunities for self-employment. For example, people who had received skills training from ActionAid in Uganda and went on to set up businesses found it difficult to compete with established artisans who could produce superior products which they sold at more attractive prices. Similarly, training programmes in RDT and ASM in India did not appear to be sensitive to the local opportunities for gainful employment, with the result that only a relatively small proportion of those who received training were applying the skills they had acquired. In contrast, Gono Kallyan Trust in Bangladesh was able to capitalize on its relatively close proximity to Dhaka by identifying market outlets for horticultural produce grown by poor farmers.

In several projects, the NGO insulated producers from local market forces by creating an artificial and temporary source of demand. ActionAid Uganda trained local unemployed youths in tile-making and purchased most of the tiles they produced for use in its own house-building programme. Women trained in printing and dyeing techniques by CASA went on to produce saris and other items of clothing, most of which were purchased by the NGO to augment its disaster relief stock. In neither case, however, was it certain that, once the NGO withdrew, the products would be competitive on the local market.

The distribution of land and other assets also conditions the options available to local NGOs. In Bangladesh a large landless population with minimal access to capital limits the prospects for rapid and enduring poverty alleviation. ActionAid Bangladesh provided credit for income-generation programmes but the degree of material improvement was relatively small, since demand was low and the investment was geared towards activities which, at best, supplemented earnings from casual labour. In such an environment, it would be unrealistic to expect substantial benefits to accrue to the poor in the absence of major structural reforms centred on the redistribution of land and capital assets. In India, by comparison, crop loans and grants for minor irrigation schemes provided by Arthik Samata Mandal were successful in raising farmers' incomes because some prior redistribution had taken place.

Another issue of importance for particular projects is the nature and extent of repression on the part of local élites. Resistance to programmes designed to strengthen the poor, or appropriation of their benefits by the rich, can clearly limit the potential impact of NGO interventions. Several of the NGOs in India encountered opposition from local politicians and dominant groups, who tried to subvert their activities. This was especially evident in the case of the fishermen's co-operatives which attempted to market fish collectively and RDT's attempts to help farmers escape from the clutches of money-lenders who controlled rural credit. Project performance in such situations has to be assessed in the context of a political environment which is averse to NGO attempts to promote social and economic empowerment.

Perhaps the most dramatic example of external factors which undermine project impact is sporadic natural disasters, to which resource-poor environments are particularly prone. Severe flooding in Bangladesh destroyed the fish-ponds excavated with assistance from GUP, while a tornado devastated houses and crops belonging to those assisted by GKT. A cyclone which hit coastal Andhra Pradesh soon after the CASA and ASM evaluations were completed resulted in widespread loss of livestock, assets, and crops. Despite these catastrophes, the people affected were able to rebuild their lives fairly quickly as a result of an immediate influx of disaster relief, and the reduction in vulnerability brought about by the NGO's interventions.

9. Cost-Effectiveness

A central question, especially for official donors but also increasingly for their private supporters, is whether NGOs offer value for money in terms of directly assisting the poor. This is only partly a question of whether particular NGOs are effective in terms of the impact of the projects they promote. It is also a question of whether the costs of NGO projects and programmes represent the most efficient use of the resources available to them.

Cost-effectiveness within NGO projects refers to the relationship between the inputs of a particular programme or project (its costs) and what has been achieved (its benefits), even where such benefits cannot be quantified in financial terms. Tracing this relationship involves, at its simplest, forming a view as to whether the costs are commensurate with the benefits. But it also involves an assessment of possible future cost–benefit relationships, and sometimes consideration of whether the money might have been more effectively utilized in funding other sorts of projects. Projects which appear to be costly at an early stage of their development may be much more cost-effective in the future.

There are major difficulties with assessing cost-effectiveness in the sorts of poverty-focused projects typical of many NGOs. In the first place, an element of subjectivity is bound to arise in any attempt to measure costs and benefits, which increases in cases—like all the sixteen projects considered here—which contain non-quantifiable objectives. Moreover, both the absence of quantifiable base-line data and the limited availability of project-specific cost data[6] mean that not even the potentially quantifiable data exist in a usable form. The upshot is that this pervasive lack of data precludes a rigorous quantitative analysis of cost-effectiveness either in the case-studies or in these summary paragraphs. None the less, the studies are able to throw light on most of the key issues.

For some NGOs, it appears novel to pose the question of whether the benefits achieved in a project justify the costs expended. The dominant view has been that the assistance given is itself largely the justification for the costs incurred: the fact that people are poor and therefore require help remains in the minds of many the main basis for providing assistance. Within this perspective, costs are largely set aside (written off), and success is perceived largely in one of two ways. Originally, success was seen to lie merely in the ability to provide assistance to as many of the poor as possible. However, nowadays it is more commonly seen almost exclusively in relation to the achievement of the objectives of the project—the provision of clean water, the increase in income, the expansion of gainful employment. Within this perspective, the overall costs of achieving the objectives set are of secondary importance, although it should be stressed that almost all NGOs make a conscious effort to keep costs to a minimum. For most of them, benefits (reduction in poverty) are the hoped-for bonus, but lack of benefits (continuation of poverty) provides no sound basis for withdrawal.

NGOs pride themselves on the low cost of their projects, frequently comparing the delivery of their services with projects promoted by official aid agencies or with government programmes. In terms of the resources devoted to them, the sixteen case-study projects certainly appear to cost less than similar types of official aid interventions. However, we are not always comparing like with like: thus, NGO projects tend to be smaller-scale and, in terms of cost per beneficiary, either broadly equivalent to, or even more expensive than, similar programmes run by host governments. One reason for this is that NGO projects tend to be more staff-intensive than similar government projects, and the employment costs of expatriate NGO personnel are higher than the equivalent employment costs of government officials in most developing countries. However, these higher costs need to be placed within a broader perspective, as the NGO projects both appear to produce greater benefits, and (largely because of this) are certainly favoured more by the poor than government projects.

As indicated, there was insufficient quantitative data to permit precise calculations of costs and benefits. However, sufficient information was obtained to permit some fairly firm judgements to be made. Broadly, the sixteen projects fall into three clusters: for five of them, it was judged that the resulting benefits clearly outweighed the costs of the intervention; in five others, the objectives were certainly achieved but at a high cost of resources and staff provided and of administrative overheads; two were evidently not cost-effective, since they did not succeed in generating significant tangible benefits; it was more difficult to judge the remaining four projects.

Cost-effectiveness might be seen more profitably by asking if benefits could be significantly enhanced by increasing costs. For a number of the projects, greater benefits might have been reaped if, for instance, the approach had been different, if more resources had been placed at the project's disposal, if the NGO personnel had been more skilled, or if there had been better project management. This leaves one with the question of the precise relationship between increasing the costs (to improve the quality of the project) in order to achieve greater benefits and (hopefully) better targeting towards the poorest.

CONCLUSIONS

If this summary of the results of the case-studies has shown anything it is surely the complex nature of societies into which NGO projects are inserted, as well as the sheer range of different internal and external factors which influence project outcomes. The results of the sixteen evaluations have clearly produced a source of information which helps to throw light on the difficulties NGOs face in their attempt to assist in poverty alleviation, as well as helping us understand better what might or might not prove to be effective. Yet there are clearly other, and perhaps even more important, lessons to be learnt, many of which probably lie embedded in the files and experiences of the increasing number of NGOs in the North and the South who are seeking to contribute to the alleviation of poverty across the developing world. This study has barely scratched the surface of an area of development which remains extraordinarily difficult to understand, and thus to address comprehensively.

NOTES

1. All four countries are considered poor enough to be eligible for IDA (International Development Association) funding, the 1989 cut-off point being an average per capita income of $700.

2. In some cases, the ODI evaluations examined the whole project, in others just a single programme component, although both are referred to as projects in the pages which follow.

3. The one exception is the community health component of the Multi-Sectoral Rural Development Programme in Uganda, although particular attention is given to the attempts to institute cost-recovery mechanisms through user-fees and income generation.

4. In the event, the assent of the local NGO proved to be the dominant consideration governing the final selection of the case-studies; projects that had been outright failures, or where there were very poor relations with the funding agency, were excluded.

5. In these countries, village-level institutions and farmers' co-operatives do exist, but the poor are usually denied effective representation in them, which renders them powerless in local decision-making.

6. It is rare for NGOs to sub-divide their overhead and head-office expenses and allocate them to different projects.

6

NGOs and Poverty Alleviation: Some Policy Implications

INTRODUCTION

The previous chapter highlighted a number of themes and issues which appear to be of central importance to project impact and which NGOs, in the North and the South, will increasingly have to address, since the 1990s are likely to be a decade in which the role of NGOs in poverty alleviation is set to increase. The purpose of this chapter is to discuss further a number of these themes,[1] grouped under four headings: questions of effectiveness, the scale of NGO interventions, relations between NGOs and governments, and, more specifically, between northern NGOs and official aid donors. The chapter also attempts to draw out policy lessons for the major groups involved in NGO development: NGOs working in the field, grant-making NGOs, host governments, and bilateral and multilateral donors who provide funding to NGO projects and programmes.

IMPROVING NGO EFFECTIVENESS

The level of resources provided to beneficiaries and the commitment of the beneficiaries to particular NGO interventions are essential components of the effectiveness of NGO projects aimed at alleviating poverty. But these factors need to be placed within an array of differing circumstances which will continually affect performance, the exact composition and importance of which will change from intervention to intervention.

This suggests that for NGO projects achieving success is more an art than a science: it lies in having the sensitivity and skill to balance the provision of resources with the sustaining of commitment. The trouble is that no NGO has the time (or the money) to practise the art with precision: money is needed both to provide physical resources and to nurture group commitment. The world in which NGOs live and have to execute their projects is far from ideal. Corners often have to be cut, which inevitably results in a less than ideal project performance. None the less, NGOs, both northern and southern, face the problem of how to improve the effectiveness of their present range of project interventions.

A basic requirement is for more information and analysis in order to guide the choice of the type of intervention which should be attempted, its form, its size, its progress, its duration, and its continuation once external support has been withdrawn.

For the generalist NGO, deciding on the form of intervention is at once both the most critical and the most difficult part of project selection.[2] It requires some understanding of both the poverty of the target group to be assisted and the nature of the society in which this group of poor people is located, including the potential for resolving gender-related questions of poverty. It also requires an understanding of the development work being undertaken and planned by the government, at least at the local level, and ideally of the nature of the role which the government expects NGOs to play in poverty alleviation. Increasingly, too, such an assessment is likely to require knowledge of the activities of other agencies working in the proposed project area, as well as the overall effect that NGO work is likely to have on government efforts in the medium and longer term.

All this suggests that NGOs need to have some sort of local, if not national, assessment of poverty and poverty alleviation into which particular interventions can be placed. Undertaking and utilizing such an assessment has the added advantage of reducing the likelihood of discrete projects being divorced from the more basic processes of development under way in the wider economy. In particular, NGOs have much to learn from different types of project carried out in the same locality, as well as from similar interventions in different localities. A major problem is that NGOs still prefer to work on their own and to draw on project experience largely from within their own organizations. There is a wealth of untapped experience from other NGOs, and often also from government agencies, either working in similar localities or utilizing similar types of intervention. Such information therefore needs to be shared within and between NGOs in a far more systematic way than occurs at present.[3]

Broader assessment is also important as there would appear to be considerable ignorance within individual NGOs, and even more between different NGOs, concerning methods of effective poverty alleviation and the relative costs of different interventions. Current weaknesses suggest that particular attention needs to be focused on the extent to which the resources (financial and human) committed to a project are adequate to achieve the objectives set, not least if the project contains (as it usually does) a growth component.

While NGOs should not simply adopt projects with low costs per beneficiary, or which are expected to produce the greatest unit quantity of benefit for the costs incurred, they should be aware of the relative anticipated costs and benefits of different forms of intervention, as well as being able to link these to the risk element and the record of project performance. For instance, there are likely to be trade-offs between keeping costs down and a reduced ability to reach the very poorest by means of finely targeted interventions, which by their nature require closer supervision and a greater investment of resources, both human and financial.

The ODI evaluations also indicate that greater care and time need to be taken in both project selection and identification. Establishing discrete projects which have the potential of benefiting the poorest requires, at the outset, that the objectives be clearly stated, even if these change over time. But it also requires greater transparency in relation to the means to achieve these objectives.

At this stage, thought also needs to be given to NGO withdrawal: in the initial preparation of the project, the issue of self-reliance and how this is going to be achieved needs to be addressed. Pre-project work ought also to address explicitly questions about the size of the beneficiary group: is it adequate (too large or too small) to nurture the community aspects of the project; is the project likely to lead to élitism among project beneficiaries or to a rippling outwards of the anticipated benefits? What all this suggests is that, in drawing up a project, the likely problems to be encountered ought to be addressed explicitly: what sorts of risks are likely to arise, and when, and what methods should be adopted to reduce them?

Greater attention also needs to be focused on the practice and mechanisms of undertaking continuous assessments of achievements and problems, and to have these fed back into the planning process. However, the processes of continuous assessment and monitoring need to be matched both to the nature of the project and to the abilities of the staff involved: there is no point in devising a sophisticated method of appraisal if none of the staff are able to undertake such assessments. Equally, there is little point in outlining detailed targets, for instance annual increases in income, if the staff are incapable of knowing whether these targets are being met.

There is no doubt that monitoring and evaluation procedures are weak in most NGOs, both northern and southern, and that few, if any, northern NGOs have worked out proper procedures for integrating the information and insights obtained from the few evaluations which are undertaken into the project cycle. However, little practical purpose is likely to be served by recommending that the monitoring of projects should become more formalized, and in particular that a greater number of evaluations should be undertaken by different NGOs, unless mechanisms for incorporating this information into the project cycle are carefully worked out. A major current constraint in utilizing whatever information is, or ought to be, available, is simply lack of time: NGO personnel do not have the leisure to read, reflect, and act upon the data which are currently available within their organizations, let alone devote time to generating, reading, and constructively acting on yet more information. The prior need, therefore, is to examine ways in which the information which does exist within NGOs can be channelled into the work of project officers; only then will it be worth while to expand the scope and number of evaluations.

That this need is urgent became increasingly apparent during the present study. The evaluations suggest a certain amount of complacency on the part of some NGOs. Beneficiaries were far from reluctant to voice their criticisms about the running of the projects—not that this is surprising, for criticism is often part of the evaluation process, even one which aims to be constructive. However, the ODI evaluations tended to be far more critical than were the local NGOs of the projects they were running. One reason for this is a high level of ignorance about evaluation and monitoring methods, and of the rich sources of information on project performance and impact that can be tapped without major effort or expense.

The case-studies also indicate that greater attention needs to be devoted to obtaining a deeper understanding of the environment or setting of the project, including the dynamics of the society in which the project is to be located. This lack of perspective not only distorts understanding of the wider world, but also down-plays the range of influences which are brought to bear on particular projects. For example, whether the national economy is expanding or contracting, or, more particularly, whether there is a history of drought or other natural disasters in the locality of the project, can have a critical bearing on project outcomes. It is also important to know whether the achievement of project objectives is likely to be at the expense of other groups (of non-beneficiaries), and if so what the likely reactions of the non-poor are likely to be, or whether all are likely to gain.

There are clearly some situations, especially in large parts of rural sub-Saharan Africa, where disparities within particular communities are not great, in which attention ought to be given to those interventions which are based upon, or build upon, the notion of 'mutual gain'. Experience obtained in executing these types of projects can be pooled to assist in building up group cohesion which, in turn, should provide an even more important asset if subsequent (more substantive) interventions involving group conflict are to have a better chance of success.

Conversely in the South Asian context, where a far more highly polarized socio-economic environment often prevails, these sorts of initiatives are more vulnerable to capture by powerful rural élites to the detriment of the poor and the disadvantaged. However, even in contexts where there are higher risks involved in pursuing a narrowly targeted approach, it may be possible for NGOs to secure the support of dominant groups for poverty-alleviating interventions if their interests are not directly threatened. When they are, as, for example, when NGOs seek to mobilize the landless in pursuit of higher wages or land redistribution, a violent backlash is all the more probable and NGOs are not always in a position to protect the communities with which they are working. For these reasons many NGOs in South Asia tend not to adopt interventions which carry high risks of direct confrontation, but seek instead to combine poverty alleviation with social uplift without provoking antagonism from dominant social groups.

THE SCALE OF NGO INTERVENTIONS

For the foreseeable future, the NGO movement will be subject to continued external pressures for further growth, with the scene set for a period of continued expansion similar to that experienced in the 1980s. These pressures originate in part in the still widely shared view that NGOs make an important, and probably significant, contribution to poverty alleviation in developing countries. They will continue to be boosted by the influential paradigm in which privatization, democracy, and pushing back the role of the state are judged to provide three key pre-conditions for development to occur. In part, too, NGO growth will be fostered by the sheer scale and perpetuation of the problems of poverty, especially in regions like Africa, where governments will continue to have insufficient resources of their own to provide an adequate or even minimum quantity of human and physical resources to promote development. Equally, these pressures are likely to be furthered by the wider fall-out from economic recession and structural adjustment programmes, with NGOs continuing to play a growing role in attempting to address some of the social costs of adjustment.

In turn, all these factors are likely to increase the amount of external funding for NGO interventions in the developing world, both from official aid agencies, and from individuals and private-sector organizations and institutions, resulting in a steady increase in NGO poverty-alleviating projects and programmes. For its part, the World Bank's newly formulated *Operational Directive* on poverty reduction explicitly envisages an expanded role for NGOs in poverty alleviation in the 1990s. It comments thus (1992: 12):

NGOs have shown that their programs can reach the poor often more effectively than programs managed by the public sector, especially when NGOs are brought into the early stages of project preparation. Subject to government sensitivities, Bank policy encourages task managers to involve NGOs as appropriate—particularly grassroots and self-help groups among the poor —in project identification, design, financing, implementation, and monitoring and evaluation.

For individual NGOs, the critical question this raises is the manner in which this continued growth should be directed. For the movement as a whole, what needs to be asked is the extent to which NGOs are capable of making, and have the means to make, a significant dent in the still substantial problems of poverty in the developing world. These questions were addressed at an international workshop held in early 1992 and entitled: Scaling-up NGO Impacts: Learning from Experience (Edwards and Hulme, 1992).

A series of factors lead us to be pessimistic that an expansion in the range and number of NGO projects will have a major impact upon world poverty and hunger. These relate to both the nature of NGO intervention and the broader institutional and political environment in which NGOs operate. As highlighted in the previous chapter, many of the weaknesses of NGO projects revolve around the problems of inadequate and insufficient resources, especially financial resources. With more money, greater care could be taken in project and beneficiary selection; NGOs would have more time to obtain a greater understanding of the dynamics of the poor in relation to other local, regional, and even national groups; more, better, or more appropriate physical resources could be provided; there would be more time for staff to evaluate and monitor projects, to design an appropriate means of withdrawal, and to decide upon the best time for such withdrawal. But the financial constraints on NGOs are usually more deep-seated and complex than even this suggests. Given the massive problems of poverty to be addressed, there is a constant tension between, on the one hand, committing more resources to fewer, better prepared, organized, and structured projects, and, on the other, extending resources more widely to reach, and hopefully make at least some impact upon, a greater number of poor people.

Pressures to spread rather than deepen are increased by two additional factors, financial and human. The first is the wish to keep the costs of helping the poor as low as possible—which is almost bound to have some adverse effect on efficient delivery. The second is the pressure to try to complete projects as quickly as possible so that scarce resources can be transferred to other areas of need. And overriding all this is the tension, within the larger NGOs in particular, of allocating resources to medium-to long-term development projects as against the channelling of funds to short-term emergencies. The desire within these organizations is clearly to devote more resources to development projects; but this is tempered by the fact that new emergencies continually occur (and old ones often recur), and also that significant increases in income (from donations) tend to arise largely from media coverage of these emergencies, pressurizing the NGOs to spend less income on development.

There are two possible routes of expansion. One is for the number of interventions undertaken to increase, be they particular projects with different communities or an intensification of the processes of intervention with particular groups of beneficiaries. This is the path of replication. Replication could arise from more new NGOs being established, or it could result from existing NGOs executing a greater number of projects. The other route is for the scale of intervention to become larger, so that each includes a greater number of beneficiaries. This is the path of scaling-up (Edwards and Hulme, 1992).[4]

Scaling-up is more likely to occur if existing NGO interventions become bigger. However, the overall impact of scaling-up is likely to be limited for four major reasons. First, scaling-up requires better performance in a number of areas of NGO intervention which have been pinpointed as key weaknesses. These include problems of project management, shortages of staff skills, and limited financial resources, all of which inhibit greater impact with current numbers of beneficiaries. Secondly, scaling-up is likely to reduce the NGOs' political room for manœuvre, narrowing the range of interventions which conflict with prevailing élites and centres of power, and raising the profile of the groups being assisted. Thirdly, the scaling-up route is increasingly likely to lead to conflict with the characteristics identified as particularly helpful to achieving success in current NGO interventions. These include smallness, community participation, and high staff to beneficiary ratios. Fourthly, the bigger and comparatively wealthier northern NGOs, with some important exceptions, have tended in recent years to move away from managing, operating, and running projects themselves, replacing this mode of expansion with the funding of smaller and more indigenously based grass-roots NGOs. In this sense, the movement towards scaling-up has often led, in practice and ironically, to a certain scaling-down. There is little to suggest that this pattern of expansion will be altered for the rest of the 1990s.

All these factors suggest that pressures for expanding and enhancing the impact of NGOs are likely to be met with the replication of the small-scale approach type of initiative. However, this route also presents problems. In particular, there are four precise and more immediate factors which are likely to constrain the continued and rapid replication of such NGO intervention, or to adversely influence its effectiveness. These relate to human-resource capability and finance, the increasingly narrow choice of projects, weaknesses in NGO co-ordination, and increases in the number of NGOs.

The case-studies in this book not only highlight the importance of the human-resource skills of NGO personnel in order to achieve project objectives, but also indicate what can go wrong if pressures to expand are not resisted when there are insufficient human skills to execute new projects. Already there is concern that the expansion of NGO projects and the emergence of new NGOs are adversely affecting performance, as more and more NGOs are born and projects are becoming over-stretched. If the rapid expansion of the 1980s and early 1990s continues into the rest of the 1990s, project performance is likely to be an even greater cause for concern.

But even if we assume both that expansion-by-replication continues apace and that there is no lowering of project performance, the overall impact of NGOs on the problems of poverty in the countries in which they operate would still only be small. One element is the individual impact of projects on the elimination of poverty of the beneficiaries concerned. As we have already observed, it is rare for NGOs' poverty-alleviating projects to enable the beneficiaries to escape from poverty: the achieve-ments, though real and important to the groups involved, tend to be of small rather than massive gains. In addition, in terms of total foreign aid and human-resource skills, NGOs account for a maximum of 15 per cent, and probably 10 per cent or less, of finance available in most developing countries. Thus even an (unlikely) doubling of resources available to NGOs would make only a marginal difference in most countries.

Furthermore, to the extent that NGO projects become more widespread across countries and within different localities, the opportunities for creating viable poverty-alleviating projects which do not conflict with and challenge dominant power struc-tures are bound to decrease, while the expanded presence of NGO projects is bound to draw attention to what is being attempted. In both cases, expansion-by-replication is likely to narrow the prospects for gains to continue to be made for the rural poor in line with what was achieved in the past.

Finally, national development is clearly something much bigger than a series of individual interventions: there are many major areas of national development in which NGOs are neither involved nor choose to work. NGOs simply do not have the resources, nor the desire, to involve themselves in important areas of national devel-opment building: in promoting the deepening and diversification of the economy through manufacturing sector expansion, in training high-level skills, in promoting the use of information technology, in building the telecommunications, road, rail, and power systems of a country, or in enhancing the foreign-exchange-earning capacity of the country. Hence NGO efforts are invariably supplementary to government in achieving the broader goals of development, even if there are other ways in which NGOs seek to influence the official agenda beyond the confines of individual projects.

NGO–GOVERNMENT RELATIONS

In addition to human resource and financial considerations, there are a range of structural and institutional constraints which are also likely not merely to limit the impact of individual interventions, but which may well lead to more substantive and deep-seated difficulties for resolving the problems of poverty. Many of these revolve around NGO–government relationships. It is within this context that a number of specific factors which tend to characterize most NGO interventions need to be considered: working with groups, smallness, face-to-face contact, and awareness-building.

In certain instances, the differences between NGO and government projects appear, at least on the surface, to be small or non-existent. Thus, a range of more technically focused NGO projects—building wells, boreholes, dams, houses, etc.—are in large measure the same types of projects which, if it had the resources, would be carried out by the government. However, even in these gap-filling interventions, the NGO almost always brings to the project a greater sense of community involvement, and a higher degree of sensitivity to local needs.

Of most importance in this context is the strong commitment to participation which usually characterizes NGO types of intervention. But this, too, needs to be viewed within a broader perspective. Even where a developing country government embraces the philosophy and approach of participation, it is at a disadvantage *vis-à-vis* the small voluntary organization in making it work in practice. There are various factors at work here. In the first place, NGOs are not normally burdened by the bureaucratic restraints which necessarily characterize state initiatives. Where services are provided and channelled to local communities by central government, they usually need to be provided on a universal basis and are commonly organized within the context of national targets and policies. Even where a particular line ministry wants to respond to a local need, it needs to cover itself from accusations of favouritism, tribalism, or regionalism and to persuade its critics, or its potential critics, that it is providing its services in a balanced way. In marked contrast, NGOs commonly have the freedom to operate in a manner they choose, and often in an area they themselves select.

But there are potential dangers in the NGO approach to which NGOs need to be alert. Thus one of the reasons why NGOs are favoured by local communities is precisely because they bring benefits disproportionately to one area or region over others. What is more, the greater and more extensive the poverty of a region, the less adequate are also likely to be the bureaucratic structures and the services that government provides. This means that NGO projects are likely to be relatively more high-cost and gains relatively less easy to achieve than those to be expected in a more hospitable environment. What this suggests is not only that NGO performance is likely to be limited to areas which government or other agencies are less able to reach, but, perversely, that NGO assistance is likely to be least effective where it is needed most.

Furthermore, it has to be recognized that NGO project expansion is far from a costless exercise for the economies and societies in which it takes place. While some resources (human and physical) for NGO projects are brought into a country, and are therefore provided as free goods, others are clearly not. Northern NGOs in particular, sensitive to criticisms of neo-colonialism, will continue to want to employ (and where necessary train) as many indigenous staff as they can, and engage local contractors, even if short-term efficiency thereby takes a dip. Where possible, they will also try to utilize domestically manufactured or processed consumer and intermediate goods: from desks and tables to cement and bricks.[5] Thus any expansion of NGO projects will necessarily entail an increase in domestic resources—human and capital—utilized by these projects. Clearly in poor countries where resources are scarce, the time will eventually be reached (and sometimes quite quickly) when the NGO use of resources will mean that fewer resources are available to be channelled to other uses. In this process, it could well happen that poor and more marginalized people could suffer disproportionately.[6]

On the human resources front, and in African countries in particular, the expansion of NGOs which is currently under way has already resulted in a significant loss of skilled personnel from the government and increased inefficiencies within the civil service either as NGOs—like official aid agencies—have poached key staff from the civil service, or as their supplementing, or topping-up, of government salaries has led those continuing in government service to devote a disproportionate amount of their time to facilitating donor projects.

One of the main reasons for this is that the larger and northern-based, or northern-funded, NGOs in particular are able to pay significantly higher salaries than can the government. To the extent that NGO expansion continues, the wage and salary distortions which NGOs (and official aid agencies) cause and contribute to will be perpetuated and become more pervasive, creating widespread problems if and when aid agencies withdraw. In addition, as NGO involvement in development projects expands, there is bound to be an increased risk of duplication of effort between NGOs and other agencies, most notably the government, in rural development interventions unless a rational deployment of human resources and technical staff emerges. For instance, in Zimbabwe NGOs employ an additional 25 per cent agricultural extension or related personnel to those deployed throughout the country by the government, yet there is little or no co-ordination of the work of the government and NGO extension staff.[7]

But the adverse consequences are more profound than simply affecting salary differentials or leading to an inefficient deployment of skills. However distinct, separate from government, and geographically isolated individual NGO projects are, NGOs operate within the overall administrative system and so are affected by government and government institutions. Like the private sector, NGOs and other donors need a well-ordered administrative system in order to operate efficiently. As numbers of NGO projects expand, the efficiency of the public administration system in general and of line ministries in particular is bound to be affected by increased defections of personnel to the aid sector, adding to the problems caused by direct defections to the private sector, while the increased numbers of NGO projects will demand an even greater degree of public service efficiency to administer. In time—and already that time has arrived in a number of poorer African countries—the level of defections will be so great as to frustrate not only the development efforts of the government but even the development efforts of the NGOs themselves. The consequence of this trend continuing is that NGOs will increasingly need to consider the impact that their interventions are having on the ability of the host government to operate in the development field. Hanlon (1991: 107) has documented an extreme case, in Mozambique, where, in his view, the effect of NGOs has been not only to create parallel institutions to those of the state but to undermine state structures and severely reduce the government's ability to assist the people: 'donors have used aid to weaken and break the Mozambican government'.

There is also the problem of lack of co-ordination. Like their official counterparts, a feature of NGO operations has been and continues to be their lack of co-operation, consultation, and sharing of information about their areas of operation, their successes and failures, and reasons for varied project performance. This has been exacerbated by the explosion in the number of NGOs in many countries, encouraged in large measure by the increased availability of funds from government and official aid donors. In many of the larger NGOs, too, there is often a recognized and acknowledged lack of intra-organization sharing of information and data. As individual NGO interventions increase in number, poor co-ordination is bound increasingly to limit effectiveness unless and until the problem is addressed in a comprehensive fashion.

Southern NGOs, in particular, tend to spend far more time and devote far more resources to promoting individual and discrete interventions than in analysing the broader policy issues which have a bearing on their mostly micro-level poverty-alleviating interventions, and in seeking to influence government policies which have a direct bearing on the lives and incomes of poor people. There is thus often substantial scope for NGOs in the south to lobby governments to influence policies and the legal framework to make it operate more in favour of the poor and marginalized over against the richer and more affluent beneficiaries of the prevailing social, political, and economic system (Bratton, 1990; Edwards and Hulme, 1992).

The precise way in which change could occur will depend, of course, on an array of issues not least of which is the nature of the southern government. However, this broader role has become increasingly important as governments have adopted structural adjustment programmes, many of which are adversely affecting different groups of the urban and rural poor. Although NGOs are often in a comparatively advantageous position to engage in such lobbying, in Africa in particular, they appear to have been reluctant to take on such an advocacy role. In Asia the influence and importance of this type of action by NGOs is of far greater importance (see Chapters 7 and 8 for examples from India and Bangladesh), even if in the last few years the contribution of NGOs to the current process of democratization in Africa is becoming the subject of growing interest and debate (Fowler, 1991).

To enhance their capability to undertake these types of activities, southern NGOs need funds both to analyse where the gaps are and the potential exists to pursue more widespread lobbying exercises for the poor, and to provide a local capability to undertake such activities. There is clearly scope for northern NGOs to fund such initiatives, and to share their expertise in campaigning with their southern partners (Clark, 1991; Vasant, 1989). In certain circumstances even more could be done in this area: in particular because they are external bodies, northern agencies often have a greater ability to raise certain issues, especially those related to human and land rights, and democracy, than do southern NGOs whose staff tend to be more vulnerable to intimidation—or worse.

But even beyond these more sensitive issues which ripple over into politics and challenge the entrenched positions of various national and regional interest-groups, relationships between NGOs and governments in the south are likely to face increasing pressure for change in the 1990s. In particular, growth in the numbers of NGOs present in a country, and in the number of projects they undertake, has led increasing numbers of southern governments to discuss the need for, and often to introduce, a more formal system of monitoring and co-ordinating the activities of NGOs. Few, however, have yet gone as far as the Indian Government, which has incorporated NGOs into its recent development plans and substantially funds some of their activities.

Most governments now require foreign (and local) NGOs to register their presence in a country, and to specify their area of development activity; many require NGOs to seek agreement from the local authorities to operate in a particular locality. To the extent that NGOs become an increasingly significant influence in a country, their potential for policy influence up to the national level is bound to increase. As this happens, it is understandable that a government will want not only to co-ordinate their development efforts but also to increase its ability to monitor, control, and put boundaries around their operations.

At the same time, and often at the instigation of official donors, governments are viewing NGOs as sub-contractors who can take on the responsibility for delivering services and implementing large-scale development projects (Robinson, 1995). What remains uncertain is the extent to which, as NGOs grow in influence and importance in the development sphere, issues of control will become the dominant motive in government action. In deciding how to draw the boundaries, governments run the risk of restricting and limiting NGOs to the extent that their independent and flexible style of operating is stifled. If they are so restricted, the NGO movement is likely to remain relatively stagnant and marginal, or even to wither. This would clearly have serious effects not only on actual and potential NGO interventions, but also upon far wider attempts to foster self-reliance and nurture community-based activities. Most NGOs would argue that if these are stifled, the potential for development for the poor dies as well.

There will therefore be an increasing need to find a compromise between competing pressures. Governments need to create a mechanism in which the insights and experience of NGOs are utilized and disseminated, while NGOs need to be sufficiently confident in the government to want to share their experiences. Clearly this is an ideal and, in practice, will continue to be far removed from reality. However, if governments believe that NGOs do have a role to play in development, they will wish to establish a mechanism which will both provide feedback from individual NGO experience to government agencies and to other NGOs, and enable NGOs to tap the experience and knowledge of the government and its various institutions.

The initial reaction of most NGOs to government interest is to try to defend their territory, fearing that to the extent that they conform and submit to the rising demands put on them by the government, their uniqueness will be threatened. To the extent that they refuse to conform to increasing bureaucratic attempts to put boundaries around their activities, they will be increasingly faced with the options of either running down their activities (and thereby lessening their influence) or—if they are northern-based NGOs—simply of pulling out.

One possible way out of this growing dilemma is for governments to institution-alize their relations with NGOs in different ways at different levels. In some countries a national register of developmental NGOs has been established, divided into local and foreign. However, if governments wish to encourage the (controlled) growth of NGOs, they need to avoid the creation of complex legislation, or the introduction of complex procedures, which inhibit NGO activity or delay the speedy implementation of their projects.

Two levels of contact are likely to be of growing importance. First, line ministries involved in particular forms of intervention—agricultural extension, water, health, etc.—need to know about current NGO activities in their field of competence, to be able to encourage further NGO involvement in localities or areas of technical com-petence where government is not involved, and to rationalize the national (and inter-national) resources devoted and planned in each area. Clearly, the type and degree of contact between line ministry and NGOs will vary from country to country—in some cases the NGO role will be dominant, in others it will be minimal.[8]

In all cases, however, it will become increasingly important for relevant line min-istries to have the ability to monitor NGO activities within their areas of competence. In many instances, it will be useful to have some sort of government–NGO liaison facility; often this may mean little more than the relevant NGOs joining a ministry–donor working group. For their part, there will be a growing onus on the NGOs working in particular fields to collaborate more, initially through exchanging informa-tion between themselves, in order that their representatives can act as the centre of contact for all NGOs involved in these fields. If this does not happen, the likelihood will increase that governments will assume a more restrictive, rather than a more supportive role, in relation to NGOs.

The second level of contact is the locality in which the different NGOs operate. In the first instance, NGOs will be increasingly called upon to obtain local clearance to work in any given area, and contact with local politicians is tending to become of increasing importance. NGOs have often been wary, and sometimes resentful, of the local authorities in the areas where they work—in some cases expressing an arrogant view that they have a right to be there because they are clearly helping the poor. To the extent that the local power structure clearly oppresses the poor, then NGOs who work to improve the position of the poor are a threat. What NGOs have often failed fully to acknowledge, however, is that unless their interventions encompass the whole community (and not just a group of beneficiaries), they are almost bound to cause tension in the areas in which they work, whatever the degree of oppression which exists. Bringing in resources from outside that otherwise would not have been avail-able can often be a major cause of jealousies across and between communities. To the extent that these jealousies exist, it will be increasingly difficult for NGOs to continue to create 'islands of development', and increasingly necessary to harmonize their development efforts with those of the government and other agencies working in the same locality.

For their part, therefore, NGOs often need to be more sympathetic to the demands which local political and administrative structures place upon them. It would be worrying if such limitations were absent, especially since governments will want to ensure that foreign NGOs in particular are not fronts for other non-developmental (religious and political) agendas they are unwilling to reveal publicly.

NORTHERN NGOS AND OFFICIAL AID DONORS

In the future there are likely to be even closer relationships developing between northern NGOs and official aid agencies, with a continued increase in the level of funding and greater NGO involvement in policy dialogue and project implementation. It is also becoming increasingly common for northern NGOs to fund projects and programmes undertaken by southern NGOs rather than to execute projects themselves, and for northern NGOs to channel funds to partners in the south, who themselves fund projects. Clearly many of the problems of project impact described in the previous chapter—and ways of resolving them—would apply with equal force to poverty-alleviating projects funded by these partners and executed by southern NGOs.

It is therefore of interest to these agencies that the interventions they fund more effectively achieve the objectives set; addressing the range of constraints which limit NGO project success is clearly as relevant to official aid funders as it is to the NGOs themselves. In terms of much current practice, it would appear that greater attention often needs to be given by official aid agencies to the following: the funding of pre-project preparation; assisting overall contextual assessment and analysis; helping assess ways in which current data within NGOs might be utilized more effectively; and assisting with the enhancing of management and technical skills within NGOs.

All this points to an enhanced role for external donors in promoting NGO institutional development with a view to enhancing their overall impact and effectiveness. This may require a greater flexibility in the type of funding that donors are willing to provide, possibly through more core funding for NGOs with a proven reputation for sound development work. A more specific initiative would be to incorporate the costs of ongoing monitoring and evaluation into NGO project funding. At the same time, northern NGOs might profitably consider providing, or increasing the level of, block grants to southern NGOs or consortia to enable them, in turn, to build up their own institutional competence.

To the extent that official aid agencies feel the need to continue to fund NGO interventions on a project-by-project basis, NGOs should be further encouraged to devote more time and resources at the outset to describing how the precise objectives of their projects are to be met, how they will be sustained after their withdrawal, pinpointing the risks involved, and discussing, however crudely, how risks could be reduced. NGOs will also need to do more to specify the management and staff requirements of projects and how these are to be met and to provide a breakdown of total costs and cost per beneficiary, perhaps also comparing these with their other interventions.

Although northern NGOs have been reticent in addressing their own shortcomings, they have been sensitive in trying to address management weaknesses and inadequate human-resource skills in the south. A widespread practice has evolved whereby individual northern NGOs pay for southern NGO staff to travel abroad on exposure-cum-training and study trips or to develop international networking contacts. However, what is often missing is provision for the enhancement of local skills for a wider group and larger numbers of NGO personnel, as well as for project managers. Just as the World Bank has highlighted the need for capacity building at the national level, so too there is a pressing need to build skills capacities within and between southern NGOs. The problem is accentuated because there is usually little liaison between the NGOs capable of funding national or regional facilities which could provide this function; it would usually be prohibitively expensive for just one NGO to fund such centres.[9]

An alternative way of addressing the same set of problems is through more targeted training. Official aid agencies have been accused of placing too much emphasis on project execution and too little time on training local people. If NGOs are serious about self-reliance in the communities with which they work, then they need to consider building in—and funding, or requesting funding from official aid agencies for—a training component in all their projects, even though the total project costs are bound to increase as a result, and the more immediate and tangible benefits arising from particular project interventions are likely to be slower in coming.

While the distancing of northern NGOs from direct efforts at poverty alleviation in some senses reduces their impact and influence in poverty projects within developing countries, the growth and expansion of NGOs in the north, and wider acceptance of the legitimacy of their role, provide them with new opportunities. One is to influence public opinion about poverty and development, and the wider policies which affect developing countries. The 1980s have already seen a growth in public education and advocacy work both in northern countries and among international finance institutions. More and more northern NGOs have channelled funds into these initiatives, and NGOs have met with success in specific campaigns.[10] The importance of NGOs in the broader development debate is set to increase, especially if individual efforts are better co-ordinated.[11] Both their legitimacy in such lobbying, and the impact of such initiatives, are likely to be substantially enhanced to the extent that they are able to make better use of the data and information contained within different NGOs.

CONCLUSIONS—A PLEA FOR MODESTY

An important theme woven through the pages of this book has been the difficulty of making firm generalizations about the role and impact of NGOs in poverty alleviation. There is still insufficient evidence of what they have achieved in the past, as there is of the differing influence of the range of internal and external factors which influence performance, to be able to draw uncontestable conclusions about the impact of NGOs in poverty alleviation.

NGOs know and recognize the constraints under which they work, and the limitations of their interventions. Yet many appear reluctant to expose their own supporters and the general public to these shortcomings and, more broadly, to acknowledge that, in isolation, even a wide array of different poverty-alleviating projects is unlikely to make a major dent in the problem of world poverty. Even when NGOs have tried to move away from a concentration on isolated projects to try to tackle more of the deeper structural problems of development, the results have frequently been limited, not least because voluntary agencies will always be vulnerable to powerful social and political forces, especially when they choose to play a more visible role in trying to resolve conflictual national issues.

Part of the reason that northern NGOs tend to exaggerate the potential impact they can make is that, historically, most have built their domestic support more on the basis of eliciting a response to the unacceptability of the extent and depth of developing-country poverty (as well as to the immediate dangers to life which emergencies bring), and less on the manner in which the projects and programmes undertaken contribute to the fundamental resolution of these problems. To the extent that the moral appeal to do something for the poor and vulnerable is used to legitimize the action undertaken, any assessment of impact tends to be set aside, or relegated to a subsidiary and secondary level.

There are practical (as well, perhaps, as moral) dangers in continuing to maintain such an approach. In the first place, it discourages NGOs from critically assessing their work, and from informing the public of the impact of their projects and programmes. And as we have seen, weaknesses in absorbing the lessons of experience tend adversely to affect future impact. One result is that this places those critical of NGOs and the whole NGO approach to development in a stronger position to be able to make use of the evidence of poor individual project performance in order to try to influence the public not merely to hold the view that NGO projects do not solve the problems of local poverty, but to question the very basis for continuing to support NGOs and to respond to the moral imperative upon which this funding is largely based. If the belief becomes widespread that the money provided makes hardly any difference at all to the lives of the poor, there would be little point in continuing to contribute to and support the activities of NGOs.

This book has argued that NGOs can, and many probably do, make a contribution to alleviating poverty and making the lives of the poor a little more tolerable, in spite of the particularly hostile environment in which they often have to work. Yet the contribution made by them is limited, both in terms of the increases in income which can be achieved in a typical NGO project, and in terms of the impact that the NGO approach to development as a whole can have on the vast problem of developing-country poverty. There is little reason for NGOs to be hesitant in acknowledging that their contribution is frequently limited, and that in each country the impact of the overall NGO effort is usually still marginal to solving the wider problems. Greater transparency by NGOs regarding both the problems that they face in project implementation and of the often major problems involved in trying to overcome world poverty would not only help to undercut the hollowness of criticisms made against them, but would also strengthen the moral basis of public support for the important but extremely difficult work which they are trying to achieve.

NOTES

1. More than a few of these dovetail with ones highlighted in a similar exercise undertaken in the Netherlands in the 1990–1 period, where nineteen projects funded by the four leading Dutch co-financing agencies across six countries were reviewed and assessed.
2. In contrast, for the specialized NGO, such as Water Aid in the UK, the form of intervention is often determined by the nature of the NGO.
3. In its 1992 *Operational Directive*, the World Bank President called upon Bank staff to produce poverty assessments for all countries which borrow from the Bank by 1994, which are to form the basis for a collaborative approach to poverty reduction by country officials and the Bank. This initiative does not lessen the need for NGOs to conduct their own analyses and undertake their own assessments of poverty in the countries and regions in which they work. Indeed if sharp differences arise between assessments made by Bank officials and NGOs, these differences could well the form the starting-point for dialogue and discussion about different approaches to resolving the problems of poverty in different contexts.
4. For a more detailed discussion of the scaling-up issue see Edwards and Hulme (1992).
5. See UNIDO (1990) for the enormous waste of poor countries' economic potential because official aid agencies continue to insist on importing even the everyday goods they require in the countries in which they work.
6. This could either be because resources are allocated administratively to NGO projects, or else because an expansion of effective demand pushes up the price of such goods and services.
7. Part of the reason for this lies in the reluctance of the NGOs to being tied down to medium- to long-term commitments of their staff and assets, arguing that to enter into such a commitment would eliminate their unique characteristics.
8. This has been the subject of an extensive research project at ODI which examines the roles that NGOs play in promoting sustainable agricultural development by acting as an interface between public-sector research and extension agencies and poor farmers in a number of developing countries (see Farrington *et al.*, 1993).
9. One recent initiative which seeks to fulfil this role is El Taller ('the Workshop'), now based in Tunis, which aims to act as a resource and training institute for southern NGOs. A parallel initiative in the north is the International NGO Training and Research Centre based in Oxford, which was founded in response to the realization that European NGOs require such a facility to enhance their own organizational capacities.
10. Clark (1991: 145 ff.) provides an excellent overview of both particular campaigns and of the future potential of NGOs in advocacy work.
11. Four large European Protestant agencies commissioned a study in mid-1992 to examine ways in which this might occur in practice.

PART II

CASE-STUDIES FROM FOUR DEVELOPING COUNTRIES

7

Bangladesh

AN OVERVIEW

The increasing favour of non-governmental approaches within the international community has been reflected in mushrooming growth for NGOs in Bangladesh. The variety of organizations and ways in which they are registered means that it is possible only to estimate the figures involved. The NGO co-ordinating body, ADAB (Association for Development Agencies in Bangladesh), reported in 1990 that it had registered around 550 local-level NGOs engaged in development activities and 316 national and foreign NGOs receiving foreign donations. With many provisos about the hazards involved in making such estimates, this suggests that throughout the country there may be perhaps 2 million NGO group members. Even if this figure is anywhere near accurate, however, the uneven distribution of NGOs around the country needs to be borne in mind. There is a high correlation between accessibility to the major metropolitan centres and concentration of NGO activity; there is also a noticeable association between density of NGOs and communities of Christians, since many of the NGO funding agencies have some form of Church links.

Uncertainty about the exact number of NGOs combines with their reluctance to publish full accounts of their finances to make it impossible to put an accurate figure on the volume of funds that they now handle. A representative of one of the largest NGOs, however, estimates that NGOs in total bring into Bangladesh US $85–100m. each year. This represents around 6 per cent of total foreign aid, in contrast to an estimate of 1 per cent in 1972–3.

While the NGOs differ from one another in style and emphasis there are certain broad trends in programme development. After the initial period of post-war reconstruction, the NGOs devised programmes for integrated community development with a strong emphasis on agriculture. By the late 1970s evidence that benefits went largely to those who were already better-off led to disillusionment with this strategy, and NGOs came to see poverty not simply as a problem of income differentials but also of the power relations which constitute rural society. Many NGOs therefore began to lay emphasis on consciousness-raising with the aim of forging class-based alliances among poor people.

For some NGOs, consciousness-raising has been the centre of their development strategy, with initiatives towards income-generating activities despised as not attacking the root problem of inequality. More generally, however, consciousness-raising

This chapter was substantially written by Sarah White, based on her longer primary research report produced as a technical working paper of the Overseas Development Institute (White, 1991).

was adopted as one element within a broader development strategy, comprising basic literacy, health education, income generation and skills training, provision of sanitation and drinking water, and family planning. This was always an uneasy compromise, with consciousness-raising expected to work and achieve measurable results just like any other kind of project. Experience showed that it did not do so, and in some cases where the poor were encouraged to confront the rural power structure they suffered severely as a result.

There is undoubtedly a process of endogenous change and reflection amongst Bangladesh NGOs, and the larger ones in particular form quite a tightly bound peer-group and have considerable influence on each other. At the same time, however, they are clearly affected by external factors, such as shifts in international politics and development fashions. Particular words ring, as it were, the bell on the donors' cash register and the till springs open. 'Credit' is certainly one of these, as is 'women' and —the latest favourite—the 'environment'. The influence of terminology should not be underestimated. Thus, even in the heyday of consciousness-raising, co-operative members and potential members were being described as the 'target group' and so allotted a very passive role (Wood, 1994), with development appearing as a kind of social engineering. It is not perhaps surprising that the term 'target group' has outlived that of 'consciousness-raising' as a key symbol amongst NGOs in Bangladesh (Sanyal, 1991).

For many small-scale indigenous NGOs a single programme focus remains, but the main trend is for NGOs to develop a comprehensive programme approach. Amongst the case-studies presented here, examples of this are given by both Gono Unnayan Prochesta and Caritas. The late 1980s and early 1990s are also seeing a new orientation towards urban programmes, breaking down the virtual monopoly focus on rural needs. Co-operatives are still the basic unit, with the dominant emphasis now on savings and credit to foster small-scale income-generating activities (Sanyal, 1991).

In recent years particularly, NGOs have given increasing attention to gender issues. For some, this has always been a central concern: for the majority, however, the influence of international donors has played a key part in the recognition of the gender dimensions of poverty and identification of women as a priority target-group. NGOs have also included gender issues in their attempts at consciousness-raising, with moves to oppose the practices of dowry-gifting and male violence against women, and to gain recognition for the contribution that women make in the household economy.

It is important, however, not to exaggerate the influence that NGOs have had in this area. In the first place it is clear that there is a wider process of social change which is bringing about shifts in gender relations, with the decline of landholding undermining the family farm and the expansion of new opportunities for business and salaried employment. The NGOs thus represent one facet of a wider process. In the second place, many NGO programmes for women are far from imaginative, and reproduce old patterns, with women being concentrated in low-budget, low-productivity areas which serve rather than challenge the established principle of male dominance.

Since the mid-1970s, a myriad of smaller indigenous NGOs have been set up. Some of these grew out of local clubs and associations; some were set up by individuals or small groups of committed people; some began as projects of larger NGOs and then became independent. This process is still taking place and has been accelerated by the volume of funds entering the country following the disastrous floods of 1987 and 1988 and the cyclone of 1991. As part of Bangladesh society, the NGOs reflect the predominant form of social relations: the formation of particularistic patron–client ties. Smaller, local NGOs may receive funding through, or on the recommendation of, or as a result of advice from, larger NGOs; and this relationship may continue with broader ties of mutual interest.

Links between the NGOs are formalized in ADAB, which aims to co-ordinate NGO activities, training, and services and act as a forum for more unified representation to the government. There are also a number of more limited umbrella organizations to assist smaller NGOs. ADAB has a national forum and local 'chapters'. Membership of ADAB is, however, restricted and membership of the local chapter does not entail that of the national federation. The history of ADAB has been chequered, with times of comparative unity, but overall it has been weakened by internal divisions and factional disputes.

The expansion of NGOs has also generated a burgeoning servicing sector which provides training or help in design of project applications and so on. Some NGOs specialize in this; some larger NGOs have special departments which contract out facilities or offer training; and there are also some straightforward commercial enterprises. The growth of a commercial side to NGO activities reflects their professionalization and their development as an alternative career sector. It clearly affects the kinds of programmes that NGOs can undertake. The development of this servicing sector is also due to the international climate that favours privatization, and so brings the drive to establish some form of self-reliant funding. Typically, NGOs regard these activities as quite separate from their development work, and as not changing the kind of agencies they are, except in allowing them more autonomy from donors. Amongst the case-studies considered here, Gono Unnayan Prochesta has been foremost in this. It has proved difficult for NGOs to keep prices at an acceptable level, however, while maintaining an ethical system of operation, as margins are generally made in Bangladesh markets by exploiting workers, adulterating products, or violating safety regulations. Leaving aside questions about the effect of business enterprises on NGOs as development programmes, therefore, the attempts by NGOs to set up commercial activities have in general been unsuccessful so far.

Looking at the wider picture of NGOs in Bangladesh points up the inadequacy of the terms in which they are conventionally characterized by donors: as conduits for the transfer of resources to the poor. Two features stand out. First, in a national context where there has been only formal democracy and an unwieldy state bureaucracy, NGOs represent a means whereby members of the élite may build up a client base, work towards directing social change, and ultimately establish a voice in local and national affairs. Second, in a situation of scarce resources and limited opportunities for commercial development, NGOs may become an outlet for the entrepreneurial spirit, as a growth area of private sector initiatives within a dominant national industry of aid.

Relations with the State

Relations between the state and the NGOs in Bangladesh are contradictory. While publicly President Ershad proclaimed his support for the NGOs, in practice they found it difficult to get government approval for their programmes. In an ADAB survey of fifty-one NGOs in August 1989, only forty-four out of 162 projects submitted to the government over the previous two years had been approved (D'Rozario, 1989). The activities of voluntary organizations have been regulated under the Societies Registration Act since 1860 (introduced under British colonial rule), which was confirmed in the Voluntary Social Welfare Agencies (Regulation and Control) Ordinance in 1961. It was not until 1978, however, that foreign funding became an issue, with the Foreign Donations (Voluntary Agencies) Registration Ordinance, followed in 1982 by the Foreign Contributions (Regulation) Ordinance requiring not only registration of all organizations receiving foreign funds, but also annual clearance of foreign-aided projects. Bringing foreign funds into the country for projects without prior approval was punishable by a fine of twice the value of the donation and imprisonment of up to six months. Another government circular prohibited government officials from serving on NGO boards or councils—including officials of semi-autonomous bodies, universities, and government schools (D'Rozario, 1989). By mid-1989, however, the system had virtually broken down and in November representatives of the major NGOs met President Ershad to discuss changes. In June 1990 a new NGO Affairs Bureau was opened under the Presidential Secretariat's Public Division, to provide a one-stop service to NGOs: the same departments will have to be circulated as before, but the Bureau itself does this within set time-limits (120 days for registering an organization, and 60 days for approving a project proposal).

Legislation is only one aspect of state–NGO relations. The position of NGOs as the darlings of foreign donors is obviously one that brings its own tensions. On the one hand, some government officials recognize that their agencies have something to learn from NGO methods of working and understand donor frustrations with the state bureaucracy. On the other hand, government employees can find it hard to have their departments' programmes compared, almost always unfavourably, with those of NGOs. There is also envy and distrust amongst senior officials of the economic resources and increasing political influence wielded by senior NGO leaders. This shows also in the practice of government officials setting up their own NGOs. While some of these may be bona fide, they are widely suspected of being a front for access to foreign funds.

Lower down the hierarchy, government employees often resent staff at a comparable level in the larger NGOs having greater flexibility in working, receiving generally better salaries, and having a higher budget for office support, vehicles, etc. None the less, for the majority of Bangladeshi graduates, government service would still be first choice since it offers higher social status and longer-term security. There is also some reciprocity: NGO salaried staff come from broadly the same social background as government officers and typically see good relations with local government representatives as an essential pre-condition for success in their work. At the local level, informal arrangements for sharing resources therefore arise.

NGOs and government at national level also have some interests in common. In its introductory publication, the NGO Affairs Bureau stated that the government welcomed NGOs' activities to 'supplement and complement government's development programme'. This reflects concerns that NGOs should not be seen as an alternative to government and raises the broader issue of sovereignty—clearly an issue in a new country like Bangladesh where the quest for a national identity is evident in numerous ways. At the same time, however, focusing this issue on NGO activities clearly disguises the government's own heavy reliance on foreign funding. Rather than indicating a concern with foreign insurgence, therefore, this seems likely to represent a more acceptable expression of the suspicion that allocations to NGOs will reduce the government's share of official external aid. In fact, however, while some NGOs are simply fronts for getting foreign funding and are not doing any serious development work, the fears of subversion from NGOs seem unfounded. The great majority are helping to do what the government has stated as its aims: as in the radical left critique, they are preventing rebellion rather than fomenting it. Very few are even encouraging their members to put pressure on the government to provide better public resources; the NGOs regard it as unrealistic to expect this to achieve anything, and attempt to meet the needs themselves.

There are also cases of direct collaboration between the state and the NGOs. The most obvious example is the NGOs' participation in the government's declaration to distribute unused government-held *khas* land to the landless. A very small amount of land has in fact been distributed, but it indicates how NGOs may enter the mainstream of policy determination. Similarly, President Ershad's 'cluster village' scheme, to bring homeless households together in a new custom-built village settlement, became part of many NGOs' rehabilitation programmes after the 1988 flood. It enabled the NGOs to distribute significant resources to clients and the government to construct at little or no cost visible and lasting (presumably) demonstrations of President Ershad's commitment to help the very poorest.

At an individual level also, some leading figures from the NGO movement have taken important advisory positions in various governments, including those post-Ershad. It is not clear what this means for NGOs as a whole: on the one hand, it could represent the state's co-option of potential opposition figures; on the other, it could mean that the NGOs' concerns and values are taken more seriously at the national level. The most likely outcome seems to be a negotiation involving some concessions on both sides.

British NGOs in Bangladesh

Bangladesh represents the second largest recipient of British aid and British overseas NGOs are strongly represented in the country. They include ActionAid, CAFOD, Christian Aid, Save the Children Fund, Oxfam, War on Want, the Intermediate Technology Group (ITDG), and Tear Fund, alongside single project foundations for which the financial resource is British, such as the Centre for the Rehabilitation of the Paralysed, or the British Airways orphanage. Two large US-based international organizations—CARE and World Vision—which have been working in Bangladesh also have British branches.

Of the large NGOs, only ActionAid and Save the Children Fund are directly operational. As elsewhere, Save the Children is primarily concerned with the health sector. The other large NGOs all fund projects through Bangladeshi partner organizations. For CAFOD, there is a single partner, Caritas Bangladesh, while other contributions go into a centralized Catholic fund, the Asian Partnership for Human Development. Christian Aid supports CCDB, the development organization of the National Council of Churches of Bangladesh (Protestant) as well as a range of smaller partners. Both CAFOD and Christian Aid tend to have a 'hands-off' approach to the programmes they support; Oxfam is more interventionist. It believes that small, local NGOs are best able to realize their own objectives if they have access to ongoing guidance and support. Oxfam has the most scope for this, as it has a well-established local office in Bangladesh, which over the years has developed a policy of aiming to support social action groups rather than organizations oriented primarily towards service provision. War On Want followed a similar approach up to the cessation of its activities in 1990, but on a smaller scale.

Bangladeshi NGOs do not necessarily know where the funds they receive come from. Thus one of the case-study organizations only discovered when an evaluation team arrived that the funds it had received for post-disaster relief came from the British Government, rather than directly from the British NGO with which it had dealt. So far, the Overseas Development Administration is careful not to be seen to be wishing to influence policy. None the less, there are fears amongst the British NGOs that accepting grants from the government on a regular basis could compromise their autonomy, that they will be less able to take a stand on issues of which the government disapproves, and that the accounting and monitoring systems of the ODA are already having a subtle effect on views of what constitutes good programmes.

The Case-Study Projects

The four projects reviewed in this chapter are intended to illustrate the role of NGOs in Bangladesh development in two ways: first, they show some approaches that the NGOs have taken to tackle poverty in Bangladesh; second, they indicate a range of NGO problems and successes in their attempts to raise the economic status of the rural poor. While the case-studies cannot be taken to represent the whole spectrum of NGOs in Bangladesh, they do highlight a number of important trends in the movement. The ActionAid project is centred on savings and credit, which form key elements in almost all NGOs' development strategies. The Gono Kallyan Trust study is concerned with agriculture and so reflects the importance of the land and its crops to the Bangladesh economy and society. The Gono Unnayan Prochesta project aims to enable the landless to gain access to another productive resource, fish-ponds, which can provide an important source of income and protein. The Caritas social forestry programme indicates the growing concern for environmental degradation and longer-term ecological sustainability.

The case-studies also introduce some of the diversity of geographical locations in Bangladesh. The ActionAid programme is sited in the far south of the country, on an island in the delta area, which has a history of neglect by government and NGOs alike. Gono Kallyan Trust, in sharp contrast, operates in the heartland of NGOs in Bangladesh, in Manikganj district only an hour and a half from Dhaka. Gono Unnayan Prochesta is sited in middle-south Bangladesh, and the field study of the Caritas programme took place in Dinajpur, far to the north.

Finally, the organizations themselves differ substantially from one another. ActionAid is an operational British NGO. Gono Kallyan Trust is a small, new Bangladeshi NGO, with a strong local orientation. Gono Unnayan Prochesta has for many years been a regional NGO, focused primarily on one sub-district (*upazila*), but is now extending its coverage to establish itself on the national scale. Caritas has seven regional offices in different parts of the country. It is one of the oldest NGOs in Bangladesh, dating from before Independence, and is part of an international federation of Catholic development agencies throughout the world.

The case-studies are based on field research between February and June 1990, in which the ODI researcher worked with two teams, each with two Bangladeshi research assistants. Co-operative groups (or *samitis*) are a central feature of NGO activities in Bangladesh and in each programme an average of fifteen *samitis* and forty individuals were interviewed. The aim was not to draw a strictly representative sample of the NGOs' activities, but to cover a range of different areas and types of *samitis*, to grasp the variety of experience. In each case, interviews were carried out in three different locations. Standard checklists were used to gain profiles of the organization, the programme, and a sample of households including both participants and non-participants in the programmes.

The method of data collection was intensive rather than extensive, relying on detailed interviews to build up a rounded picture of the programme and how it fitted into the wider opportunities that households face. None the less, the questions underlying the study included the following: What are the aims of the project? Does it achieve them? Does it reach the poorest? Is it managed efficiently? What does it cost? Is it sustainable? Can it be self-reliant? At the same time, the study aims to move beyond this view of NGO effectiveness as primarily an issue of aid administration, and to set the NGOs and their work in their broader social and political context.

ACTIONAID BANGLADESH DEVELOPMENT CENTRE PROGRAMME

The core of the ActionAid Development Centre programme is to encourage savings and extend credit to the poor, particularly women, organized into small groups (*samitis*). The stress is on self-reliant development, with the view that lack of capital is the key constraint that keeps people in poverty and dependence. Savings are collected at weekly meetings where there may also be some discussion of health and education issues. Small loans are given to four or five *samiti* members at a time. The size of loans increases in set steps of Tk.200, and they are repayable in weekly instalments. Availability to the *samiti* of subsequent loans is dependent on all members repaying existing ones on time.

The Development Centre programme operates in three *upazilas* (sub-districts) in southern Bhola, the largest island lying in the delta formed in the mouth of the Ganges, Brahmaputra, and Meghna rivers. The total population of southern Bhola is estimated at 500,000, of whom more than 50 per cent are landless. In December 1989 7,755 were registered ActionAid members, belonging to 385 registered *samitis* with a further thirty-two in preparation. The programme is, however, constantly being extended. The recurrent annual budget in 1989/90 was Tk.4,772,000 of which 66 per cent was staff costs, with the balance for transport, stationery, and other materials. Loans are given from a revolving fund of Tk.7,500,000.

ActionAid Bangladesh has seen a considerable degree of success in achieving its aims. Most of its clients come from the target-group, the landless poor, although they are not generally the very poorest of all. There is an efficient system for the collection of savings and the issue of credit, with a loan recovery rate of over 90 per cent. The high demand for loans indicates that they are of some benefit to households, but a common complaint is that they are too small to make a significant difference. The programme as a whole is individualist in orientation and relies on high pressure from staff and the other members to repay on schedule. This can mean heavy costs being borne by member households which are in difficulties with repayment. The utility of the loans is also restricted by the fact that many of the activities they finance— particularly for women—are of extremely low productivity. The relatively small impact that the programme makes on poverty as a whole points to the limitations of an approach which concentrates solely on credit.

The ActionAid Development Centre Programme occupies an equivocal place within the overall NGO scene in Bangladesh. On the one hand, it acts as a useful test-case for the efficacy of credit as a development intervention, and as such is of great significance, as provision of credit has an increasingly dominant place in NGO programmes in Bangladesh. On the other hand, however, ActionAid is unusual in being a foreign operational agency, in a context where most foreign NGOs are funding Bangladeshi partners rather than running programmes of their own. While it has only one expatriate member of staff (the Director), ActionAid's style is therefore distinctive. First, it has resisted the more general pattern amongst NGOs of adopting a broad range of programmes, and has placed maximum emphasis on credit as the agent of change. Second, it has an unusually tight management style with a rigorous policy of reporting and monitoring and a strong emphasis on cost-effectiveness. An evaluation of ActionAid's Development Centre programme, therefore, must in part consider some of the relative advantages and disadvantages of the operational involvement of foreign NGOs.

There is no doubt that the ActionAid Bangladesh Development Centre Programme is achieving its objectives in many areas. On the whole it is reaching the poor. It has good loan recovery rates. It has meant for some people a substantial increase in income and an enlargement of options, especially where larger loans have been given, and has inspired in most of its members the confidence that they can do something to improve the position of their families.

These achievements are in large part due to the ingenuity of *samiti* members in turning what they are given to good use. Alongside this, the discipline within ActionAid among both staff and *samiti* members is clearly a central factor in the programme's effectiveness. As with the Grameen Bank, the system of payment by small weekly instalments limits the potential to divert repayments into consumption. Beyond this, the programme's strength lies in its simplicity, its focus on the delivery of a single service, and its relatively high staff–client ratios.

The most serious potential constraint to the usefulness of the programme is the small size of the loans. While concerns about poor people's ability to repay are real, many are in fact still having to resort to outside loans to cover their credit needs, and so are incurring punishingly high interest rates. To keep to tight restrictions on the volume of loans may be to condemn *samiti* members to remaining in poverty: while they may become less poor than they were, on these amounts of capital there is little potential for making the move out of annual deficit.

The most serious shortcoming is that the programme is not in general reaching the very poorest—those whose absolute level of income is simply too low, who are in chronic deficit for most of the year. For them the ideal of self-reliance is a long way off. The non-credit aspects of this programme (health education and some teaching for children) point up the chronic paucity of state provision. The question clearly arises whether the economic ventures of individual poor households will ever be enough to make a significant impact on rural poverty. There has been some shift towards tighter targeting of clients, as seen in the differences in membership between the older established and the newer *samitis*; in the former there were some who were clearly better-off, with tin-roofed houses and surplus assets to hire out. On the whole, membership is fairly unstable; only four of the *samitis* interviewed had seen no change in membership and they were all less than one year old. In two cases the *samiti* split as members making regular savings and repayments left to set up on their own. This clearly has negative implications for *samiti* coherence and solidarity.

Although gender issues do not figure in the Development Centre objectives (the emphasis is rather on families and domestic concerns of health, nutrition, and education), the programme clearly has gender implications. To make regular payments either means that a woman is gradually building up capital of her own or that she has to ask her husband or son for money, and so implicitly challenge the cultural ideology of women's exclusion from economic affairs. This does not necessarily mean that the woman has rights over the use of the money she saves. One woman told, for example, how her son insisted she leave the *samiti* after four years of membership, and she had to give to him the full Tk.900 of savings that she withdrew. Some see *samiti* membership as being a new kind of female service to the household. In some cases, changes go further than this, as the loan capital enables women to mobilize their own labour. The potentially positive impact of the programme in terms of gender is, however, limited in two ways. First, credit alone does not widen higher productivity opportunities for women, so the rational household choice (let alone male authority bias) is usually for the husband or son to use the loan. Second, for any but the absolutely lowest-productivity businesses, some access to male labour for marketing is also a prerequisite.

The Development Centre programme has an overall contradictory character in relation to gender. While on the one hand it draws women slightly closer to the market place, on the other hand it clearly relies on the prevalent cultural system in which women are schooled to accept authority and sacrifice themselves for their families' good. The risk of a programme bringing new resources into a situation of inequality—that it will reinforce existing power relations—is the same in relation to gender as it is to class. Without a positive commitment to enlarge women's room for manœuvre, the overall impact can therefore be to reinforce existing gender inequalities. There is a danger of further institutionalizing this through the privatization of programme administration on to *samiti* members. Hard questions need to be asked about whether this would be possible if the clients were primarily male, and what messages are being given if the end result is that women are doing work for ActionAid at less than anything near a living wage.

Despite the wish of ActionAid to foster solidarity amongst the poor, the Development Centre programme is strongly individualist. The vast majority of loans are taken on an individual basis, with just a few cases of joint agricultural projects, particularly amongst Hindus. In our field study, only once did a member say that their *samiti* was thinking of putting the Tk.600 loans to a common fund to rent a rice-mill, but even she did not mention this in the follow-up individual interview, and others rejected the idea—they had their own plans, or their husbands would not agree. Experience of other organizations is similar. Joint projects undertaken by, for example, Grameen Bank *samitis* have been much less successful than their individual ventures. ActionAid sees this individualism as arising out of the social and cultural environment, but this is also reinforced by the structure of the programme itself. The pressure which ActionAid puts on members to make payments on time makes *samiti* members likely to be stricter with one another. The *samitis* are formed for collective policing, not for collective solidarity.

There are only isolated cases of *samitis* becoming involved in local social issues, or moving towards federation between different *samitis*, which might strengthen their voice. A few have managed to call a community hearing to resolve a particular dispute. A temporary federation of *samitis* was formed in one union, to make joint applications for *khas* land, and a few households were successful. Potentially, the formation of such a pressure group could improve *samitis*' access to public resources rather than struggling, as they do now, to provide for all their needs themselves. Nevertheless, most members say they are now closer to one another than they were before. In some cases there is a lot of mutual support, often reflecting good relationships that pre-date joining ActionAid. The hierarchical internal structure and set patterns for loan amounts and access clearly reduce the scope for conflict but they also contribute to the considerable difference in degrees of understanding and participation in meetings between leaders and members. This may be intensified if ActionAid persists with plans to pass some of the administration on to members, over whom the organization will not have the same power to restrain unfair practices as it does with paid staff. There are many mixed Muslim/Hindu *samitis*, including within the same group, and no apparent sense of tension. There is also one mixed male/female *samiti*, though men and women are in separate groups within it.

The rhetoric about the *samitis* themselves taking the lead is very strong. In practice, however, particular *samitis* are far from autonomous. On the contrary, members are strongly impressed by the need to obey the rules. The claim that the 'members decide' reflects ActionAid's hopes for the future, rather than the present reality. Past experience and members' comments play a part in the reformulation of the programme, but it is the senior staff who make the revisions. Rather than changes being initiated by *samitis*, there is often a time-lag as field-level staff and *samiti* members adjust reluctantly to changes in the rules they have learnt. When these issues were discussed with field-level staff they pointed out that rules were indispensable to their work and that people expected them to arrive with a ready-made programme. This is clearly both realistic in field practice, and reflects the overall stress of the programme on targets, a tight management system, and the achievement of clearly defined objectives.

These points indicate a more general trend: the disjuncture between the perceptions of members and those of the organization. What was most impressive in conversations with *samiti* members was the great sense of hope that if they make sacrifices, obey the rules, and save diligently they will achieve success for their families. People do not join a *samiti* as a rational economic calculation, and many have no clear idea of what they have saved or what kinds of amounts they will end up with, or how the value of money will change these five years on. There is no sense of labour as being a cost, nor any calculation of net rather than gross returns. And that rain comes, or animals die, is simply accepted: the loss is not seen as a ground to reflect on whether the loan was of benefit.

The point that 'the members decide' appears also in relation to the life of the *samitis*. ActionAid's plan is to withdraw after five years, or at most ten. All the members interviewed, however, hoped to continue their *samiti* if the worker extended it, with few plans for alternative methods of organization. Some talked, as primed, about seeing 'if we can stand on our own feet', meaning, it seems, individual economic self-sufficiency, not running the *samiti* themselves. So the ideas for gradual ActionAid withdrawal do not come from the members themselves. Rather, they clearly reflect the current development philosophy, which is common to the majority of NGOs in Bangladesh, and is initiated from the top down. Thus even the loosening of control and opening up of *samitis* to more self-definition by the members becomes a new technique for testing by an external, in this case expatriate, agency.

GONO KALLYAN TRUST HORTICULTURE AND AGRICULTURE PROGRAMMES

The aim of Gono Kallyan Trust (GKT)'s programmes is to provide technical support and advice for small groups of poor people, particularly women, to take land on lease for horticultural or agricultural production. The produce is divided into three shares according to inputs: land (the landowner), labour (the *samiti*), and capital (GKT).

The objectives are to increase consumption, particularly of vegetables, and to enable the poor to gain access to land and by working together to raise income and lay a basis for self-reliant development and broader socio-economic change.

GKT was formed in 1986 and started work in Saturia Upazila, Manikganj, the following year. It operates in ten unions of the *upazila* and in 1989/90 had an annual budget of Tk.1,300,000 (excluding relief and rehabilitation), with thirty-four staff members, of whom eight are women. In that year, 50 per cent of its ordinary programme funds came from two British NGOs, Christian Aid and War on Want, which also supplied the lion's share of the emergency funding. By June 1990 GKT had 110 *samitis*, forty of them under 9 months old, with forty-seven for men and sixty-three for women, and an average of twenty members in each. Most of the *samitis* meet weekly, though some meet fortnightly or monthly. They all collect savings and most begin to look almost immediately for land which can be used for joint cultivation projects. GKT also gives crop-seed loans and supplies vegetable and tree seedlings on an individual basis; it has three nurseries for the cultivation of seedlings, on leased land. GKT also has shallow tube-wells (STWs) and deep tube-wells (DTWs) with which it provides irrigation on a 25 per cent crop-share basis.

The annual floods in Bangladesh in 1987 were exceptionally heavy, and the 1988 floods were a national disaster. In April 1989 Saturia suffered a tornado that wrought massive destruction of buildings, machinery, trees, and crops, killing many people and severely injuring thousands. Nevertheless, in its first three years GKT saw considerable progress in moving towards its objectives. The senior staff are dedicated and experienced, and their commitment is reflected at the lower levels also. GKT is largely working with the poor—those with less than one acre of land. Most of the work on joint projects is fitted around *samiti* members' ordinary occupations, so that the crops they produce represent additional income, rather than replacement of existing sources. GKT's provision of access to technical and capital inputs means that the landless and land-poor are beginning to figure in the local land economy, which is still the basis of rural society. Rapid expansion in the number of groups also means, however, that there is now a need to consolidate and strengthen management and particularly technical capacity.

The case of GKT thus raises a theme central to the history of Bangladeshi NGOs: the complex interconnections between disasters and development. On the one hand, NGOs' development work has suffered severe setbacks through natural disasters, which have caused widespread economic and social damage, and have meant the suspension of normal activities. For many NGOs, two years of development efforts from mid-1987 to mid-1989 had to be diverted into relief and rehabilitation. On the other hand, the present NGO movement in Bangladesh was born out of the human disaster of the war of Independence in 1971, and NGOs have expanded rapidly in both size and number with the massive in-flow of funds following the 1987 and 1988 floods. For GKT the disasters have meant access to many additional resources, in particular agricultural machinery. At the same time, the tornado destroyed its rented office and all its records, thus both frustrating the general programme and providing the means to enlarge the organization.

The ultimate aim of GKT is self-reliance, both for the organization and for the *samitis* that it sets up. GKT intends, therefore, gradually to hand over all productive assets to the *samitis* and perhaps to encourage the formation of a central federation to take over the distribution of fertilizers and pesticides. The NGO has a strong ethic not to raise funds by increasing its share of agricultural output, or by supplying irrigation or power tillers for a profit. It may therefore move into different businesses to finance its development activities. The hope is to establish a broader base, including a training centre, and then to extend to other areas, in every case setting up semi-autonomous GKT cells, each staffed and run by local people.

That much of GKT's strength derives from its grounding in the locality is clear. Its formation in 1986 grew out of a long-standing commitment: some of the staff set up an NGO in Saturia in 1975. This enables it to take advantage of many opportunities that outsiders might never have heard of. At the same time, the experience of senior staff, and particularly of the co-ordinator, has been a crucial factor, as shown partly in their care to foster good relations with major national NGOs, through which they have gained access to resources far beyond those they could have achieved on their own. The STWs, DTWs, and power tillers have been important for GKT's credibility as a technically competent organization and at the same time have meant that *samitis* can back up their requests for the lease of land with their ability to provide new technology to enhance production. The experience of GKT shows how smaller NGOs can mobilize a relationship with a larger NGO patron to serve their own advancement.

The GKT Horticulture and Agriculture Programmes have as yet brought relatively small economic returns to their participants. They have, however, considerable potential in terms of raising the incomes of the rural poor and enlarging their access to land. Clearly the chance to cultivate land has a very wide appeal. This is not simply economic, but also a sense of gaining a stake in a society for which land is a key symbol, and of taking control at a basic level: the ability to produce one's own food. On the other hand, the experience of other NGOs demonstrates that problems over joint resources commonly arise as time goes on and the sums involved increase. This is particularly the case if this development takes place at the same time as the introduction of significant new assets such as the STWs and DTWs, which tend to have an individualizing impact on *samiti* unity, and to supersede the importance of other *samiti* functions.

The proximity to Dhaka is an important factor that predisposes local landowners towards sharecropping. The sons of wealthier people tend to look outside agriculture to commerce or services for employment, and have little experience or interest in working the land. This not only helps GKT's programme, it also intensifies its wider impact, which is to put pressure for change in the terms of sharecropping contracts. The predominant form of sharecropping in Saturia is still for the sharecropper to bear all the costs and the landowner to take half the crop. While this is exploitative under normal conditions, it becomes acute in the case of rice, which needs heavy irrigation. To some extent, therefore, the shift in technologies is putting pressure on the old system, but activities such as those of GKT help to hasten the process.

GKT's aim is to establish written leases, but this seems to be happening only in a minority of cases so far. Amongst the *samitis* interviewed, only three had a lease arranged for a period of three years, and one for five, giving the *samiti* some security so that it can capitalize on profits or make up on losses in the following years. In the majority, however, land is given only for a single season. In two cases the landholders had refused to renew the lease the following year, in one because they were not satisfied with the returns, and in the other because they saw the profits were good, and wanted to take back the land to gain maximum returns themselves. Some land-owners also take back land because they want to plant a crop that the *samiti* does not or cannot, and some *samitis* voluntarily give up land when they see that a crop does not do well there. In one case, land leased from a school had been planted with spinach, and was shortly afterwards dug up by the school authorities for use in an earth construction project. In most cases *samitis* take small parcels of land from several owners at different times. In only two *samitis* were the members themselves owners of joint project land, though in a few cases members were former sharecroppers of the land.

There is widespread appreciation of the joint cultivation projects, despite the fact that in a significant number the yields have been disappointing. Reasons for this satisfaction are clear: most of the work is done in 2–3 hour stints, fitted around other employment or household labour, and only very rarely did *samiti* members report that they had lost income from other sources because of time spent on the project. The second positive factor is that the work is available to both men and women, whereas agricultural employment is in the main reserved for men. For women in particular, therefore, the GKT projects offer an opportunity to use their labour to earn income. Thirdly, the value of this income is increased because the crop is available all at one time and not in small daily amounts which go to immediate expenses. On the other hand, the projects do carry some opportunity cost. Women with small children are particularly likely to be unable to take part. While in the majority of *samitis* all participate, in three of them projects were run by a smaller (and varying) number of members. Of the sixteen *samitis* interviewed, all but two had joint projects; one of these was very new, and both were looking for land to establish projects.

Of the fourteen *samitis* with joint projects, six complained that poor timing or the amounts of seed or other inputs supplied reduced the size of their harvests. Some of these (particularly with the supply of seeds and fertilizer) reflect problems that are outside GKT's control. STWs are similarly not always available at the right time, or water is not supplied in the required amounts. Women's groups are the most likely to suffer irrigation problems, as they are less able to insist on timely application of water. Complaints regarding irrigation are seen as a chronic and unavoidable factor; as GKT is supplying the water free there is no limit to demand.

Some landowners are dissatisfied with the amount of labour put in. They complain that women do not work properly because they are not familiar with agriculture, or that men do not give the work the necessary attention because they are doing other work for an immediate wage. This is clearly a potential problem area since *samiti* members regard any return on the project as profit, while at the same time they know that they will personally receive only a small share of the crop, and are therefore not highly motivated to get the best possible return if other income-earning opportunities compete for their time. This may mean that landowners will in future be less ready to give land to the *samitis*.

The first years of the programme have been something of a honeymoon period. GKT has been able to distribute resources far beyond its normal programme capacity, and has offered new access to technology and other inputs, which have promised greatly increased yields in income. That GKT does in fact produce better harvests will be a key factor in landowners' continuing readiness to give their land, since under GKT's scheme the landowner's share of the crop is cut from the customary half to one-third. As the number of *samitis* expands, a strong method for management of capital inputs will become increasingly important.

Not all the staff are strong technically. Part of the difficulty in this area stems from the fact that, amongst a generally stable workforce, it is the technical staff that GKT has found it difficult to keep, as they can more easily find other jobs in government service or with other NGOs. This also has an important financial aspect. At present, the three-shares system means that GKT provides a substantial subsidy to the *samitis*. In its crop share, GKT in general makes at best a marginal profit over the costs of its inputs, even excluding overheads. In the projects for which reliable figures were available, it was found that GKT made an average of 40 per cent over material input expenditure, excluding the cost of power-tiller ploughing, and of 18 per cent when an imputed cost for the power-tiller was included. Where returns are very low GKT forgoes its share. Improved returns on projects are therefore vital if GKT is to be able to sustain the programme, let alone achieve the self-reliance that is its aim.

Not all the produce is marketed: potatoes and rice in particular are often kept for consumption within the household. In general, however, there are problems of *samitis* selling to intermediary traders and thus not realizing as high profits as they might. Women are in a particularly weak position as they are excluded from the weekly market and so have to sell produce through their sons or husbands or to traders who come to their homes. At present GKT possesses no storage facilities and therefore has to sell at the lower prices prevailing after harvest in the local market. GKT is aware of these market constraints and has held discussions with one of its *samitis* of vegetable traders about the possibility of their undertaking wider marketing. It also has longer-term plans for setting up a cold-storage plant and perhaps a Dhaka outlet for *samiti* produce.

Much of the success of the GKT programmes lies in the NGO's distinctive style of operations. The first element in this is a commitment to essentials, as shown in the simplicity of its office—mud floors and tin-sheet walls—with all the workers, including the co-ordinator, sharing rooms. Shortage of funds means that staff pay has been low and with long backlogs for some senior staff. Working methods are also highly flexible, showing a readiness to respond to people's needs, adapting usual practice if necessary. Thus instead of providing inputs in return for a share of the crop, GKT may give a loan to the *samiti* to cover the costs of cultivation. Or if extraordinary circumstances mean that repayments of loans cannot be made on time, GKT will reschedule them. This reflects the organization's small size and local basis: it is able to make its programme respond to people's actual situations, rather than being primarily oriented towards its own programme and putting it into operation.

The second element in GKT's style is its bold entrepreneurial initiative, with an eye for making the most of whatever opportunities present themselves. Thus GKT has accumulated fifty STWs, fourteen DTWs, and five power-tillers, most of them acquired on loan or through special technical assistance funds, or on an instalment basis from the NGO in which the co-ordinator used to work. Some were also reallocated to it when the original recipient organization proved incapable of using them effectively. It is here that the interrelations of disasters and development are at their most evident: most of this equipment was originally provided through relief and rehabilitation programmes to larger organizations. GKT has also earned some money through the sale of seeds, seedlings, and fertilizer, irrigation water, and hiring out the power-tillers. In these ways it has managed to set up and extend its programmes despite the donors' original caution.

The GKT programmes give contradictory messages on gender issues. On the one hand, they have succeeded in bringing women out of the household and into field cultivation, at a higher level than before. The women have also clearly grown in confidence in being able to talk with men about cropping practices. There is still, however, more dependence in the female than the male *samitis* on GKT workers for cultivation advice, and the women were generally much less able to say what inputs had been given and the days of labour, and were less clear in the way they reported the projects they had undertaken. There is also the question of what happens to resources when they enter the household: the one who earns is not necessarily the one who has the say.

The most serious shortcoming of the programmes for women is, however, that the agricultural projects at present give only an additional, not a main, source of income. In view of women's generally very restricted employment opportunities, projects either need to become much larger or to be supplemented with other forms of income (e.g. from operating power-tillers, rice-mills, etc.) if they are to become a means of real economic advancement for women.

GKT has shown boldness in the appointment of women as nursery managers. Interestingly, also, it is the only one of the four NGOs reviewed here that shows no gender bias in the scale of benefits gained through the main projects. Both in terms of the total amount gained, and when controlled for crop type, women's and men's earnings in the joint projects come to almost exactly the same. On the other hand, in employment on a casual basis GKT follows existing market values in giving women lower pay than men. In addition, the new technology which is so central to its programme approach, is still overwhelmingly in the hands of men. As *samitis* come themselves to take over the technology, there is a clear danger that the present relatively equal gender balance will be upset, and the control over major assets, and thus bargaining power, will shift to the male advantage.

GKT has no rhetoric of consciousness-raising. Its strategy is clearly pro-poor, but it aims first to establish some economic security as a sound basis for social and political change. The joint cultivation projects, however, clearly have a powerful social as well as economic impact. Unlike many NGO joint projects which come to rely on one or two members to keep them going, the GKT's agriculture and horticulture programmes depend on collective working, which forms a strong force for welding groups together and greatly reduces the potential for mistrust and suspicion to develop. Thus all groups reported that relationships had improved since they had formed the *samiti*, and most were engaged in some social welfare in the village. Some *samitis* also co-operate in other areas, some of this pre-dating GKT membership. One (male) *samiti* shows a possible way forward: the members have invested the income from their joint project in the *samiti* savings, and aim to build up the capital to take land on a mortgage for joint cultivation, and perhaps even buy land eventually.

Tensions over the amount of labour put into the joint projects were not voiced within *samitis*, though they could clearly be a source of problems. In one case the members running the project admitted that they had deliberately kept others out in order to get better returns for themselves. This problem may increase as the growing number of *samitis* wanting land puts more pressure on the amount of land available. There were also a couple of cases where joint cultivation between a men's and a women's *samiti* had led to problems of unequal labour participation and the men taking decisions without properly consulting the women. In both cases they intend to work separately in future. On the other hand, there are some examples of mutual help between different *samitis*: for example, a men's group had passed on land to a women's group to cultivate, when the women's land was withdrawn. This sense of corporate identity may increase as *samitis* begin to take over all land within a STW or DTW command area.

On the other hand, in providing material inputs and organizing for joint projects almost immediately after groups are formed, GKT is going against much of the accepted NGO wisdom about the importance of building up maturity before making any major intervention. Two factors mitigate the potentially disruptive effect of immediate access to major inputs: first, that GKT has so far only handed over particular inputs on a project-by-project basis; and second, that cultivation is undertaken jointly, so that everyone is directly involved.

GKT's plan to hand over STWs and other capital inputs to the groups to manage themselves is certainly desirable in terms of building up *samitis*' self-reliance. However, *samitis* need considerable maturity before this can be done, otherwise the new resources are in danger of being captured by more dominant individuals in the group. GTK is aware of this. In the newest group interviewed, for example, the plan was to have *samiti* members farming the land as they do now (largely as sharecroppers) but to share out the GKT inputs including the STW according to the size of landholding.

GONO UNNAYAN PROCHESTA FISHERIES PROGRAMME

Gono Unnayan Prochesta (GUP)'s fisheries programme aims to provide the material inputs and technical support needed to enable *samitis* of women, landless men, and marginal farmers to gain access to disused ponds and develop them for fish cultivation to increase incomes and improve diets, as well as to develop and strengthen *samitis'* solidarity and ability to work in co-operation. Fishing and fish trading are ancestral trades for some sections of both Hindu and Muslim communities. The national dish of Bangladesh is *mach-bhat*, fish and rice, and fish is the most important source of animal protein, but fish production has been dropping with the seasonal drying out of surface water sources due to irrigation, and rising prices have put fish purchase beyond the scope of poorer people.

About 14 per cent of total fish production comes from purpose-built ponds, but only half the area under ponds is cultivated at present, and the average yield is extremely low, partly because of the disincentive effects of multiple ownership. The idea of *samitis* of landless and marginal farmers taking over these unused ponds is not a new one. The First Five-Year Plan 1973–8 included a programme for Reclamation of Derelict Tanks, and since then there have been a number of government and non-government initiatives towards co-operative fish cultivation. GUP *samitis* began their first pond projects in 1976, and fisheries have formed a separate sector since 1988. Most of the ponds are taken on lease for 11 years, during which time any profits are divided, 75 per cent to the *samiti* and 25 per cent to the pond owners. GUP begins by re-excavating the ponds to make them appropriate for use and this provides employment for the landless. It provides training and advice to *samiti* members, supplies fish fingerlings for stocking the ponds, and monitors fish catches and markets to prevent the glutting of markets.

The NGO's integrated development approach means that the fisheries programme has no *samitis* of its own, but provides technical support to established *samitis* belonging to other programmes, whose core functions are savings and credit, though they may also be involved in handicrafts, cultivation, or livestock production. While fisheries constitute a separate sector in programme terms, they therefore rely for day-to-day administration on general *samiti* motivators and extension workers. Fisheries thus represent for the *samitis* just one of a number of options and forms of involvement with GUP.

In 1990 145 ponds were held by GUP *samitis*, sixteen by institutions, and a further thirty-five were run by GUP directly. The ponds are located in six *upazilas* of three districts, though the majority are in GUP's home *upazila*, Rajoir in Madaripur district. GUP's main work is with its 476 *samitis*, covering approximately 8,000 families, with a broad range of programmes, encompassing agriculture, livestock, functional education, tree plantation, sugar-cane processing, handicrafts, a bakery, community health, credit, youth participation, legal aid, a Peace Centre, and a Training Centre. In addition, there is an emergency programme for year-round readiness to respond to disasters. As a major employer in the area, GUP has a considerable voice in local affairs, particularly in the *khas* land distribution and in the post-1988 flood 'cluster village' programme. It has also given training to workers from the Bangladesh Rural Development Board (BRDB) and government employees from other parts of the country. It sees no competition with BRDB, as the two are oriented to different client groups.

GUP has a strong interest in agriculture, and emphasizes the introduction of new crops, new varieties, new breeds of livestock, and new methods of cultivation. In the 1970s it was involved with the supply of shallow tube-wells (STWs) for irrigation, and is returning to this now with a number of deep tube-wells which are to be supplied to *samitis*. In 1990 GUP had a total of 235 staff, and an annual core pro-gramme budget of approximately Tk.20,000,000, a small part of this generated through its own activities. It also receives some funds in kind, for example wheat from the World Food Programme (WFP), in addition to some inputs from UNICEF and other international agencies, including a number of foreign NGOs.

The main funding comes from a consortium of four NGOs, of whom the largest donor is the British agency, Christian Aid, which funds approximately 25 per cent of the core programme budget. While GUP is one of the most senior among Bangladesh NGOs in terms of its length of operation, before the 1987 floods it worked in only two *upazilas*. With the emergency programme it moved to other areas in 1987, and greatly expanded its working area and number of clients in 1988. Before the 1988 floods it had 132 *samitis*; in 1990 it had 476 in eleven *upazilas* in six districts. Rather than looking towards withdrawal now the emergency period is over, GUP is moving towards setting up permanent operations in these areas. The people, it says, have asked its workers to stay, and there are clearly strong dynamics towards expansion. The NGO feels that its regional focus has kept it marginalized to some extent in relation to the major national NGOs.

While the GUP fisheries programme has generally had a positive effect on the village environment, providing larger and cleaner sources of water for domestic use and an increase in total fish production, it cannot be said to have been successful in achieving its overall aims. The programme was badly hit by the floods of 1987 and 1988, when many *samitis* sustained substantial losses from which they are only now beginning to recuperate. This aside, however, there are many problems within the programme itself. Three of the eighteen ponds examined in this study are no longer operational. Many *samiti* members are far from being amongst the poorest. *Samiti* coherence and solidarity are poorly developed. Many pond projects were started in *samitis* which were still new, and where it has largely fallen to one or two members to take responsibility for them. Technical support has been weak, particularly in the crucial initial stage of re-excavation.

While most *samitis* have seen some net profit, the scale of this is small: the overall annual average gain per member from pond cultivation is only Tk.69, excluding re-excavation costs which are, in any case, heavily subsidized by GUP, with few *samitis* in practice repaying their re-excavation loans. Looking only at *samitis* and years that had shown a profit, in more than 50 per cent of cases they had gained less than Tk.100 per member per year. Individual benefit is clearly greater where there are smaller numbers of members; there is also more benefit for those who are also pond owners, who not only get an additional share of the profits but also have a substantial asset brought back into service. While the conventional wisdom sees multiple ownership as itself a problem, it seems rather that the capital involved in re-excavation is a highly significant factor in deterring more intensive pond use by the owners. There are too few fisheries staff to provide the necessary back-up and support. Records both at the *samiti* level and within GUP itself are unreliable and highly unsystematic. There is a noticeable tendency for returns to decline over time, as is also the case with care for pond maintenance.

Fish cultivation is increasingly common amongst Bangladeshi NGOs. On the one hand, it represents a way that landless people can gain access to significant productive resources which are often lying unused. On the other hand, it is also a part of the drive on the part of NGOs to achieve some measure of self-sufficiency: if well developed, fisheries can be a means for NGOs, as well as *samitis*, to generate substantial income. In GUP, as in other NGOs, fisheries have developed in the last few years, from being an activity which some groups were involved in, in a more informal way, into a full programme in their own right. Increasingly, fish cultivation is seen as a specialist area, which requires its own resources. There can, however, be problems with organizations that are not primarily technically oriented moving into higher-cost and higher-technology interventions. Alternatively, the technical orientation, and particularly its business potential, can sometimes take over from the social and become an end in itself.

The support that GUP has given in establishing written leases, supplying fish fingerlings and loans for fish cultivation, and providing training, has to some extent overcome potential bottlenecks. Even so, the pond projects are not bringing in such returns to owners that they are likely to renew leases when their time runs out. There is little doubt that the main attraction of the programme for pond owners is the promise of getting their asset reconditioned without cost. The programme would be unlikely to be sustainable if this facility were withdrawn.

None the less, overall many members have gained through belonging to GUP *samitis*. All but two of the *samitis* studied, both female, had received fisheries training but in a haphazard way. The provision of relief, including charity from GUP in individual misfortunes and some compensation for pond losses in times of disaster, has been of benefit. Credit has also been of use to individuals, although this has disproportionately benefited those who were already better off. *Samitis* still look to GUP in the expectation of help, though older *samitis* complain that they no longer get the personal attention and support that they used to in the early days.

Overall, the level of savings in the *samitis* has been low, but savings do not seem to be a very high priority. Most of the older *samitis* have given loans to members, and all but two of those studied had taken GUP cash loans, which were divided unequally between members, with the most going to the wealthier members and the *samiti* officials. This difference is also visible between *samitis* by economic status and by gender, sometimes reflecting self-limitation by members themselves. Generally there is little pressure on repayment, reflecting GUP's flexible attitude, but this could lead to friction within the *samitis*.

The most serious constraint is GUP's poor management. This is shown both in the technical and financial handling of pond projects and in the very limited development of participation and solidarity within *samitis*. There is a great disparity between *samiti* members in degrees of social and economic benefit, with those who are better off from the start tending to gain most.

There are two clear points in the programme at which the intended social and business or technical priorities can conflict. First, poor social development of the *samitis* tends to mean that pond projects in practice become the province of one or two better placed members, and people are made *samiti* members because they have shares in a pond. Second, the concern to develop the ponds as business ventures may result in *samitis* selecting as members only those who clearly have the means to contribute, thus excluding the poorest. There is no evidence that the GUP *samitis* have challenged existing vested interests in fish production. GUP is committed to develop marketing and to move out of production into processing fish, and this could enlarge the *samitis'* share in overall profits from the fish sector. Any such move, however, would also require much fuller solidarity and commitment to the group if benefits are to be generally shared. As they stand, the pond projects do not serve as a basis for mobilization of the poor, or a move towards social change.

Problems with mis-budgeting have arisen through schemes being drawn up by staff or local volunteers who have no special training. GUP recognizes that there have been problems, and has introduced measures to tighten up on-site approval procedures. As a result, the number of new projects was reduced from fifty-nine in 1989 to twenty schemes implemented in 1990. In this, GUP has clearly resisted the pressure to re-excavate more in order to fulfil targets and demonstrate greater achievement.

Just three staff cover 196 ponds, and mis-budgeting and mis-siting are possible consequences. This situation has been exacerbated by a frequent change-over of staff, as technically qualified officers have left to take up opportunities elsewhere. Fisheries staff admit that they cannot get around to all the ponds and that this limits the quality of support they can give. Most of the practical follow-up falls to the extension worker.

Reporting is an acknowledged area of weakness in GUP. There is no sense of any active monitoring of pond performance, input costs against output, at either the *samiti* or organizational level. The lack of readily available accounts within the *samitis* clearly leaves the way open for misunderstandings and distrust to develop between the few who take responsibility for maintaining the ponds and the other members.

The long-term aim of GUP is that *samitis* should become independent and register with the government as *Samabaya* (co-operative) *Samitis*. So far, however, there are serious questions about whether the *samitis* would be ready for this step. Membership is unstable, and this clearly has negative implications for solidarity. In some cases, however, there was the reverse problem: *samitis* had become mini institutions in themselves, with other relatives taking their place as older members died. In general, the calling of meetings and attendance are erratic. The irony of the ponds being taken in part to foster group solidarity becomes clear when the projects have outlasted the active life of the *samitis* without entirely breaking down.

Nevertheless, *samitis* do show some signs of building up mutual support. One marginal *samiti* had extended Tk.2,000 to its cashier to mortgage land, which he is now farming on a sharecropping basis, giving half the profits to the *samiti*. The oldest *samiti* had built up substantial capital through savings and various projects over the years. Instead of keeping the money in a common fund, however, the members had several times divided the *samiti* funds among themselves, realizing amounts of approximately Tk.500 each at a time. GUP has also made some moves to build up mutual support between *samitis*. In one union, fifty-two *samitis* came together to take a rice-mill as a joint project, each with between one and three shares worth Tk.1,000 each. A handicrafts *samiti* had also invested Tk.5,000 of its savings in a new Women's Programme shop. On the face of it, this is impressive evidence of joint mobilization, although it is clearly far too early to say what the final outcome will be.

There are, however, some questions as to how far ordinary *samiti* members, and even *samitis* which do not have particularly forceful leaders, will have a voice in the joint projects. There are already allegations of unfair practices and capture of the rice-mill by dominant personalities. It may be that over time the projects will stabilize and poorer members will exercise their numbers to assert their voice. There is clearly a danger, however, that these joint projects might primarily become a means of mobil-izing *samitis'* savings for the benefit of particular individuals or factions. There is only limited evidence of the basic group strength and habits of participation on which such an investment ought to be built.

CARITAS BANGLADESH SOCIAL FORESTRY PROGRAMME

Older villagers in Bangladesh can still remember the time when they would have laughed at the idea of having to pay for firewood: trees were in plentiful supply and wood was there for the taking. Now, in some areas, even the straw left in the fields after harvest is sold. Electricity is limited largely to urban areas and *upazila* headquarters, and Bangladesh has few resources of coal or oil to draw on. Most cooking, and the boiling of rice before husking, is done over fires in clay hearths. Wood and bamboo are basic materials in house construction and furniture. Wood-fuel is used in huge quantities in brickfields, since as a delta area Bangladesh has little stone or rock, so mainly bricks or brick chippings are used to construct any permanent structure. At the same time as consumption of fuel is increasing, its supply is dwindling. The pressure of poverty means that trees are cut down and sold in times of shortage; a growing population needs more and more land for housing; the drive to increase agricultural production has resulted in the clearing of forest areas; numbers of cattle are declining, so the alternative fuel of dried dung is increasingly scarce.

Wealthier rural households often have their own cattle (and thus dung-fuel), and they usually have trees or bamboo or, if not, can afford to buy them in. Poorer households, however, are pushed into using ever more marginal sources of fuel. While more land under cultivation means some increase in straw, this is undercut by the common high-yielding varieties having a shorter stalk than local varieties. The need for fuel puts pressure on alternative uses of paddy husk and straw, such as cattle fodder and roofing materials. An increasing amount of time has to be spent in fuel collection, and cooking becomes more arduous and hazardous.

The primary aim of the Caritas Social Forestry Programme is to motivate people, in particular its *samiti* members, to grow more trees around their homesteads. It also encourages them to plant on government or institutions' lands, such as school playing-fields, roadsides, and embankments. While fruit-tree varieties predominate, particular encouragement is given for people to plant fuel-wood and timber-tree varieties, in line with the government's priorities: from 1982 to 1987 a Community Forestry Programme aimed to build up the area under tree cover. The Caritas programme involves general discussion of the importance and benefits of trees; training in methods of planting and grafting, and seedling care; the supply of seedlings at a subsidized rate; and support for the establishment of village-based nurseries. Caritas has encouraged its *samiti* members to plant trees around their homesteads since the mid-1970s; a separate programme in social forestry was launched for three years on a pilot basis in 1986 and this was enlarged and extended for a further three years in 1989. Within the Caritas annual budget (1989) of Tk.266,011,567, the social forestry programme is a very small component, commanding an annual budget of only Tk.2,008,349 which is wholly funded by CAFOD.

Caritas Bangladesh is an autonomous Bangladeshi Catholic foundation and receives funds from all over the world, predominantly from Catholic sources. As a member of the international Caritas federation, Caritas Bangladesh benefits from wider exchange on a relatively equal level with its sister organizations in other countries. Caritas has a central office and training centre in Dhaka, plus seven regional offices in different parts of the country. The structure and programmes are similar in each regional office, with some variation according to the size of area covered. In each region Caritas concentrates its work in particular *upazilas*, typically three or four, within which work is again focused on particular unions.

While Caritas has in recent years tightened its targeting on the poor, its approach still shows signs of its earlier community-development orientation. Caritas believes that working with all levels of society is important in order to disarm any potential opposition to its focus on the poor, especially in view of the suspicion that tends to surround Christian organizations. It also aims to mobilize the more wealthy to work for the good of the poor in their community. Locally, it works in quite close co-ordination with government, and sees a good relationship with the *upazila* authorities as important to its ability to operate. *Samitis* also cater for different client groups, including some relatively wealthy people, though only landless and women's *samitis* are eligible for the full range of support that Caritas provides.

Programmes cover a broad range, from projects to build roads and bridges, through the provision of pumps for drinking water and latrines, agricultural and fisheries development, and preventive health care, to feeder schools for young children, skills training, housing, and emergency relief. Development Extension Education Services (DEEDS) is the core programme to which many of the other programmes are linked. Under DEEDS, small groups are anchored by regular savings, and given training, subsidized access to various material inputs, and loans. The aim is to have a men's and women's *samiti* in every village, the men's being divided into 'landless' (less than 0.5 acre), 'marginal' (0.5–3 acres), 'youth' (not class-specific), and 'credit unions', while the women's are not sub-divided although Caritas now recognizes that class also divides women.

The DEEDS programme has changed considerably over time, reflecting the trend towards more homogeneous groups oriented towards savings and credit for smaller income-generating activities, characteristic of the NGO movement in Bangladesh as a whole. The next move is similarly in line with current trends, as Caritas plans to withdraw from the *upazilas* where it has been working, and hand over to a federation of the *samitis*. Caritas will then remain in those areas only in a supportive or advisory role, and move its main programme to new *upazilas*.

The main *samiti* development programme at present covers twenty-eight *upazilas* under twenty-one districts. As both the government and other NGOs are similarly working to motivate people to grow more trees, it is difficult to determine what the specific impact of the Caritas forestry programme has been. Alongside these interventions from outside, there also seems to be a strong dynamic from within village society itself towards a heightened awareness of the importance of trees, as people realize how much they have lost through the widespread felling and non-replacement of trees over the past twenty years. While this makes the task of evaluation more complex, the fact that so many different agencies and social trends are working in the same direction is undoubtedly positive, and helps to make each particular initiative a success.

The social forestry programme was badly hit by the floods of 1987 and 1988, when a large number of seedlings were lost. Damage by livestock is another significant constraint, not so much to planting but to the survival of trees. Local estimates put the survival rate at 50 per cent, though Caritas surveys in Birol and Sardar *upazila* came out at 78 and 70 per cent, respectively, for Caritas seedlings. Caritas nationally puts the figure at 68 per cent (1988–9).

In the area visited, the primary aims of the Caritas social forestry programme were being achieved: people were being motivated to plant trees, there was beginning to be acceptance of new varieties and the economic value of fuel-wood and timber, and small nurseries were being established in the villages and were producing considerable profits. The impact of the programme spreads well beyond its immediate clients, as others see what is happening and come and learn from them.

The underlying tendency of the programme is to bring greater benefits to those who are already relatively well-off. This is partly because *samitis* do not generally include the very poorest people, but more fundamentally, it is due to the essential requirement of land on which to plant trees. Amongst the poor, some do not even own the land on which they live, and many others are already using to the full the little space they have. The stress on fuel-wood and timber also fits the interests of the more wealthy more closely than those of the poor. People's first priority is to have fruit for consumption and sale. Poorer people have adapted to the use of marginal resources for fuel; it is those who are better-off who are still using the traditional sources of wood, bamboo, and cattle dung. It is also those who have a relative surplus of land who can afford to set some aside for fuel-wood or timber trees.

The Caritas programme raises two issues which are central to current thinking and strategies amongst Bangladeshi NGOs. The first is the need for sustainable development. The disastrous floods of 1987 and 1988 are widely believed to have been caused, at least in part, by environmental degradation and specifically by deforestation. NGOs have seen much development work literally washed away in the floods, and so recognize environmental sustainability as a crucial aspect of development. At the same time, there is growing emphasis on the importance of clients becoming self-reliant, and of NGOs beginning to generate some of their own finance. The primary thrust of Caritas' social forestry programme is thus to encourage people to plant trees around their homes, and so grow more of their own fruit, fodder, and fuel-wood, for consumption or sale. It also aims to foster village-based nurseries, and so a degree of local autonomy in seedling supply. Equally, through the establishment of its own nurseries Caritas can recover part of its programme costs.

The second issue concerns the target-group approach which has been favoured by Bangladeshi NGOs since the late 1970s. This is now being reconsidered, in view of the interconnection between different groups within the rural economy and a belief that farmers with small and even middle-sized holdings should not be excluded from NGO support, in order to arrest their decline into landlessness. The argument for broadening the range of potential clients is particularly strong in the case of environmental programmes, where the greatest impact is clearly to be made by encouraging all classes of people to participate. Similarly, if production of fruit, fodder, and fuel is increased overall, this should help bring prices down and reduce pressure on the marginal resources now being used for fuel and fodder, such as rice-husk and straw, leaving these to the very poor who cannot either grow or buy alternatives.

The Caritas social forestry programme in Dinajpur has gone some way towards achieving its ends of raising the motivation of the poor to plant trees, and so laid a foundation for environmental conservation, improved diet, and a rise in incomes. The scale of its impact has, however, been modest, resulting primarily in a few more trees being planted around individual homesteads. The more ambitious aspect of the programme—to foster collective planting projects—has yet to be implemented to any significant extent, and the aim to reorient demand from fruit to fuel-wood varieties has met with only limited success. Its nursery programme has, however, helped to broaden seedling supply and to form profitable businesses for some marginal landowners.

The main constraint in terms of the programme's impact on poverty is the centrality of land in a tree-planting programme. At this point the overall programme objectives are in contradiction to Caritas' priority for the poor. The capacity of the poor to plant more trees very quickly reaches a limit. Unless there are secure ways for a group of poor people to gain longer-term tenure of land, the in-built bias of the programme is always going to end up by favouring the wealthier. If the focus on the poor is to be retained and strengthened, there will have to be a widening of the programme into secondary areas such as marketing, which are less dependent on landholding, or some more active mobilization towards the poor gaining for themselves more secure access to the crucial productive resources.

The budget for the social forestry programme also acts as a constraint. Social forestry has, for example, considerably less status than the fisheries programme, which has a staff member of assistant field-officer level in every *upazila*, while the social forestry programme has only an organizer (who is a semi-volunteer). The organizers are paid as volunteers and have no margins, for example, to fund a trip to the regional office; at the same time, the regional social forestry officer finds it difficult to insist if the organizers do not achieve what he would like. This constraint is compounded by confusion over the responsibilities of social forestry organizers. Central office staff argue that the organizers should be working only within a target union; the Central Social Forestry Officer says that they should gradually move out from this base in succeeding years; the organizers themselves believe that they have responsibility for the whole *upazila*.

The programme as it stands has something of a split personality: it is technical but largely implemented through non-specialists; it aims to contribute to major environmental changes but its practical implementation is typically low-key. The Central Social Forestry Officer is a horticulture specialist rather than a forester, and many of the regional forestry officers and organizers have no scientific background. Since the basic motivation for acceptance exists, the question clearly arises whether the technical side of the programme could usefully be upgraded. This would mean fuller training for organizers and the regional and central social forestry officers, so that they can act more effectively as technical resource persons, leaving the basic motivational discussions to the DEEDS workers.

CONCLUSIONS

This section summarizes the main achievements of the four case-study programmes, and reflects on their effectiveness in achieving their stated aims of raising the economic status of the rural poor. It also returns to the issues of the NGOs' character and approach that were raised in the introductory section, and suggests some common directions in which the case-study findings point.

Evaluation Difficulties

The four case-studies indicate a number of practical difficulties in the process of evaluation. Project records are not usually such as to provide reliable background data, and so lead to heavy reliance on clients' recall. More fundamental, however, are the unsatisfactory conditions under which interviews are conducted. They take place usually on first introduction to people and are strongly interviewer-led. Respondents rarely know the context in which evaluators come, and so they construct one for them, shaping the information they give in line with the assumed power and interests of the evaluators and calculations of the gains and risks of different forms of response. The limitations of data gathered under these circumstances point to the importance of the NGOs themselves strengthening procedures for ongoing self-monitoring.

In assessing the impact of a project, one of the greatest difficulties is to judge the difference that the project has made. This is clearest in the case of the Caritas social forestry programme, where it is simply one of a number of similar programmes run by the government and other NGOs. But in the other examples also, it is important to remember that the project represents only one of the opportunities open to village people. It may not therefore be valid to attribute all changes to the impact of NGO intervention. A business newly started or extended with credit from an NGO, for example, might well have been undertaken anyway, using an alternative source of funding.

A third point that comes through strongly in these case-studies is the limits to NGO control. The most striking aspect of this is the natural environment. The disastrous flooding in Bangladesh in 1987, 1988, and 1991 has hit NGO development efforts extremely hard, both in terms of their work programmes having to be set aside for relief and rehabilitation, and in setbacks to the income-generating projects that they had fostered. Seedlings planted under the Caritas social forestry programme, fish in ponds stocked under the GUP fisheries programme, crops planted under the GKT horticulture and agriculture programmes, were all swept away in the floods.

Reaching the Target-Group

The NGO projects reviewed all have similar aims. First, they are intended to benefit those most in need: the landless and land-poor. While the primary criterion for defining the target-group is economic, gender is also a significant variable in affecting poverty among households and access to resources within them. The second major aim is to raise the incomes of the target group, which is to be done by securing their access to key resources. This involves: encouraging savings and providing credit; arranging for share leasing of land and fish-ponds; supplying technical advice and training, and some key material inputs. The third aim is that the income-generation projects thus fostered should become self-sustaining, rather than reliant on continued support from the NGOs. The fourth aim recognizes that poverty has social as well as economic dimensions: it is to promote solidarity amongst the poor.

All of the NGOs form *samitis* (co-operatives) as the basic unit with which they work. This is both an administrative convenience—dealing with individuals would require considerably more staff time—and intended to promote group solidarity. *Samitis* generally meet weekly, though some meet fortnightly and some monthly, and an NGO organizer is usually present. Instability in *samiti* membership is a feature common to all but the newest NGO (GKT). In some cases this is because members move to another NGO which seems to have more to offer; in most they simply withdraw from NGO involvement as circumstances at home change or they argue with other members. *Samitis* also break up altogether: this tends to happen either early on when they do not receive the immediate benefits they expected, or much later, when there are significant joint assets over which arguments arise. Members not obeying the rules, particularly where there is a high degree of collective responsibility as in ActionAid's programme, is also a common cause of *samiti* break-up. Former members sometimes rejoin later on. Changes in *samiti* membership mean, on the one hand, that more people are reached by NGOs than present membership figures portray. On the other hand, however, it clearly undermines group solidarity.

Samitis are typically stratified according to gender and class, although there are some mixed-gender groups and there is a tendency for NGOs to regard class differences as less significant amongst women. *Samitis* also commonly divide according to community (Hindu or Muslim) but this is more often a result of neighbourhood links than NGO policy.

Overall, the NGOs reviewed here are predominantly working with the landless and land-poor. Many *samitis* are not, however, as economically homogeneous as they appear. The strictness of targeting varies considerably between organizations. ActionAid has the tightest procedures for client selection, while both GUP and Caritas still show evidence of their early community-development approaches. Both these organizations recognize this institutionally, with separate groups for the landless and marginal farmers. In practice, there is a significant minority of small landholders within landless groups, and members of marginal farmers groups may extend into the middle rung of Bangladesh rural society, whose landholdings support year-round self-sufficiency in food-grains. There is a tendency for NGOs to represent their clients as poorer than they actually are. In none of the four cases are NGO clients, in the main, from amongst the very poorest.

There are several reasons behind this. In the first place, while NGOs recognize structural factors of poverty—such as the low land–person ratio, shortage of employment opportunities, restrictive gender division of labour, and inadequate state provision of education and health care—they can make only piecemeal attempts to remedy these. In the second place, while the new forms of access offered by NGOs fit the enterprise strategies of some poor households, they do not tackle some key obstacles faced by the poorest. These include ill health—one of the most common causes of economic decline in Bangladesh is chronic deficit, which prohibits setting aside capital for business; poor kinship, neighbourhood and patronage links; and a lack of skill or aptitude to manœuvre in relationships and the market.

Households such as these may show little observable difference from others of the poor in terms of material assets, but the odds are clearly weighted against their being able to achieve self-reliant development. If dependence on the NGO is to be avoided, their capacity to absorb inputs for productive use is likely to be extremely low. On the other hand, their comprehensive rehabilitation could drain NGO resources through consumption subsidies. By contrast, those households whose members are healthy, include able adult males, have at least some economic margins, and include someone with a head for business and personal politics will typically show better returns on NGO investment and form a sounder base for NGOs' expansion of their budget and activities.

There are further factors which undermine the NGOs' stated aims of strict targeting on the landless. First, there is no clear division between the landless and those with very small holdings. Landless people may sharecrop land for part of the year, or mortgage land in return for a loan. Smallholding farmers may have to work on others' land for part of the year, supplement their holding by leasing more land in, or even lease out their land and so receive only half of what it could produce, because of lack of (particularly male) household labour to work it.

Whatever the difficulties in defining a target-group, few NGOs wish to follow the alternative means of selection, which is to limit the scale of their programme so as to make it too marginal to be of interest to any but the very poor. Vertical linkages across

Bangladeshi society mean poorer clients may themselves approve the inclusion of some higher status members. These factors all combine with the observation that smallholding farmers are vulnerable to decline into landlessness, to loosen the NGOs' strict definition of the poor and widen the scope of their targeting.

The practicalities of NGO working also contribute to this tendency. NGOs have an ambivalent relationship with the better-off people in their working areas. Whatever their rhetoric, in practice most NGOs operate through an accommodation with the existing power-structure. Most NGO workers are from the middle class, and so find their natural peers among the middle and larger landholders. Institutionally also, having links beyond the poorest, and being seen to have something to offer other groups, can be an important help to NGOs operating in that area. In the projects of both GKT and GUP, for example, the NGO as guarantor is an important factor in the *samitis* gaining leases for land and fish-ponds, and being able to retain them.

Across all the income-generating projects, joint or individual, there is a tendency for the greatest benefits to go to those who are already better-off. This is true both in terms of the scale of resources that clients receive from NGOs, and in the returns they get on their use of them. Men receive larger loans, have privileged access to new technology, and are more likely to be involved in more substantial joint projects, than women. Men with some education and existing business or landholding see more benefit than the landless.

In terms of gender relations, the NGOs' practice has been contradictory. On the one hand, they have taken positive steps to integrate women in the development process. The proportions of female members in the study programmes are 87 per cent for ActionAid and 52 per cent for GKT; female *samitis* account for 44 per cent of *samitis* in GUP. National figures for Caritas were not broken down by gender, but women's *samitis* made up 42 per cent of those in the three Dinajpur *upazilas* where the field-study took place. Targeting women makes sense in terms of NGOs' commitment to work against existing patterns of disadvantage. It has two further attractions: first, it is a high priority with donors; and second, the gender division of labour means that most women's work is based at home and so they can attend *samiti* meetings during the day, while many male *samitis* have to meet at night, which is both less convenient and more hazardous for NGO workers.

Where both policy and culture have tended to make women invisible, simply to recognize their presence by targeting them may be seen as a step forward. The potential for this is stronger in programmes like those of GUP and GKT, which involve women moving into activities in which conventionally men have predominated: horticultural and agricultural production and fish-farming.

Overall, however, few NGOs have chosen to accommodate their programmes to existing power relations. Poor women in Bangladesh have always made an economic contribution to their households. At the same time, as the number of landless households is rising, poor women are seeking new means to contribute to household income. The NGOs have incorporated this into their programme approach, and have extended the opportunities facing women. In most cases they have not, however, had the boldness to recognize how fundamentally the changing economic conditions call

into question the established ground-rules on gender. NGO programmes thus reproduce a family welfare orientation for women, with a stronger economic emphasis for
men. While there are exceptions, there is a clear tendency for projects for women to
be less well funded than those for men. Income-generation projects for women use
predominantly very simple technology, are intended to provide supplementary rather
than major sources of income, and involve participation in the market at only the
lowest rung, where women may produce more goods but have little control over their
disposal.

Changes in Income

All the NGO *samitis* are anchored by savings. Most of the households were already
setting aside money when they could, but *samiti* members say the discipline of contributing a regular sum makes them save more than they would otherwise. Women in
particular say that they value the extra security of having cash out of the house, and
thus invulnerable to plunder by other family members. Savings are generally made as
insurance for the future rather than for a specific purpose, and few *samiti* members
keep a close tally of the sums they have deposited.

The scale and regularity of savings differ considerably from case to case, and
person to person. The ActionAid programme places most emphasis on savings, with
a norm of Tk.5 to be paid regularly each week. The other organizations are much
more flexible, with levels falling to Tk.5 per month, and rising to Tk.20 per week,
though the weekly average would be Tk.2–3. Savings are also less regular, as members
may miss weeks when they are under financial pressure. In GUP, particularly among
better-off clients, their highly marginal level of savings seemed to represent a membership fee to the NGO *samiti*, rather than a significant resource in itself. Savings held
thus vary greatly between clients, length of membership, and the different organizations,
but they can represent significant sums: some interviewees from ActionAid development centres had up to Tk.2,000 in their accounts.

All four NGOs provide credit to their clients, although GKT has done so only on
an experimental basis. Demand for credit is high. Loans may nominally be given to
samitis, but in practice the great majority are utilized individually, and repayment is
the individual's responsibility. The size of loan given to an individual ranges from a
minimum of Tk.200 to a maximum of Tk.5,000, the average being around Tk.900.
Interest rates vary, from the top rate of ActionAid's 17.5 per cent per annum to the
lowest of GKT's 5 per cent. The predominant pattern is for them to be heavily
subsidized: an average interest rate on a bank loan would be 16 per cent p.a., while
GUP and Caritas charge a maximum of 12 per cent p.a., and a minimum of 6 per
cent. The extent to which NGOs are subsidizing credit is in fact even greater than the
differences in interest rates make it appear, since a large number of smaller loans
means relatively higher transaction costs. Even ActionAid, charging an interest rate
slightly higher than that of the commercial banks, does not cover its costs.

Repayment practice varies sharply among the NGOs. ActionAid is strict, and the
system ensures that *samiti* members put pressure on one another to keep payments to

time. This pays off, with a very high repayment rate: more than 90 per cent of loans are paid within twenty-four hours of falling due. The other NGOs are much more flexible. This has both costs and benefits. On the one hand, some ActionAid members clearly undergo hardship to keep up repayments. On the other hand, non-repayment to time in the other NGOs undermines the establishment of a revolving loan fund, and thus prospects of sustainability. More immediately, extended non-repayment is also one cause of *samiti* break-up.

There is a tendency for those already in a position of advantage to capitalize on this in access to credit. Leaders tend to get larger loans than ordinary members, small-holding farmers than landless, men than women. Some of this is due to institutional bias, but also significant is the effect of the members' actions themselves. The *samiti* typically decides which of its members will receive how much of each joint loan, and so is responsible for the bias that occurs. *Samitis* may also lend to members from their own group funds.

In such cases they are more conservative than when using the NGO's funds: usually lending either according to power in the group or in line with the amount of savings held. Loan use exacerbates these patterns in loan allocation: the person who takes the loan may not have use of it, but may pass it on to someone else, who often has some kind of power in relation to them. The larger the resources involved, the less likely they are to stay in the hands of a subordinate person. Thus, in line with the usual pattern in Bangladesh, the smaller loans in ActionAid's credit programme are predominantly used by women, while the larger ones are likely to pass into the hands of male family members (Goetz and Sen Gupta, 1994).

The variety of uses to which credit is put, and the NGO practices surrounding its issue, make it very difficult to generalize as to the efficacy of credit as an NGO development intervention. The high level of demand is witness to its being appropriate; and in defraying some of the need to take other, higher interest loans from non-institutional sources it is almost by definition a success. The evidence shows that at least part of the capital is deployed in the income-generating schemes for which it was borrowed, though it is difficult to be certain that those activities would not have been undertaken with money from another source if funding from the NGO had not been forthcoming. With this proviso, it appears that NGO credit can be a significant factor in leading to the accumulation of assets, extending people's market involvement, and encouraging them to undertake new activities, resume ones that have lapsed, or extend enterprises in which they were already engaged.

For Bangladesh NGOs in general, joint projects have proved to be far less success-ful than individual income-generation schemes. This holds true for the projects reviewed here. The annual average income per member from a GKT joint project is Tk.418; from the GUP's fisheries programme, at most Tk.130, and −Tk.9 when all costs are included. In terms of technical inputs and expertise, and in management, joint projects place considerably greater demands on both NGOs and the *samitis* themselves. Joint projects are, therefore, less common than individual projects: in both the ActionAid credit programme and the Caritas social forestry programme, joint projects are an option, but in neither have they been taken up on a significant scale. If they do take place there is a high chance of their becoming dominated by a minority of the participants. When joint assets become substantial there is frequently dispute over their control. In most of the cases reviewed here the returns to individuals have been marginal, and in a few mismanagement led to considerable losses for the *samiti*, though the NGOs may discount their own costs in order to soften the blow to the *samitis*.

Social Benefits: Learning and Solidarity

In the projects reviewed, NGO organizers lead group discussions on topics such as possible income-generating programmes, health care, the importance of education, nutrition, sanitation, and so on. Amongst women's groups more time is spent on family welfare topics: in men's groups economic-oriented discussions of the project predominate. As thoughts of consciousness-raising have declined, there seems little vision of where the teaching component might proceed, and there is thus a marked tendency for this element to dwindle over time.

Results of more formal training programmes organized by NGOs appear to be mixed. There is a strong tendency for a single member in each *samiti* to become the one who attends training, despite the stated aim of this being shared between members. Where literacy is low and training is still classroom-oriented, this specialization is not a surprising outcome. On-the-job advice seems to be at least as useful as training sessions, and is usually needed to supplement any more formal training given. Even where NGOs are moving into more technical areas, they commonly lack the resources to give practical training programmes.

The NGOs' aim of building up solidarity amongst the poor is still some way from achievement. Flux in membership indicates a lack of common group identity, leaders tend to become entrenched, while most members settle back into taking a considerably less active part. For the NGOs there therefore appears another, immediate concern: with the tendency for *samitis* to break and re-form, how much is it realistic to expect to achieve within the life-cycle of a *samiti*?

While many *samitis* undertake some common welfare functions, joint social action or participation in local issues is rare. This reflects the orientation of the NGOs themselves, which lack a clear vision of where enhanced solidarity might take their clients. A possible exception to this is GKT, whose programmes involving joint work have a potential for bonding members together and an underlying dynamic which could reorient access to land by class and gender. As yet, however, it is too early to say how well GKT and its members will be able to carry this broader programme through. None the less, while the more ambitious aim of building solidarity among the poor may still prove elusive, there is no doubt that coming together and having some input from outside has helped to raise many members' self-confidence.

Participation

The NGO style has the notion of a high level of participation as a key element. Whereas superiors in government offices are addressed as 'Sahib' or 'Moshai' (sir,

Muslim/Hindu), those in NGOs are addressed as 'Bhai' or 'Dada' (elder brother Muslim/Hindu). While in Bangladesh hierarchical relations exist between brothers, this is still a significant difference. Interestingly, the government/NGO distinction does not hold for women, who in both cases are called 'Apa' or 'Didi' (elder sister, Muslim/Hindu). The use of family terminology accurately suggests the relatively personalized, charismatic character of NGO leadership, compared with the systems of government bureaucracy. It also expresses a degree of informality within a structure in which everyone knows their place.

Two of the ways in which NGO programmes are often claimed to be more participatory than official ones are their relatively small size and their local orientation. This study shows that in practice the tendency is for NGOs in Bangladesh to become large-scale and nationally based. It is perhaps no coincidence that it was the smallest, newest NGO with the strongest local links (GKT) that seemed able to respond with most flexibility to the particular needs of the poor in its area. Taking a pessimistic view, this might suggest that the costs of success as an NGO—growth—are the undermining of the very factors that underlay its effectiveness in the first place. GUP seems a clear case where expansion has led to a fall in the quality of relationship which programme participants at first enjoyed with the NGO staff.

The existence of an NGO style suggests that the common claim that NGO interventions are each unique is overdrawn. Of the programmes reviewed here, GKT's is the only one that does not appear in various forms in different NGOs within Bangladesh and beyond. On the other hand, the importance of personalities and individual commitments should not be underestimated: they come through as significant factors in all the case-studies. To transplant a programme to another social context or to extend it on a different scale, cannot fail to change it. Such a process is most likely to be successful when it develops out of the self-monitoring of a programme itself, and incorporates the flexibility to adapt to the new context.

The current priority placed on self-reliant development has emphasized the importance of participation at the *samiti* level also. As the slogans go, it is the *samitis' samiti*, the members' NGO. Somewhat contradictorily, this rhetoric issues from the top down, rather than representing a groundswell of members' self-confidence. None the less, the NGOs are taking practical steps towards members taking more organizational responsibility. Foremost in this is Caritas, with its plans to withdraw from present areas of operation and hand over to *samiti* federations. It is also evident, however, in ActionAid's loosening up of its rules for *samiti* organization, GKT's plans to hand over management of inputs to *samitis*, and GUP's fostering of union-wide joint projects.

There are two findings to note in relation to this development. First, *samitis'* decisions are by no means necessarily more equitable than NGOs' procedures. In these studies, *samitis* have been seen keeping out poorer people in order to safeguard their own interests; dividing loans by power in the group and by savings (which often serves as a proxy for wealth); and refusing to lend out *samiti* funds at all for fear that members will not be able to repay. *Samitis* being left with the responsibility to bank their own savings has led to savings being kept at home and used by leaders, and in one case to the savings being lost when used as an unsuccessful bribe. In a situation of scarce resources, loosening institutional control can mean leaving the more vulnerable open to the risk of resources being captured by the less scrupulous.

The second finding is simply this: the members do not want the NGOs to withdraw. The push towards member control comes from national and international development theorizing, not from the clients themselves. This point is considered in more detail below.

Administration

The NGO style in Bangladesh, as elsewhere, is caught in the tension between a voluntary and a professional ethic. This is clearly evident in NGOs' moves to become more technically proficient, although they have difficulty retaining technical staff and few have the funds available to establish fully proficient technical back-up. All the organizations reviewed in this study have paid staff working on a full-time basis who see NGO work as their chosen career. At the same time, they all also work through volunteers, local people working in their home areas, who are often given a small honorarium for their services—a practice justified in terms of their relatively low expenses in working from home, the fact that they are working for the development of their own community, and the fact that they gain experience from doing the voluntary work which stands them in good stead for gaining paid employment in future.

It is typically the volunteers who attend group meetings and are responsible for *samiti* development. While administrative posts are filled by regular staff, the primary work of NGOs is thus dependent on the good will or desperation of volunteers, and hence vulnerable to their possible disillusionment and shortage of time because of their need to take other work to make some income. This inevitably affects the quality of service which clients receive.

The issue of staffing is inevitably tied to that of administration costs. Figures for administration are difficult to come by, since the government ceiling of 10 per cent on receipts for administration leads NGOs to include administration within programme costs and to enter only the unavoidable minimum under the 10 per cent heading. Only ActionAid makes available a breakdown of data on costs. For June 1989 it calculated staff costs of Tk.24 per member per month, making an annual total of approximately Tk.288, which represents a deliberate drive towards cost reduction, since the figure for December 1988 was approximately Tk.480 per year. Overall, there is little doubt that, as a sector, the NGOs are comparatively well-resourced: NGO staff tend to have higher salaries than government officials at comparable levels, and to have better back-up resources. In the rural areas, one can tell immediately where there is an office of a major NGO by the number of vehicles, particularly motorcycles, that it has in its compound.

A clear finding of the case-studies is the inadequacy of NGO systems for recording, let alone effective self-monitoring. This has costs both in programme efficiency and in terms of project achievement, as improperly kept accounts, particularly in joint projects, can easily lead to distrust among *samiti* members, and even suspicions of

NGO workers. At the same time, a common complaint amongst staff in the larger NGOs is that an increasing amount of their time has to be spent at their desks, rather than out in the villages with the people. The problem is that the records are not kept for use in the local office, but to justify themselves to head office, and ultimately to demonstrate accountability to donors.

The root of this problem is not, of course, simply technical, it reflects tensions between different levels of NGO management and the funding and operating NGOs. While the terminology is of partnership, the equality and mutual trust which this implies are a great deal to achieve within hierarchical organizations or funding relationships. Progress towards fuller partnership would seem to be an important corollary of more satisfactory forms of record-keeping being instituted.

Self-Reliance and Sustainability

In the late 1980s and early 1990s, self-reliance and sustainability have come to be priorities amongst Bangladeshi NGOs. This reflects, in part, their level of vulnerability if outside funding were to be cut or withdrawn in future. To guarantee some independence as institutions, therefore, the NGOs have begun to set up business wings to generate some internal funding, though few of these have so far proved successful. The issues arise also in relation to project costs, and whether these could be cut or recovered from clients, and to establishing programmes as self-financing units, which could potentially become autonomous of the NGO and managed by clients themselves. The establishment of revolving loan funds, which require no further injection of outside capital, gives the clearest example of this so far. Finally, concerns for self-reliance and sustainability apply also to the income-generating projects undertaken by NGOs' clients, namely, that they should be run on a genuinely economic basis without continued reliance on the NGOs' support.

Issues of self-reliance and sustainability may be presented in purely technical terms, as aspects of NGOs' efficiency, or more politically, as nationalist priorities in an overall context of foreign dominance or the touchstone of a radical commitment to help the poor and not simply foster a new dependence. The tensions in this are seen very clearly in the case of Caritas, as it debates the form that its handover of power to the *samiti* federation should take. Everyone recognizes that to withdraw is risky: those at the top feel that it is a risk that must be taken, if Caritas is to put its commitment to fostering self-reliance into practice. At another level, however, the issues of self-reliance and sustainability also call radically into question the nature of NGOs themselves and their role in the wider context of the development of Bangladesh.

It is clearly worth while for income-generating projects fostered by NGOs to aim at self-reliance: the continued presence of the NGO cannot be guaranteed, and its capacity to assist others will be limited if it has to be continually servicing existing clients. In these terms, both ActionAid's credit programme and Caritas's social forestry programmes have relatively good prospects of fostering self-reliant development projects amongst their clients. Four factors seem important in this. First, they both have relatively modest aims. Secondly, these are appropriate to clients' demands and, thirdly, extend rather than replace existing activities. Fourthly, they are both oriented predominantly to the individual household, rather than attempting collective economic co-operation. Added to this, ActionAid's savings and credit programme is outstanding amongst Bangladesh NGOs in the singularity of its focus. With a few concessions to health and educational needs amongst the poor, it aims primarily to provide an efficient, targeted banking service. Its strictly limited intervention and tight procedural discipline contribute both to programme efficiency and to reducing any danger of clients' dependence.

By contrast, the projects sponsored by GKT's horticulture and agriculture programmes and GUP's fisheries programme are comparatively heavily reliant on continuing NGO input. They are more ambitious, first, socially—aiming at gaining access for the landless to major productive resources—and, secondly, technically. Thirdly, while they as yet provide only marginal gains in income, they involve a majority of clients taking up activities of which they have little experience. Fourthly, they envisage co-operative working among members, and this is in tension with the social structure in which collective identity is predominantly oriented towards the family/kinship group.

These projects are intended to be self-sustaining and there is no reason why they should not become so in time. At present, however, they are heavily dependent on the NGOs for subsidies, and for day-to-day project management and technical advice. The NGOs are also significant as guarantors. This is seen most clearly in the case of GKT, where the NGO inspires the landowners with confidence that its more technical approach to cultivation will produce better results, and it may take some time and effort before the landowners are ready to see the *samitis* on their own as capable and trustworthy.

Turning to the NGOs themselves, the issues of self-reliance and sustainability become more complex. The availability of foreign funding has shaped the Bangladeshi NGO style in ways which would not be easy to sustain from internally generated sources. The NGOs have become substantial institutions with a pronounced tendency to expand both the range of their programmes and the geographical scope of their working area. The donors have therefore played a contradictory role: on the one hand, they extol the virtues of self-reliance, on the other, their provision of funds has moved the NGOs into a position where self-generation of the funds to keep them going is simply impracticable. This may spiral further as NGOs receive larger and larger funding from official donor agencies and become increasingly top-heavy as more and more time and energy are spent on servicing donor requirements.

Similar contradictions are evident at the local level also. While, on the one hand, NGOs state their aim as fostering self-reliant development among the poor, on the other, they build themselves up as institutions that look set on staying. With one voice they go to the poor with something to offer; with another they say that the poor should stand on their own feet. Whatever the rhetoric, the institutional logic of NGOs does not favour their continual divestment of hard-won *samitis*.

Income-generating projects for the poor should, of course, be founded on a sound economic basis. At the same time, the limitations to such programmes have to be squarely faced. The poor are not poor because they lack the wit or will to change their situation. To focus simply on their own efforts may be implicitly to support the structures which keep them poor. A fundamental dilemma faces NGOs here. As long as they stay in the shallows of helping the disadvantaged while failing to threaten the entrenched interests that make them so, their work can continue uninterrupted and even supported by the élite. Their institutional interests, and their belief that the poor are best served by their continued presence, thus lie clearly with adapting to, rather than challenging, the existing power structures.

Ultimately, however, poverty is a question of power, and political changes are required if the poor are to have some voice and if the structural factors which underlie their situation are to be tackled. Improving the economic situation of the poor may be a necessary part of this, but it can never be sufficient. For the NGOs this does not mean rhetorical claims about consciousness-raising or class alliance, still less does it mean a head-on confrontation which can only bring damage to the weaker party. What it means is the vision and flexibility to see the opportunities, to see the points at which exploitation occurs and how they can be redirected. It means a sense of overall direction which, at the same time, stays alive to the particular, local, possibilities for change.

8

India

Voluntary agencies in India have a history of involvement in a wide range of social welfare and development work which stretches back to the last century. In this respect they have firmer foundations than their counterparts in most other developing countries. India is also of interest for this study because of its intractable problems of rural poverty and the apparent limitations of government poverty-alleviation programmes.

AN OVERVIEW

There is widespread agreement among development practitioners, government officials, and foreign donors that NGOs play an important role in helping to alleviate rural poverty in India,[1] complementary to that of government, both in terms of providing additional resources and in making government programmes more effective. This view has formed the basis for a sustained increase in the level of funding from government sources and official aid donors. It is also a view shared by many NGOs, although some see their role in terms of empowering the poor rather than in implementing development programmes.

In a country the size of India, with major differences between individual states and regions, NGOs are characterized by a rich diversity of approaches, traditions, and activities, rendering the task of generalization problematic, if not impossible. They cover most areas of the country and their activities affect a significant proportion of the population living in poverty. A number of studies have identified a particular set of attributes with which they are associated, but there is relatively little information on their aggregate impact in alleviating poverty.[2]

Estimates of the number of NGOs active in rural development in India range from less than 10,000 to several hundred thousand depending on the type of classification that is used. Nearly 20,000 organizations are registered with the Ministry of Home Affairs for foreign funding, although the list does not distinguish between religious organizations (such as mosques and temple management committees), commercial bodies, and voluntary agencies; only half of these fall into the NGO category. In addition, there are many others which derive their financial support from internal sources, such as businesses and private donations. A realistic estimate of the number of NGOs actively engaged in rural development in India would be in the 15–20,000

This chapter was substantially written by Mark Robinson, based on his longer primary research report produced as a technical working paper of the Overseas Development Institute (Robinson, 1991a).

range, including local and regional branches of national organizations which operate as NGOs in their own right.

Aggregate numbers reveal only part of the picture as there are significant variations in the number of voluntary agencies in different states, with a marked concentration in the south of the country. For example, a directory produced by the Council for Advancement of People's Action and Rural Technology (CAPART) in 1990 listed 470 NGOs in West Bengal and 373 in Tamil Nadu as compared to 77 in Madhya Pradesh and 11 in Jammu and Kashmir. To some extent these reflect differing patterns of poverty, but also historical factors (such as areas of Christian missionary influence or Gandhian activity) and the priorities of foreign donors. Some districts possess dense networks of NGOs, which overlap and compete for clients, while in others there are hardly any NGOs active on the ground.

NGOs in India can be grouped into six categories according to their scale of operations and the location of their head office:

• large indigenous NGOs working in several states in different parts of the country;
• large indigenous NGOs working in most districts of one state;
• medium-sized indigenous NGOs working in a large number of villages in one or two districts of one state;
• small indigenous NGOs working in a group of villages in one locality (the most common type);
• large international NGOs with in-country representation providing funding and support to indigenous NGOs;
• small international NGOs working directly in one or two localities.

Comparatively few possess the staff or financial resources to work intensively at the state and national levels, although it is these organizations which are best-known in government and donor circles. A number of the larger NGOs perform an intermediary role in channelling resources from donor agencies to small local NGOs, and are not generally involved in project implementation. Most international NGOs have no direct representation in the country and prefer to work through intermediaries, although several have regional offices.

NGOs are generally reluctant to divulge detailed accounts, but some of the larger national ones have budgets amounting to tens of millions of rupees. One survey reported fifty-four NGOs with annual turnovers in excess of Rs. 1m., although this is probably an underestimate. The same survey found that nearly half the respondents had budgets below Rs. 250,000, which provides some support for the view that the majority of Indian NGOs are small-scale and localized (Nath, 1989).

Recent estimates suggest that the amount of foreign funds coming into the country for use by NGOs each year is in the region of Rs. 9bn. (US$ 520m.), up from Rs. 5bn. in the mid-1980s. In quantitative terms, this is equivalent to approximately 20 per cent of official aid flows, which stood at $2.4bn. in 1991. A further Rs. 500–700m. is provided by the government. When individual and corporate donations are added in, an annual income figure of Rs. 10bn. would seem a reasonable estimate of the total available resources, although this does not take into account unofficial payments or contributions in kind by project beneficiaries. This figure is double the government's annual expenditure on IRDP, and 10 per cent of its overall budget for poverty alleviation and service provision, which indicates that the resources mobilized by NGOs are important but essentially supplement those provided by the government.

Evolution and Approach

The fundamental objectives of NGO activity in rural India are poverty alleviation and the empowerment of the poor, primarily through small-scale development projects. Some NGOs have chosen to tackle the symptoms of poverty manifested in low educational standards, ill-health, poor sanitation, and inferior housing by means of social welfare programmes. Others, among them the four NGOs examined in the present study, have concentrated on enhancing the asset position and income-earning potential of the poor through land-improvement schemes, credit, and skills training. An alternative approach has been for NGOs to empower poor people to demand resources from the state or to challenge injustice and exploitation.

The foundations for the contemporary voluntary agency movement were created in the pre-Independence period, some of them associated with the social reform movements of the late nineteenth century, largely concerned with educational and cultural matters and only tangentially with the question of poverty. Christian missionary groups established a network of hospitals, schools, and welfare services for the poor in the first half of the twentieth century. A third tradition was the Gandhian approach, which combined social reform with village development activities (Alliband, 1983).

The Christian and Gandhian approaches continued to predominate after Independence. In the early post-Independence period, disaster relief and food-for-work programmes came to be associated with Christian organizations in particular. Social welfare provided critical back-up for public service provision in the 1950s and early 1960s, and agencies steeped in Gandhian values emphasized village self-reliance and provided the foundation for development activities centred on small-scale agriculture and cottage industry. The integrated development approach became popular in the late 1960s and early 1970s, with NGOs combining health and education with economic programmes in pursuit of poverty alleviation. It was also at this time that funding from international NGOs began to make its mark.

During the latter half of the 1970s, a more radical trend emerged, with social action groups taking the view that poverty was a structural phenomenon which had to be tackled head-on through the active mobilization of the rural poor. They abjured violence but the thrust of their activities was confrontational, initiating struggles over issues such as land reform, wages, and bonded labour, while another dimension of their work rested on empowering the poor to demand efficient delivery of services from the state and pressing for the implementation of progressive components of government legislation. With liberal foreign funding, social action groups proliferated throughout the late 1970s and early 1980s, and established themselves as the dominant type of NGO in some states, notably Tamil Nadu and Bihar, in sharp contrast to the programme-focused approaches which had found favour from the 1960s (Unia, 1991). By the mid-1980s, however, their relatively limited economic achievements led to a questioning of the basic tenets of this approach. At the same time, there was growing criticism of the lack of participation by the poor in the design and implementation of NGO integrated development programmes.

From the mid-1980s, a further trend emerged within the NGO movement, emphasizing the importance of a professional approach based on sound management, planning, and co-ordination. A parallel development was the creation of resource agencies which work directly with the poor but also provide support services to other NGOs in the form of training, evaluation, and documentation. These agencies are usually financed by core grants from foreign donors and payments for staff training from individual NGOs. Intermediary agencies responsible for channelling funds from foreign donors to small national NGOs in some cases also provide these types of services, for example, in assisting with evaluations.

In recent years there has been an element of convergence between these various approaches, with NGOs seeking to combine project-specific development work with active organization of the poor. Reflecting this greater uniformity, community organization is now treated, for the most part, as an essential prerequisite of the successful introduction and implementation of specific programmes. Similarly, most NGOs now recognize that organizational work among the poor cannot be sustained without material improvements derived from programme-specific activities.

Most NGOs work through groups, though with considerable variation in purpose and approach. Some, notably the Gandhian agencies, chose to work through existing village institutions (*panchayats* or *gram sabhas*). But these are invariably dominated by the rural élite, and most NGOs therefore prefer to form groups which exclude the wealthier members of the village community. In some cases, caste or tribal affiliations constitute the basis for group formation, while others, particularly the social action groups, restrict their membership to the landless or marginal farmers. Another approach is to include all the poor, irrespective of caste or class. In some cases membership is defined by a common occupation, such as farming or fishing.

This diversity of approach has tended to make co-ordination difficult to achieve, since there are often sharp differences of perspective and orientation. At the local level, these differences are sharpened by competition over areas of operational activity, especially where there are dense networks of NGOs, and by personality conflict. Another difficulty is the preoccupation of many local NGOs with projects in the villages where they are already working, and their failure to perceive the need for or the potential benefits of sharing insights or resources with other organizations. Rivalry over scarce government resources and official patronage also hinders co-ordination at the local level.

Nevertheless, some networks have been established at the state level to present a common front in negotiations with the government over legislation and policy formulation.[3] Some NGOs have sought to form networks with specific advocacy objectives such as trying to encourage the government to introduce a guaranteed employment programme nationally. Other networks have been formed by foreign donors, although these can also have the effect of creating or widening divisions between groups of NGOs. More recently, there has been an initiative to establish an NGO network at the national level. A number of the larger and more established NGOs formed the Voluntary Action Network India (VANI) in 1988 as a common platform, initially to exert pressure on the government to amend or revoke contentious items of legislation, but now with an expanded remit to provide resource materials and organize conferences on foreign funding and strategic issues of broader NGO concern. Co-ordination between NGOs remains relatively weak, however, and this results in a duplication of effort and limits their potential impact on a larger scale.

Foreign Funding

The bulk of voluntary agency activity in India is funded by international NGOs. German and Dutch agencies account for the largest share, while British NGOs contribute about 5 per cent of the total. Foreign funding agencies display a marked preference for projects which centre on community development, incorporating a range of sector components, among them agriculture, credit, health, and education. At the same time, they also tend to support activities that are popular in their own countries: women and environmental development were popular in the 1980s, with the result that some national NGOs have tailored their programmes accordingly. International NGOs work for the most part in collaboration with national NGOs, acting as a conduit for funds, and comparatively few are involved directly in project implementation.

Funding mechanisms fall into four categories. The first is where the donor operates exclusively through an intermediary agency in India which is responsible for identifying suitable projects, liaising with partners, and monitoring and evaluating their activities. German and Dutch agencies such as EZE, Misereor, and CEBEMO generally work through established intermediary organizations or umbrella groupings. The second type is the consortia model favoured by the churches, where donor agencies pool their funds, usually in the form of block grants, which are then distributed by an intermediary agency. Caritas India performs this role for the Catholic agencies and CASA (Churches' Auxiliary for Social Action) for the World Council of Churches.

The third approach is that favoured by Oxfam, Save the Children Fund, and NOVIB, all of which have in-country offices, staffed mainly by Indian nationals, forming part of the parent organization and performing a role similar to that of an intermediary agency. Oxfam tends to favour small agencies, viewing its project support as catalytic and aimed at encouraging innovative approaches. In each region it establishes priority sectors or identifies specific social groups for special consideration. In Karnataka, for example, women and nomadic tribals receive particular attention, with social forestry as a key sector. There is also provision for non-project initiatives, such as training, networking, and inter-project visits, with the purpose of encouraging cross-fertilization of ideas between individual NGOs and promoting institutional development.

A variant on this approach is where the funding agency assumes a more active role in project planning, implementation, and evaluation through an in-country office. ActionAid UK favours large-scale integrated rural development projects, some of which are designed and initiated by its own personnel and later develop into quasi-autonomous agencies in their own right. In the case of existing partner agencies, ActionAid is rather more interventionist and encourages a degree of uniformity in terms of sector priorities, programme objectives, and monitoring.

The fourth model does not involve an intermediary agency, and relations between donor and recipient operate on a one-to-one basis. Projects are submitted directly to the funding agency which processes the applications in its head office. The main form of contact with project partners is through periodic tours undertaken by desk officers of the agency concerned. Christian Aid, for example, channels most of its funds to Indian NGOs bilaterally.

Official donors have proved increasingly willing to channel a proportion of their bilateral aid funds through NGOs, usually in the form of co-financing to international NGOs. Some have explored the potential for direct funding of Indian NGOs, but the government has tended to discourage this. Moreover, official donors lack the staff resources to monitor small grants directly or to develop a sufficiently detailed knowledge of the voluntary sector, with the result that most prefer to channel funds through NGOs from their own country.

Legislation governing the receipt of funds from abroad consists mainly of the Foreign Contributions Regulation Act (FCRA), which applies to voluntary agencies, religious associations, and companies alike. The Act was introduced in 1976 in response to government concern about the increasing volume of funding coming from overseas sources, some of which, it was alleged, was being used to fund subversive organizations. It compels all organizations wishing to receive funds from abroad to register with the Home Ministry, to submit audited accounts on a half-yearly basis, and to provide details of each individual contribution. Failure to comply can result in the withdrawal of the FCRA number and a government investigation. A 1984 amendment extended the definition of political organizations barred from receiving foreign funds, obliged recipient organizations to specify in advance the bank involved in the transaction, and provided the government with further powers to inspect audited accounts.

Liberal foreign funding has undoubtedly encouraged a proliferation of small agencies and enabled others to expand quickly. There are cases where rapid growth has diluted the effectiveness of the implementing agency, which in turn raises the prospect of the funding being terminated. A related problem is that the availability of funding encourages unscrupulous organizations to apply for support without adequate vetting. Individuals offer their services as consultants to NGOs, giving advice on appropriate sources of funding, and assistance in drawing up proposals and writing reports. Few donors adopt a strategic approach in their country programmes, and in many cases funding decisions tend to be *ad hoc* and reactive. The four case-studies indicate that different types of foreign funding can influence the organizational effectiveness of local NGOs, and certain types of institutional support may be more appropriate than project-based grants in helping them to achieve their objectives.

Relations with the Government

As NGOs have grown in size and influence, their activities have brought them into closer contact with government, the implications of which have been the subject of extensive debate. A dominant consideration here is the increasing volume of programme funding from government sources.

The government has long recognized the positive NGO contribution in the field of social welfare, and provided limited funds to support these activities, but it has only been in the latter half of the 1980s that the NGO role in rural development has received explicit recognition. The Seventh Five Year Plan (1986–90) marked a watershed. The work of voluntary agencies was considered as complementary to that of government in offering the rural poor a range of choices and alternatives, at low cost and with greater participation. The plan document provided for an active NGO involvement in the planning process and Rs. 1.5bn. were allocated from government funds for a wide range of anti-poverty and minimum needs programmes. A semi-autonomous body called the Council for the Advancement of People's Action and Rural Technology (CAPART) was created to administer these funds, which include a small proportion of bilateral aid.[4] To be eligible for CAPART funding, agencies have to be registered with the government for at least one year and working in rural areas.

Many NGOs seek government funding in preference to foreign aid principally because it obviates the need for registration under the Foreign Contributions Regulation Act. A strong nationalist tradition has in any case always existed among Indian NGOs, which abjures foreign funding on the grounds that it undermines their independence and limits their freedom to determine programme priorities. At the same time, the legitimacy derived from government funding can provide them with a degree of protection from harassment from vested interests.

Against this, dependence on official funds leaves NGOs susceptible to changes in government policy, and can result in programme modification to accommodate official priorities. It can also lead to co-option, whereby voluntary agencies tone down their social and political objectives in order to secure financial support. In practice, however, there is not such a sharp dichotomy between organizations in receipt of government as opposed to foreign funds, since most seek a blend of funding from both sources.

Another dimension of the relationship with government is in the realm of programme replication. The government has frequently sought to replicate voluntary initiatives on a larger scale, especially in the case of technological innovation, health care, and education. Related to this, there is a growing tendency for government bodies, particularly at the district or sub-district levels, to ask NGOs to implement specific programmes or schemes. Government officials believe that if NGOs are made responsible for project implementation, the administrative costs will be lower, and the scheme will be executed with greater efficiency and with the active participation of the intended beneficiaries.

Local co-operation leads to NGO representation on consultative committees, for example, those responsible for determining government funding priorities or for preventing atrocities against tribals and scheduled castes. Contacts with local government officers and bank officials provide them with information on funding and can help safeguard their projects. However, relations with local government are not always cordial, and there are numerous instances of obstacles being placed in the way of voluntary agencies, either out of official jealousy or to contain efforts at mobilizing the poor.

While the government has been increasing the level of funding that it provides to NGOs, it has also sought to regulate their activities more closely. Over the years, an elaborate legal framework has been devised. All voluntary agencies with seven or more members are compelled by law to register with state or central governments under the Societies Registration Act, 1860 (or the corresponding state act), as a trust under the Indian Trusts Act, 1982 or, in the case of religious organizations, the Charitable and Religious Act, 1920. This is a formality which rarely poses a problem, but registration is essential for NGOs wishing to apply for grants through CAPART or to receive foreign funding.

The government has also attempted to establish a regular forum where NGOs and officials can interact and exchange views. In 1985 it backed a proposal from a group of voluntary agencies for the formation of a National Council of Rural Voluntary Agencies, with corresponding state councils, whose main purpose would be to investigate complaints in regard to official obstruction and harassment and look into allegations of NGO mismanagement and misuse of funds. The proposals met with widespread opposition (much of it co-ordinated by VANI) on the grounds that they would constrain the autonomy of voluntary agencies, and the government decided not to put forward legislation.

Clearly, closer co-operation with government has had its costs. While the government has provided an increasing level of financial support to voluntary agencies and has encouraged their participation in policy formulation, it has also placed a number of restrictions on their freedom to function independently. It is less clear, however, whether increased co-operation has resulted in greater development effectiveness; several of the case-studies attempt to throw light on this question.

The Case-Study Evaluations

In some ways, NGOs in India are analogous to the proverbial iceberg, with a small group of agencies (usually represented by a handful of charismatic individuals) assuming a high public profile and known to government and foreign donors, whereas the vast majority are virtually unknown outside the area in which they are working. It is therefore tempting for supporters and opponents alike to make judgements about the overall impact of voluntary agencies based on the well-publicized performance of a few prominent organizations, whereas the picture is far less clear-cut on the ground.

Evidence on the impact of individual project interventions is surprisingly limited. It is unusual for NGOs to disseminate detailed information about their activities, even though a large number of evaluation studies are conducted each year, either at the behest of donors or on the initiative of the implementing agency. The pitfalls of particular types of intervention are thus not taken on board by others. Those reports which do receive a wider circulation tend to concentrate on operational concerns related to programme goals or strategic orientation. Evaluations attempting to gauge impact are of variable quality and often fail to distinguish between changes in economic status attributable to the NGO and the broader changes taking place in the local or regional economy.

With these considerations in mind, the four case-study evaluations attempt to identify the reasons for the success or failure of poverty-alleviation programmes where NGOs combine income-generation with community organization. The four organizations differ in their approach to rural development. RDT, the largest of the four, exemplifies the integrated approach from a broadly secular perspective. CASA, though founded on Christian principles, shares the secular approach but places greater emphasis on social development objectives and community participation. ASM combines elements of the Gandhian approach with a distinct atheist philosophy, and promotes development activities which are designed to benefit the village as a whole. Unlike most NGOs, the Kanyakumari District Fishermen Sangams Federation (KDFSF) was created as an apex body to co-ordinate the activities of existing fishermen's associations.[5]

RURAL DEVELOPMENT TRUST: CROP LOANS SCHEME

Background and Context

The Rural Development Trust has been promoting development activities in the Anantapur district of Andhra Pradesh since 1969. Its Community Organization Programme forms a key component of an integrated rural development project which includes health, education, skills training and, more recently, ecological development, covering some 280 villages in the district. Credit is provided to small and marginal farmers through village associations (*sangams*) for investment in agricultural inputs, enabling them to cultivate their land more intensively without having to rely on high-interest loans from money-lenders. The case-study examines the impact of the credit programme on the economic and social status of poor households in six *mandals* (administrative divisions) in Anantapur district where ActionAid UK was the main funding agency.

Anantapur district is located in the drought-prone region of Rayalaseema. The harshness of the local environment cannot be overstated: vegetation cover is sparse, consisting mainly of scrub and thorny undergrowth, and rainfall is low and intermittent, with an average of one in every four years declared a drought year. The main cash-crop, groundnut, has undergone a substantial increase in acreage over the past twenty years. Millet is the major food crop, although there has been a marked decline in production in recent years. Paddy is also grown during the winter season. Most people living in the area are engaged in farming, with 80 per cent of the workforce classified as cultivators or agricultural labourers. Land ownership is highly skewed:

farmers owning less than 5 acres account for the majority of cultivators, but a relatively small share of the total cropped area. Agricultural labourers constitute one-third of the rural labour-force, but most own some land. Agricultural work is mainly restricted to planting, weeding, and harvesting during the June to December groundnut season, which typically generates two to three months of employment.

The main impediments to removing poverty are the environmental constraints, the uneven pattern of land distribution, and the limited availability of off-farm employment. Farmers with less than 5 acres of dry land cannot meet their basic consumption needs without undertaking casual wage labour. The majority of small and marginal farmers are below the poverty-line. Even in a good year, they can only just make ends meet from groundnut cultivation: when the rains fail, yields are barely sufficient to cover the costs of inputs. Sharecroppers secure only marginal returns from leasing arrangements with the added benefit of fodder. Only the minority of farmers, with access to irrigation, can be assured of higher incomes from paddy cultivation.

The RDT was formed in 1969 by a former Jesuit priest, with the initial aim of improving irrigation facilities for poor farmers; community wells were constructed during the 1970s through an extensive food-for-work programme. The programme was discontinued in 1978 with a reorientation and expansion of the project in favour of an integrated development approach. This also marked the launch of an extensive child-sponsorship programme funded by ActionAid UK. Health, education, and community organization were established as the key sectors of the project, with a separate women's programme from 1982, and skills training from the late 1980s. A massive ecological programme started in 1988, which combines water harvesting measures and social forestry with employment generation, is now the largest component of the project in terms of funding and human resources.

The Community Organization Programme (COP) was born out of the realization that many poor farmers failed to benefit from the irrigation programmes of the early 1970s. It was founded on the assumption that poor people had to be more explicitly targeted for development assistance. The target population included small and marginal farmers with less than 5 acres of land, and the landless. Its objectives were as follows:

• to create an awareness among the rural poor of their common social and economic problems and to provide them with the means to overcome these through the formation of village associations (*sangams*);
• to improve the income levels of poor farmers through the provision of credit and extension in appropriate agricultural practices;
• to promote increased self-reliance by enabling poor people to manage programmes themselves on a sustainable basis.

For ease of administration, *sangams* were formed on caste lines, and became the focal unit for all the sectoral programmes, especially health and education, and later credit. All those below the poverty-line (roughly 60 per cent of the population) or with a child in receipt of sponsorship, were eligible for membership.

RDT regards development as a long-term process, in which economic and social change are equally important. Poverty is thus seen both as a structural phenomenon arising from inequalities in the distribution of wealth and assets and as a social phenomenon characterized by poor education and a limited awareness of individual potential. Long-term poverty alleviation is intended to address basic needs at the local level, namely for food, clothing, shelter, knowledge, and services, as well as social and political rights. In this context, the *sangam* is intended to act both as the starting-point for village development activities and as a forum for uniting poor people. In short, the *sangams* were conceived as enabling people to achieve an awareness of common problems for collective action, and thus as the pivotal unit around which other programmes would function. The administration of credit at the local level is considered to be the joint responsibility of the *sangam* and village-level field staff.

A central Community Credit Fund (CCF) was established soon after the formation of the *sangams* in 1980. For the first three years, it was built up by annual contributions from RDT (in effect from ActionAid) of Rs. 60 per family on which individuals could draw to meet petty expenses, provided they had no record of default. After 1986, the CCF evolved into a fully fledged crop loans scheme and RDT's contributions gradually increased each year in line with a matching amount from the farmers, with loans carrying an interest rate of 11 per cent, on a par with that charged by the commercial banks. Farmers were entitled to borrow on a regular annual basis at the time of sowing in June, rather than intermittently according to specific needs. The credit was used primarily for the purchase of inputs such as fertilizer, pesticide, seeds, and bullock hire for ploughing and labour expenses, with the aim of enhancing production. Individual contributions steadily increased, in some cases to Rs. 200, with RDT continuing to provide a matching amount. This allowed the CCF to grow quickly, enabling individual farmers to borrow up to Rs. 1,500 provided they repaid regularly and in full. The CCF was designed to become self-sufficient once the amount available for loans reached an optimal level in relation to farmers' needs, which was estimated at Rs. 2,000 for a 5-acre plot. The programme also aimed to make the *sangams* increasingly self-reliant so that over time they would be able to assume greater responsibility for credit management.

In the 135 villages covered by ActionAid the target-group population amounted to 13,800 households (70,000 people), out of a total of 24,800 households. Assuming that some 60 per cent of the population can be classed as poor, the number of families reached by RDT was equivalent to 6 per cent of the rural poor in Anantapur district (population 2 million). Sixty-four staff were employed in administering the COP, divided between three field offices; eight community organizers were responsible for supervising the work of forty-nine field-workers who interacted with the *sangams* on a regular basis, in administering the Community Credit Fund.

The main cost incurred (Rs. 1.4m. in 1989) was for administration and staffing. With 5,765 borrowers, the average cost per beneficiary worked out at just over Rs. 200 per head in 1989, although this included provision for non-credit activities. Further costs were incurred by borrowers in terms of the opportunity cost of attending regular *sangam* meetings and making repayments, but these were offset by lower interest rates compared to those charged by money-lenders and the accessibility of the credit.

Nevertheless, they suggest that the credit scheme was expensive to administer relative to loan size, even if the credit disbursed ultimately had a positive impact.

Programme Assessment

Changes in cropping patterns and improved economic status. From 1986 CCF credit encouraged a rapid shift towards groundnut production on the part of small and marginal farmers. Alongside the supply of credit, a land reclamation scheme initiated by RDT in the wake of the 1985/6 drought also enabled many farmers to extend the area under their cultivation. Factors external to the project also had a bearing on the trend towards groundnut cultivation. One such was the demonstration effect exerted by larger farmers with access to institutional credit who had been steadily increasing the amount of land under groundnut in response to the favourable market price arising from increased demand for edible oils.

The most visible effect of this shift in cropping patterns has been increased incomes for the majority of farming households. The returns on groundnut cultivation were found to be three to four times higher than for traditional food-grains. The cumulative effect of three successive good crops of groundnut after 1986 undoubtedly raised the incomes of target-group farmers substantially, enabling many households to cross the official poverty threshold (Rs. 6,400). It is questionable whether such changes are sustainable in the longer term, however, given the continued vulnerability of farmers to drought and crop failure and their limited capacity to save. While groundnut production is more profitable than food-grains, yields varied considerably according to rainfall, soil type, seed quality, extension advice, and the aptitude of individual farmers. Farmers also benefited to varying degrees depending on the size of their landholding, their possession of assets, and the nature of leasing arrangements.

Evidence of improvements in the economic status of beneficiaries was seen in the form of improved food consumption, more regular purchase of clothing, and the acquisition of basic household utensils. Farmers were also able to purchase bullocks and small plots of land, and clear off outstanding debts to money-lenders. The sale of groundnut provided farmers with cash to purchase rice which became the main food staple, and although nutritionally inferior to the traditional millets, was perceived to be a higher status food. A further factor was the availability of subsidized rice from the government, at prices below the cost of traditional food staples. Families tended to eat more varied and regular meals and having to go without food at night during the lean season became a thing of the past for most people.

Increased income from agricultural production to some extent enhanced farmers' ability to cope with calamities, such as drought and sickness. Seed saved from the previous year's harvest provided security in times of need; small amounts could be sold if the need arose. Moreover, many of the poorest families no longer migrated out of the area in search of temporary employment during the lean season, as returns from groundnut cultivation were sufficient to meet household needs if supplemented with additional income from wage labour.

Distribution of benefits.   Small farmers owning between 2 and 5 acres of dry land (the principal target-group) were the main beneficiaries. Those with a pair of bullocks or access to irrigation gained relatively more than those without such assets, since the costs of ploughing were also incurred by those without bullocks. Marginal farmers owning less than 2 acres, sharecroppers, and tenants gained less: their capacity to generate a sufficiently high yield to repay the loans is lower than that of farmers owning more land, even in relative terms. They also depend to a higher degree on income from agricultural labour for their family needs. Nevertheless, the extra income generated from groundnut cultivation was considered to be important.

Returns for sharecroppers are generally too low to generate a significant level of income. Many marginal farmers using crop loans for sharecropping were primarily interested in the fodder value of the crop. Landless agricultural labourers, who constitute around 11 per cent of the target population, benefited least of all. Such people cannot invest in land; borrowing for sharecropping is unremunerative as the returns are low; a number are simply too poor to borrow with their limited capacity to repay. Nevertheless, those landless beneficiaries with non-agricultural sources of income— such as basket-making, mat-weaving, leatherwork, and the sale of hides—were able to purchase raw materials in bulk at lower prices using CCF credit. A significant number used their loans for consumption purposes, to benefit from the marginal saving on bulk purchases of foodstuff. And a number of former bonded labourers managed to pay off their debts and take up cultivation.

Other factors have had an influence on local employment opportunities. A gradual expansion in the area under irrigation has led to an increase in the demand for labour. In particular, the availability of employment on irrigated paddy and groundnut land owned by richer farmers has helped to reduce out-migration. At the same time, the tendency for small and marginal farmers to take up groundnut cultivation on their own plots reduced the availability of labour during the June–December groundnut season, and may have contributed indirectly to an increase in wages.

Widows of small farmers who joined the *sangam* following the death of their husbands used the credit to purchase assets for other members of the household to cultivate the land or leased it out on a sharecropping basis. Since they rarely have any independent means of support once their husbands die, the income derived from cultivation of the family plot with credit from the CCF played a critical role.

A small proportion of borrowers became relatively better-off through being able to double-crop as a result of acquiring land or access to irrigation facilities. Others had access to non-agricultural income such as remittances, but few could be considered wealthy. For farmers owning 5 acres and above the loans available through the CCF were relatively incidental to their overall investment needs. Most in this category, especially those with land under irrigation, borrow from institutional sources, notably co-operative societies and the nationalized banks in the range of Rs. 2–4,000, as compared with the Rs. 700–1,200 available through the CCF. For them loans under the CCF were useful in so far as there was a matching contribution from the RDT together with the other advantages related to timeliness and low interest.

Social development.   The purpose of the *sangams* is threefold: to facilitate discussion and action on issues and activities for the benefit of the community, to practise democratic processes in decision-making, and to develop local leadership qualities. However, the field investigations suggest that most of the *sangams* fell well short of these objectives. They primarily functioned as credit groups, bringing farmers together to discuss issues such as size of contributions and repayment problems, facilitating loan distribution, and providing an organizational structure for repayment. Some provided a forum for the exchange of information on agricultural practices such as cropping patterns, use of fertilizer, and seed varieties. There was little sense of ownership attached to the crop loans scheme, although the *sangams* varied considerably in terms of the beneficiaries' involvement in the administration of credit. Many continued to depend on RDT social workers to disburse credit and to collect repayments, which had important implications for the sustainability of the scheme.

Sangams varied considerably in their capacity for independent action and decision-making. In a few instances they fulfilled a broader role in providing a forum for collective action. In one case, the *sangam* enabled its members to seek redress of outstanding grievances related to the distribution of surplus land by the government. In another, members petitioned the government for permission to cultivate a substantial tract of land owned by temple authorities. However, these were the exception rather than the rule.

Although in most cases members were unable to explain the broader purpose of their *sangam*, there have clearly been some important qualitative benefits from *sangam* membership, especially for the scheduled castes. Many reported that the practice of untouchability had diminished, and better education of their children assisted in this process. Coming together as a group has given members greater confidence to approach local government and bank officials. Such changes are indicative of enhanced social status for scheduled caste villagers in the wider community, although not all of these can be attributed to the existence of the *sangam*.

Sangams clearly perform an important role in bringing poor villagers together in a common forum where they are able to articulate and discuss shared problems, which is not the case with *panchayat* councils, where the poor are usually denied effective representation. Nevertheless, it is not evident that all members participate equally in *sangam* meetings. The landless members in particular do not play an active role, as discussions often relate to the interests of farmers owning land, who have been the principal beneficiaries of the programme. Moreover, *sangam* leaders exercise a fairly dominant role in meetings and have a tendency to speak on behalf of others. This has a positive side in so far as leadership among the poor is developing, but also a negative dimension as regards limits on participation.

Advantages of the crop loans scheme.   Aside from its direct benefits, there were a number of benefits related to the CCF as an alternative source of credit. The most important one cited by farmers was reduced dependence on money-lenders. The majority of small and marginal farmers (and to a lesser extent middle-income farmers) have traditionally depended on private money-lenders (usually big landlords) for the bulk of their credit needs, mainly for consumption purposes (especially following crop failure) and for marriages and festivals. Many marginal farmers and agricultural labourers were tied into bonded labour contracts as a result of incurring debts which carried high rates of interest (typically 24 per cent).

With the spread of groundnut cultivation farmers began to borrow for seed, fertilizer, bullock hire for ploughing, and labour costs. To secure a loan they had to make frequent visits to the money-lender, in the process wasting time that could have been spent tending crops, and where the money-lender lived outside the village incurring additional travel costs. The need to petition for loans was also a demeaning process which reinforced traditional caste and patron–client relations. The provision of a loan was commonly made conditional on farmers having to work on the landlord's plot before working on their own land, thus incurring delays in sowing and harvesting. Even when the money-lender finally agreed to a loan, it often came too late to enable a farmer to purchase seed and other inputs at the optimal time, i.e. at the onset of the rains. Output was reduced as a result.

In addition to reduced dependence on money-lenders, loans from the CCF were timely, as they came just before sowing in June, and they carried a lower rate of interest. The matching contribution from the RDT was clearly regarded as an important benefit, especially since higher contributions by farmers were matched by the RDT, enabling them to increase the amount they could borrow over time fairly quickly. In some cases, access to CCF credit had encouraged farmers to approach banking institutions for additional loans for agricultural purposes. There were, in addition, several cases where families had two, and in some cases three, members taking loans from the CCF for the same piece of land which was farmed jointly, giving them access to quite substantial sums.

However, for a significant proportion of farmers interviewed in the study, the volume of credit available through the CCF failed to meet their full requirements, and many continued to borrow from money-lenders and banks to supplement the CCF loans. This was especially true of middle-income farmers who had ready access to institutional credit. Other farmers borrowed from the CCF for their agricultural needs and resorted to money-lenders for loans to cover marriage expenses and dowries, although there was an element of fungibility between these two sources of credit, and their end use was not always clearly demarcated.

Some costs were incurred in moving away from money-lenders to the CCF. The patron–client system contained an element of reciprocity and was not purely confined to rent extraction by rapacious money-lenders, especially where the money-lender was also the local landlord. Some farmers complained that the CCF was more inflexible in demanding repayments within a fixed time-schedule irrespective of crop performance. In times of drought some money-lenders would waive interest payments or stagger repayments, in return for labour commitments or other favours. The reciprocal dimension of the patron–client relationship therefore helped to explain the propensity of some poor farmers to continue taking loans from the money-lenders, particularly where the latter rely on a regular supply of casual labour during the harvesting season.

Sustainability. A major impediment to achieving a self-sufficient revolving credit scheme was the vulnerability of small and marginal farmers to crop failure as a result of drought, which is a recurrent feature in the area. Even if the CCF had been built up to an optimal level, a severe drought would have led to widespread default and depleted resources within the fund. If the RDT contributions had been discontinued, the scheme would have been in danger of collapse. By 1988 the cumulative amount of outstanding dues had reached Rs. 1.06m., shared among 2,272 borrowers, giving an average of Rs. 466 per borrower.

Three relatively good years from 1986/7 were followed by poor and uneven rainfall in 1989/90. Marginal farmers in particular repaid their CCF loans only by the sale of seed, leaving none available for the next sowing season. There was evidence that many such farmers were preparing to borrow from private money-lenders to fulfil their CCF obligations, since failure to repay would have debarred them from future loans.

A related issue was their dependence on income from cash-crop production. There are two aspects to this. Good returns are related not only to favourable climatic conditions, but also to the prevailing market price for groundnut, which is subject to fluctuations resulting from local variations in output as well as to longer-term trends in national demand for groundnut oil on the domestic market. Should a cheaper substitute become available, groundnut prices, and hence farmers' incomes, could be adversely affected, although it would be theoretically possible for them to switch crops again. Present trends indicate strong demand for groundnut oil, but there is no guarantee that this will hold for the longer term.

One consequence of the transition to groundnut production has been an increase in the amount spent on inputs, especially artificial fertilizers and pesticides purchased with credit from the CCF. This spending may raise production in the short term, but there are also some disadvantages. There is clearly a greater risk involved when the costs of investment are higher: in drought years production may be insufficient to cover input costs, and lack of rainfall can actually cause the fertilizer to damage the crop. A shift from food to cash-crop production also has implications for household expenditure patterns, rendering them susceptible to price inflation. Such considerations are important when considering potential sustainability in the longer term.

In theory, *sangams* were responsible for the administration of loans from the CCF. Most were capable of disbursement, but their involvement in loan recovery varied enormously. NGO staff did the hard work of physically collecting repayments. A number of borrowers interviewed did not know how much they had borrowed or the rate of interest on the loans, but nevertheless acknowledged the benefits of the scheme. For these reasons it was judged that the withdrawal of the direct support of field staff would in many cases result in the collapse of the scheme and perhaps the *sangam* itself.

A number of other problems with the mechanics of the scheme raised important questions about its longer-term existence. Farmers were still under the impression that their own contributions to the fund would continue to be matched by the RDT. In some cases they had been pushing for higher levels of individual contributions, underlining the importance of the incentive effect of the RDT matching contribution, which amounted to a subsidy as there was no mechanism for retrieving the organization's inputs. Since farmers had come to expect continuing contributions from the RDT, it was evident that they would lack the incentive to persist with the scheme if these were discontinued. This was borne out in practice in late 1991: when RDT decided to end its contributions, the majority of the *sangams* voted to terminate the scheme.

Strengths, Weaknesses, and Lessons

Two factors that may have played a role in the success of the crop-loans scheme up to 1991 were the community organizations and the quality of programme staff. As noted above, village *sangams* played a functional role in bringing poor farmers together to discuss their credit needs and to facilitate the administration of the scheme. Yet field staff exhibited varying degrees of commitment to the programme. Although they proved capable of administering credit and ensuring a certain level of repayment, this did not prove central to the success of the programme. Rather, success was primarily attributable to the fact that loans from the CCF provided a viable alternative to high-interest credit from money-lenders.

One of the limitations of the programme was that the benefits accruing to landless labourers were relatively marginal. While some opportunities for wage employment were created by the ecological development programme during the lean season, the needs of the landless were not specifically addressed. Although a number of *sangam* members acquired assets under the government's Integrated Rural Development Programme (IRDP), there was not a systematic effort to secure subsidized loans for non-agricultural income generation for the landless.

The major limitation of the programme lay in its lack of sustainability, which was directly related to the harsh environment in which credit was being introduced, although it was hoped that the ecological development programme would provide a longer-term solution to these problems. Another weakness relates to the role of the *sangams*. Most were not directly concerned with social issues and few displayed the potential to become self-reliant. A further limitation was the reliance of the programme on refinancing from external sources, and the fact that the CCF did not fully meet current credit requirements. Little attempt was made to encourage farmers to take out loans from banks or to make more use of government resources, which reinforced their reliance on the CCF and, by implication, on funding from foreign donors.

In many ways the Community Organization Programme was unique in terms of its scope and approach. Few other NGOs were likely to have been able to mobilize resources on a comparable scale. However, the very success of the CCF in raising the productivity and incomes of small farmers underlines the importance of alternative sources of credit, while the limitation of the programme in terms of sustainability in a drought-prone environment points to the need for NGOs considering credit provision to incorporate compensatory mechanisms as an insurance against crop failure under such circumstances.

CHURCHES' AUXILIARY FOR SOCIAL ACTION (CASA): PHASE III PROGRAMME

The project is located in the delta region of the Krishna river in coastal Andhra Pradesh, and is administered from two programme offices in Machilipatnam (Krishna district) and Bapatla (Guntur district). Phase III began as an integrated rural development programme in 1981 following three years of relief and rehabilitation work in the wake of the 1977 cyclone. The programme gives equal emphasis to the process of community organization through the formation of self-reliant village associations (*sangams*), and to mobilizing resources from the government and the nationalized banks for the promotion of income-generating activities and infrastructural development. Priority is given to assisting the landless and small and marginal farmers, especially tribals, *harijans*, and economically backward castes. In the thirty-two villages covered by the programme, some 3,000 households have received assistance from CASA, although the organization has now withdrawn from half of these villages. This study evaluates the overall contribution made by the programme to poverty alleviation and enhanced social status among the rural poor in coastal Andhra.

The programme has achieved its overall objective of bringing about a sustained improvement in their economic and social conditions. Substantial resources have been mobilized from the government and local banks at relatively low cost. The majority of the programmes taken up by beneficiaries have brought about an increase in incomes, often by a substantial amount, and this has invariably resulted in better food consumption, higher expenditure on clothing, food, education and housing, land acquisition, and increased savings.

Sangams serve as the focal point for promoting village unity, planning and executing development activities, and fostering self-reliance among the poor. Prospects for the longer-term sustainability of the programme are favourable, as evidenced by the villages where CASA has already withdrawn. The very success of the approach adopted in Phase III, with its emphasis on constructive collaboration with local government officials, has much to offer in terms of a model for NGO development strategies more generally, although this will depend on political conditions and resource availability in different parts of the country.

Context, History, and Structure

In contrast to the dry interior region of Andhra Pradesh, the east coast districts are comparatively well developed. Krishna and Guntur districts experienced fairly rapid agricultural growth during the 1980s, although there are significant disparities between inland areas and the relatively inaccessible coastal strip. The latter is subject to periodic cyclones, the most recent being in May 1990, when there was extensive damage but relatively few deaths, unlike the 1977 cyclone which killed 40,000.

Agriculture is the main occupation of people living in the area, with two-thirds of the workforce engaged full-time. An extensive canal network around the Krishna river enables most farmers to double-crop, although there are supply problems in the delta itself. Much of the land on the coast is highly saline and offers little scope for cultivation. The main crop is paddy, often grown in rotation with a cash-crop such as pulses, groundnut, or vegetables.

Small and marginal farmers owning less than 5 acres of dry land (or 2.5 acres of irrigated land) account for approximately half the cultivated area, although the extent of landlessness is comparatively high, with 44 per cent of all workers in both districts classed as agricultural labourers. Wages tend to be higher than in the semi-arid interior region, and are among the highest in south India, excluding Kerala. Off-farm occupations include rickshaw-pulling, maintenance and repair services, and artisanal activities.

The population of the two districts is extremely heterogeneous, the majority being Hindu, although there are pockets of Christians and Muslims, and a small tribal population. The dominant castes are the *kammas*, whose power and patronage derive traditionally from the ownership of land, although they have begun to invest in small businesses and real estate. Most of the tribals and the scheduled castes are landless agricultural labourers, although some are marginal farmers. The backward castes, who mainly consist of small farmers and fishing communities, account for more than half of the rural population. Poverty is perpetuated by several factors: restricted access to productive assets such as land, capital, and livestock; exploitation by money-lenders lending money at exorbitant rates of interest; landlords who pay low wages or promote unfair leasing arrangements; government programmes which are not sufficiently responsive to the needs of the poor; and widespread illiteracy and ignorance about civil and economic rights.

CASA is a large national NGO representing about twenty major Protestant churches. It nevertheless maintains a secular approach and works with all communities regardless of religious affiliation. The focal unit of its Phase III programme is the *sangam*, representing the interests of poor households on a common economic basis rather than on caste lines, and aiming to promote unity through a process of awareness-building, in order to resolve community disputes and problems, to enable individuals to approach government and bank officials for financial and technical assistance, and to empower the poor to challenge caste discrimination and economic exploitation. Such community organization always precedes economic activities, on the grounds that without effective popular participation, income-generation programmes cannot succeed. CASA staff perform a catalytic role, encouraging villagers to form *sangams* and identify new sources of income and employment. The philosophical premiss on which Phase III is founded is that the poor should be encouraged to shape their own development priorities and to mobilize, as far as possible, external sources of finance for income-generation activities.

Phase III has three main elements: community organization, economic activities, and common village programmes. Community organization provides the entry-point for most development activities in the villages adopted by CASA on the basis of non-formal education, which includes informal issue-based discussions on topics such as indebtedness, land rights, and drinking water, developing functional literacy training, and learning about banks and government institutions. However, as with the RDT project, the aim in forming village *sangams* is not only to promote unity and awareness among the poor, but to encourage the emergence of a strong village leadership independent of the dominant social groups which traditionally monopolize local affairs.

Economic programmes are selected and approved by the *sangam*. Once approved, CASA staff (and later on the *sangam*) assist them in approaching the bank for subsidized credit.[6] This is used to purchase assets for income-generation purposes in three categories: new activities (such as rickshaw-pulling, small businesses); those which supplement existing sources of income (for example, dairying and goat-rearing); and those which enhance an existing activity (e.g. crop loans, or the purchase of catamarans).

A number of features are common to all the adopted villages. If none already exist, CASA provides materials for the construction of community halls by unpaid voluntary labour. These serve as the place where the *sangam* can meet and where non-formal education classes can be conducted. In certain cases, CASA will approach the local administration to secure funds for roads, drinking-water facilities, schools, or houses. CASA's role is generally restricted to staff support, liaison with officials, and follow-up, although it often contributes an additional subsidy from its own funds to speed up the flow of benefits.

In 1989 CASA Bapatla spent £19,500 on common programmes and subsidies for village-specific programmes. This compares with £45,000 raised in loans from banks and £69,000 in the form of grants and subsidies from the government. *Sangam* members' contributions in cash and voluntary labour (excluding savings) were £7,600, making a total of £141,100 for programme expenditure. In CASA Machilipatnam the comparable sums were £21,000 on programmes, with government contributions of £36,000, and £87,300 from bank loans; £19,000 came from *sangam* members giving a total of £163,300. In the same year funding from Christian Aid for the two programmes amounted to £57,200, covering the full costs of the Machilipatnam programme, and 50 per cent of the Bapatla programme. CASA's expenditure on administration in both districts was only 10 per cent of the total budget in 1989, and the figures show that CASA mobilizes from the banks, the government, and voluntary contributions more than six times the amount of resources it expends from its own funds.

Programme Assessment

The Phase III programme has substantially succeeded in achieving its main objective of promoting self-sustaining development initiatives. Overall CASA's role has been to ensure that government programmes are responsive to the needs of the poor, efficient in their implementation, and effective in alleviating poverty.

Community organization.   Apart from serving as a vehicle for implementing development programmes, the *sangams* provide a forum for resolving disputes and redressing
grievances. The formation of such groups has helped the poor to identify common
problems and cut across intrinsic factional divisions, despite attempts by vested interests to undermine their unity. Through a process of non-formal education CASA
staff have sought to raise the awareness of *sangam* members about community problems. In addition to functional literacy, members have also learnt how to approach
government and bank officials directly and how to secure loans and subsidies and to
ensure that they receive good quality assets. The increase in their self-confidence and
self-esteem is highly valued.

In some cases, the *sangams* have taken awareness-building a stage further and
challenged the structures that continue their exploitation. In one village the *sangam*
entered into direct conflict with the local landlord over land rights. In others *sangams*
have managed to pressure the government into providing families with fisheries and
surplus land for cultivation. *Sangams* have also fought for the legal rights of their
members and challenged instances of caste discrimination. Some have struggled successfully for better wages and working conditions.

After the May 1990 cyclone and in strong contrast to 1977, when people concentrated on meeting individual rather than collective needs, many *sangams* approached
local government officials for immediate emergency assistance, and organized committees to collect and distribute food and relief materials. In some instances, they
drew up damage lists for insurance purposes.

The development of a strong *sangam* leadership has been instrumental in ensuring
that the poor have an effective channel of communication with outside officials and an
ability to withstand the attempts of vested interests to undermine their efforts at
promoting unity. The new leadership has displaced traditional modes of decision-
making in the *panchayats*, which excluded the vast majority of the poor. Most *sangam*
presidents are energetic individuals strongly committed to the *sangam* and with a
good standing within the community. All the *sangams* interviewed met regularly,
usually once or twice a month. The level of attendance inevitably varied from village
to village, and while high in the early phase, was not consistent, especially during the
peak agricultural season.

Women have made significant strides as a result of being able to participate in
sangam affairs. This was more apparent in villages where *mahila mandalis* (women's
associations) had been formed to enable them to meet separately to discuss issues
which impinge on family relationships and gender relations. Nevertheless, in those
villages where there are no *mahila mandalis*, women are guaranteed equal representation in the management of the *sangam*.

Visits to other villages where CASA has been active have enabled women to learn
from the experiences of others and discover that their own situation is not unique. In
the past women rarely ventured outside the village, but they now have the confidence
to go to the nearest town or a neighbouring village without their husbands. Women
have often been instrumental in pressuring government officials to provide house-
sites, safe drinking water, and other infrastructural facilities designed to benefit the

community as a whole. This is a direct reflection of their increased self-confidence and heightens the respect they receive from the men in the community. Women have also been encouraged to start up revolving savings schemes funded by regular contributions ranging from Rs. 5 to Rs. 10 per week. As well as contributing towards household welfare, these schemes have served as an important vehicle to bring women together to discuss other common issues.

Women have played an active role in tackling the problem of *arrack* (locally-brewed alcohol) consumption, which is endemic in many villages, since in many cases they have been the victims of their husbands' drunken violence. Their own status has improved as a result and reductions in *arrack* consumption have led to dramatic improvements in household expenditure and savings in some villages.

Despite these successes, the process of establishing *sangams* has not always been easy. It has proved less difficult to set up viable *sangams* in villages where there is a greater degree of homogeneity in terms of caste (i.e. in tribal or scheduled-caste communities) or occupation. Where the village community is composed of several castes which differ in terms of economic and social status, dominant groups, fearful that their privileged position within the community will be eroded, try to subvert their formation by exploiting factional rivalries or by accusing CASA of pursuing religious goals. This is especially the case in villages which are closer to urban centres and therefore more susceptible to external political pressures.

Economic impact. A number of different income-generation programmes have been taken up by *sangam* members in the CASA-adopted villages, for the most part through a loan with a subsidy component via the IRDP. Most have resulted in increased disposable incomes, in some cases by significant amounts. Of a sample of forty-four people who took loans for economic programmes, twenty-five (57 per cent) experienced significant increases, and eight (18 per cent) a marginal increase in income; six (14 per cent) reported that they had experienced no change in their economic status while three reported a loss. Only in a minority of cases did the programmes fail to yield the intended benefits, usually on account of factors beyond the beneficiaries' control, such as premature death of an animal or illness in the family. It has proved more difficult to establish sustainable economic activities in the remote coastal villages where poor communications and a weak effective demand for goods and services limit their potential.

For very poor people, increased income will tend to be spent on a greater quantity and a better quality and range of food consumed. Nearly half of those interviewed reported similar changes in eating habits to those recorded in the RDT project. The trend towards rice consumption is most marked for the landless and marginal farmers, since small farmers with more than 2 acres of land grow enough for their own consumption needs. Increased income from non-farm activities has accelerated the trend and the increased purchasing power of the landless in particular.

Aside from rice, most beneficiaries reported eating more varied foods. It is now common for families to eat vegetables every day, and meat several times a month. Dairy beneficiaries tend to keep some milk for their own consumption, usually for making into buttermilk, although many will use it as a nutritional supplement for young children. In short, increased incomes have contributed towards greater food security; most families no longer have to lead a hand-to-mouth existence.

While food continues to account for the major share of the expenditure of poor households, many find that they now have surplus income to spend on other items. Children's education is a priority, with some opting to send their children to residential schools in towns and bear the costs of fees, books, clothing, and transport. Education is seen as a passport out of poverty, providing access to secure and relatively well-paid employment outside agriculture, and with it higher status.

Most of those interviewed now spend more on clothing, whereas they previously bought clothes only out of necessity, many of them second-hand. Household utensils are another important item of expenditure, and a number of households have also purchased luxury items such as jewellery, electrical goods, and bicycles. Improvements have also been made to houses. In the case of those with government housing, they have added verandas and new roofs, or replastered the walls. Others have built new mud-walled houses with the proceeds from their income-generation activities.

Acquiring land is often a major priority for poor rural households. Land gives security as a fixed asset and gains in value over time. With cultivation it can provide an additional source of income and improve a household's economic status. Eleven respondents (22 per cent of the total), including a number of formerly landless labourers, said they had invested in land with savings from economic activities supported by credit. Land acquisition was especially notable in the case of those who had invested in sheep-rearing and catamaran-fishing.

Many beneficiaries had opened fixed deposit accounts with banks. Of those interviewed, one-fifth reported that they had savings in bank accounts, in a number of cases amounting to several thousand rupees. These savings are used to cover marriage expenses, the cost of children's education, or for purchasing assets, and also as a reserve fund to be drawn on in case of emergencies, especially for medical expenses which can be a big drain on family resources. In addition, by having fixed deposits with the bank, beneficiaries are automatically entitled to take loans without collateral security. Prior to the take-up of various economic programmes, indebtedness to money-lenders was rife. Access to bank credit has freed beneficiaries from this dependence on the money-lender: the vast majority have been able to pay off their debts to money-lenders completely. This has an important psychological dimension.

A common coping mechanism of poor villagers in the lean agricultural season is out-migration in search of work in other areas, often several hundred kilometres away. Whole families used to migrate for three to four months at a time in search of employment to secure enough income for survival. The take-up of self-employment and other income-generation programmes has helped to reduce out-migration. More work is also now available locally from economic activities supported by credit.

It would be an exaggeration to suggest that all the positive developments observed in the well-being of *sangam* members are attributable to CASA's intervention. At least two other factors have contributed. Coastal Andhra has developed relatively quickly in comparison with drought-prone districts further inland, due mainly to especially rapid agricultural growth. Increased irrigation has enabled many farmers to grow two, and sometimes three, crops, which in turn has increased the amount of work available to landless labourers. An expansion in the net sown area under paddy has also contributed towards a change in diet: with two crops of paddy even marginal farmers can produce sufficient rice to meet household needs. The second factor is the rice-subsidy scheme introduced in 1983. Families below the official poverty-line are entitled to 25 kgs. of rice per month at a subsidized rate (roughly half the market price). Many beneficiaries, in particular landless labourers, cited this scheme as an important addition to their household requirements.

The success of the programme is also evident from the influence it has had on the approaches adopted by other NGOs in the vicinity and the willingness of villages in the area to become involved. Several NGOs have simply replicated the CASA approach. Other villages in the project area, having seen the progress in the CASA villages, have approached CASA with a view to securing some form of assistance, or have independently established *sangams* of their own. Moreover, some *sangams* have provided individuals in neighbouring villages with information about government programmes and the benefits of forming community organizations. Several villages were adopted by CASA following a request from the inhabitants. In other cases CASA turned down requests on the grounds that the villages had already achieved a certain level of development and were not in need of its support. The government has also approached CASA on occasion with recommendations that it begin work in a particular village.

Distribution of benefits. While the majority of beneficiaries have experienced marked improvements in their economic status as a result of taking up income-generation programmes, there are variations according to individuals' initial asset holdings and the geographical location of the village. Three main groups are covered by the programmes: agricultural labourers, small and marginal farmers, and women. Although those already in possession of land or animals are in a better position to benefit from particular economic programmes, a substantial number of the very poorest (wage labourers and marginal sharecroppers) have been brought above the poverty-line as a result of new or supplementary sources of income. The rate of success tends to be higher in peri-urban villages where opportunities for non-agricultural activities exist, and where communications and access to marketing facilities are better.

Households that depend exclusively on income from agricultural wage-labour are invariably among the poorest (excluding the sick and the destitute); female-headed households where the husband is sick or has died suffer the greatest hardship, especially if the children are too young to go out to work. The acquisition of an income-generating asset such as a buffalo or flock of sheep, or regular work from a new activity, has in many cases carried households above the poverty threshold. Earnings from rickshaw-pulling supplemented by agricultural labour can more than double household income. Prawn cultivation can triple or quadruple it if the tank is well maintained, but this is an exceptional case. Income from dairying has been much more variable in the case of landless households, since earnings depend on access to fodder and the level of milk production. Some households have experienced deferred benefits if a calf dies. In some cases, where milk production has been consistently low (largely in sandy soil areas), families have experienced a net loss in income.

Marginal farmers and sharecroppers have benefited in two ways. Recurrent credit in the form of crop loans from a commercial bank is both cheaper and more accessible than loans from money-lenders, and supplementary income derived from dairying or other economic activities supported by bank credit and subsidies can provide for household consumption needs during the lean season or in the event of crop failure. Some farmers have increased yields by applying more inputs, but in general credit has not contributed significantly to output, which is contingent on a range of other factors. Production on smaller plots has to be supplemented by other sources, usually earnings from agricultural labour, or from a supplementary income-generating activity such as dairying.

Securing an independent means of livelihood through loans for a range of economic activities has resulted in a marked improvement in women's social, and to a lesser extent economic, status. An independent source of income (albeit marginal in some cases) has given women greater economic security and the confidence to deal with their husbands on a more equal footing. Women who were previously confined to work in and around the house have the opportunity to use their time more productively. As a result of taking up income-generation programmes which provide full-time employment, others have stopped going for agricultural labour, which is hard and poorly paid, and they perceive this as an important change for the better.

Cost-effectiveness.   Overall the project data lead one to conclude that the Phase III programme is highly cost-effective in terms of resource mobilization. However, it is difficult to assess the aggregate value of benefits arising out of the different programmes taken up by *sangam* members—a protracted process which was not feasible in the time available and in view of the constraints imposed by the lack of data.

The most profitable activities with the highest cost–benefit ratios are catamaran-fishing and prawn cultivation (rates of return range from 30 to 70 per cent, excluding the imputed cost of labour). At the other end of the scale, dairying is not always profitable (net income ranges from Rs. 0–400 per animal), and without subsidies a number of such ventures would actually be loss-making. In the case of crop loans, the principal benefit lies not in increased incomes, but rather in reduced transaction costs.

Sustainability.   *Sangams* are encouraged to identify their own priorities and programmes of action. CASA gets the *sangam* started and provides orientation through non-formal education and awareness-building. Once it is well-established, CASA withdraws but continues to play a supportive role.

In those villages where CASA had withdrawn up to five years previously, the *sangam* was continuing to play an active and important role. Members are very clear about its role and purpose and view it as an organization owned by and representing the interests of the community rather than as an institution imposed from outside and of little importance to them. In general *sangams* display a remarkable degree of self-reliance. The only exceptions are remote coastal villages, where it has proved difficult to implement self-sustaining economic programmes because of poor communications or inadequate local resources. While many activities have been undertaken by the *sangams*, they have not fully overcome the tendency to depend on outside assistance. They continue to look to CASA to provide them with resources and infrastructure, or to secure these from the government on their behalf.

As for the economic programmes, the majority are progressing satisfactorily in those villages where CASA has withdrawn. Repayment rates are high, ensuring a regular flow of subsidized credit from the banks. Where individuals have used up their subsidy entitlement, they continue to borrow from banks to replace or upgrade existing assets, having established secure credit ratings. The *sangam* provides advice and support to those wishing to take out loans for the first time, and uses its standing with the bank to facilitate access to credit. Examples of failure are relatively few, although in such cases (some calf-rearing beneficiaries and those buying fishing canoes) individuals have experienced difficulties in securing access to new loans, and have turned to CASA for direct assistance.

Strengths, Weaknesses, and Lessons

The reasons for the success of the Phase III programme in coastal Andhra are threefold. First, with the formation of self-reliant community organizations which articulate the interests of the poor, both in defence of their rights and in seeking external support for their own development initiatives, not only is the process of development participatory but people actively discuss and shape their own priorities as individuals and for the village as a whole. *Sangam* members invariably deal directly with bank and government officials, only turning to CASA for advice and logistical support. CASA's emphasis on developing self-confidence and understanding of official procedures has ensured that *sangams* will continue to have ready access to institutional credit.

Secondly, and critically important, there is the close relationship which CASA has established with government officials and the banks. The goodwill of bank officials responsible for making decisions on loans was initially cultivated by close personal contact on the part of programme co-ordinators, who persuaded them to extend credit in small amounts for the purchase of income-generating assets under the IRDP. Regular repayment has ensured the continued availability of credit and improved the banks' lending record, although the government's decision in 1990 to waive outstanding loans to poor farmers resulted in the banks adopting a more cautious stance, which reduced the volume of credit available to CASA's clientele.

The third reason is the calibre of the programme staff. The field staff are mostly graduates from regional universities with a personal knowledge of the area. All exhibit a high level of motivation and satisfaction with their work, even though salaries are low compared with government jobs, which also offer greater security. Staff turnover is low, ensuring continuity in the organization.

Mention has already been made of the problems encountered in some of the remote coastal villages, which are largely due to factors beyond the control of CASA. A further set of limitations applies to the implications of maintaining a close relationship with government, which is necessary in order to ensure a continued flow of resources to eligible beneficiaries. On the one hand, CASA's desire to challenge injustice and exploitation may be toned down in order to avoid disrupting its relationship with officials. On the other hand, the support of individuals within the government can also provide CASA with a degree of protection where dominant groups attempt to undermine its work. On balance, the success of the programme justifies the approach adopted by CASA, which is shaped by the requirements of its constituents and by the local socio-political situation.

Secondly, there has been a growing tendency for the government to ask CASA to implement particular programmes with official funding. This stems from the reputation it has developed. CASA has agreed to implement several government programmes but has also turned down a number of requests, since it is well aware of the potential danger of becoming purely a sub-contractor for the government.

The approach taken by CASA in the Phase III programme is by no means unique in India, or for that matter in Andhra Pradesh. Many organizations have chosen to concentrate on mobilizing resources from state and central governments and banks in preference to relying on foreign funding agencies. CASA has simply proved more capable than many others of mobilizing a large volume of credit and subsidies which are then used in a highly effective manner.

THE KANYAKUMARI DISTRICT FISHERMEN SANGAMS FEDERATION

The Kanyakumari District Fishermen Sangams Federation (KDFSF) co-ordinates the activities of thirty village-level co-operative societies (*sangams*) working with traditional fishermen in the southernmost district of Tamil Nadu state. Their main purpose is to secure the best price for the fish catch and to provide collective marketing facilities, thereby eliminating the middlemen and raising the incomes of member fishermen. They also facilitate access to institutional credit for their members, as well as providing a forum for discussing the problems of fisherfolk and evolving collective solutions. At a wider level, KDFSF is concerned with the allocation and management of the fast depleting fish resources, and with identifying opportunities for alternative sources of employment. The Federation also provides training in the use of outboard motors, and campaigns on wider policy issues of concern to fishing communities.

The evaluation found that there has been a significant improvement in the economic and social conditions of the fishing communities as a result of the activities of the *sangams*. They have succeeded in obtaining better prices for their catch by controlling fish sales, which also ensures immediate payment. Improvements in boat design and a trend towards motorization of traditional craft have enabled some fishermen to go further afield in search of more productive fishing grounds. With the help of the *sangams*, the fishermen are in a better position to obtain credit from the banks for the purchase of craft and gear. There has also been a significant reduction in their indebtedness, with reduced dependence on traditional money-lenders and increased bargaining power.

At the same time, the *sangams* have failed to give adequate consideration to the problems of poor fishermen as a whole. In particular, they have not fully addressed the problems of casual labourers, who are excluded from membership of the *sangams*. Moreover, they have not tackled pressing social problems in the villages and have done little about the problem of seasonal migration.

Context, History, and Structure

Kanyakumari district is located at the southern tip of India in the state of Tamil Nadu. The 40 km. coastline extends from Kerala in the north to Kanyakumari town where the Arabian Sea and the Indian Ocean converge. Some 120,000 fisherfolk are spread among forty-four coastal villages, accounting for approximately 8 per cent of the total population in the district. Most of the fishermen are Roman Catholics from the backward caste community. Their religion distinguishes them from the predominantly Hindu local population, although there are also pockets of Muslims.

There are marked differences in fishing practices along the Kanyakumari coast in line with local variations in the continental shelf and in fish breeding patterns. To the north, the shelf is narrow and fishing is restricted to six months in the year; the fishermen from these villages migrate to Kerala in the off-season. Further south, the shelf widens out and rocky reefs provide good breeding grounds; at the same time, rougher sea conditions limit the use of outboard motors.

Most of the fishermen rely on traditional techniques using catamarans (constructed out of logs tied together with rope) and special nets and equipment, although there are variations in the combinations of gear used in the different villages, with corresponding variations in income. Fishermen owning catamarans employ casual labourers under different systems of remuneration based on a share of the catch proceeds. Annual production of fish in the district is approximately 50,000 tons, about 15 per cent of the total for Tamil Nadu, although there is evidence of a downward trend as a result of over-fishing. The fish caught include high-value export varieties (prawn, lobster, cuttlefish, and squid) and demersal fish used for local consumption. The peak months are June through to October, when most of the export species are landed.

Several different marketing systems conform to the demand for the various species. Export varieties are processed in factories in Kerala. High-value fish are transported to major urban markets in south India; this trade is dominated by a single large merchant in Kanyakumari district. Cheaper varieties of fresh fish (about 40 per cent of the catch) are sold in local markets in Kanyakumari and southern Kerala. Half the fish landed in Kanyakumari is dried and salted locally, mostly by the fishing families; this is sold directly to fish merchants and distributed in wholesale markets in Kerala and Tamil Nadu.

A large proportion of the district's fishermen are heavily indebted to money-lenders who are also fish merchants. Traditionally they took loans at high rates of interest (typically 36 per cent) and were obliged to sell their catch to the merchant or his appointed agent at low prices, plus a commission fee corresponding to 5–10 per cent of the value of the catch. These bonded fishermen inevitably found it difficult to repay the principal, let alone the interest payments on their loans, and consequently became indebted for life.

Alternative employment opportunities are limited, although some people travel to Nagercoil (the district capital) and other towns each day for work. Migration further afield during the lean season (October to March) is a widespread phenomenon; in some villages up to two-thirds of the fishermen migrate during the lean season, since there is no alternative occupation.

The first independent *sangam* was formed in Kanyakumari district in 1974 under the auspices of the Kottar Social Service Society (KSSS), the development arm of the Catholic Church, which has been active in the fishing communities since the late 1950s. Initially influenced by the Marianad co-operative experiment in Kerala, a group of young fishermen in Mel Manakudi village formed a group to sell their fish collectively and persuaded the local bank to lend them money to pay off their debts to the money-lenders. Other *sangams* followed their example and registered under the Societies Act to distinguish them from the government-sponsored co-operatives which were either defunct or dominated by wealthier fishermen. By 1981 there were nine *sangams* with 530 members.

The Kanyakumari District Fishermen's Sangams Federation (KDFSF) was formally established in 1983 to co-ordinate the activities of the individual *sangams* which continued to grow in number and membership, despite entrenched opposition from traders and middlemen who faced diminished profits and a loss of patronage. By 1990 there were thirty societies in twenty-six villages, with a total membership of 2,500 fishermen or approximately 12.5 per cent of the total number of traditional fishermen in the district. The central purpose of the KDFSF *sangams* is to liberate the traditional fishermen from the clutches of exploitative middlemen and to provide them with a collective identity. Membership is initially restricted to those fishermen who own craft and gear and who have independently repaid all their debts to the money-lenders.

The members' daily catch is sold at a beach auction organized by the *sangam* auctioneer, who receives a salary of a percentage of the daily catch. His receipt detailing the sale price can be immediately encashed at the society office by the fisherman or any member of his family. This system reduces the fisherman's effort and ensures a reasonable sale price and immediate payment. The *sangams* collectively market export varieties of high-value fish which are sold in bulk to the export agencies through competitive tender.

Each *sangam* employs a salesman (more than one in the larger *sangams*) and an accountant. The Community Development Officer (CDO) is the main link between the Federation and the *sangams*. Each CDO (eight in all) is in charge of four or five villages and plays a crucial role in the motivation and day-to-day administration of the *sangams*, monitoring the fish auction and the settling of accounts, arranging bank loans, supervising repayments and convening meetings of the *sangam* executive. They also mediate disagreements or problems within the *sangams*, or between individual *sangams* and the Federation. The CDOs are supervised by two senior field staff who are in turn responsible to a chief executive based in the main office. The activities of the Federation are governed by a board of trustees consisting of the presidents of each of the *sangams*, who elect a chairman and an Executive Committee responsible for determining policy and overseeing day-to-day affairs.

Other NGOs have also been active among the fishing communities in Kanyakumari district, in most cases in a single village and with a limited programme. The Community Health Development Programme has been implementing health, sanitation, and nutrition programmes as well as providing training, education, and self-employment programmes for women. Shantidan has been actively organizing women fish vendors and petty traders, thereby complementing the work of the *sangams*. Oxfam and Misereor have been the principal funders of KDFSF and village programmes and have contributed towards the salaries of the CDOs and the construction of community centres containing offices, a meetings hall, and fish storage facilities. The *sangams* are intended to be self-financing. A percentage deduction from the members' catch generally covers administrative costs, and some make significant profits.

Programme Assessment

Economic impact. The *sangams* have clearly achieved their economic objectives. Control over the marketing of the catch has increased the members' bargaining power, and payment is settled without delay. Members no longer pay commission fees to the merchant's agents and are not compelled to sell their fish at low prices to pay off their debts. Their increased incomes have enabled them to increase their savings, regularize their food intake, and invest in craft and gear; some have been able to purchase outboard motors and plywood canoes. However, economic disparities within the communities have increased as membership is denied to heavily indebted fishermen, labourers, and women fish vendors.

Factors such as the level of motorization, trawler activity, and fish stocks crucially influence income-earning capacity and condition the types of support provided by the KDFSF. Remittances from the considerable number of migrants to the Middle East were a significant factor influencing the lifestyle of the fisherfolk, by enabling families to purchase craft and gear and invest in housing construction, but aggregate statistics on the size of these remittances were not available; in any case, remittances virtually ceased in the wake of the Gulf War.

The most visible effect of *sangam* activities is in the increased price of fish, in some cases for non-members as well. There has also been a steady increase in the volume of fish caught by *sangam* members, reflecting the investment in better-quality equipment.

The income and expenditure pattern of a sample of four villages over the 1987–9 period indicates that the incomes of *sangam* members were higher than those of non-members by as much as a factor of fifteen, reflecting both the higher prices received by members and the fact that they generally own more craft and gear. Consequently the quality and quantity of food consumed by fishermen and their families have improved, but not dramatically since the basic diet (rice, tapioca, and fish) has remained

TABLE 8.1. *Changes in craft and gear ownership of* sangam *members,*
based on four sample villages

Name of village	No. of fishermen	Before joining sangams				Asset pattern (1990)			
		Numbers of				Numbers of			
		Cats[a]	OBMs[b]	Canoes	Nets	Cats	OBMs	Canoes	Nets
Vavathurai	7	12	0	0	16	13	1	0	24+2hl
Khizhmanakudi	8	14	0	0	19	16	0	0	31
Kadiyapatanam	7	9	0	0	2+1hl	8	2	0	3+1hl
Enayam	11	23	2	0	40	6	11	8	41

[a] Cats = catarmarans; traditional village-made fishing craft.
[b] OBMs = craft fitted with outboard motors.

substantially unchanged. *Sangam* members have also used increased incomes for purchasing household utensils and clothing.

There has been a significant improvement in the craft and gear ownership pattern of individual fishermen since the formation of the *sangams*, as shown in Table 8.1. In addition to increases in the quantity of fishing assets there have been qualitative changes in terms of the larger capacity of the recently introduced trammel nets and the replacement of cotton by nylon nets which are both lighter and less visible to fish.

Members are able to purchase fishing requisites (primarily nets and tackle) from the Federation's marketing centre at subsidized prices. Although they also buy from other sources, this facility helps to keep a check on prices and prevents artificial scarcities.

Higher incomes have also resulted in increased savings. The *sangams* have encouraged members to increase their personal savings through small revolving funds within the *sangams* and by opening bank deposit accounts against which they are able to borrow for other needs. In all the four sample villages, twenty out of thirty-two members interviewed reported savings in excess of Rs. 10,000; nine had savings in excess of Rs. 25,000. Some of them intended to use their savings for the purchase and maintenance of fishing equipment, others to repay old debts, or to cover marriage expenses of their daughters and for meeting special household needs.

Motorization has long been a contentious issue. An earlier attempt in the late 1960s met with failure as the engines were unsuitable and costly to maintain. The KDFSF has therefore resisted the spread of outboard motors (OBMs) because of their high running costs, unreliability, and risks of operation. They are also blamed for accelerating the depletion of fish stocks. But many fishermen are strongly in favour of OBMs, which enable them to travel greater distances to deeper fishing grounds and compete more effectively with trawlers; even so the catch is not always sufficient to meet running and maintenance costs. Government subsidies are available for those wishing to invest in the new technology. Fishermen claim that they have increased their individual catch as a result, but they are also aware that motorization may further deplete the inshore fish resources. In Vavathurai, for example, fishermen reported that the average daily prawn catch on catamarans using outboard motors was 100 kg., compared to a normal catch ranging from 16 to 30 kg. on unmechanized craft.

The KDFSF now accepts the trend towards motorization as inevitable, and has provided training in engine maintenance and repair. It hopes to encourage the use of indigenously produced diesel engines pioneered by the South Indian Federation of Fishermen Societies (an umbrella body) but has not been very successful to date, as the fishermen prefer to take their chance with the more expensive imported kerosene engines. The provision of OBM training has in turn encouraged the members to acquire engines and canoes, although the scarcity of credit is seen as a major hurdle in this regard. Despite the training, for which there continues to be strong demand, some of the fishermen interviewed displayed little understanding of the operational costs of OBMs.

Access to institutional credit has been a major difficulty for the traditional fishermen. Previously most of them were unable to obtain bank loans because they lacked collateral, and were forced to resort to money-lenders. The *sangams* have facilitated access to bank credit for the purpose of acquiring craft and gear. Of twenty-seven fishermen interviewed twenty-six had taken loans from the banks, seventeen of them through the IRDP. With the backing of the Federation, members are able to borrow up to Rs. 5,000 (at 4 per cent interest with a subsidy component) under the IRDP but this is not sufficient to enable them to purchase good equipment: a new catamaran costs Rs. 7–8,000, a kerosene engine Rs. 19,000, and individual nets can cost several thousand rupees. Some members therefore continue to rely on private money-lenders to top up credit from the banks, or for consumption purposes (notably dowries) which the banks will not fund.

The *sangams* attempt to restrict bank credit to purchase of craft and gear, but in practice some fishermen have put their loans to other consumption uses such as marriage expenses, repayment of old debts to money-lenders, house repairs, illness, etc. In some cases IRDP loans were used to repay old debts and to meet marriage expenses, thus illustrating the fungibility of bank credit and the ease with which it can be used for unproductive expenditure.

It was not possible to estimate the level of repayment for the *sangams* as a whole owing to lack of data. Repayment levels are fairly good where the *sangams* are closely involved in loan supervision; in such cases, a percentage (normally 5 per cent) share of the daily catch is usually deducted by the *sangam* for the repayment of bank loans. But there is uncertainty about the daily catch associated with increased competition, a declining resource base, seasonal fish movements, ill health, and other personal problems: repayments are especially poor during the lean season. The problem was exacerbated by the V. P. Singh government's announcement of plans to waive outstanding loans from the commercial banks, which generated a tendency to withhold repayment. Political interference by influential merchants who resent the *sangams* has also encouraged individuals to default on their loans. A further difficulty is that government co-operatives receive a large share of the available bank credit even though they are controlled by vested political interests. The lack of an alternative source of credit in addition to that available from the commercial banks remains a major hindrance to the development of the fishing communities.

Social impact. Like other *sangams*, the fishing co-operatives provide a common forum for their members, and there has been increasing emphasis in recent years on non-formal education by means of seminars on issues such as indebtedness, the local power structure, and the fishing economy. The balance of power within the fishing communities has clearly shifted in favour of the traditional fishermen with the formation of the *sangams*. Patron–client ties have weakened and the dominance of the merchant money-lenders has been undermined. The *sangams* now play a key role in resolving village disputes, as illustrated by a recent case of an engine being stolen from a fisherman: the *sangam* tracked down the thief and confiscated his craft and gear. Prior to the formation of the *sangam* there was no mechanism in place to deal with village disputes: the fishermen were divided between competing factions allied to individual merchants. The unity created by the *sangams* has quite clearly been advantageous from the point of view of the fishermen, who stress the importance of the social progress achieved.

The Federation makes representations to the government on behalf of the fishermen, for example in lobbying for subsidies on outboard motors and kerosene. It also co-ordinates campaigns, most notably to secure a government ban on in-shore trawling during the peak breeding months.

Nevertheless, there are many social problems within the fishing communities which have not been addressed by the *sangams*: for example, endemic alcohol consumption, women's status, shortages of drinking water, inadequate transport facilities, poor sanitation, and illiteracy. School drop-out rates are high in the sample villages. Although education has not featured strongly among members' concerns, they increasingly recognize the fact that education offers the possibility for their children to secure employment outside fishing, which many believe has limited prospects. Child labour is prevalent in all the villages, but again this issue has not been tackled by the *sangams*.

As noted earlier, migration during the lean season is commonplace, and has probably increased in recent years, mainly because of the unavailability of fish and the rough sea during this period. The *sangams* have not properly addressed this issue, although it is recognized to be a problem since family life and normal *sangam* activities are disrupted. During this period, receipts from the daily catch of fishermen who do not migrate are barely sufficient to cover the administrative costs of the *sangams*.

In general, the *sangams* do little about the needs of non-members (women fish vendors, labourers on catamarans and canoes, heavily indebted fishermen, and those without adequate gear or craft) and tend to concentrate on serving the needs of existing members rather than of the community as a whole. In some villages non-members were unable to explain the purpose of the *sangam*. Others view the *sangam* members as a separate category of rich people. For their part, some *sangams* are reluctant to admit new entrants because of potential management problems. In a number of cases this has led to the formation of new *sangams* within the same village.

Distribution of benefits. The KDFSF acknowledges that the economic activities of the *sangams* are primarily of benefit to asset-owning fishermen who are not necessarily among the poorest in the fishing communities. The evaluation found evidence to confirm this. Sangam membership is restricted to debt-free owners of craft and gear—about 10 per cent of the district's fishermen. The majority of members have managed to acquire new fishing assets and have the means to maintain their existing assets; in some cases, they own two or more catamarans with different combinations of gear. Motorization has given rise to further differentiation, which in turn has widened the gap between craft and gear owners and casual labourers with no assets.

While they recognize the latter's difficulties, *sangam* members refuse to incorporate them on the grounds that it would be more difficult to find crew if labourers acquired craft and gear of their own. Furthermore, members argue that those without at least one craft and set of gear do not deserve to be considered as active fishermen, and that their situation demonstrates a lack of initiative. A previous attempt to extend membership to labourers met with no success because of difficulties with loan repayments. Assetless fishermen are considered a liability for the *sangams* and are treated as potential competitors in the context of declining fish stocks.

Despite the restrictions on membership, non-members have been able to increase their bargaining power through the functioning of the *sangams*. They are becoming increasingly aware of their exploitation by middlemen and try to secure prices for their catch comparable with those received by *sangam* members. They are also able to buy good quality fishing gear (nets, tackle, etc.) at reasonable prices from the Federation's marketing outlet. Contact with *sangam* members helps them to learn how to use modern techniques to their best advantage.

Labourers also benefit to some degree. Higher prices have in turn increased the value of their share of the daily catch, and immediate payment has been especially beneficial in enabling them to raise the quantity of their food intake and regularize their consumption patterns. As a result, labourers generally prefer to work with *sangam* members. This has affected the ability of other non-member fishermen to attract good workers and has encouraged them to pay their share of the proceeds without much delay. The tied labour system is thus no longer so widespread and labourers have more choice over whom they work for.

In general, the status, needs, and problems of women seem to be unrelated to the existence of the *sangams*, although in some the fish vendors are able to purchase fish on credit and pay back what they owe from their earnings in the market later in the day. Vendors buy their fish direct from the fishermen, and do not appear to enjoy any particular preference in the local markets. They frequently encounter problems in transporting their fish to the market by bus (the conductors and other passengers try to prevent them loading their fish). Because of the lack of adequate storage facilities they often incur losses when there is an excess supply of fish.

Sustainability. Sustainability may be considered from several angles. First, as regards the capacity of the *sangam* to manage its activities without the support of the Federation, all the *sangams* are essentially self-financing. Some operate revolving credit funds for small-scale loans. The benefits realized (higher prices and bigger catches) generally exceed the administrative costs. However, smaller *sangams* find it difficult to cover staff costs and other day-to-day expenses, especially during the lean season. Some asserted their ability to function independently, but it is difficult to visualize their complete independence from the Federation, which continues to play a supportive role that is valued by the membership. Moreover, the amount of credit secured from the banks through the *sangams* is not sufficient for the members' needs and this limits the scope of the *sangams* and their capacity to increase the size of the membership.

A related issue is the fishermen's ability to subsist on income from their daily catch, which is subject to the vagaries of fish availability, sea conditions, and seasonal variations, as well as the quality of their craft and gear. Trends in fish stocks are the topic of heated debate and there is no conclusive evidence of a consistent decline. Nevertheless, it remains the case that, with the increasing numbers of active fishermen (as a result of population growth) and the trend towards motorization, competition is increasing, which may in turn result in overfishing. It is therefore difficult to predict the long-term prospects for traditional fishing in the district, but many fishermen are convinced that their offspring will have to find alternative sources of employment in the future.

Strengths, Weaknesses, and Lessons

The *sangams*, with the help of the KDFSF, provide a service that is unrivalled by other NGOs in the district. They have been instrumental in replicating their organizations so as to accommodate more members, despite restrictions on membership, as well as helping to set up *sangams* in neighbouring villages at their request. The Federation has responded positively to requests whenever it has found there is scope for a viable *sangam*. In their current form they offer a model which could be replicated in other parts of coastal Tamil Nadu. The KDFSF was identified by the FAO's Bay of Bengal Programme as the only NGO capable of providing competent support and technical assistance to traditional fishermen in the state.

The success of the programme is intrinsically related to the purpose and composition of the *sangams*. They have an organic link with the fishing communities, and their programme of activities reflects their needs and aspirations. The Federation differs from most NGOs in that it performs a supportive role primarily concerned with co-ordinating the activities of the *sangams* themselves, formulating policy, and providing a channel of communication with government and funders. Participation flows from effective representation and extends beyond programme implementation into the decision-making process. KDFSF staff work closely with the fishermen, and most are recruited from the fishing communities, which provides them with a real understanding of their problems. From this organic link stems a strong commitment to the aims and objectives of the organization, which provides the second major reason for its success.

There are a number of limitations to the *sangams* in their present form. They concentrate too narrowly on economic issues and fail to address pressing social problems in the fishing communities. There are no systematic attempts at awareness-building or discussions of social problems at the village level related to housing, health, and education. In general they are passive about the serious problem of seasonal out-migration. Moreover, they have ended up creating a new class of middle-income fishermen with access to bank credit which gives them the opportunity to acquire new craft, proper gear, and outboard motors, thereby further widening the gap with marginalized groups (a large proportion of the women, labourers, and indebted fishermen) who have only benefited to a limited degree from the formation of the *sangams*. A reluctance to give serious consideration to women's needs and to find ways of helping non-members is a further limitation, although they recognize the need to reassess the thrust of their activities.

The main limitation from the point of view of the members is that credit is insufficient to meet their requirements, with the result that they are still obliged to borrow from money-lenders or draw on their savings to meet their investment needs. Limitations on the availability of credit in turn act as a constraint on expanding the membership.

Overall, the project demonstrates convincingly the success of an approach which focuses narrowly on a particular sector, namely small-scale fishing, where the principal causes of poverty and exploitation have been clearly identified and appropriate programmes to respond to them have been introduced. Such a model highlights the importance of appropriate organizational structures designed to promote participation, and of interventions which draw upon existing skills and knowledge within a narrow field of economic activity. At the same time, the fact that benefits have primarily accrued to asset-owning fishermen points to the importance of anticipating from the outset the distributional consequences of such a narrowly focused intervention.

ARTHIK SAMATA MANDAL: AGRICULTURAL DEVELOPMENT PROGRAMMES

Based originally on Gandhian principles, Arthik Samata Mandal (Organization for Economic Equality) (ASM) began work in the Krishna delta region of Andhra Pradesh providing emergency assistance to the victims of the 1977 cyclone. It subsequently set up health, child-care, and educational programmes in about 100 villages. Agricultural development programmes were also introduced with the aim of improving the economic status of poor farmers. The evaluation was primarily concerned with assessing the impact of these programmes on the rural poor in the Srikakulam and Koduru divisions of Krishna district, most of whom are marginal farmers, lease-holders, and agricultural labourers.

Background and Project Description

At the time of the 1977 cyclone, the situation of the poor was especially dire. Most were landless labourers dependent on casual wage-labour at meagre rates of pay which were barely sufficient to meet their basic subsistence needs. Full-time work was available only for a few months in a year. Landless households often went without food during the lean season, or were forced to borrow money from landlords at high rates of interest, resulting in widespread indebtedness.

By way of an entry point, ASM set up crèches in a number of villages to assist working parents by providing child-care facilities during working hours, plus some elementary education and nutritious food for their children. It also promoted economic programmes involving simple investments with reasonable returns, and these were supported not only by ASM itself but also by small loans from banks and government subsidies. The overall aim was to create model villages by means of integrated socio-economic programmes comprising not only agriculture, irrigation, animal husbandry, and fisheries, but also education, woman and child welfare, and care of the elderly.

ASM operated largely through existing farmers' co-operatives originally set up by the government to facilitate the process of land redistribution, but it has also played a role in setting up *mahila mandalis* (women's associations) in a number of villages. While concentrating on the needs of marginal farmers, agricultural labourers, and the scheduled castes, who constitute approximately 50 per cent of the total population in the villages where it is working, the organization aims to involve the whole village community in its development activities.

The main emphasis of its economic programmes is on agricultural development, since agriculture is the main source of employment and income for the rural poor. A large proportion of the intended beneficiaries obtained small amounts of land (0.2–1 acre) in the redistribution programmes of the 1960s and 1970s. But such small amounts of land, with no irrigation, were insufficient to employ them full-time, and with no opportunity to procure fertilizer and other inputs, yields were poor and incomes had to be supplemented by casual wage-labour. ASM concentrated on three complementary programmes: land levelling, irrigation development, and the provision of crop loans. It also encouraged farming households to adopt new farming methods and to diversify into non-traditional crops like sericulture and prawn cultivation.

Tractors were provided to level the uneven terrain and enable farmers to plough deep enough to make the soil suitable for intensive crop cultivation. Using water from the canals and drains, a series of lift irrigation schemes and feeder channels were constructed in the Koduru villages to pump the water up to the fields. In Srikakulam division, where much of the land was on islands (*lankas*) in the Krishna river, the emphasis was on tube-wells powered by diesel engines. Schemes covering more than 1,000 acres were funded through a combination of grants from ASM's own sources and subsidies from the government, with labour provided by the beneficiaries. Responsibility for the maintenance of engines and pump-sets has gradually been transferred to the farmers' co-operatives in recent years.

The crop loans scheme began in 1981. On the basis of collateral deposited by Oxfam in the local banks, marginal farmers were encouraged to borrow small amounts each year to purchase crop inputs with the object of not only enhancing productivity and promoting food self-reliance but also reducing dependence on traditional money-lenders. ASM staff members liaise directly with the banks in securing the loans in order to eliminate interference from intermediaries and unnecessary expenditure, and explain banking procedures and the terms and conditions of the loans to the farmers. For the purposes of repayment, a group loan guarantee system was introduced; farmers are organized into groups of three and held jointly responsible for outstanding dues. In the event of any irregularity or default, ASM assistance is withheld until payment has been made.

An additional component of ASM economic programmes has been an initiative to promote off-farm employment by means of credit from the nationalized banks. Collateral of Rs. 100,000 deposited with the local banks has enabled people to take out subsidized loans under the IRDP for activities such as brick-making, dairying, poultry-raising, cycle repairs, and fish-vending. In some cases, this was complemented with skills training by ASM. Individuals in real need of assistance (through extreme poverty, physical disability, or death in the household) are given direct support from ASM's own funds.

A major thrust of the overall project has been on the provision of health, child-care, and educational services to the rural population,[7] not only through the crèches but also through preventive health programmes in the villages. In Srikakulam there is a twenty-bed hospital with a qualified doctor supported by thirteen staff members, which provides round-the-clock treatment to people from the surrounding villages; it treats an average of forty patients per day. Besides providing elementary education for pre-school-age children, ASM staff members also conduct non-formal and supplementary education classes for working children and adult education programmes. Each programme is administered by a co-ordinator assisted by field-workers and part-time volunteers based in the villages who form the point of contact with the co-operatives and women's groups, making a total staff complement of 120.

Impact of the Agricultural Programmes

Evidence from the field investigations indicated that crop loans, land levelling, and irrigation development have all made a major contribution to improving the economic status of poor farmers, primarily as a result of higher incomes from increased yields. Others have benefited from the incremental income generated from off-farm employment supported by subsidized bank credit under IRDP. In those villages where the focus was exclusively on irrigation, thirty-six out of forty-eight households interviewed said that their standard of living had improved as a result of the programmes; only five households reported no change.

In general, beneficiaries preferred to invest additional income in fixed assets like land, livestock, and housing improvements, or to use their savings for dowries, with comparatively marginal changes in lifestyle and living conditions. Several reported that they now spend more on clothing and education for their children. As with the other projects, food consumption has improved both in quality and quantity. Landless agricultural labourers have benefited from consumption loans to give them food security during the lean season when little work is available.

Other changes are reduced dependence on landlords for work and credit, a better understanding of financial matters, and the ability to plan for the future. All these point to increased self-reliance and greater economic security. All the farmers are interested in acquiring more land; they sometimes borrow from the landlords for this purpose in the expectation of being able to repay the loans from the extra income derived from crop cultivation.

In response to questions about the benefits brought about as a result of ASM's intervention, people referred primarily to the economic programmes, but child-care, supplementary education, and health-care were also seen as important. Irrigation was cited by fifteen respondents, crop loans by twelve, and access to credit or a new source of income (such as sericulture) by eleven.

Crop loans.   These are provided by the commercial banks to marginal farmers recommended by ASM for a period of nine months. Loans are disbursed when the paddy is transplanted in September and repaid after the second harvest in June, which in this area is usually of a cash-crop like black gram. Half the loan is paid direct to the suppliers of seed and fertilizer to ensure that the credit is used for cultivation purposes. Even so, some spend the money on consumption needs, paying off private debts and marriage expenses.

A 1988 evaluation of the scheme estimated that 2,882 loans were disbursed in the 1981–7 period, involving 535 farmers, many of whom borrowed from the banks on a recurrent annual basis. The cumulative amount borrowed was Rs. 5.5m., giving an average loan size of Rs. 1,900. Repayment rates averaged 79 per cent, considerably higher than the usual level, probably because of the close involvement of ASM staff in facilitating access to institutional credit.

The crop loans scheme has resulted in a number of tangible benefits for marginal farmers, the most important being to raise yields from 15–18 to over 25 bags per acre through the use of fertilizer and improved seeds purchased with credit. Secondly, leaseholders have gained access to bank credit which was previously denied to them because of a lack of collateral. Many increased the amount of land under lease, which has raised their income, although landlords have tended to increase their share of the crop as yields have risen. Average net income from leasing-in 1 acre of land is Rs. 1,500; on more than 2 acres, the return is greater than the potential annual income from casual wage-labour. Leaseholders also tend to supplement income from cultivation with casual wage-labour.

Thirdly, bank interest rates at 11 per cent are considerably lower than those charged by the money-lenders—36–50 per cent. A related benefit is that bank loans are timely. However, they are not always sufficient to cover all the costs of inputs with the result that some farmers have had to supplement bank credit with private loans or reduce the amount of fertilizer used, which could adversely affect yields.

While crop loans have clearly been of benefit to these farmers, they constitute a relatively small proportion of the total farming population in Koduru and Srikakulam divisions. And the number of borrowers declined from a peak of 511 in 1984 to 285 in 1987. Interviews with farmers suggest that this is a result of their reluctance to repay existing loans following the government's announcement of its plans to waive loans for small and marginal farmers.

Land reclamation and irrigation. Project data indicate that 1,394 farmers have benefited from lift irrigation and 1,121 from land reclamation. With these facilities farmers are able to grow two crops a year in paddy-growing areas, with a consequent increase in income. In the *lanka* lands which are unsuitable for paddy cultivation, irrigation has enabled cash crops such as vegetables, bananas, turmeric, and maize to be grown, as well as increasing production of pulses and other traditional crops. Even very small plots of land can produce a good income from high-value cash crops.

The perennial supply of water has allowed some farmers to go in for sericulture, whose potential returns far exceed those of other crops. The net income from each crop of 60 kg. of silk averages Rs. 2,600, and farmers have been able to produce four crops a year. A proportion of the net proceeds is used to repay loan capital of Rs. 9,500 from the bank (with the help of Rs. 3,000 of subsidy from the sericulture department of the state government). Sericulture provides regular employment for women who have received basic training in silkworm-rearing. It has also encouraged farmers to move their houses to the *lanka* lands in close proximity to their fields.

A number of farmers in the coastal belt switched from paddy to the more lucrative prawn cultivation once lift irrigation was installed, using the saline water in the creeks and drainage channels. The investment for this is high—Rs. 5,000 for excavating the tanks and a further Rs. 5,000 for feed and other inputs—and the risks are also higher. The potential income from two crops is Rs. 12–15,000 a year, enabling some farmers to purchase land and extend the area under cultivation. But abandoned tanks in one village where prawns had been cultivated since 1978 suggest that they do not always yield the expected dividends, and some farmers have sold their land and returned to casual wage-labour.

Self-employment programmes. ASM self-employment activities funded with credit from the banks under the IRDP include dairying, sheep-rearing, brick-making, fish-marketing, tea stalls, and cycle repair shops. A 1984 study found that 39 per cent of the 260 beneficiaries who had received loans in the previous three years had started new businesses which were generating good returns, while 37 per cent continued to rely on agriculture as their main source of employment, and supplemented their income with brick-making and fishing during the lean season. These activities are heavily concentrated in and around the ASM office in Srikakulam, and there has been no systematic attempt to encourage a more widespread take-up of credit for off-farm employment.

Factors external to the project have also contributed towards the improvements that have taken place. Most importantly, land redistribution in the 1960s and 1970s, though not substantially reducing the landholdings of the rural élite, since most of the redistributed land was owned by the government, laid the basis for a fundamental shift in the balance of power between rich and poor. Once the farmers gained access to credit and irrigation, they were able to make rapid progress and reduce their

dependence on the landlords. Another external influence has been a general improvement in the physical infrastructure of the region, with an expansion of the canal
network, rural roads, and the electricity grid. Power and a regular supply of water are
essential for the development of lift irrigation, and roads facilitate the movement of
crops to nearby market towns, which has in turn enabled farmers to expand their
range of crops. An expansion in the canal network has also led to an increase in the
amount of land under double-cropping and in opportunities for employment. It
remains the case, however, that the benefits of economic growth only percolate down
to the poor very slowly and that without a concerted effort on the part of ASM to
enhance the productivity of marginal farmers through investment in irrigation and
facilitating access to crop loans, the changes that have been observed would not have
taken place.

Distribution of benefits.   The main beneficiaries of the economic programmes are formerly landless marginal farmers (owning between 0.5 and 2 acres) and leaseholders.
Most are from the scheduled and backward caste communities, while the remainder
are economically backward even if further up the caste hierarchy. While a small
number of the households interviewed owned more than 5 acres, none could be
described as wealthy, and there was no evidence that larger farmers had managed to
capture programmes designed for the poor.[8]

Progress has been dramatic for households which gained access to land and subsequently to productivity-enhancing inputs through crop loans and irrigation. Among
leaseholders, the least well-off were those who leased only 1 or 2 acres, which would
generate comparatively little income. The number of landless labourers is very small,
but those who continue to rely on casual wage-labour as their primary source of
income have not experienced any significant improvements. Nevertheless, in line with
its objectives, ASM has been successful in directing benefits to the most disadvantaged sections of rural society.

Women have benefited indirectly from an increase in household income. In some
cases widows and women abandoned by their husbands have received training in skills
such as small business activities (tailoring, leaf-plate-making, book-binding) with the
aim of providing them with an independent source of income, although it was not
possible to evaluate their impact or list the number of women who subsequently
found employment.[9] Sericulture loans are taken in women's names since they assume
the prime responsibility for rearing the silkworms. This has enabled women to contribute directly to household income without having to go in for casual wage-labour
in the fields.

In line with its secular beliefs, ASM aims to dispel popular superstitions on myths,
caste practices, and women's place in society. While there was evidence that ASM
had successfully mobilized people against caste discrimination (through participation
in anti-caste rallies and attendance at inter-caste marriage ceremonies), these activities
tend to be periodic and do not form an intrinsic part of its development work.
Through its promotion of issue-based discussions in *mahila mandalis*, ASM has been
able to challenge some of the accepted norms regarding women's subordinate role in

rural society, although it is not clear whether this has been the case in all the associations.

Discussions with villagers suggested that the farmers' co-operatives and *mahila mandalis* play a fairly restricted role. They meet only periodically, usually at ASM instigation, to discuss development programmes. In the past the co-operatives brought farmers together for land distribution and provided voluntary labour for land-levelling, digging channels, and constructing pump-sheds. But their current role appears to be exclusively tailored to programme implementation, rather than as or-ganic village-level institutions integral to the lives of their members. The few excep-tions are co-operative societies headed by charismatic leaders with political influence who are able to motivate their members to work collectively or take joint decisions—especially noticeable in societies involved in developing *lanka* lands for scheduled caste farmers.

Understanding of banking procedures varied considerably between villages. Where ASM's involvement had been confined to providing irrigation facilities, the farmers generally displayed little knowledge about the range of government subsidies and grants, despite the project's apparent emphasis on resource mobilization. Even in those villages where farmers had been taking crop loans on a regular basis, they tended to depend on ASM staff to act as intermediaries. There was also a widespread tendency for people to rely on the personal intervention of the ASM Secretary in times of need, rather than on problem-solving within the community. This further undermines the capacity of the village-level organizations for independent action and it is evident that traditional concepts of patronage die hard.

Cost-effectiveness. Funding for most of the ASM programmes derives from Save the Children Fund UK. In the financial year 1989/90 a grant of £113,000 (Rs. 29,380,000) was provided to cover core programme costs mainly for health, education, child-care, and vocational training. Oxfam was instrumental in getting the crop loans programme off the ground after the 1977 cyclone and ActionAid provided support for the health and educational programmes in the early 1980s.

ASM has calculated that, over the period 1978–88, expenditure on development programmes (inclusive of administrative costs of 12 per cent) amounted to Rs. 92,820,000 spread over 100 villages. This gives an average expenditure per head of Rs. 460 (based on an estimated target population of 200 per village). Before 1985 income-generation schemes such as poultry-raising, dairying, fish-ponds, and kitchen gardens were supported by one-off grants. Thereafter ASM sought the help of the commercial banks in providing subsidized credit for this purpose. Lift-irrigation schemes are funded by special grants from Save the Children Fund and Norfolk Overseas Aid, while the crop loans programme draws on a revolving fund of Rs. 100,000 deposited as bank collateral by Oxfam.

Sustainability. While the economic programmes have had a positive impact on incomes and well-being, there are several question marks over their potential sustainabil-ity in the longer term. These relate to ASM's style of management and popular involvement in village-level organizations. Programme decisions tend to be imposed from above and the involvement of senior programme staff is relatively limited. While the Project Secretary's personal involvement in programme implementation provides villagers with a direct channel of communication and has enhanced effectiveness, it may undermine their longer-term capacity for independent action and initiative. This is compounded by the fact that the farmers' co-operatives play a relatively restricted role in educating and motivating their membership.

ASM monitors the programmes that it initiates closely to prevent procedural delays and other problems and to ensure financial accountability. Unless ASM staff keep in constant touch, the programmes tend not to yield the expected results, although some farmers have been taking up sericulture and other new agricultural activities without any material assistance from ASM. While villagers are capable of managing the programmes, they sometimes have difficulty in approaching banks and government institutions. Responsibility for implementation is only transferred to the co-operatives once the programmes are up and running—usually after three years. New methods of cultivation (such as sericulture) and the repair and maintenance of diesel engines require some technical knowledge; there is little training and a limited understanding of new techniques could clearly restrict the potential impact.

All the irrigation schemes are capable of being sustained over a long period because farmers value the benefits they have generated and have a close interest in ensuring that engines and pumps function efficiently. A recent decision to transfer responsibility for engine maintenance to individual farmers or groups of farmers is likely to induce a greater sense of ownership.

Crop loans and IRDP loans are difficult to sustain without consistent follow-up and continued subsidization. Many beneficiaries are unfamiliar with bank and government procedures, and there does not appear to have been much effort on the part of ASM to increase the number of farmers taking crop loans, or to offset the decline in the number of active borrowers following the breakdown of the group guarantee system. The government's policy of loan waivers and the consequent non-repayment of loans have greatly affected the continuity of programmes as the banks are reluctant to release fresh loans. Without a more active campaign to persuade farmers to repay, the future of the scheme must be in some doubt.

The Krishna delta region was struck by a major cyclone in May 1990 which destroyed crops, houses, and roads. Six months on much of the damage had been repaired, and cyclone relief grants from ASM and the government had enabled farmers to plant a fresh crop, overhaul engines, and purchase new materials, with comparatively minor losses. Regular programmes were disrupted as a result of post-cyclone relief work but there were signs of their being restarted as things returned to normal.

Potential for replication.   ASM has convincingly demonstrated that improved access to institutional credit and productivity-enhancing assets can significantly raise the incomes of marginal farmers. Crop loans provide an effective mechanism for marginal farmers to invest in productivity-enhancing inputs, providing that some form of collateral or guarantee mechanism can be put in place. At the same time, experience would suggest that the longer-term continuity of both the crop-loans scheme and lift irrigation would be better served by encouraging farmers to participate actively in all stages of the planning and management. Existing village organizations would appear to have a limited capacity in this regard, and this points to the need for reorientation and revitalization if they are to play a more active role.

In the larger irrigation and land reclamation schemes ASM has been successful in mobilizing government finance, bank loans, and farmers' contributions with relatively small inputs from external donors. Save the Children Fund has been involved in the planning and management of nearly all of them, and this points to the potential in scaling-up small interventions by collaborating closely with local government institutions. All recurring costs are met by the farmers and they seem to have little difficulty in covering these from their increased incomes.

Strengths, Weaknesses, and Lessons

Some 3,000 poor farming households have seen their incomes increase as a result of investing in inputs which enhance productivity on leased or redistributed land with the help of crop loans secured through ASM from commercial banks. Irrigation and land levelling have expanded the area under cultivation, and enabled farmers to grow a wider range of crops and to increase output. Self-employment programmes have provided an additional source of income for a small number of households.

While the agricultural programmes have generally been a success, there are limitations on their sustainability in the longer term. In this regard, the objectives of fostering self-reliance and independent initiative appear to have been only partially fulfilled. ASM's close supervision certainly contributed to the initial success of the economic programmes, but since few of the farmers' co-operatives have formed effective links with banks and government institutions their capacity for resource mobilization in the future may be constrained. Although the project has convincingly demonstrated that targeted inputs in the form of credit and subsidized investments can raise poor farmers' output and incomes, it also illustrates some of the limitations of relying on existing village associations as a point of contact for programme implementation without ensuring that they play an active role in promoting community participation.

The changes brought about in the lives of poor farmers in the Krishna delta illustrate the importance of targeted economic programmes which can effectively deliver benefits to the poor with a minimum of leakage to wealthier groups. A good working relationship has developed between ASM staff and farmers, and villagers have gained confidence in the positive intentions of the organization from its health and education programmes. A strong faith in the benevolence of ASM, and of the head of the organization in particular, as 'provider in times of need', has cemented this relationship.

ASM has also established good channels of communication with bank and government officials, and maintains cordial relations with local politicians. These links have undoubtedly contributed to the success of the crop loans scheme, and have encouraged banks to increase the volume of lending to marginal farmers and leaseholders who are generally excluded from institutional credit. IRDP loans have been procured through similar channels and have enabled ASM to secure a reasonable share of the government subsidies available to disadvantaged groups.

Strong leadership has given direction to the programmes, and shaped the philosophy of the project as a whole. However, a reliance on charismatic leadership with limited delegation has weakened the capacity of senior staff to play an effective role in project management and to provide accurate feedback. This is reflected in the poor quality of records maintained by the organization, and the lack of reliable data concerning the current scope and impact of the economic programmes. For example, there is no clear information on the number of people currently benefiting from the crop loans scheme, and cumulative lists of beneficiaries invariably exaggerate the programme impact. Monitoring takes the form of verbal reporting and observation, with only scanty written records. This in turn weakens programme performance and masks difficulties which have emerged in the course of implementation.

The rather poor prospects for the sustainability of the crop loans scheme give cause for concern. The hierarchical style of project management finds its reflection in the weak organizational basis of the farmers' co-operatives and *mahila mandalis*. While some groups display a genuine potential for independent decision-making and self-reliance, the majority possess little autonomy. In the short term this may not unduly affect performance, but it does lay the future course of activities open to question.

On the positive side, the project points to the effectiveness of targeted economic interventions under close supervision. It also highlights the centrality of land as a productive asset in strategies for poverty alleviation. This suggests that NGOs may need to pay greater attention to the land question and participate more effectively in public debate over land reform. In some cases they may need to encourage the landless to be more involved in activism, especially where land has been alienated or where there have been clear abuses of legislation on land ceilings.

ASM's attempts to work through existing village organizations without any consistent focus on group dynamics and capacity-building highlight the limitations of such organizations in managing collective assets and credit programmes or in effecting social change. This experience draws attention to the need to build social development objectives into economic programmes and the importance of organizational work and training in developing genuine community accountability.

CONCLUSIONS

The case-study evidence presented here indicates that NGOs play a catalytic role in terms of enabling poor communities to define their own development priorities, and are innovative in their willingness to experiment with new ideas, but that their activities remain supplementary to those of government, and in some cases duplicate existing services and programmes. Their record in alleviating poverty is uneven, although the evidence suggests that their performance is better than that of government. On the negative side, NGOs lack continuity, they often work in isolation from, and sometimes in opposition to, one another, which fragments their effort, and many depend heavily on external funding agencies. Managerial competence and technical expertise are often weak or poorly developed, which reduces their potential impact. Nevertheless, the evidence suggests that NGOs continue to make an important contribution to rural poverty alleviation in India.

An important caveat to bear in mind when attempting to assess the impact of NGO programmes is that many choose to work in remote areas, characterized by harsh environmental conditions and poor communications. They also encounter resistance from entrenched vested interests which fear a loss of influence and income as a result of the poor gaining greater independence. It is to their credit that NGOs are able to achieve anything at all under such circumstances, and instances of failure should ultimately be judged in this light.

Reaching the Poorest

All four case-study evaluations conclude that the projects have contributed towards an overall improvement in the economic status of the rural poor, expressed in terms of higher incomes and greater security of employment. However, the conditions of the very poorest have not changed dramatically, since they were invariably beyond the reach of economic programmes. Benefits from these programmes tended to correspond to the initial asset-holdings of different groups of the poor, reflecting the unequal structure of rural society, expressed in differential access to land, capital, and resources. The case-studies indicate that NGO programmes generally achieved higher levels of success with people owning some land and fixed assets and living in relatively developed areas with readily accessible markets. Yet although such people were not from among the very poorest, they could not be classed as well-off; even in the Indian context, they remained poor in that they generated little surplus beyond that necessary to cover their subsistence needs, and were for the most part among the bottom 40 per cent of the population in material terms.

Since they work within the existing structure of rural society, NGOs promoting economic programmes cannot hope to bring about a more equal distribution of wealth and assets although they can improve the situation of the poor in relation to wealthier groups, or prevent the gap growing wider. But, even if the returns to the poorest are low in comparison to the less poor, they can nevertheless be regarded as an achievement. And there were some exceptions. The landless did benefit when they received or invested in fixed assets, especially land. In the CASA Phase III programme, surplus government land was used for prawn cultivation, resulting in considerable increases in income for former casual labourers. Redistributed land formed the basis for targeted investments in small-scale irrigation by ASM, which raised crop production and in turn generated higher incomes and security of employment. The acquisition of income-generating assets (such as rickshaws, fishing craft, and dairy cattle) through improved access to subsidized credit was found to be effective in several of the projects.

The poorest also experienced marginal improvements through less direct means. For example, loans provided by RDT in Andhra Pradesh enabled the landless to purchase raw materials and food in bulk, resulting in small net savings. The poorest also benefited indirectly through increased opportunities for employment brought about by more intensive cropping patterns (as in RDT) or a higher share of increased production (for example, with the labourers on fishing craft belonging to *sangam* members in the KDFSF). Although the not-so-poor were the prime beneficiaries in the four projects examined, these examples illustrate that some benefits also accrued to the poorest.

NGOs recognize that women are among the poorest sections of rural society because of their domestic responsibilities in addition to searching for opportunities to increase household income. Several NGOs organized women into separate groups in recognition of the fact that their needs were different and that they were unable to air their problems freely in the presence of men. However, the case-studies showed that economic programmes tended not to cater explicitly for women, especially where they concentrated on enhancing the productivity of existing assets, and the incremental income was often marginal.

Types of Benefit

The case-studies have shown that the impact of projects also refers to broader criteria than the purely economic, such as improved health and nutrition standards, better education, and increased mobility. Monetary benefits derived from NGO interventions may sometimes appear marginal, but for the poorest the fact that they no longer have to endure periods without food or now consume better food can represent a critical improvement. A further set of criteria, less amenable to quantification but nevertheless an important social dimension of project impact, are captured in the notions of increased self-respect, improved quality of life, higher social status, and reduced dependence. For the poor, many of whom experience discrimination on the basis of caste, gender, and ethnicity (in the case of tribals), such qualitative improvements were found to be as important as material benefits. Some were a direct consequence of enhanced economic status (such as self-reliance associated with material security and an independent source of income), while others stemmed from group participation and collective decision-making.

In the Indian rural context, the emphasis placed by NGOs on functional literacy and group cohesion is designed to improve the independence of the poor from dominant social groups and to protect the material gains they have made as a result of NGO interventions. In several of the projects the collective solidarity of the poor proved important in enabling them to stake their claim over redistributed land and to demand minimum wages in line with government legislation and better working conditions. The NGO has to play a mediating role in order to minimize conflict and to ensure that project participants have the rights of redress through the legal system and protection on the part of law-enforcement agencies. Nevertheless, it generally proved easier for the NGOs to work effectively when dominant social groups were persuaded that an improvement in the material well-being of the poor would not threaten their own position, or when programmes were introduced for the benefit of the community as a whole.

Costs

NGOs pride themselves on a low-cost approach, but the case-studies have shown that, while their programmes may be cheap in cash terms, they are costly in relation to the number of people they benefit. By implication, the incremental cost of finer targeting may prove prohibitive in relation to the level of benefits, since larger numbers of staff will be required, although programme success is associated with an adequate level of resources, both human and financial. The administrative costs of revolving credit funds were especially high since they required close supervision and monitoring, as the RDT crop loans scheme illustrates. In contrast, the fishermen's co-operatives were largely self-financing, as they covered most of their costs from a fixed share of the catch. The approach favoured by CASA was one of the most cost-effective from the point of view of the NGO, since it used small amounts of money to lever a large volume of resources from government and the nationalized banks.

An additional consideration is that of the cost-effectiveness of NGO programmes. In the face of the paucity of data, it was difficult to come to firm estimates, for example, of the incremental benefit derived by farmers from institutional (NGO and bank) credit as opposed to non-institutional (from money-lenders) credit. While in all four projects there were identifiable benefits, it was not always apparent that these exceeded the costs incurred by the NGO in every case.

Reasons for Success

The case-studies demonstrated that the successful implementation of economic programmes was contingent on the active participation of the intended beneficiaries in shaping programme content and design. Effective participation, usually through the group approach, also provided a stronger basis for self-reliance in the longer term.

NGOs in India have concentrated their energies on creating village-level groups or associations. Group formation has become something of a creed for Indian NGOs, with the aim of promoting collective solidarity (especially since the poor are usually denied effective representation in existing village-level institutions) and to ensure that benefits arising from development interventions are targeted more effectively. In all four case-studies, NGOs favoured a group approach, centred on the formation of new village associations (*sangams*), although in one (ASM) the NGO chose to work with existing farmers' groups and village institutions. There were relatively few groups which included the wealthier villagers, although there were a number in which the poorest did not play an active role, which limited the potential benefits that could be gained by casual labourers and women.

Groups were found to have been successful in credit and marketing initiatives, by providing a structure for repayment and distribution. This was especially striking in the CASA Phase III programme. However, success was not purely contingent on group participation: in the RDT and ASM projects poor farmers benefited from economic programmes introduced with minimal participation. Although needs were correctly identified and a level of success was achieved, there were some doubts over their potential sustainability, since the beneficiaries continued to rely on the NGO to take decisions on resource allocation and programme administration.

A second determinant of programme success was the commitment of NGO project staff with low turnover and tenacity in the face of difficulties in the field. NGO staff have to work long and unsociable hours, the conditions of work are difficult, there is no security of employment, and the levels of pay, particularly for field staff, are generally low. Where staff had a close affinity with the beneficiary group because they came from the same area their level of commitment tended to be greater. Staff working for NGOs with religious underpinnings exhibited a strong moral commitment to their work. An incentive structure with the possibility of mobility and reward, backed up by good training, further reinforced this commitment. The most effective staff perceived their role as facilitators rather than providers, promoting participation and encouraging people to take decisions for themselves rather than treating them as passive recipients of benefits after the fashion of government programmes.

Thirdly, the quality of leadership also played a part. All the NGOs were headed by charismatic or capable leaders able to motivate their staff or manage the programmes effectively. Strong leadership was also associated, however, with a failure to delegate and a tendency towards top-down decision-making at the expense of both staff and beneficiary participation.

Rather more difficult to explain were situations where an identical programme was introduced in two similar communities but in one the activity failed to take off whereas in the other it became a profitable enterprise. It is unclear whether differential success can be explained by entrepreneurial flair, historical circumstances, or purely chance factors.

Such results raise important questions regarding the potential replication of successful programmes, even among relatively homogeneous communities in comparable agro-climatic areas. While participation, staff commitment, and effective leadership are all essential ingredients of project success, external factors also have a role to play. Some of these (such as the prevailing level of effective demand) can be anticipated and incorporated into programme design, but ultimately they are subject to a degree of uncertainty. Approaches found to be successful in one area cannot be adapted wholesale in another if the social and economic context and the organizational capacities of the NGO are very different. An important exception were the two CASA programmes operating in coastal Andhra, which have adopted similar approaches with a high degree of success, probably because they are both supported by a national

NGO which has the capacity for organizational learning and possesses the necessary technical expertise.

Agriculture, Credit, and Income-Generation

NGO interventions in this sector are designed to enhance the economic status of poor households by raising crop production through a range of activities, among them credit provision, technical advice on cropping patterns and inputs, small-scale irrigation, storage facilities, and marketing. The case-studies indicated that the NGOs registered considerable success, with increases in output, crop diversification, and an expansion in the cultivated area contributing to increased incomes. Nevertheless, it proved difficult to promote a sustained increase in output without a continued inflow of external resources, especially in semi-arid areas where recurrent drought is a major problem. The RDT case-study illustrates some of the difficulties of working in a drought-prone environment. It demonstrates how NGO credit enabled poor farmers to purchase fertilizers and other inputs which raised productivity and hence household income, although output was heavily contingent on climatic factors. Credit also encouraged poor farmers to take up cash-crop cultivation where the returns are higher, although the risks are also greater when farmers invest more heavily in inputs.

The four case-studies indicate that credit from NGO sources or loans from commercial banks facilitated by NGOs offer a number of specific advantages over non-institutional credit related to the terms and conditions attached to the loans, which were often as important as the impact of the credit itself. The most important of these were ease of access, timeliness, lower interest, and reduced dependence on money-lenders, all of which result in decreased transaction costs and improved self-reliance.

Three of the NGOs studied facilitate access to credit from the commercial banks by underwriting the loans, depositing collateral, or opening up channels of communication between bankers and poor borrowers. One of the most important features of this activity is to improve the access of the poor to rural banking institutions and to heighten their understanding of banking procedures. From the point of view of the banks, the involvement of the NGO improves repayment levels and enables them to meet government lending targets.

In terms of sustainability, institutional credit offers longer-term security over NGO credit, as banks are a permanent part of the local socio-economic infrastructure whereas NGOs are only a temporary presence and there is no guarantee of programme continuity following their withdrawal. However, default is treated less sympathetically, and access to credit is still determined in the final instance by the willingness of local bank officials to lend to the poor. A further problem with bank credit is that the availability of subsidized loans (under the terms of government programmes) is a function of government policy, and policy shifts can adversely affect poor borrowers. In addition, imprudent policies can affect the functioning of both bank and NGO credit, as the loan waiver announcement of the V. P. Singh Government starkly demonstrated. These reflections lead to the conclusion that NGOs play a significant but essentially supplementary role in credit delivery alongside the official banking system, but that their role in facilitating access to credit and educating their clientele about banking procedures is likely to remain important for the immediate future.

The main problem in coastal Andhra, as in many parts of India, is a shortage of land. For this reason, NGOs have sought to promote new sources of income for the landless and marginal farmers to supplement or replace income from wage-labour and agricultural production, through the provision of credit, subsidized inputs, and skills training. Increasingly, NGOs have been accessing government resources under the IRDP and facilitating bank loans on behalf of their constituents. Income-generation programmes promoted by NGOs broadly fall into three categories: enhancement of an existing activity (agriculture, fishing); creation of new sources of income and employment to replace an existing activity (rickshaw-pulling, provisions shops, petty trading, repair services, etc.); or creation of new sources of income and employment to supplement an existing activity (dairying, animal husbandry, food processing, social forestry, basket-making, weaving, etc.). Many NGO income-generation programmes have fallen short of their objectives, either because the level of income they produce is very low, or because the benefits of these activities cannot be sustained without external assistance. Evidence from the four evaluations points to some of the reasons for this differential performance.

An important conclusion is that new off-farm income-generation activities are more likely to succeed when project participants have been involved in the process of identification and selection. A greater sense of ownership and commitment comes as a consequence of groups discussing the merits and drawbacks of new activities, which in turn provides a necessary but not sufficient condition of programme success. This leads to the conclusion that when new activities are introduced by the NGO without proper consultation they are susceptible to failure, although benefits can result in the short term from top-down interventions.

A second finding is that sensitivity to market opportunities is integral to the success of income-generation programmes. Proximity to market towns, and the quality of local communications and local infrastructural facilities, are all crucial determinants of programme success. Obviously it proved more difficult for NGOs to create new sources of income and employment in villages where demand for services is low and transportation difficult, although there were exceptions to this, as in the case of prawn cultivation, promoted by CASA and ASM, where high prices and local conditions rendered it economically viable, despite the remote setting. Similarly, the general level of economic development is a further determinant of the potential for new sources of income and employment: the level of effective demand for goods and services in a less developed region is invariably lower than in more prosperous areas with a more intensive level of economic activity.

A third consideration is the level of technical expertise required for a new economic activity. From the perspective of the beneficiary, the ability to master a new skill is an important determinant of programme success. Where training is inadequate or the technology too complex, the risk of failure is greater. A related observation is that programmes which enhance an existing activity rather than introducing a completely new one stand a greater chance of success in terms of impact and sustainability.

Individuals vary in their capacity to take up and sustain new income-generation activities. As noted earlier, those already in possession of assets and capital had a far greater chance of successfully developing new business ventures than landless labourers who were forced to start from scratch and acquire new technical skills and capital. The capacity of the poor to adapt to new activities was found to depend not only on skills training but also on confidence building and functional literacy to enable them to compete effectively in the market-place.

The most elusive group in this respect are women from the poorest households for whom the prospects of developing new skills and sources of household income are restricted by their class and gender. Small-scale income-generation schemes for women generally focused on handicraft production and skills training. Women's income-generation programmes had in several cases been tagged on to projects with broader objectives and had accordingly suffered from poor planning and implementation. In several cases, small-scale enterprises for women had foundered on the lack of local demand for the goods they produced and problems of transportation when the markets were further afield. Women were often forced to compete with established businesses run by men who had ready access to marketing networks and the necessary technical expertise. The evaluations found that income realized on these activities was often quite marginal (and in some cases negative when the opportunity costs were taken into account) and at best provided supplementary income rather than secure sources of employment.

Only in programmes seeking to promote new sources of income and employment, or those where women had access to productive assets, were the concerns of women addressed more directly. In some cases these were confined to training initiatives, where women were provided with new skills but with uncertain employment prospects. In other programmes, the income-generating potential of new activities was limited, particularly where they provided a supplementary income, the classic examples being dairying and calf-rearing. The overriding impression is therefore that women's needs were not fully addressed by the NGOs, programmes designed for women formed a peripheral part of their overall concerns, and where they were included, they emphasized traditional types of work characterized by uncertainty and low remuneration.

A final point to note in this regard is that income-generation schemes by their very nature involve risk and experimentation, and a certain level of enterprise failure is to be expected. At the same time, this should not detract from the fact that the costs of failure are high, not only in terms of the material losses incurred by the poor, but also because they undermine the willingness of people to experiment with new activities. Unfortunately, the lessons of failed schemes are rarely absorbed by other NGOs, largely because the experience tends not to be recorded and shared. This points to the need for improved co-ordination and information sharing, and for assistance to help NGOs develop their technical and managerial capabilities, in order to maximize their impact and improve the quality of their interventions.

NOTES

1. This chapter is more narrowly concerned with those NGOs that are involved in development activities which aim to improve the social and economic status of the poor, either
through direct project interventions or by means of campaigning, training, research, and
documentation. NGOs provide support to the poor through grass-roots membership organizations such as village-level bodies, women's committees, co-operatives, slum-dwellers'
associations etc.). In India the terms NGO and voluntary agency are used interchangeably.
2. An enormous amount has been written on NGOs in India, but few studies examine their
impact in any detail. The bulk of the literature has been concerned with debates over
funding, partnership, classification, and relations with government.
3. The Federation of Voluntary Organizations for Rural Development in Karnataka (FEVORD-K)
and the Association of Voluntary Agencies (AVA) in Tamil Nadu are two examples of such
networks.
4. CAPART was created in September 1986 from the merger of two existing organizations,
PADI and CART, with the twin aims of promoting NGO involvement in rural development and promoting new technological innovations through NGOs.
5. Absent from the NGOs involved in the study are any social action groups, even though
several have explicit social development objectives. Such groups see themselves as distinct
from programme-oriented NGOs and consider their activities to be less amenable to impact
evaluation. Their exclusion is not intended to diminish the importance of their contribution,
which has certainly been influential in the Indian NGO movement and undoubtedly benefited a significant number of people (see Unia, 1991, for a discussion).
6. Subsidies are provided to the rural poor through the government's Integrated Rural Development Programme (IRDP). To be eligible for a subsidy, a family must be earning less than
the officially designated household poverty-line (Rs. 4,800 in 1990). Under recently introduced legislation, tribals and scheduled castes are entitled to a 50% subsidy on loans, and
all other 'weaker sections' (the landless or those owning less than 1 acre of land) to 30%.
7. The ODI evaluation was primarily concerned with the economic programmes supported by
ASM, and only addressed the health and educational programmes where these have directly
contributed to improvements in people's economic status.
8. The 1988 crop loans evaluation found that 27% of the households interviewed had annual
incomes below the official poverty threshold, and 47% were in the Rs. 6,400–10,000 range.
The 26% who were earning in excess of Rs. 10,000 per annum could be considered comfortably off: 85% were from the backward class community, compared with 11% from the
scheduled castes.
9. A 1988 ASM report indicated that of twenty women who had already completed training in
book-binding, sixteen had found employment in different printing presses; no details of
income were given.

9

Uganda

For years, voluntary agency intervention in Uganda has been dominated by relief work: in some parts of the country development work is still difficult, in others it has had to be abandoned or halted as new emergencies have arisen. But with emergencies becoming an almost permanent feature of many parts of Africa in the past decade, the selection of Uganda as one of the countries for a study of NGOs active in poverty-alleviation projects is of particular interest, as it shows some of the range of constraints under which NGOs struggling to promote development have to operate. It also discusses other issues of interest to NGO approaches. These include: experimentation with new approaches and techniques; the difficulty of reaching target-groups; and questions about the sustainability of NGO projects. In addition, the case-study highlights the impact of external factors (war conditions, a dilapidated infrastructure, and a retreating state) on a non-governmental movement witnessing rapid expansion.

Following a general overview of the role of NGOs in contemporary Uganda, the bulk of this chapter reports the results of four evaluations of projects undertaken in 1990. Each of the projects has a (funding) link with British NGOs, although only two projects have had a direct operational input from a British NGO. The projects were chosen in consultation with Ugandan NGOs, and were not selected at random. In defining a methodology to conduct the evaluations, care was taken to involve partners at the outset and to develop a research programme that would answer the NGOs' perceived needs, as well as to help answer the more general questions raised in this cross-country investigation of projects.

OVERVIEW

Any assessment of NGOs in Uganda has to be based on fragmentary data and anecdotal evidence. One of the many results of civil strife, war, and economic chaos in Uganda is the absence of reliable information on most aspects of social and economic life. The world of NGOs is no exception, and this clearly impairs any attempt to evaluate their general contribution to poverty alleviation in the country. Generalizations are also complicated by the diversity of NGO activity, and by problems of definition. Thus, in many regions of Uganda, there are numerous forms of voluntary and reciprocal exchanges within different localities: collective and co-operative labour practices not only continue to flourish, they also adapt to change. In addition, NGOs themselves have evaluated the impact of their activities in only a handful of instances.

This paper was substantially written by John De Coninck, based on his longer primary research report produced as a technical working paper of the Overseas Development Institute (De Coninck with Riddell, 1992).

The central role of the state in the evolution of Uganda's political economy, its traditionally authoritarian nature, and its specific desire to control development have had an important influence on the characteristics and development of the non-governmental movement. The early colonial period witnessed the establishment of some of the NGOs which are still very active in the country. As in the neighbouring countries, the churches assumed much of the responsibility for embryonic health and education services, well before the state moved into these areas; church-based NGOs continue to form an important section of the non-governmental movement in the country. The colonial government's attitude to these NGOs was ambivalent: on the one hand, missions relieved it of some of its responsibility for health and education, particularly in the rural areas and, through a network of prestigious secondary schools, inculcated appropriate attitudes in the indigenous élite. On the other hand, the diffusion of some of these services fostered the emergence of nationalist movements, which, in turn, spawned new types of non-governmental voluntary associations with a clear political agenda—the urban associations, trade unions, and co-operatives which spearheaded political opposition to colonialism.

In the 1960s the relative prosperity of newly independent Uganda favoured a rapid development of NGOs: church-based organizations found their work increasingly aided not only by the funds available to their parent congregations in Europe or the United States, but also by a new breed of NGOs which developed funding relationships with them. Thus, the early activities of Oxfam and CAFOD, for instance, were almost exclusively linked with various churches, whose expatriate priests and administrators seemed to provide foreign non-governmental funders with a measure of accountability and social familiarity. Simultaneously, however, increased public revenues allowed the state to extend its role in the provision of services. To some extent, the role of NGOs was therefore circumscribed (government now took direct control of church schools) and mostly confined to traditional fields: welfare, charitable work, and the provision of health facilities. Even if, during Uganda's golden era, the state had little choice but to leave the extension of these services to NGOs, including the churches, especially in the more remote rural areas, the assumption was always that NGO involvement would be transitional, pending state takeover once resources allowed.

The advent of the Amin regime in 1971 signalled the gradual isolation of Uganda from the international NGO movement at a time when the basis for its spectacular worldwide growth of the 1980s was being laid. As economic collapse was accompanied by gross abuse of human rights, most foreign NGOs withdrew support or kept well away. Meanwhile, and contrary to developments in a number of neighbouring countries, the new regime could not allow an indigenous NGO movement to evolve. Largely by default, therefore, the churches continued to play a prominent role in the non-governmental movement in Uganda, reinforced by the recourse of non-confessional NGOs to church structures, then considered the only means to reach the general population.

The 1979 Liberation War and the fall of Idi Amin heralded a period of intense interest in Uganda on the part of the international community: offers of help poured in and international NGOs were not to be left behind. During 1979 and 1980, for example, a number of British-registered NGOs (ACORD, Oxfam, ActionAid, Save the Children Fund) swiftly established or re-established a physical presence in the country. The rapid changes of regimes during that time, and the widespread feeling that Milton Obote's return to power had been fraudulently engineered, appear to have done little to undermine international NGO interest. By 1980 more than fifty foreign NGOs were active in the context of the Karamoja Emergency, later followed by similar operations in the West Nile region and in the infamous Luwero Triangle.

As the political, economic, and security situation deteriorated further in the early 1980s, NGOs, together with the churches, again assumed a substitutive role for state services. A missionary hospital, for instance, had by now become the main national referral and training facility in the country—in spite of its isolation in the north of the country—and the churches increasingly focused on the upkeep of the local infrastructure, such as health centres and even main roads. These years proved to be trying times for NGOs: the practical difficulties of work in a country riven by political instability and with an infrastructure close to collapse were enormous and costly. Political and security considerations also hampered, or even profoundly altered, the nature of programmes—as the ACORD and ActionAid case-studies described here demonstrate.

The advent of the National Resistance Movement (NRM) government in 1986, and the return to a degree of political stability in most of the country, constitute the current phase of NGO activity. Besides the more obvious division into local and expatriate NGOs, and setting aside their sectoral interests, NGOs active in Uganda today could be grouped as follows:

- Localized indigenous organizations include the large number of self-help voluntary associations known to exist and small, usually unregistered, groups working in one or two villages. The wide range of activities in which they are involved include communal agricultural work, the protection of a spring, or forming parent–teacher associations. These organizations are usually not dependent on external funding.
- Larger local agencies normally have their own staff: they often work at regional or even national levels and sometimes receive funds from external sources. Some may be involved in their own project work or, in a few cases, be service agencies. They often attempt to promote grass-roots groups (as service organizations), although some have developed their own operational programmes. A number have the capacity to work in emergency situations (church organizations, Uganda Red Cross).
- Non-operational expatriate agencies have usually established a funding link with local NGOs, but generally do not maintain a representation in the country.
- Operational expatriate agencies maintain an office with their own staff in the country. Though they may fund local structures as well, they generally implement their own programmes, which may be of a short-term, rehabilitative, or disaster relief nature, as well as long-term development work. Their budgets tend to be the largest within the NGO sector, apart from a handful of agencies funding the churches, and they often have strong links with official donors.

No accurate estimate exists of the number of NGOs active in Uganda, although several hundred have applied to the government for registration. Estimates of income at their disposal are, not surprisingly, even more uncertain. Ministry of Planning figures indicate disbursements of approximately $9.5m. in 1987/8, and slightly less the following year, but these are considerable underestimates. Indeed, the cumulative disbursements in Uganda of British NGOs in the last few years exceed this sum, and some individual programmes involve considerable expenditure. In 1988/9 and 1989/90, Oxfam alone spent £3.8m.; and SCF spent £1.6m. in 1989/90. ACORD's Uganda budget in 1991 was approximately £750,000. In 1990 the Overseas Development Administration's support to UK NGOs' work in Uganda alone amounted to approximately £3m. The European Community's contribution to NGOs (working in Uganda excluding relief programmes) was ECU 2.7m. in 1989.

Relations with the Government

Since their return, or establishment, *en masse* in 1979, expatriate NGOs have benefited from almost complete freedom of action, so long as the perceived basic interests of the state are not threatened. NGO criticism of successive regimes has generally been muted, especially since government rhetoric has consistently been pro-development and has stressed the needs of the common man. What is more, the recent thrust towards liberalization and privatization of the economy has helped to bolster the role of NGOs in national development, with foreign NGOs benefiting from large-scale support from bilateral and multilateral agencies. The only challenge has come when, in one or two instances, NGOs have confronted the political authorities directly. The response has then been swift: the Obote 2 Government, for instance, forced NGO representatives to disprove reports of atrocities in Luwero.

One consequence of this *laissez-faire* attitude has been far less NGO impact on public policy and policy debates (with the possible exception of health-care) than growth in numbers might suggest. For its part, the government has provided little guidance, assistance, or encouragement to NGOs. However, this freedom of action has now been questioned by the NRM Government for two main reasons. First, the rapid growth of NGOs has led the authorities to demand a measure of control (from an administrative and security perspective, rather than a developmental one). Secondly, the new administrative and political initiatives (see below) are intended to reach down to the local level where NGOs are predominantly working. One result was the 1989 NGO Registration Act, which created a Registration Board under the authority of the Minister of Internal Affairs to register NGOs and monitor their work (mainly by attempting to control their access to the local population). To date, however, the NGO movement in Uganda does not represent a challenge to the political authorities and the main local NGOs remain urban-based Western-type agencies. Government attempts at control are also severely hampered by limited administrative capacity.

The NRM Government has introduced an entirely new pyramidal structure of

Resistance Councils and Committees from village level to the National Assembly.[1] The RC system has increasingly been seen by development agencies—and particularly by NGOs—as an ideal (and often indispensable) vehicle for development work at the local level: Resistance Committees (RCs) can, in other words, articulate local interests and needs, allocate resources equitably, and be held accountable by constituents. A major problem remains, however, in that the new structures have been established without the necessary resources to discharge most of their functions: RCs do not generally have access to technical expertise, do not generate their own finances (except through fines and other *ad hoc* levies), are open to corruption (especially so long as most RC officials are not overtly remunerated), and generally lack experience. Of the four projects described in this chapter, three programmes depend, to a greater or lesser extent, on active support from the RCs.

Co-ordination between government and NGOs at other levels is, however, limited. Ministries tend to compete among themselves for NGO resources and NGOs often complain about not being consulted or informed when decisions affecting their work are taken by government. A range of co-ordination fora has, however, been established. First, there are a series of monthly meetings for both local and foreign NGOs convened by the Aid Co-ordination Secretariat in the Prime Minister's Office. Issues discussed are normally of a practical nature, such as operational difficulties in areas affected by insecurity, duty-free restrictions imposed on NGOs by the Ministry of Finance, and immigration and exchange-control regulations. Secondly, there is the National Council for Voluntary Social Services (NCVSS). Within the NGO community the Council is considered to be of limited effectiveness, as a result of lack of resources and administrative constraints, and is viewed by some NGOs as promoting an outmoded social welfare thrust to development.

NGOs themselves have also attempted to share common problems and sometimes co-ordinate activities through DENIVA (the Development Network of Indigenous Voluntary Associations), which defines itself as 'the consortium of all local NGOs and grassroots community groups actively engaged in development-oriented programmes in Uganda'. Emergency operations in a particular region and specific sectoral interventions have strengthened co-ordination efforts; of these, perhaps the most promising has been the Uganda Community Based Health Care Association (UCBHCA), set up in 1986 to co-ordinate community-based health-care work throughout the country at the instigation of NGOs active in this field.

In many instances, co-operation between NGOs and government mirrors an unequal relationship between a state whose administrative capacity is so limited and its level of organization and co-ordination (between the various ministries with which NGOs communicate, for instance) so reduced that NGOs can, if they wish, take advantage of their position. Yet lack of co-ordination reduces NGO effectiveness: their initiatives are often poorly integrated with those of the government, information does not always circulate, experiences are not discussed, and efforts are sometimes duplicated. It is therefore not surprising that reservations have been expressed (by government as well as by some NGOs) about the emergence of parallel structures. Emergency programming has provided perhaps the most extreme examples of NGOs constituting a state within a state; this was especially visible during the Karamoja relief operations in the early 1980s.

Related to this issue, and reflecting the practice of official aid agencies, a number of NGOs pay or supplement the totally inadequate salaries of government personnel involved in their programmes. Similarly, NGOs have attracted civil servants into their employment. Working for an NGO often provides sufficient income to meet all immediate family needs (this is rarely the case in government service and in much of the private sector), provides some social prestige, and consequently has become a sought-after form of employment. Thus, as government resources dwindle, NGO programmes become more all-encompassing and acquire a higher profile, in part by default. In performing these ever-expanding functions, however, most NGOs espouse the principle that the poor have to be brought into the existing development process.

Viewed within the perspective of privatization, NGOs are frequently perceived by bilateral and multilateral donors in Uganda as more efficient and more reliable than government agencies, at the very least complementing at grass-roots level whatever can be achieved through official development assistance by the government. In addition, in the early 1980s and at times of political upheaval, funding NGOs provided some donors with a political insurance policy, providing assistance without giving political legitimacy to the regime.

Thus, most bilateral donors, including Britain, channel some of their resources through NGOs,[2] and the European Community has fully funded a number of European NGOs' activities in the country. To date, the most formalized collaborative venture between official donors and NGOs is the PAPSCA initiative,[3] while NGOs have been given an important role in World Bank-funded proposals to reconstruct northern and north-eastern Uganda. The attitude of official donors to local groups has been much more circumspect. There are, as yet, few direct contacts (especially with grass-roots organizations) and the intermediary role of a foreign NGO is still usually seen as indispensable to ensure adequate management and accountability.

The Rise of Local NGOs

The recent expansion of the local NGO sector has stemmed in large part from a greater degree of political freedom in the country. Other influences have been the experiences of Ugandan returnees with NGOs (and other donors) outside the country, and the increasing desire, on the part of foreign NGOs, to find local like-minded partners to whom funding and training can be extended. The state has also sponsored an emerging network of often constituency-based Development Associations, which are frequently led by local political figures. These factors go some way to explaining the emergence of local, often urban-based, agencies (quite distinct from localized voluntary associations, now increasingly acquiring a formal status) whose institutional and operational models have been inspired by Western NGOs and which often depend on one or two highly trained members of the élite.

This growth has, however, been met with a degree of scepticism among Ugandans: in the get-rich-quick culture that has developed since the advent of Idi Amin, altruism has, at times, become suspect, especially in the eyes of the urban population. A few cases of financial improprieties among local NGOs (and the churches) have done little to remove the suspicion that some local NGOs are mere fronts for other types of activities. Similarly, the sometimes flamboyant lifestyle of NGO expatriate personnel, living in the smartest neighbourhoods and driving ostentatious four-wheel-drive vehicles, has led to a questioning of the primary motive for establishing an NGO. In official circles, too, local NGOs are sometimes perceived as competitors with government for scarce resources and patronage, as superfluous to the RCs, or as agencies whose close links with foreign NGOs can undermine national integrity (especially when the origin of their funds is unclear).

Most local NGOs remain primarily project-oriented and involved in welfare-type activities. Increasingly, however, other types of agencies are emerging: on the one hand constituency-level associations; on the other, development agencies (some with a service capacity providing training for local NGOs). A few local NGOs have established their institutional credibility and have attracted interest on the part of official as well as non-governmental agencies.

The relationship between local and foreign NGOs is not without its difficulties: indigenous NGOs resent what they see as the hegemony of international NGOs (made all the more powerful by their access to official donors) in spite of their rhetoric of partnership, their differing reporting and other requirements (forcing local NGOs to be more accountable towards donors than to their target-groups), and their emphasis on project-related activities rather than on institution-building. Foreign NGOs, on the other hand, complain of the poor administrative capacity and lack of institutional maturity of local NGOs and of cases where local NGOs are disguised fronts for private business ventures.

The explosion of Western-type NGOs appears to have been matched by a rapid increase in the numbers of grass-roots groups, although such growth is impossible to quantify. Their isolation, their limited resources, their inability to use the most fashionable development jargon, and an institutional profile quite unlike that of well-established NGOs, all limit their access to external support. In comparison with other African countries, the local NGO movement generally remains small and highly dependent on foreign funding.

The Particular Place of the Churches

The churches continue to play a prominent role within the NGO movement in Uganda. While in large measure this involvement is historical, it also reflects the churches' access to financial resources, their political leverage, and, increasingly, the breadth of their programmes. Both Catholic and Protestant Churches maintain a centralized facility to plan activities and liaise with donors. Most local dioceses, however, have developed their own activities and established direct links with funders—often under the personal leadership of a bishop. This decentralized approach (much favoured by foreign donors who often spurn the central co-ordination offices) goes some way towards explaining the diversity of approach and the range of activities promoted. Thus, some large Catholic missions—often staffed by expatriate personnel —retain a reputation for their paternalistic and evangelizing stance and for their isolated and insular approach to development. Increasingly, however, church-linked activities are attempting to move away from project-oriented activities with a narrow geographical and technical focus towards programmes with an innovative content and a participative methodology.

The churches' involvement in health delivery is especially significant: their pioneering work in relation to the AIDS epidemic, in particular, has received much support inside and outside Uganda, as have their activities in the general field of primary health care. Churches, however, collaborate little with each other, with the important exception of co-ordinating medical supplies, and, equally, little with non-church-linked NGOs (or indeed the government).

Sectoral Interests and Target-Groups

Issues of power and control have been less prominent in the agendas of NGOs than their attempts to address the symptoms of poverty. While areas of activity have tended to follow development fashions, they encompass a wide range of relief, welfare, rehabilitation, and development work. Programmes with a sectoral focus (especially in water, health, agriculture, and education) coexist with multi-sectoral programmes of the type illustrated by two of the case-studies. NGOs have recently placed more emphasis on income-generating activities (including credit) and research (into landlessness, AIDS, and the financing of primary health care), with women's activities now attracting attention (women's groups, women's legal education, and networking). NGOs have tended to move away from programmes geared to the provision of inputs and increasingly to engage in programmes stressing community participation and the training of agents of change.

Many NGOs tend to assume a commonality of interests within their target population and often fail to look for signs of social differentiation. Where NGO targeting occurs, it tends to focus on clearly identifiable groups facing exceptional difficulties. These would include war and AIDS orphans, displaced persons and refugees, and the disabled (including an estimated 450,000 children nationwide). In selecting target-groups, a number of NGOs have also attempted to concentrate their activities in the more remote areas, reflecting the country's deep regional differences—and especially the North–South divide.

Although they have been active in a wide variety of domains, NGO efforts have been most prominent in the two areas of health services delivery and disaster relief, and this has largely informed the perception of them among the general public. In some instances, attempts have been made to link relief efforts with food-for-work and other rehabilitation schemes, followed by development activities, particularly where the necessarily short-term (and often dependency-creating) impact of relief has become evident. NGOs have proved themselves able to react swiftly and to raise substantial resources in such circumstances, but their record has not always been an unequivocal one, as has been particularly illustrated by the 1979–82 Karamoja famine. Intra-agency competition, a limited understanding of local conditions, and the insistence on employing inexperienced expatriate personnel, disregard for local authorities and local expertise, the adoption of an authoritarian approach, a willingness to act unreservedly as UN subcontractors, a general lack of self-criticism, and logistical incompetence all contributed to severe shortcomings in an operation which, furthermore, fostered the worst forms of dependency. The arrival of the NRM has not signalled the end of NGO involvement in emergency situations: since 1986 NGOs have participated in disaster relief (for both Ugandans and refugees) in northern and eastern Uganda, in western Uganda, and again in Karamoja in the late 1980s and, more recently, for Rwandese refugees in the south-west of the country.

THE UGANDA WOMEN'S FINANCE AND CREDIT TRUST[4]

This study is the result of fieldwork conducted over a five-week period in April and May 1990. Altogether forty-seven clients (including twelve groups) and three prospective clients were interviewed on the basis of a wide-ranging questionnaire whose content reflected the lack of any previous evaluation and was jointly devised by UWFCT and ODI. To complement these interviews, discussions were held with most Trust employees, and the relevant UWFCT programme officer accompanied most field visits. The main research findings were presented at a one-day workshop held with Trust staff in June 1990.

Origins, Structure, and Character

The Uganda Women's Finance and Credit Trust (UWFCT) grew out of an initiative on the part of professional Ugandan women concerned with the plight of poor women with no access to formal financial institutions. It was founded in 1984 as an affiliate of Women's World Banking (WWB)—the organization created in the wake of the 1975 Mexico conference to promote women's access to credit and banking—and started work in earnest in mid-1987. Its activities centre on the provision of credit facilities to women or women's groups wishing to initiate or expand micro-businesses. It also provides business management training, and a range of technical and other extension services to its clients.

The Trust's early aspiration was to launch a loan guarantee fund. However, funding constraints and the high rate of inflation combined to prevent this. Gradually, the Trust altered its approach by placing lending to women at the centre of its activities. The Trust received its first injections of funds from the Dutch agency NOVIB in 1987 and 1988. Other donors have included Christian Aid, the European Community, the Swedish development agency (SIDA), Experiment in International Living (EIL), the United States Government, and a few local industrialists.

Its immediate objectives are listed as the following (Status Report, 1988/9: 2):

(a) To cater for the financial interest of women in the middle and low income sectors of the economy, whose interests are not catered for by existing financial institutions in the country.

(b) To help these women expand their micro-businesses as a means of employment for themselves and others by giving them loans and other accompanying services using simple unbureaucratic and yet effective procedures.

(c) To provide technical assistance for those involved and encourage the upgrading of traditional technologies, applications of appropriate technology and better management techniques.

(d) To encourage better management skills, leadership, and legal awareness among women, using both formal and informal but intensive personal training.

(e) To encourage saving, communal co-operation, and other good banking practices among women entrepreneurs.

The Trust's target-group was later defined as poor women who have not gained access to formal financial institutions. A condition for Trust support is that funded projects be at the very least mainly owned and operated by women. Thus by mid-1990 120 projects run by individual women or women's groups had been granted loans, directly affecting 400 women and their families. Over 300 additional projects had been identified for support. The Trust had also run seminars and workshops, and staff members had given lectures in many parts of the country. Provisional accounts for the 12 months ending June 1990 indicated that USh.27m. had been lent; income stood at USh.64.9m. (of which USh.55.8m. came from grants or donations, mostly from abroad).[5]

By 1990 the Trust was concentrating its activities in the central region in and around Kampala, two areas in the East (Mbale and Kamuli), and Masaka in the West. It employed eleven staff, mostly project officers with combined geographical and sectoral responsibilities. In addition, part-time co-ordinators worked in two of the areas.

Loans are at the core of the Trust's activities. They are made available to women (individuals and groups) in both urban and rural areas who have no access to institutional finance. No collateral is required, but two individuals have to volunteer as guarantors, and 10 per cent of the money loaned is usually required as a deposit from potential creditors. A wide variety of income-generating activities are considered appropriate for lending, in the fields of agriculture, crafts, and small-scale industrial activities such as baking, carpentry and tailoring, or service activities (commerce, nursery schools).

Loan applicants are required to invest in the Trust's savings scheme for at least three months before their application is considered. Basic management training is required and the project officer makes monthly visits to the beneficiary after the loan is made. Loans are disbursed in tranches, each instalment being approved once previous funds are checked as having been spent in accordance with the project proposal. In mid-1990 interest rates charged on borrowing stood at 30 per cent per annum, until recently well below the rate of inflation.

The repayment record has been consistently good. On the first twenty-three loans financed by NOVIB, for example, the repayment record as of mid-1989 was as follows: fifteen on schedule or fully repaid; four rescheduled; two written off (including one where a dairy cow died), and two non-applicable (still in the normal grace period). Technically, only one other client, out of the 121 total, had defaulted by mid-1990, although there were thirty-odd clients in arrears but still repaying their loans (this was in part due to the Trust's limited administrative capacity to undertake the necessary follow-up).

Complementing the loans is the Trust's emphasis on business training. Specific training is extended to group leaders, while one-day awareness seminars have also been run, focusing on banking and credit and involving both beneficiaries and other NGOs and institutions in related fields. UWFCT has recently devised its own curriculum for its prospective clients. The Trust started its own savings scheme in February 1988. By mid-1989 more than 1,500 women had joined, although about 600 accounts were dormant, possibly because the holders had saved in the expectation of near-instant credit.

The government has expressed support for the Trust's activities which are viewed as supplementing government efforts aimed at increasing rural productivity and self-sustaining development through the use of locally available resources. The only concrete and tangible government support, however, has been specific tax-free privileges for its two vehicles, valued at approximately USh.4m.

The Trust expects its activities to have a long-term impact through (UWFCT files):

the increased direct participation of women in the economic life of the country; lending institutions being more amenable to financing women's micro-projects; greater acceptance of women in the country's business communities; development of a network of professional women; and transformation of the UWFCT into a viable credit and savings institution and, subsequently, into a fully-fledged bank.

Future plans include a limited extension of the lending programme and the coverage, by initiating lending activities in more areas of the country.

UWFCT expects to become financially self-sufficient (through interest earnings from the Loans Fund) by 1998. In the mean time, budgets for the three years to 1993 anticipated expenditure of $415,000–$435,000 per annum, mostly to be covered by external grants. The Trust also intends to revive its loan guarantee scheme with UWFCT and WWB acting as part-guarantors (75 per cent) for loans granted by commercial banks to women wishing to initiate or develop income-generating activities.

Assessment of Current Activities

At the project level, the Trust has succeeded in making a range of unique services available to disadvantaged women. It has launched a bank, with which depositors identify closely, and has extended credit to women who had no access to formal financial institutions. Some savings have been mobilized and, although still relatively few, most of the projects funded by the Trust can be termed 'successful' (75 per cent in our sample). Of the 25 per cent which could be considered 'failures', eleven were too new to be judged. Most projects have also resulted in gainful employment, although two-thirds of respondents reported an increased workload.

Successful projects appear to be associated with two important factors: first, adequate project identification and subsequent support from the Trust resulting in the timely availability of inputs and the development of an activity with an assured market, and second, commitment on the part of a client (including a significant contribution to project costs) and the development of an activity either building on her existing technical skills or at least not requiring hitherto completely unknown skills. Conversely, the main causes of failure stemmed, on the one hand, from the Trust's and client's performance: poor project identification leading to an over-optimistic prognosis and insufficient technical assistance (this includes marketing problems, investment in the production of a single risk-prone product, lack of raw materials including agricultural and veterinary supplies and poor agricultural practices). On the other hand, some failures were also due to unfavourable external factors (such as climatic conditions for agricultural projects, and social factors, such as illness).

At the institutional level, a genuine local NGO has been established and is flourishing in spite of the teething problems to be expected in the early years of any new organization, as well as those stemming from the uncertain Ugandan environment. UWFCT has been able to retain the services of a highly motivated and committed staff willing to work in sometimes arduous circumstances with minimal resources, an essential requirement if the Trust is to fulfil some of its long-term objectives, such as making other lending institutions more amenable to extending credit to women involved in micro-enterprises.

The Trust's work has clearly had an impact on its clients' status and feeling of self-confidence: just over four-fifths of respondents saw their future as brighter than it would otherwise have been. Approximately two-thirds stated that the project had increased their self-confidence and independence, although a number of respondents were heavily reliant on UWFCT moral support, sometimes to the point of dependence. In most cases their business development had successfully tackled cultural constraints: men were said to be supportive in about four-fifths of the projects, but 35 per cent said that the local community was envious. Confidence in the future was also expressed in terms of expansion and diversification plans for many of the respondents, with six planning to approach other financial institutions to finance them, while another seven expected to use their own profits or savings.

The social impact of the Trust's work was enhanced by its spread effect: 91 per cent of the respondents, for instance, had informed other people about the Trust. Working with groups also spread the Trust's impact, and most of the groups visited were felt to be genuine groupings engaged in a viable venture. Of the women interviewed, only three (6 per cent) said that their particular initiatives would have taken off without the support of the Trust, while another 22 (47 per cent) that ongoing businesses would just have survived.

Reaching poor women. There is some clear evidence of success in reaching the target-group. In the first place, the majority of projects visited were owned and managed by women: in only three cases, could it be said that men controlled the business. Within Uganda's cultural context, this constitutes a considerable achievement. Secondly, the great majority could be classified as belonging to the poor (though not necessarily the poorest): two-thirds of the clients had no other regular source of income besides the Trust's project, and did not have access to other forms of institutional lending. Typically, project holders live in peri-urban or rural areas, and are subsistence farmers with several dependent children; most are married with husbands also involved in farming, retired, or working away from home. However, between one-third and one-quarter of the clients interviewed did not belong to this group. They were part of a first generation of beneficiaries selected in the early days when staff constraints meant that the current practices of rigorous selection and supervision were not practised.

To a large extent, UWFCT's success in reaching poorer women can be ascribed to the staff's diligence in the selection of clients. This is due largely to UWFCT's main institutional achievement: its ability to retain the services of a motivated staff willing to work in difficult circumstances with limited resources. Approximately half those interviewed had heard of the Trust by word of mouth, a quarter through talks given by UWFCT staff, and the remainder through personal contacts with a staff member or an existing client. This individual approach (the Trust has so far abstained from publicizing its lending activities widely) allows a personal relationship to develop between staff and client constantly reinforced by regular follow-up visits—a source of strength (though not without its problems) to the lending programme. The evaluation confirmed that the Trust is universally perceived by clients as receptive, open, and supportive. They do feel, however, that its centralized structure makes it distant from those outside Kampala, and as a result sometimes slow to respond.

Provision of credit. Credit amounting, on average, to USh.280,000 per project, was made available for a wide range of purposes. Of those interviewed, only one client was about to default, and the evaluation strongly suggested that the repayment record would continue to be good. The loan disbursement procedures adopted by the Trust and the clients' ownership of the projects are probably the main factors accounting for this achievement, although clients criticized the lengthy processing of applications, which took between 3 and 11 months to complete. Three procedures have been adopted to reinforce high repayment rates: first, the drawing up of pre-feasibility studies jointly by the client and a UWFCT staff member; second, disbursement of a loan in kind or, when in cash, for specified physical items or services, such as building materials, veterinary support, or transport costs; third, the disbursement of funds by instalments.

Promotion of management skills. Management skills are imparted via formal seminars and also through regular follow-up visits, when progress is reviewed and particular problems are discussed. All the clients interviewed had benefited from these, many receiving more than one visit per month, although a few (in more distant locations) had received only one or two visits in the course of the previous year. The vast majority argued that this support had been very useful. However, in a number of cases it was stated that records were kept at the Trust's insistence rather than because they were seen as intrinsically important for the project's success, and various concepts discussed during training sessions (interest payments, own labour as a cost item, etc.) were not clearly understood. Interviews suggested that UWFCT's effectiveness in providing technical assistance could be enhanced by three factors: first, the development of specific regional approaches stemming from the identification of common problems and needs (such as landlessness and opportunities for off-farm employment, or crop specialization and diversification); second, access to other credit schemes' experiences through field visits and access to technical information; and third, better technical information being put at the disposal of programme officers (for instance on piggeries, or on ways of minimizing risks on agricultural projects).

Savings mobilization.　　Thanks to its personal approach, the Trust has succeeded in launching an institution with which depositors identify: 'it is our bank', they often said. Of some importance, however (and perhaps corroborating a point made above about gaps in business training), none of the respondents saw the return on their deposits with the Trust (15 per cent) as insufficient (at the time of the survey, the inflation rate approached 100 per cent). A number of reasons were given for wishing to save with the Trust besides the requirement to save to become eligible for a loan. These ranged from mobilizing resources, being forced to save for the future, being assured that the money would be secure and not embezzled, and, more generally, depositing with an approachable, user-friendly institution in contrast to the commercial banks. There is little doubt that a more decentralized structure would enable UWFCT to mobilize additional savings, and most people who expressed an opinion deplored the fact that deposits and withdrawals had to be made either in Kampala or in the course of a staff member's visit.

Longer-Term Impact

The long-term impact of the Trust will mainly be a function of three related factors: the quality of its programme, the existence—or otherwise—of alternative credit delivery systems, and UWFCT's ability to influence policy-makers and donors.

Two immediate constraints must be mentioned here. The first relates to the Trust's limited resources in relation to the number of people it wishes to assist, and to its capacity to expand. The second relates to a lack of clarity regarding policy issues such as the definition of target-groups, long-term operational strategies, and the exact nature of its assistance. A more decentralized structure could enhance the planned participation of clients in the Trust's work, such as in project selection and monitoring, and reduce any metropolitan bias in the UWFCT's relationship with its beneficiaries. Lack of appropriate technical advice also stems from the limited resources at the Trust's disposal. With only one vehicle available for fieldwork, for instance, Programme Officers normally have to rely on public transport to reach clients, in many cases walking miles from one client to another. The General Manager is over-burdened with routine administrative tasks, and offices are noisy and poorly equipped.

The reluctance of donors to finance the high level of overheads (ranging from 89 per cent to an estimated 81 per cent by 1995) is much regretted. The Trust argues that donors must recognize the special circumstances in Uganda arising (until recently) from a highly inflationary environment and an unfavourable exchange rate. What is more, there appears to be little scope for expanding local fund-raising since this would only be possible if the Trust adopted a higher political profile, which it considers would compromise its independence.

Little information is at present available to throw light on the effectiveness of other credit programmes targeted at Uganda's poor, although credit provision to the disadvantaged has, in recent years, attracted the attention of NGOs, the government, and the banking sector. The most comprehensive of these has, perhaps, been the Centenary Rural Development Trust Ltd (CERUDET), established by the Catholic Church in 1984. Under the CERUDET scheme, loans are granted to applicants for a variety of projects without security, the local Church Committee being expected to apply sufficient peer pressure to ensure repayments. As with UWFCT, this credit programme is complemented by a savings scheme. A Rural Farmers Scheme has also been run by the main commercial bank, using donor funds. However, the scheme has run into a number of difficulties, including poor supervision, lengthy administrative delays, and a high default rate. For the time being at least, it is clear that the Trust's initiative cannot be replicated by government: apart from the limited resources at its disposal, its extension staff—plagued by low morale, limited skills, and thus uncertain commitment—would be unlikely to take on the role of UWFCT field staff.

The remaining issue concerns UWFCT's ability to expand its operations and to influence the work of other like-minded agencies. The Trust's effectiveness is increasingly recognized: an implementing role for UWFCT in the context of an IFAD-funded programme with the Ministry of Agriculture in Masindi District was under active discussion in 1991, and other independent assessments have confirmed the strength of the UWFCT. At present, however, UWFCT has only a limited capacity to expand its activities without compromising its approach.

Conclusion

The costs of implementing UWFCT projects have undoubtedly been high in relation to the credit disbursed (approximately 50 per cent in 1988/9). Part of the reason for this certainly lies in inefficiencies within the UWFCT, yet of crucial importance have been the Trust's determination to reach women who would not otherwise gain access to credit (especially in remote rural areas) and the emphasis placed on training, regular follow-up visits, and technical assistance (at a time when government extension services have collapsed). The high rate of project success and the spread effect manifested in a number of locations where projects exist, the innovative nature of the Trust's work in the Ugandan context, its ability to reach its target-group, and the likelihood that overhead costs will soon begin to fall, place these high costs in their wider perspective.

Even though the Trust's approach entails relatively large overheads in servicing a relatively small number of clients and, in view of Uganda's current economic situation, a heavy reliance on external donor support, there are, at present, no prospects of the clients paying for these costs. They appear justified to the extent that a necessarily onerous multi-pronged approach favouring close contact with the target-group would seem indispensable to meet objectives.

THE WEST ACHOLI CO–OPERATIVE ENGINEERING UNION (WACU)

The selection of the WACU workshop as one of our four case-studies was based on three factors. First, although the workshop was never, in the strict sense, owned and operated by the Agency for Co-operation and Research in Development (ACORD), the level of assistance provided assimilated it closely to the ACORD programme in northern Uganda. ACORD's involvement, and its recent withdrawal, provides one of the few examples of an initiative now operating (albeit with great difficulty) without NGO support. Second, over the 1980s, development activities in northern Uganda have constantly been threatened by political instability. Third, the scale of the project brings into focus a series of questions relating to appropriate institutional and technological choices as well as to the impact of the national macroeconomic environment on an initiative with regional ambitions.

This evaluation was inevitably constrained by the aftermath of the civil disturbances which have affected all aspects of life in northern Uganda in recent years. Fieldwork could not take place during periods of workshop closure, information gathering was hampered by the lack of documents owing to looting and losses during the war years, and travel in the rural areas was precluded.

Apart from documentation still available in Gulu and ACORD's records, the material presented here stems from discussions with workshop staff, Ministry and co-operative officials, and ACORD personnel in both Gulu and Kampala. Fieldwork conducted in Gulu in November 1990 was complemented by an assessment of technical issues relating to ACORD's support to the workshop, undertaken by an engineer formerly attached to the workshop as a trainer.

Origins, Structure, and Character

The Engineering Workshop attached to the West Acholi Co-operative Union (WACU) is located in Gulu town, the main administrative centre in northern Uganda, 350 km. north of Kampala. With a surface area of 15,000 sq. ft., it is by far the largest industrial unit currently operating in the town, indeed possibly in the whole northern half of the country. The present workshop is essentially the product of assistance provided by ACORD since 1980, at a time when proposals were drawn up for a multi-sectoral long-term programme consisting of three interrelated components as listed in the Agreement signed in late 1981 by ACORD and the Ministry of Co-operatives and Marketing. The aims were: first, to increase agricultural production in Gulu and Kitgum districts through the provision to farmers of locally manufactured agricultural implements; second, to promote the development of appropriate designs and skills for the local production of agricultural implements; and third, in a later phase, to diversify production, to cover non-agricultural fields.

For the workshop this meant supporting an existing structure—the Co-operative Union—rather than starting a manufacturing base from scratch. Originally built in 1963 and owned by Asians, the workshop and its equipment had been allocated,[6] following their forced departure in 1972, to the District Co-operative Union. The facilities included stores, an office, sheds, and residences, as well as four lathes, welding plants, and various smaller items. The Union's original intention in applying for the allocation of the workshop had been to use the facilities to service its cotton ginneries. By the time ACORD's support began, the workforce had been reduced to fourteen (four of whom had some technical training). The machinery could no longer be maintained and production was confined to welding work and vehicle repairs. Nevertheless, the workshop was still open. ACORD's assistance was planned to cost about £250,000 for an initial two-and-a-half years (later extended by six months). It was to include managerial and technical support and the provision of heavy equipment and other tools plus the raw materials needed for the production of agricultural equipment, mainly ox-plough spare parts. These raw materials, imported from Kenya, were to be sold to the workshop for local currency.

Materials and tools started arriving in early 1981, followed by a VSO volunteer seconded to ACORD as a technical adviser in September. The existing equipment was repaired, the first plough spares produced and the workforce reorganized pending the arrival of heavy equipment (lathes, pedestal drills, a power-press, etc.) in early 1982. By then, a whole range of plough spare parts was being produced and design work on prototypes had started. Turnover had increased from USh.30,000 in January 1981 to USh.140,000 in November. Demand for spare parts seemed buoyant and this was confirmed by figures provided by District Agricultural Offices citing a demand in both districts in excess of 100,000 items.[7]

Further progress was made in 1982: by mid-year, complete ploughs were being produced and a toolbar had also been designed. Turnover had reached USh.500,000 in June, and eight additional workers had been hired. Over the following two years, production continued to expand and diversify (with groundnut-hullers, ox-carts, and service work on such diverse items as road-graders and ferries). A shop was opened adjacent to the workshop, and marketing drives were launched in the two districts. A second expatriate adviser was appointed to upgrade existing technical skills and further diversify output. In 1984/5, forty-seven tons of steel were processed annually, and 3,000 plough spare parts and 220 complete ploughs produced.

Although production growth and product diversification demonstrated considerable progress, the workshop was proving a victim of its own success and was facing fundamental problems which compromised its sustainability. As a 1985 evaluation put it (Roberts, 1985: 29–30):

The problems which ACORD has encountered have been essentially two in number. They concern the orientation towards servicing local farmers which ACORD originally set for the workshop, on which only qualified success has been registered, and the long-term viability of the workshop as a self-reliant, i.e. financially solvent, enterprise . . . The first problem is essentially a problem of distribution or marketing . . . ACORD has felt frustrated by the difficulty of reaching the poorer farmers of the more outlying districts.

Marketing trips eased this problem to some extent, but the workshop's productive capacity remained under-utilized as there was no network of private traders developing to take the workshop's products to distant villages. This also underlined ACORD's limited success, up to then, in linking its assistance to the workshop with a comprehensive agricultural extension programme. For the workshop, the marketing constraint was compounded by the seasonal nature of the demand for agricultural tools, leaving it to survive on servicing work from September to March, while demand was difficult to meet at other times. It had insufficient capital at its disposal to carry large stocks of finished products, and therefore started seeking bulk orders from elsewhere in the country. Cash-flow difficulties led to erratic loan repayments to ACORD and to difficulties in raising the local cover for a $60,000 IDA hard-currency loan, negotiated on its behalf by ACORD for the purchase of steel in Kenya.

These constraints in turn reflected the greatest single obstacle facing the workshop: the poor calibre of its management, which was to prove an intractable problem for years to come. The immediate problem stemmed from lack of the management skills which rapid growth demanded. Training in neighbouring Kenya for the manager and the despatch of a management adviser by ACORD in 1984 did little to alleviate these difficulties. It soon became clear that production successes and the level of outside assistance (ACORD had been a 'fairy godmother', the management adviser argued) had in effect concealed the consequences of a large accumulating debt and deep-rooted management deficiencies.

By 1985 the workshop was far from the degree of self-sufficiency that ACORD had envisaged five years earlier, and proposals to rectify this situation were soon overtaken by events. Political coups and managerial problems marked the beginning of a long period of uncertainty, from which the workshop was to emerge into a radically changed environment. Most crucial for its long-term prospects was the near-annihilation of the cattle population in northern Uganda as a result of continued civil conflicts: in Kitgum district, for instance, cattle numbers had dropped from 158,000 to just 2,000 in two years. Almost overnight, the market for ploughs had disappeared.

Through ACORD's good offices, other NGOs provided some relief. Thus a 1,000 plough order was secured from Oxfam and a $64,000 grant obtained from USAID to purchase the necessary raw materials. Orders for brick and tile machines were also received from ActionAid and the 1988/9 estimates predicted the use of 175 tons of steel to manufacture, among other things, 4,000 ploughs and 3,000 shares. By the end of 1988, the workshop employed eighty-one staff.

In 1988 seven years of day-to-day assistance provided by ACORD through its technical adviser came to an end. However, its support to the workshop continued through attendance at management committee meetings, logistical back-up (especially for purchases outside Uganda), and the provision of foreign-exchange facilities and contacts with other agencies as potential customers. The departure of the technical adviser, however, immediately led to fears about the consequences of the high turn-over in trained staff, and, perhaps more importantly, about the workshop's loss of its political umbrella. Indeed from 1989, the workshop increasingly became the object of tussles among prominent residents. Relations with the Union management also became strained, and 1989/90 saw a number of investigations by the Ministry of Co-operatives and the office of the District Administrator to investigate allegations of embezzlement and support for rebels.

The financial situation continued to be very precarious: losses mounted (with many debtors untraceable), and overheads remained high as a consequence of previous output levels. Orders were tenuous, reflecting the high production costs, the lack of expertise in other markets, and the competition from low-priced imports. By February 1989 twenty-two staff had already been made redundant, and in March the senior foreman was murdered. At 31 July 1989 total turnover for the year was a mere USh.13.2m. (475 ploughs had been produced in 1989), well below the planned level of USh.77m.

Although peace was gradually returning to northern Uganda, 1990 was to prove perhaps the most difficult year yet for the workshop. By the time of the evaluation, it had to adapt to a much reduced level of support from ACORD, severe market constraints, a cash position that did not allow the salaries of a reduced workforce to be paid regularly, demoralized managerial staff, and uncertainties stemming from official investigations. These led to a devastating closure of the premises by the local political authorities for a period of two-and-a-half months. Workshop estimates suggest that the closure resulted in the loss of USh.50m. of the USh.70.6m. orders expected for 1990/91. Closure could not, however, mask the underlying problems that the workshop was continuing to face, especially the lack of markets, aggravated both by the failure to open a representative office in Kampala and competition from donor agencies.[8]

An Assessment of the Project

Lack of data prevents accurate quantification of the workshop's overall economic impact. However, up to the mid-1980s, considerable progress had clearly been made in producing agricultural implements that were in demand in the region, using appropriate designs, developing local manufacturing skills, and minimizing the use of foreign exchange. By 1989, tens of thousands of spare parts and hundreds of complete ploughs and various other implements had been produced, and a general engineering capability was available to the region at large. Employment had been provided, at one point, for 100 people. At the time of the evaluation, an order *in extremis* for forty brick-making machines financed by CIDA and valued at USh.500,000 each had just been received. Moreover, all the local government departments, institutions, and public services continue to depend on the workshop for service and maintenance. All this is undoubtedly positive.

Over the years, however, ACORD has spent almost £500,000 on the workshop: such an investment can only really be justified if it leads to the establishment of a manufacturing facility with viable long-term prospects. After 10 years, the workshop is still in existence and, had its local market not entirely—and totally unexpectedly— vanished, it might well have thrived. Yet, because of the scale of its operations and the rigid nature of its technology, the workshop has found itself especially vulnerable to external factors, with the uncertainties of the late 1980s bringing this particularly to the fore.

ACORD based its strategy on the provision of agricultural tools. However, the main constraint on agricultural production may well have been weeding and harvesting, rather than ploughing, while marketing constraints were also shown to be significant for Acholi smallholders. More fundamentally, however, ACORD placed most emphasis on assisting an existing institution, which was to lead to critical problems for the whole enterprise. As Roberts had already noted (1985: 27):

The ambitious objective which ACORD has set for the workshop would only make sense were ACORD in a position to control the management of the enterprise. Yet it appears that ACORD has been unwilling to entertain more modest expectations of the workshop (and a more modest conception of its own role in relation to it) because of the central place which the workshop has occupied in ACORD's conception of its entire northern Uganda programme, as the centre-piece of the (itself notionally central) agricultural development programme.

In a sense these tensions illustrate the cultural difficulties which ACORD—as an NGO—was experiencing in dealing with what should have been a business initiative. The advantages expected to come from linkage with the Co-operative Union (such as access to credit from the Co-operative Bank and marketing through the co-operative structure) did not materialize, nor did support from the Union's parent Ministry. The government was especially reluctant to intervene in local political struggles and to resist the importation of ploughs which were heavily subsidized (either directly or through an overvalued exchange rate). In effect, as one official put it, the Ministry 'has stood back because ACORD was there'.

Research by ACORD into alternative technological approaches to the manufacture of agricultural equipment was also limited. Once made, the implications of the choice of a relatively capital-intensive technology plus the infrastructural requirements were profound, if down-played by the protagonists. Clearly, too, far too much was expected of the rehabilitation of the Ugandan economy. Similarly, the managerial implications—and the wider political consequences of establishing a large semi-parastatal plant in a small town—did not feature prominently in ACORD's early thinking.

By 1990 the workshop's technical capability had been severely circumscribed as a result of declining standards on the shop-floor, management constraints, and equipment deficiencies. By the end of the year, only one skilled and two semi-skilled machine operators (who had been trained by the ACORD technician) were still at the workshop. Of the rest, five had been suspended for using equipment on private work or embezzlement, four had failed to return from leave, probably for security reasons, three had been made redundant as a result of decline in production, and one had been killed and one injured in the fighting. Declining technical skills led to falling standards. On the accounting side, none of the five staff trained in costing remained, leading to the ironic situation where an order for brick-machines was recently rejected by the customer as being too cheap!

Future Prospects

By the end of 1990, the sustainability of the workshop seemed to be compromised by a series of interlinked factors. First, the changing market and the ability to exploit opportunities. While the workshop retains an ability (unique in northern Uganda) to mass-produce simple items, and has proved able to develop new products, these potential strengths have been undermined by poor machine maintenance, deteriorating product range and quality, and, especially, production increasingly oriented towards items with a low technological content at the expense of items which would fully use the equipment available. Secondly, the general quality of the management (and of the staff in general). The management was clearly demoralized by investigations and the prospects of an end to the (now limited) support provided by ACORD. The leadership appeared ill-equipped to deal with skills problems, in spite of its undoubted commitment. It also seemed to be inflexible in approach, however, and dogged by a bureaucratic approach to problem-solving. Partly as a result, labour relations were poor.

Third was the institutional context. In theory, the Co-operative Union consisted of five departments: a cotton ginnery, a ranch, the workshop, the transport department, and the education department. Of these, only the workshop remained as a revenue earner: the ginnery was destroyed, the ranch ceased to exist, and all the vehicles of the transport section were looted in 1987. There can thus be little optimism for the future as long as the workshop remains a constituent part of the Union, which is unlikely to attract management of the right calibre, given the poor remuneration, past practices, and the current Co-operative Union sub-culture in Uganda.

THE BUSOGA MULTI-SECTORAL RURAL DEVELOPMENT PROGRAMME[9]

This study was based on fieldwork conducted in 1990 in eleven out of fifty-one project areas (forty-five of which currently have a functioning aid-post), selected in consultation with MSRDP staff in Jinja, and reflecting varying degrees of community participation and leadership, commitment and skills of service providers and quality of service delivery, and proximity to the necessary infrastructure (essentially urban centres and hospital locations). Some preference was also given to aid-posts with income-generating activities designed to provide additional funds for health services. Interviews were held with five groups: aid-post staff (in charge of curative services); outreach workers (mostly village health workers involved in primary health care activities); members of the Development Committee and other community leaders; personnel associated with income-generating activities; and members of the community with no direct involvement in the medical programme. To complement this fieldwork, discussions were held with MSRDP personnel at central level and with government health staff.

Origins, Structure, and Character

The Multi-Sectoral Rural Development Programme (MSRDP) is an initiative of the Busoga Diocese of the Church of Uganda in the eastern part of the country. Launched shortly after the fall of the Idi Amin regime in 1979, it covers the three administrative districts of Jinja, Kamuli, and Iganga with an approximate combined population of 1.5 million. There are few other NGOs working in the area, especially away from the corridor along the main East–West road linking Kampala to the Kenyan border. The population of the fifty-one MSRDP project areas (each roughly corresponding to a sub-parish) is estimated at 440,000. The MSRDP commits itself to reaching all members of local communities, whether or not they belong to the church. The programme currently comprises seven sectors (agriculture, animal husbandry, and afforestation; health; women's projects; youth projects; water and sanitation; income-generation; and communications and training).

The original goal of the programme was to foster 'an increased measure of self-sufficiency in the things of everyday life in all our households in Busoga', and to show, by example, what could be achieved. The promotion of self-sufficiency entailed a programming approach which stressed the sustainability of the activities it pro-moted and, as a pre-condition of this, the participation of local communities in programme affairs. According to the Bishop of Busoga, who has continued to monitor and guide the programme, this long-term educative approach was not appreciated at the outset by funders, who stressed the achievement of quantifiable goals. It was also an approach that was to be undermined by the early provision of free (or highly subsidized) relief items and other commodities. The only viable option was to adopt an integrated approach. Self-reliance was to be promoted through a range of interlinked activities, supported by professional staff at diocesan level who provided technical back-up and training services.

The initial phase of the programme was scheduled to last for three years, but political instability led to its extension for another two years. A second phase covered the years 1985–8 and, after an interim period of two years, a third phase covering 1990–5 was launched in mid-1990. This is described as the ultimate one in the current programme, and is planned to be the last to receive foreign funding.

Growth has been rapid in the intervening years in order, according to the diocese, to meet the demand for services and to make up for the slow rehabilitation of the government infrastructure. As of late 1990, the programme employed 180 staff mem-bers (including 135 community-development extension workers in the project areas and central-level staff, but excluding staff attached to medical units, most of whom are paid by their local communities). With its breadth and scope, the programme is unique in church-managed development programmes in Uganda.

The medical part of the programme is by far the most developed, and was the primary focus of the evaluation. These activities began in 1980 with support for the establishment of aid-posts in ten of the project areas. Initially, these were principally concerned with the provision of curative services, as it was felt that preventive health-care issues could only be addressed to people with access to curative services. These are centred on the aid-post, a facility intended to belong to the local community. Its physical structure will have been erected through community contributions (although cement and roofing materials are normally provided free or, more often, at subsidized rates by the MSRDP), and its staff (typically a nurse or midwife and a nursing aid) will have been appointed and are paid by the local community, mostly through user charges. The MSRDP only provides aid-post practitioners with limited medical refresher training; the local communities are expected to identify suitable, already-trained personnel.

Services provided vary from area to area: most aid-posts function as dispensaries, providing treatment for the most common diseases. Some ten units also provide maternity services and have a maternity ward. The quality of the staff and of the physical facilities also differs from area to area and, although many of the posts have up-grading plans, they usually consist of three or four small rooms constructed with simple local materials. Most posts are situated in remote rural locations: communications are extremely poor, and there is no water or electricity. Sterilization of equipment is carried out with a small charcoal burner. Furniture is usually sparse, typically a bed or two, a desk, a couple of benches, and a medicine cupboard. Each aid-post is managed by a health sub-committee with a chairman and treasurer, the nurse or midwife in-charge acting as secretary. The committee supervises staff, the purchase of drugs, the building programme (if any), and other expenditure. It also has the critically important role of deciding on the level of user charges.

In accordance with its general philosophy, MSRDP aid-posts are meant to be financially self-sufficient. All expenditure (including staff salaries) has to be covered through user charges or other forms of income, such as special projects or community donations, although there is access to some subsidized drugs from the MSRDP central pharmacy. Apart from some assistance with building supplies and supervisory services, no other subsidies are currently extended to aid-posts for their curative work.

In addition to staff with responsibilities at or around aid-posts (nurses and non-medical staff, extension workers), personnel carry out supervisory duties (whether of curative or preventive activities) at two levels. First, local supervisors are appointed from among aid-post staff to supervise eight to ten units: they are provided by MSRDP with motorcycles to tour the aid-posts in their area on a regular basis, to provide advice, monitor, and alert MSRDP offices if need be. Secondly, in Jinja, the programme is co-ordinated by a doctor (seconded from government service) and a small team of employees, all externally funded. There are no expatriate staff, although a project manager for preventive work was originally provided.

Most (but not all) of the drugs and equipment used by the MSRDP aid-posts are provided by the central pharmacy in Jinja. These drugs originate from a number of sources: foreign donors (the UK-based Busoga Trust has until recently been providing £1,000 worth every 3 months), the Joint Medical Stores, and government stores (the Essential Drugs Programme). The pharmacy is meant to be entirely self-financing with aid-post purchases (at cost plus transport and administrative charges) replenishing a revolving fund (originally funded by the German Ministry of Overseas Development) used to make further drug purchases.

The MSRDP regards the aid-post element as a successful part of the overall programme, noting that 'this is one specific institution through which the programme has made an impact on the local community in all project areas' (1990/5 Phase 3 document, p. 35).

The aid-post also provides the focus for preventive work. This has been based on two initiatives: the Community Health Services project (CHS) funded by CARE International, and the Family Life Education Project, funded by USAID (first through Experiment in International Living, and then through Pathfinder, two US-based NGOs). The CARE project has shaped the present MSRDP preventive health activities in most respects. It had six objectives: to increase the immunization coverage of children under the age of 1 to 50 per cent (against diphtheria, polio, measles, and tuberculosis); to increase the immunization coverage of women of child-bearing age against tetanus; to increase the capacity of the project's village health-workers and health-unit staff to be active health educators; to increase the knowledge and skills of households in the administration of oral rehydration therapy; to support co-ordination efforts with other programmes elsewhere in the country; and, finally, to promote the sustainability of project activities by helping to develop the management capacity of local communities, and to promote CHS's full integration into the government programme.

The project has provided allowances for the field-workers it has trained in areas such as teaching mothers to make rehydration solutions. Bicycles have also been provided by the project to transport supplies to aid-posts. It was envisaged, however, that this support would be short-term, with each aid-post expected to raise sufficient funds to sustain preventive as well as curative services. A baseline survey was carried out in January 1986 in the areas to be covered by the CHS project, with a second evaluation survey in mid-1989. The latter survey indicated that village health-workers were actively promoting immunization and other preventive practices. The rate of increase in immunization was seen as disappointing, however, although it did indicate that substantial progress had been made in mothers' understanding of preventive measures. Their ability to prepare rehydration fluids was limited, however.

The CHS project has been complemented (and to some extent superseded) by the Family Life Education Project (FLEP), which is specifically concerned with the dissemination of family-planning knowledge and techniques, mainly through village health-workers trained to teach local communities child-spacing and to sell contraceptives (half the proceeds going in theory to the health-worker, the rest to the aid-post). AIDS-related activities have now been incorporated into the project, even if Busoga currently appears to be somewhat less affected by the disease than some other regions of the country.

The medical sector of the MSRDP collaborates with the government health department and, indeed, has received government assistance, both through tax exemptions for medical (and other) supplies and, more importantly, through the provision of staff seconded to some of the aid-posts, of immunization equipment and vaccines, and, in some areas, of drug-kits supplied through the District Medical Office. Training materials have also been provided and government officers have participated in some of the training sessions organized by the MSRDP. Collaborative planning is encouraged through monthly meetings of MSRDP and government personnel at district level. The government has recently launched its own community-based health-care programme in one sub-county of Jinja district (not covered by MSRDP).

Evaluation Results

All the posts visited in the course of the evaluation were in operation and providing a range of preventive and simple curative services. At the time of each (unannounced) visit, at least one member of the medical staff was present, although some of the posts were clearly treating very few patients. The MSRDP units compared favourably with other health facilities in the area (where these existed) and were usually preferred by the local communities. A wider range of drugs (and occasionally better facilities) was the only factor which attracted clients to private clinics or pharmacies, although this applied only to certain areas, even if some were also able to lower prices by offering partial treatment.

The MSRDP aid-posts generally provide a range of services of direct use to the local communities, especially in those areas where alternative facilities are either non-existent or grossly inadequate. Only three of the posts visited are situated in or near a town or large trading centre, where the very few government facilities are in existence. The quality of services in the latter is, furthermore, severely compromised by low staff morale, shortages of drugs, high unofficial fees, and other forms of corruption.

Local community members interviewed particularly appreciated the provision of immunization services and the consequent reduction in certain diseases, especially measles, whooping cough, and tetanus, and the provision of simple and generally effective treatment facilities close to their homes (on average 3 km. away) by friendly and understanding staff and at reasonable cost. Treatment on credit was especially valued, as well as dentistry and maternity services where these existed. Most of the community leaders interviewed expressed pride in their involvement with the aid-post and considered it an impressive asset for their local communities. It constituted, in their eyes, a facility which worked, which was run on local contributions, and which exemplified community dynamism. In some areas, the buildings are also used as a meeting-place or a community hall. Village health-workers and medical staff have a recognized social position in their respective communities (although they are generally poorly paid) and are regarded as an asset. It is also apparent, however, that the social impact could, in many cases, have been far greater with more community involvement: of the eleven posts visited, only five seemed to enjoy the active support of the whole community.

Criticisms focused on the periodic shortages and the narrow range of drugs, poor attendance by non-resident and casual staff, understaffing, and the lack of equipment and facilities. These criticisms are echoed by the practitioners themselves. Those interviewed complained of lack of accommodation, poor and delayed salaries, inadequate drug supplies, poor community support, inadequate income, and competition from other health units. Extension workers made the same comments and, in two cases, complained of the rudeness of aid-post staff.

The MSRDP medical programme has resulted in employment for medical staff, ancillary staff, and, where these are now supported by the post, extension staff. Numbers per aid-post range from five to ten, making an approximate total for all MSRDP aid-posts of 300–400 people sustained by their local communities through the provision of medical services.

Explaining performance. Performance varies considerably from post to post. Based on the number of patients attending, the quality of staff appears to assume a critical importance. Of the posts visited, the four best performers all benefited from the services of a qualified, confident, and respected health-worker and, for two-thirds of those visited, health staff were described as committed and effective. In the remaining third, staff had either recently been appointed or were demoralized by low pay and poor community leadership or were otherwise poorly motivated. Two-thirds of the posts visited are in remote areas far from main roads, so the work demands not only long working hours and perseverance (especially in preventive work), but also often entails social isolation and rudimentary living conditions, as well as occasional harassment from inexperienced committees.

At two of the aid-posts with the largest numbers of patients, an outreach service had been launched, with outposts providing curative services one or two days a week. In addition, all of the four best performers provided either maternity and/or dentistry services, and the ability to do so (only two posts provided dentistry and seven others maternity services) enhanced their performance in the eyes of patients. The provision of maternity services was often cited by the medical staff concerned as the first priority to improve effectiveness, and also to increase income.

The location of the post and the level of competition from other facilities also affected performance: three of the four best performers were far from urban centres and experienced little competition from the private sector (despite the isolation, however, they had managed to retain the services of committed staff: in other posts distance compromised staff quality). The emergence of private clinics and pharmacies is a recent development in most rural areas in Busoga; as some of them obtain free supplies diverted from government facilities, they pose a further threat to MSRDP aid-posts.

Performance also depended upon the attitude of the community and the quality of its leaders. The three most successful posts had permanent structures built, in part, through community contributions, and had attempted to start income-generating projects to enhance the post's income. The poor performers lacked effective community leadership, and local community members stated that they had never been approached to participate in building up the post. In these cases, committee members expected to receive free medical treatment and high expectations of outside assistance to sustain the post were expressed.

Cost recovery and sustainability. All MSRDP aid-posts charge for their curative services, but preventive services are generally free. Charges are generally acknowledged to be lower at the MSRDP post than elsewhere. In addition, all the posts visited provided credit for those unable to pay immediately and, in certain cases, payment in instalments was accepted (apart from one instance where the practice had been banned by the committee). One of the posts visited accepted payment in kind where necessary, and, in certain cases, sick patients were treated free of charge. For preventive services, where a patient is deemed able to pay, an initial consultation fee of USh.100 is levied for family-planning advice. Contraceptives are charged for, but many posts provide them free where it is considered essential to encourage users who could not otherwise afford them. All immunization services are free, apart from one case where a fee of USh.20 was charged for replacing lost vaccination record cards.

The interviews indicated overwhelmingly positive responses to cost-sharing. Two-thirds of respondents in all categories felt this was a good system, only 6 per cent were opposed to it, and the rest did not express a view. These responses should be set in the context of medical services having been available only at a fee (whether officially or not) for perhaps the last 15 years (in the case of church-run facilities, a small fee has always been charged) and of non-Western types of treatment having always been paid for, often quite highly. Cost-sharing fits well in a fee-for-service culture: it is widely accepted that nothing is free in this world and most respondents saw cost-sharing as necessary to provide an adequate service to improve the health status of the local community. The main criticism of the system was not the exclusion of some people because of lack of money, but because of lack of money at a time of illness. The resultant partial treatment was considered dangerous by some. If most people had access to the aid-post, it was generally accepted that some sections of the community were excluded from medical care because they could not afford the charges (though this was acknowledged to be less so than for other health facilities for the reasons already mentioned), or because they put a low priority on health. These included old people without relatives who could help, widows, and young people who had recently dropped out of school. Estimates of the size of this population varied from just a few to as much as 25 per cent. Proposals to improve the system included accepting labour in lieu of cash, reducing charges to attract more patients, granting credit during lean agricultural seasons, charging lower fees for common ailments, introducing government subsidies (through the provision of free drugs to MSRDP posts rather than to government units), charging committee members for treatment, educating the community about the need for charges, and levying a small amount for family-planning services.

Various attempts had been made—and more are planned—to initiate income-generating activities to supplement the revenue from user charges. All this is encouraged by the MSRDP and no outside assistance had been provided. Past or planned projects included crop cultivation, tree nurseries, brick-making, poultry-keeping, selling firewood, starting a canteen, and even straight fund-raising.

Six of the aid-posts had started a project which later collapsed (because of poor weather, lack of capital, limited land, the departure of concerned staff, or poor management). The main reason given for the absence of any form of income-generating project was lack of capital, but poor community involvement was clearly a major factor. In almost all cases, the projects were not really community projects: labour was provided by members of the committee, but there appeared to be a good deal of confusion about whether the proceeds should go to the committee members or to the aid-post, indicating the limits of genuine community involvement in the post. Fees are accepted as necessary for a good quality service, but if an aid-post is considered as in any way belonging to an outside agency (such as the church) or to the practitioners and/or the committee members, contributions for an income-generating project are—not surprisingly—viewed in a different light. Experience indicates that the benefits are more likely to accrue to particular individuals than to the community as a whole.

As a result, in only three of the eleven posts visited was the level of income said to be sufficient to meet an adequate level of expenditure. In the absence of other income-generating projects, aid-posts have to rely entirely on user charges for treatment and, where applicable, for maternity services. In some instances, contributions were received for construction work and, in a few cases, for other projects. The number of patients is thus the critical factor in ensuring financial viability. Large numbers of patients also guarantee low charges: the post with the highest number of patients (600 a month) had one of the lowest average fees per patient (USh.136) while, conversely, the post with the lowest number of patients (forty) charged as much as USh.490 per patient, further weakening its market position.

The main items of expenditure for the eleven posts visited were drugs (33 per cent), staff pay (15 per cent) and construction costs (13 per cent). Other expenditure (about one-third) was accounted for by other supplies, such as charcoal for sterilization purposes, transport, rent, and water-carrying. The allocation of resources was in some cases a source of conflict between staff and committee members: the latter tended to emphasize the need to improve buildings (and to pay for entertainment allowances), while staff placed more emphasis on immediate expenditure items such as drugs and salaries.

Eight of the eleven posts visited had made a profit over the previous six months. In only three cases, however, was this of any size—from USh.5,000–8,500 per month. Three posts had made a loss. In other cases, a very small surplus had been achieved by keeping expenditure to the absolute minimum, often at the expense of service. Overall, average monthly expenditure of USh.27,405 was just below monthly average income of USh.28,650.

Aid-posts have adjusted to their small revenue base in different ways. Some make very small purchases of drugs at a time. Wages are generally low, typically

USh.1,500–4,000 per month, and often paid late (several months' delay for three of the posts). This clearly plays a major role in low morale, in absenteeism (and thus fewer patients), and occasionally in the taking on of private patients. Physical facilities are poor in some of the posts and, in two cases, the post is indebted to local community leaders.

Long-term sustainability will clearly depend upon the local community's perceptions, which will stem in part from their level of involvement in the post's affairs; of the community members interviewed, less than one-third said that they had made any contribution in labour or money to the establishment (or the running) of the post. Generally, the post was perceived not as theirs but either as belonging to the church or, sometimes, as a quasi-private facility run by the practitioners and the Development Committee. Even among the community leaders interviewed, very few appeared to regard the post as their ultimate responsibility, and there was a strong tendency to seek solutions to problems through requests for external assistance. For instance, in response to questions about cost-sharing, almost one-fifth of those interviewed (a higher proportion than for the general public) stated that medical services provided by the MSRDP should be free. Those who ought to be the best informed about the general principles underlining the MSRDP programme appeared to be the most resistant to them.

The longer-term prospects for the aid-posts visited were gauged by using the following criteria: number of patients; factors contributing towards general performance (as outlined above); the profit/loss position; the existence of other income-generating projects; and the level of community support. On this basis, only two of the eleven posts failed to have made at least some progress towards sustainability. Here long-term prospects were severely hampered by the poor quality of service, resulting in limited numbers of patients (only two or three per day) and low income levels, by the lack of other sources of income, and by the poor level of community support. Using the same criteria, two other posts had uncertain prospects.

The sustainability of the posts and their outreach work is also contingent upon the provision of efficient support and supervision by the MSRDP. The central pharmacy constitutes one element of this support: the revolving fund it administers (now amounting to USh.1.6m.) has registered a good measure of success in making available a supply of reasonably priced drugs. The pharmacy has, however, faced a number of problems. A poor repayment record by posts which have been granted credit has forced it to suspend credit facilities (except for recently established posts); rapid increases in drug prices both from government stores and from the private sector, at a time when drug donations from abroad are no longer made, have resulted in a reduction of 50–75 per cent in the consumption of certain items in the past two years. Bureaucratic delays and the use of the revolving fund for purposes other than the purchase of drugs have led to occasional frustrated visits by aid-post staff wanting to purchase supplies.

The support provided by supervisors appears to be effective: routine visits are made regularly, often on a weekly basis, and supervisors are well placed to evaluate and advise on problems encountered by their colleagues. The rapid growth of the

MSRDP aid-post network, on the other hand, reduces the effectiveness of the support from the Jinja-based staff and of training undertaken at the Naminage centre. Few Development Committee members, other than the office holders, for instance, have benefited from training sessions. The posts' record-keeping is poor and reflects the lack of adequate management training for staff and committees; clinical training could also be improved.

The costs involved in running this supervisory and support structure are significant (approximately $3,300 per post per annum), particularly salary and vehicle charges. Moreover, it does not seem feasible for these to be borne by the MSRDP itself, as is currently planned for the post-1993 period, especially in view of the general failure of centralized income-generating schemes.

The Broader Context

The provision of health facilities constitutes one of the main areas of NGO intervention in Uganda and, because of its approach and its well-established character, the MSRDP provides an important illustration of this type of NGO intervention. Its innovative character lies in having established a successful network of aid-posts whose curative work relies almost entirely on community participation, mostly through user charges. A number of church-based programmes elsewhere in the country have followed this example.

The attempt to sustain preventive work through income generated by curative services is of immediate relevance to many other NGO programmes in the country. MSRDP's experience in this respect remains limited and no definite conclusions can be drawn at this point. Nevertheless, a successful community-based approach to curative services does appear to provide one route for tackling (possibly only in part) the problem of recurrent costs incurred by preventive programmes which are so far usually borne by external funding.

The MSRDP experience is also relevant to current attempts by the government to introduce cost-sharing in the provision of medical services. The planned attachment of local committees to government health units is said to have been directly inspired by MSRDP's work. In Busoga itself, the government established its own network of primary health-care workers in one sub-county in 1990. These are fully supported by local communities and an extension of this scheme is currently under consideration.

THE ACTIONAID MITYANA PROGRAMME (AMP)[10]

Fieldwork for this evaluation took place in November–December 1990. It involved visits to different aspects of the programme both within the current target area and that in which ActionAid was phasing out its programme, complemented by visits to other relevant technical training institutions, and by interviews with artisans in the informal sector in order to gauge the programme's impact.

Origins, Structure, and Assumptions

The ActionAid Mityana Programme (AMP) is the oldest ActionAid intervention in Uganda. Originally conceived as a programme of assistance to the educational sector (mostly to primary schools), AMP has now developed into a multi-sectoral initiative around Mityana town, 72 km. west of Kampala, with teams of extension workers travelling to outlying districts. The project area covers a total area of 1077 km.^{2} and an estimated population of 73,200.

ActionAid describes its overall policy as 'working with the poor in the target area to improve their quality of life through encouragement, awareness raising, training and support'. The programme's strategy is to address the three causes of poverty in the area—lack of awareness, lack of skills and facilities, and lack of external support—(1990/1 plan and budget):

through an empowerment process which will involve constant dialogue with individual community members and interest groups, awareness raising, training, exposure to more efficient production methods and improvement or making available basic facilities. [. . . support will be provided if] it will lead community members to sustainable development rather than create a dependency syndrome.

Initially established in 1981, the programme's turning-point came in 1987, both in terms of its institutional link with ActionAid (following the establishment of an office in Kampala and of a fully fledged ActionAid Uganda programme), and in terms of its content and methodology, which took the form of a move away from a perceived over-emphasis on education to embrace a broader concept of development. Work in agriculture increased, and a community-based health-care programme was launched, followed by the establishment of a Technical Skills Training Unit. Work in the education sector nevertheless continued to expand. In late 1988 it was also decided to concentrate resources in a smaller locality, and, more importantly, to phase out free handouts and other dependency-creating practices, as well as to increase collaboration with the government.

By 1990 the AMP comprised four operational programmes: in agriculture, education, community-based health-care, and technical skills development, including a Women in Development scheme. The 1990/1 budget was £498,000 including support costs. The staff establishment stood at seventy, including twenty-seven field-workers.

Overall programme sustainability is expected to be achieved within eight years via a combination of handover to government extension services and the development of sustainable programme activities for local communities. Earlier plans to transform the AMP into an independent local NGO (SHEDA) affiliated to ActionAid have been abandoned, although SHEDA has come into existence and is currently developing a programme similar to AMP in a neighbouring area.

The fourth operational programme, the Technical Skills Training Unit (TSTU), was the focus of the ODI case-study. Its aim has been 'to increase local revenues by encouraging non-agricultural economic activities' whose practical skills are generally lacking in the target area as a result of the academic bias of school curricula and Uganda's isolation, which denies most people exposure to the technologies and expertise available in other countries. In addition to general training in construction and design, the Unit adopted a Skills Development and Income Generation Programme, whose main components are support for village polytechnics, a women-in-development programme, a credit and business-management programme, and the introduction and dissemination of new technologies (using the AMP site for design and testing work).

Evaluation Results

Support to institutional training.   At the time of the evaluation ActionAid had been supporting village polytechnics for three years, and was planning to expand from two institutions to one in each of the four zones of the target area. Although village polytechnics are not at present eligible for government assistance and thus have to rely on other sources of income, their promotion forms part of government policy. The aim of the new ActionAid plan is to stimulate local communities to start up and maintain village polytechnics through which new skills can be introduced. It was planned that each polytechnic should receive assistance for a period of five years on a cost-sharing basis: each would be required to set up an income-generating project to ensure its sustainability.

Two polytechnics were initially assisted by ActionAid (at Kyankowe and Namukozi), and both have received similar types of assistance. This was scheduled to end in December 1990, after which only limited help was to be made available. ActionAid's involvement with Kyankowe is now regarded as a test-case for the district, where its approach remains unique. The polytechnic was inspired by the local Member of Parliament, who provided the land, and it opened in May 1988 with sixty trainees taking two-year courses in tailoring, bricklaying, and carpentry, in addition to agriculture, a compulsory subject for all. The minimum entry requirement is completion of primary school education (P7). Fees are moderate at USh.3,700 per term.

The chairman of the management committee was emphatic that the polytechnic could not have got off the ground without ActionAid's assistance (free building materials, salaries for the five teaching staff, and tools and equipment such as sewing-machines and training materials)—even though the precise terms under which the assistance has been made available were never entirely clear to the school authorities. As a result of internal decisions (and in part reflecting what it sees as the poor management record of the institution), ActionAid support was withheld in June 1990. This decision took the school by surprise, and its dependence on outside assistance was fully exposed: at the time of the evaluation, no teachers had been paid since that cut-off point. The future prospects for the school appeared all the poorer since earlier plans (developed by the previous principal), which included the development of on-site cottage industries to finance a revolving fund to purchase tools for hire to graduates, had failed to materialize. The income from school activities appeared to be very limited. At the time of the evaluation, the school was attempting to secure some support from the district education authorities.

Namukozi school was established in April 1988 to provide technical skills to girls who had dropped out of school. The original intake of ten (mostly single mothers) were taught weaving, embroidery, and home and business management, in addition to tailoring, over a two-year period. A further seven girls joined the school in April 1989, and seventeen the following year. The fee of USh.4,500 a term covers tuition and some materials.

ActionAid's assistance to the school covered the purchase of four sewing-machines, plus materials and salaries for the three teachers. In addition, management advice was provided and the school was given contracts to produce school uniforms for the AMP education support programme. In June 1990 this assistance ceased and the services of the business adviser were terminated. Like Kyankowe, the school faced severe financial difficulties, with income from production insufficient to meet running costs. As a result of difficulties in raising the fees, or because of pregnancies among the students, the number of trainees has dropped: only sixteen first-year and one second-year student were at the school when it was visited.

The project has also run into problems because it was increasingly seen as a family business rather than a community project. The original premises were at the manager's home (the project was his idea initially). The lack of community involvement (in part because parents are living in scattered homesteads, Namukozi being close to Mityana town) was only partially corrected by the (delayed) establishment of a management committee.

Attempts were made to judge the broader impact of the polytechnics by following the career-paths of students who had completed their training. Of the original intake of sixty at Kyankowe, thirty-two completed their courses (nineteen in tailoring (all girls), four carpenters, and nine builders (all boys)). Of these, four of the girls were able to afford their own machines and ten were said to be employed as tailors; five had neither taken up nor abandoned the trade. Of the four carpenters, two had found employment in workshops in Kampala, one was able to buy tools and set up his own business, and one was not practising. Of the nine builders, one went to Kampala, two started work in the area, and the whereabouts of the remainder was unknown.

Of the original intake of ten at Namukozi, seven completed the course (two dropped out because of pregnancy). Of the seven who completed, four have access to a sewing-machine (three on hire) and the remainder are not practising their trade (in two cases because no machine could be found). Girls have been advised to start working in their own villages because of the limited demand in town.

A total of fourteen graduates (eleven from Kyankowe and three from Namukozi) were able to be traced, while four graduates from a similar institution (Naama training school) were also interviewed. Of these eighteen graduates (seven men and eleven women), fifteen were practising their skill as their major and full-time occupation, two were practising their skills part-time, and one had failed to practise at all, because of the lack of equipment. Overall, thirteen were tailors, two carpenters, and three builders.

All the graduates interviewed who were practising their skills were working in the target area, or, in two instances, within Mityana town. Of these, eleven (73 per cent) were running their own businesses but with little knock-on employment effect; only two of them employed some six workers. All eighteen graduates interviewed had found the training useful, singling out income generation as the most significant benefit, and thus meeting the main objective of the TSTU's assistance. Nevertheless, 28 per cent (all female graduates) would have liked training in home management and 22 per cent (mostly males) complained of lack of training in business management.

Levels of income varied greatly from one skill to another. Of the twelve tailors, six were earning an average gross income of USh.36,000 per annum, three an average of USh.76,000, and the remaining three earned an average of USh.220,000. On the other hand, the two practising builders were earning an average of USh.650,000 a month, and the practising carpenter reported annual earnings of USh.1.2m.

ActionAid's TSTU programme was based on the assumption of opportunities for non-agricultural income generation in the target area. If all the fifteen graduates were working within the target area (and none of these claimed to have had any problems in marketing his or her products or services locally), others had certainly left the district. From records available at Kyankowe Polytechnic, for instance, out of nine masons who had graduated, only two were working in the area; the rest had left, for reasons unknown, but it is likely that at least some did so because of local market constraints.

Graduates interviewed identified four major problems. Three groups of four respondents each (27 per cent) named lack of tools and/or equipment, lack of spare parts, and lack of credit facilities as a major constraint. Three (20 per cent) complained of lack of technical advice. Those who complained of lack of spare parts were tailors who had hired old sewing-machines, whose spare parts were expensive and difficult to obtain. The tailors also cited the lack of credit facilities to buy their own machines (instead of hiring). When asked about their future plans, the most frequent response (7 graduates (45.7 per cent)) was a wish to buy tool-kits or sewing-machines, even though none of them had the capital to do so. Second in importance (20 per cent), was the wish to establish their own business rather than be employed. But again, they lacked capital to buy the machines. 13.3 per cent wanted to change their work location to make use of perceived better market potential, and the final 20 per cent had no plans at all.

There is no doubt that the village polytechnics supported by ActionAid appeared to meet a need in the Mityana area, especially in rural areas where artisans are seldom to be found. Although they suffered from high drop-out rates, most of their graduates ended up practising their skills and providing a useful service to their local communities. Nevertheless, four additional factors are relevant. In the first place, many practising graduates are constrained (or unable to practise) because of the lack of start-up capital: no credit and/or savings schemes were associated with the training. Secondly, training is not provided in the real world, while the absence of income-generating activities within the polytechnics compounds this disadvantage. Thirdly, none of the practising graduates interviewed kept business records. Indeed, one-quarter of them singled out the lack of business management as one of the deficiencies of their training. Finally, although time and home management appear to be high priorities for women graduates, the curriculum did not offer such training. Thus, ActionAid appears to have adopted a high-risk, somewhat inefficient and highly subsidized strategy to promote the dissemination of technical skills.

The evaluation also tried to judge the impact of the ActionAid intervention by means of analysis of parallel training and other job opportunities. Eleven small-scale enterprises were contacted to compare training mechanisms within Mityana's informal sector with the service provided by the village polytechnics. They included a bricklayers' association (fifteen young members), two brush-makers, a tile-makers' co-operative society, two tinsmiths, a baker, a weaver, two carpenters, and a tailor. All of them, except for one brush-maker and the tile makers' co-operative, were located within a 4-km. radius of Mityana town.

Of the informal sector workers interviewed, only one (the baker) was not training other people. The others had trained a total of thirty-one people over the preceding year (ranging from two to twelve people at a time) for periods of between a month and a year. The type of training provided contrasted sharply with that offered by the technical institutes in three major ways. First, it was entirely practical and on the job; second, it offered only one skill (excluding formal business management); and third, the training period was far shorter (half as long as that in village polytechnics for tailors and carpenters, for instance). Training by local artisans appeared to be very efficient and, what is more, was undertaken without external assistance. Thus, one informal sector tailor interviewed in Mityana town trained twelve girls within a year, and using only one machine. In sharp contrast, Kyankowe village polytechnic produced a total of nineteen tailors at the end of a two-year course, using fifteen machines and two instructors. Similarly, Namukozi village polytechnic produced only seven tailors at the end of a two-year course, using four machines and three instructors.

The training offered by artisans, while not imparting these skills formally, provided a course within a real business environment. Moreover, with the exception of the tailor, whose trainees were each paying a fee of USh.20,000 per annum, other artisans gave training free of charge and either provided some pocket money to the trainees or allowed them to take on private orders.

This broader perspective therefore suggests that the question needs to be raised whether it would not be a better use of money and resources to support existing artisans in disseminating technical skills rather than to finance the replication of village polytechnics in the rest of the target area.

Support to individuals and groups. ActionAid's support for the dissemination of new skills and technologies has reached an advanced stage in relation to fibro-cement roofing (FCR) tiles, utilizing a new technology in the locality, introduced through ActionAid's efforts. After initial experimentation at the TSTU workshop, seven local people were trained in the technique over a two-month period in late 1988. Of these, two were helped to establish their own tile-making businesses with an interest-free loan repayable over two years (the others continued as roofers). The loan (worth approximately USh.400,000) was made in kind to cover the purchase of the necessary equipment, the construction of a shed and curing tanks, and a first consignment of raw materials (sand, cement, and sisal). In return, the producers agreed to sell their tiles at prices controlled by ActionAid (to ensure that profit levels would be reasonable and the tiles affordable). A large proportion of the production was guaranteed a market by ActionAid for its school construction programme.

ActionAid has clearly provided a product which is appropriate for community buildings in the target area. Fibro-cement tiles have a higher content of local materials than the nearest roofing substitute (iron sheets). They are more durable, quieter in the rain (a special advantage for classrooms), and easy to manufacture. In addition, ActionAid's approach to decentralized production is innovative. The two enterprises established are producing on a regular basis (one is particularly well run), and they have created eight jobs. Production at both sites started in mid-1989. In the first few months, demand was low: in spite of the subsidies offered, the new technology did not attract prospective customers. By early 1990, however, both workshops reported that they could not satisfy demand. One entrepreneur then increased capacity to produce 200 tiles per day, although he complained of the small profit margin allowed by the pricing structure.

In the long run, it is the competitiveness of this new product *vis-à-vis* iron sheets which will determine its sustainability. At the end of 1990, the cost of tiling was USh.3,378 per square metre, compared with USh.2,810 for iron sheeting. By the time of the evaluation, the price differentials were cushioned by ActionAid orders (close to half the production of one workshop), and all school construction work within a 10 km. radius of Mityana is now expected to use FCR tiles, which are likely to remain a top-of-the-range product for relatively well-off individuals in town. In the target area demand will in all likelihood be restricted in the medium term to communal buildings (in most cases supported by AMP). This lack of demand will present special problems for the two entrepreneurs trained by ActionAid, once the subsidies are withdrawn. The loans provided by ActionAid have still largely to be repaid; a decision has already been made to extend the repayment period.

The TSTU has been closely associated with a Women in Development (WID) initiative, which started as a pilot scheme in two parishes in 1989, and was later extended to the whole population of the area. It has had three main objectives: first, to raise awareness of the need for the full involvement of women in development; second, to train members of at least eight women's groups in general and specific leadership and development issues; third, to make available to group members simple appropriate technologies for home improvement.

In 1989/90, with the help of twenty Resistance Committees, awareness-raising meetings were held for both women and men, and six new women's groups were formed. Training sessions were held to discuss problems raised by the groups, such as time management, upbringing of children, home management, child nutrition, AIDS control, first aid, and ways of starting an income-generating project. In addition, AMP provided training in planning, budgeting, and leadership skills. Eight educational trips to other groups were organized for 161 women, and 303 home visits were conducted. Demonstration sessions were held to promote mud-stoves, maize-strippers, and groundnut-shellers. Income-generating activities have been identified by the six groups, including feeding brickmakers, smoking fish, making pancakes for sale to schoolchildren, setting up a piggery, and vegetable-growing, on either a group or individual basis.

During the evaluation, ten women's groups (with memberships ranging from six to twenty-five) were visited, eight of which had been receiving support from ActionAid; the remaining two were unassisted. Most of the AMP-assisted groups cited three main reasons for setting up their group. Of major importance was the impetus provided by ActionAid. Other factors were to better themselves in health and agriculture, to learn other useful skills, and finally to share experiences, socialize, and show an example to other women. Training in time saving and home care, as well as visits to other groups, were cited by group members as having been especially useful. The introduction of mud-stoves has also been successful, with half the members in some of the groups using one.

In spite of the decision to offer only training and advice, some of the groups were formed specifically because members expected material assistance from the programme. Not surprisingly, the degree of commitment to these groups is limited, and members complain of poor attendance at meetings, especially when there is no ActionAid presence. Five of the eight groups suffered from poor organization (poor membership fee records, failure to contribute to group funds from craft sales, limited attendance); the advantages of group membership thus remain unclear. The other three groups, on the other hand, could be considered well organized.

Some of the groups visited were very dependent on ActionAid. In one instance, members unanimously declared that the withdrawal of AMP support would lead to the group's demise, and most bemoaned the fact that ActionAid no longer provided agricultural inputs. In another instance, while great difficulties were encountered in raising the annual membership fee of USh.500, raising USh.5,000 as part payment for a pig was not seen as a problem, if ActionAid provided the rest.

Members generally considered the groups more useful as a means of learning than for collective work. In all the groups the main activity continued to be traditional crafts (making mats, baskets, etc.) which ActionAid has encouraged through its training schemes. As an economic venture, however, crafts have been plagued by marketing problems. Four of the groups began other activities: three have joint agricultural projects, using borrowed land, one raises pigs, while the fourth is engaged in tailoring (using a sewing-machine bought at half price from ActionAid).

Unassisted groups have benefited from having been formed without external assistance to meet a perceived need. Indeed, both the unaided groups visited displayed a greater degree of initiative than the others. Thus, one is attempting to generate income to help local orphans acquire education, clothing, and better health. It has managed to borrow land to grow yams and tomatoes, raising USh.22,000, of which USh.1,000 per term has gone towards school fees. The group would like to have access to credit to start a poultry project. The other unaided group is based in town and is of very recent origin. Its ten members have started craftwork and baking cakes. It also rents a sewing-machine, and aims to teach sewing skills to school drop-outs. The group faces difficulties in marketing its crafts, but its baking is more successful. Future plans include setting up a poultry farm if credit becomes available.

In summary, ActionAid's assistance has clearly helped a number of women's groups develop. In most cases, however, the economic prospects remain poor for the main income-generating activity (traditional crafts). However, other initiatives have been launched and the training provided has been highly appreciated by group members. A number of new ideas have been adopted, the most striking of which is the adoption of improved mud-stoves. But the programme appears to be facing two problems. One stems from the persistent view that ActionAid is a provider of inputs, thus fostering an attitude of dependence which seems all-pervasive. Secondly, these women's initiatives seem to be isolated from other parts of the programme, and the rationale for separate WID activities remains unclear.

Other sectors. In 1988 the TSTU provided two weeks' training in carpentry skills for eighteen teachers, in order to promote the dissemination of these skills among the school population (as encouraged by government), and to enable teachers to undertake simple school repairs and maintenance themselves. The eighteen schools to which these teachers belonged were later supplied with tool-kits. Ten of these schools were visited during the ODI evaluation, three of them happened to have carpentry teachers who had not been trained by the AMP.

Of the seven teachers trained by the AMP, four felt that the training had been insufficient. Some said that they did not know how to use some of the tools provided by ActionAid; one of the schools visited had never used the tools, probably reflecting a low level of technical self-confidence on the part of the teacher. The remaining three teachers had acquired some carpentry knowledge prior to the ActionAid course. Nevertheless, all the teachers (including the one who had never used the tools) said that they were practising some skills, whatever the standard. As for the impact of the programme outside the schools, three of the teachers interviewed were already training some school drop-outs in their own workshops, whereas one was employing other people. Three teachers were producing household furniture in their own workshops, generating an average income of about USh.7,100 per month.

Ten roofers were also trained at the AMP workshop to use FCR tiles for schools and houses. Six were traced during the evaluation exercise. With the exception of a roofer from the experienced group, all found the training very useful in extending their range of skills and giving them new business opportunities. Indeed all but one of those interviewed had become full-time roofers, and were self-employed in the vicinity of Mityana town. Each was employing between two and seven employees, and all estimated that their income had increased as a result of their training. Their main problems stemmed from the lack of tools for the younger roofers, while all five of them complained of lack of jobs because of a recent drop in the quality of 'ActionAid tiles'.

The main contribution of the TSTU to the community-based health-care programme has been the training of twenty-two local masons in well-digging and spring-protection techniques. Three dispensaries have also been built, with AMP providing free raw materials and furniture. Of the twenty-two masons trained by the AMP (in 1988), ten were still practising their new skills at the time of the evaluation. The drop-outs appeared to have given up in the face of the time and effort required to mobilize communities. The relatively high drop-out rate is likely to have also been caused by the fact that the masons were selected by ActionAid. Now the choice of candidates is left to the local communities. Interviews with three of the still-practising trained masons (who had together protected twenty-four springs and dug one well) indicated that all found the training useful, although further training would have been welcomed in health-related fields. All three, however, practised their skills part-time, usually because there were not enough sites.

Artisans in the informal sector. A rapid survey of artisans in the informal sector provides a few elements of comparison with unaided artisans and groups of artisans. The artisans interviewed indicated that they received a sizeable gross income ranging from USh.800,000 to USh.2.4 m. a year (even if most of the figures need to be treated with caution, since none of the artisans interviewed kept any account-books).

Through their activities, employment had been created at an average of just under four jobs per enterprise, or, if trainees are included, seven per enterprise, by no means a negligible figure for Mityana. Five enterprises were selling their products at their places of work (carpenters, brick-layers, tile-makers, and the tailor); the two tinsmiths sold at their place of work as well as in town. In two-thirds of the cases, therefore, the local market was sufficient to absorb all the production, supporting the TSTU's presumption that there is already a local market in the target area for non-agricultural products. The remaining four enterprises (a baker, a weaver, and two brush-makers) were selling only part of their products in the vicinity of Mityana.

Generally, Mityana's informal sector gives the impression of rapid growth. Of eleven small-scale enterprises visited, nine (82 per cent) cited the lack of credit facilities or working capital as their major business constraint. Few of these artisans currently qualify for AMP attention as they operate outside the target area. Yet they could provide a self-sustaining conduit for effective skills dissemination (especially if they were assisted with the acquisition of business skills, design work, and new product development), as AMP's experience with springs and well technicians has ably demonstrated.

The Wider Context

Several characteristics of ActionAid's programme in Mityana combine to make it a programme of interest in the broader context of NGO initiatives in Uganda: its rigorous definition of a target area; its development of a separate extension structure; its multi-disciplinary approach; and its attempts to move towards a participatory approach. Yet, as with other NGOs adopting a change-agent approach, ActionAid is faced with a seemingly insurmountable problem: the adoption of a methodology relying heavily on salaried field-workers which, in itself, is unlikely to become sustainable. The development of productive activities which can be sustained by local communities or government services therefore provides an avenue which could be fruitfully explored by the AMP. To some extent, the AMP has got round this problem by working through farmers' and other groups, and by stimulating community awareness by the creation of committees. Such an approach appears to be beneficial, though difficult to implement, especially if the programme continues to strive to sever all links with the past approach based on delivery of inputs and subsidies.

Too rigid a definition of the target area can lead to a down-playing of the influence of external factors. Thus, the exclusion of urban artisans from the programme because they work outside the target area provides an example of this island approach. However, the AMP area is very dependent upon services provided by Mityana town, just as the town's present development results to a great extent from growth in the hinterland.

The AMP argues that in its target area poverty is not due to exploitation by the rich or to climate, but to lack of awareness and training. Hence it is argued that the causes of poverty are unique to a particular environment, and no general rules can be developed for all ActionAid programmes. Its current policy is to exclude the affluent, but it does not seem to have actively sought out and identified the most vulnerable, thereby leaving it open to the criticism that it has adopted an indiscriminate blanket approach which does not sufficiently take into account the considerable social and economic differentiation within the target area.

ActionAid lays emphasis on baseline studies, situational analyses, and focused group discussions to analyse the causes of poverty, and to identify qualitative and quantitative indicators to measure its impact. Even if less progress might have been registered in this regard in the AMP than in other ActionAid programmes, the emphasis placed on these issues is certainly welcome in the wider context of NGOs which have often justifiably been accused of management sloppiness.

The greatest obstacle to effective impact for the AMP remains, however, the legacy of its earlier approach of providing free or subsidized inputs. This legacy continues to undermine its relationship with its target population, whose perception of the programme remains largely unchanged.

CONCLUSIONS

Providing accurate assessments of the effectiveness and efficiency of NGO projects in Uganda is constrained in a major way by lack of information, as well as by uncertainty surrounding quantifiable objectives, costs incurred, and programme benefits. Nevertheless, if the case-studies have demonstrated their capacity to provide a service that would not otherwise be available, the NGOs have also illustrated the lack of emphasis placed on monitoring and evaluation mechanisms. In part this stems from a lack of resources and a shortage of necessary skills, and, more generally, from the low priority accorded to the collection of this information. Atypical in this respect has been the analysis undertaken by the AMP project: although it is too early for a judgement on its longer-term impact to be made, it has highlighted some of the potential pitfalls of management by objectives and of bureaucratization in rural development programmes of the type the AMP is attempting to implement. These factors, and the range, scale, and variety of different forms of NGO intervention, clearly limit the possibility of making generalizations about the impact of NGO projects in Uganda.

Lack of hard data, however, does not mean that comments on efficiency and effectiveness cannot be made. In general, the case-study projects have been effective in achieving at least some of their initial goals. In most cases, the more tangible objectives set have been attained: a functioning workshop has been rehabilitated and expanded in Gulu, aid-posts have been built in Busoga, springs have been protected and classrooms renovated in Mityana, although the proliferation of programme objectives —for instance in relation to MSRDP, ACORD, and AMP—created important management constraints. On the other hand, the sustainability of these initiatives remains uncertain, especially when high project costs (including administrative overheads and other programme delivery expenditure) are set against the size of the target population and their ability to meet the costs in the future.[11] Nevertheless, the case-studies do suggest quite strongly that it is only possible to reach this population effectively if a necessary minimum level of resources is made available: the UWFCT study probably provides the best example of the need for considerable expenditure (other than directly on the credit programme) to ensure that the poor are reached in an effective and sustainable fashion.

Money, though, is by no means everything. Social benefits and, in most cases, a degree of flexibility have enabled the projects examined here to adapt to the changing circumstances of the Ugandan environment. Thus, where development activities have (often) been engulfed by civil disturbances, the NGOs studied have proved able to switch to relief operations, as the ACORD case-study demonstrates. Such flexibility, however, often comes at a price: the run-down character of Uganda's infrastructure has forced the larger agencies to develop their own alternative structures—an expensive exercise in itself, particularly when it involves expatriate personnel. The case-studies have also illustrated how initiatives have frequently been vulnerable to factors outside the control of the relevant NGO, a vulnerability on occasion enhanced, rather than mitigated, by the design of the programme.

In view of the costs involved it could well be that (with the possible exception of the MSRDP) the NGO programmes studied could only be fully justified if their impact goes beyond their immediate project confines: innovation in terms of approach and objectives has often been in evidence, but any potential for replication remains to be exploited. Wider problems of limited co-ordination among NGOs and with other bodies are clearly relevant here: experiences are insufficiently shared, resources are duplicated, and too little is learned from mistakes.

In sum, both the evidence of the case-studies and the wider literature suggest that NGOs active in Uganda can claim to have made a significant contribution in three main areas. In the first place, their relief activities have undoubtedly contributed to alleviating widespread suffering throughout much of the turbulent recent history of the country. What is more, relief efforts have also renewed confidence in the future and, in some cases, self-respect, and possibly even a measure of security. Secondly, NGO involvement in long-term development programming has, in certain areas, provided facilities and services which would not otherwise have been available, particularly in the health and sanitation fields. Finally, NGOs are demonstrating to those concerned that, to be successful, development projects must meet a real need, must demand a high level of participation from the intended beneficiaries (including in the planning of activities) and an active contribution in their implementation and management, and must rest on the utilization of local resources and skills.

Reaching the Poorest?

It is in this context that some further reflections can be made. First, in relation to target-groups. The four NGO projects examined here have often been successful in reaching some of the least accessible areas of the country: all demonstrate an ability to work, either directly or indirectly, in small, sometimes isolated, and occasionally virtually cut-off rural communities.[12] However, their ability to reach the poorest of the poor has been more questionable. In the first place, the detailed social analysis necessary to identify this group (and an examination of issues of power and control rather than symptoms of poverty) has not been carried out. What has been more common is for the target-group to be perceived in rather negative terms as excluding the affluent. This not only makes for a somewhat unfocused approach (most noticeable in the ACORD and MSRDP programmes), but also tends to present the target population as poorer than it is. If the record of NGOs in Uganda in reaching the poorest might well be better than that of official donors, the case-studies also show that reaching the poorest is far from easy or straightforward. The manufacture of ox-ploughs, for instance, is only indirectly relevant to the poorest farmers in Acholi (though a larger supply will be of some benefit, mainly through sharing and lending arrangements). Similarly, while the introduction of fee-paying medical services in Busoga by the MSRDP does often exclude the poorest, the NGO approach—small-scale and face-to-face—allows for the effects of this exclusion to be mitigated through credit arrangements, the field staff's intimate knowledge of the local population, and payments in kind.

Similarly, the uneven record of NGO programmes with an economic focus in attempting to reach Ugandan women and answering their specific needs is also confirmed by the case-studies. While UWFCT and the MSRDP focus on women, the gender implications of the encouragement of ox-ploughing were only addressed by ACORD some years after the launch of its programme (and then only partially), and the gender-sensitivity of some of the AMP initiatives has often been too narrow.

Part of the reason for these weaknesses lies in the pressure on NGOs to produce quick results. NGOs tend to involve themselves with those sections of the population with whom quick results are likely to emerge. In part, this is the product of official funding agencies emphasizing quantified objectives, often at the expense of a participatory methodology. In part, however, it is sometimes a consequence of what one might term increased bureaucratization within NGOs: a growing emphasis on things like baseline studies, quantified objectives, the monitoring of specific indicators, etc. may well go some way towards improving the management and efficiency of projects, but they can also reduce flexibility and response to changing local realities. Furthermore, the case-studies confirm the importance of what could be termed the social self-perception of the NGO: the NGO personnel running projects are themselves part of the local élite, who tend to mix socially with the rich and who often work with local government officials and other powerful community members. This necessarily has an influence on projects, the way they are executed, and the manner in which benefits are distributed.

Scale, Sustainability, and Replicability

While most long-term development programmes implemented by NGOs in Uganda are small-scale, NGOs have increasingly been trying to scale up their activities: two of the case-studies—the ACORD and MSRDP programmes—provide examples of NGO programmes with regional ambitions. In both cases, however, success has been limited. A single—albeit central—element of their multi-sectoral programmes registered progress (the engineering workshop and the health programme, respectively) but neither agency can claim to have had the broad impact it had envisaged at the outset. A major reason for the limited success lay in management constraints: the AMP objective of attempting to reach over 50,000 people in a three-year period appeared, for instance, to be beyond the capacity of the staff to service such a large initiative. In one case, too, the political implications of attempting to promote a sizeable initiative were not sufficiently understood.

Programme sustainability, though clearly important, also appeared to be problematic. Two particular issues can be highlighted. First, although the participation of beneficiaries was acknowledged as all-important, the level of participation ranged from mediocre to poor. Second, project success was often critically related to the quality and input of the staff currently servicing the projects—but how long can this commitment be sustained? The case-studies indicate that if staff commitment and the desire to involve target-groups cannot ensure the long-term sustainability of programmes, neither can they guarantee the sustainability of the operational NGOs themselves.

At the programme level, long-term prospects were undermined, to a greater or lesser extent, by the following factors:

- lack of income generated, either because activities failed to meet their objectives, or because they were dominated by social welfare objectives which do not lend themselves to financial autonomy;
- inappropriate project design or implementation methods;
- lack of sufficient thought given to the institutional setting of the project, or little consideration given to institution-building;

• factors external to the project, such as political instability and deteriorating economic performance in the region of the project. Interestingly, the programmes assessed appeared to be relatively unaffected by direct government interference, while they also benefited little from government support.

From an institutional perspective, long-term prospects tend to be undermined where they are dependent on one or two key individuals (usually the founder members), and where they overwhelmingly rely on one or two external funding sources. The UWFCT case-study suggests, furthermore, that pursuing financial autonomy objectives too rapidly could undermine the development goals of the organization. This sort of dilemma is very common, particularly among projects designed to provide a service rather than to develop income-generating activities.

It is too early to assess the replicability of the projects studied (and of most NGO development projects in Uganda) because of their relative youth. None the less it should be noted that the issue of replication does not figure explicitly in the design stage of most programmes, even if the geographical extension of activities sometimes constitutes one of the objectives. The greatest potential for replication would appear to lie in the medical field. Elsewhere, the relative lack of co-ordination among NGOs, together with generally poor communications with the government, restrict the potential for learning from experiences and thus for the replication of successful programmes.

Specificity and Innovation

The case-studies generally support the view that in some respects the NGOs in Uganda have made their mark by default: decreasing resources at the disposal of the state have curtailed its effectiveness in providing services, while official aid programmes have tended to focus on areas of little immediate concern to NGOs (infrastructure, industrial rehabilitation, etc.). They also provide less evidence of participation and innovation than the conventional wisdom might have suggested. They all indicate the importance that the NGOs attach to participation, but the practice is different. Participation at the planning stage often remains elusive, although the UWFCT case-study is a noteworthy exception in this respect. Accountability to donors is in practice often of greater importance than accountability to the beneficiaries, often because of the need to continue to receive funds or to increase their flow. This tends to undermine group participation. Participatory evaluation and monitoring mechanisms are still a rarity: accountability to target-groups is most often conspicuous by its absence.

The innovative nature of an NGO approach has other limits in Uganda. Although increased emphasis is placed on group formation and group dynamics, traditional community development approaches often prevail. Many agencies have been reluctant to experiment with types of intervention outside their traditional domain. Thus work with individuals, rather than with groups, generally remains out of bounds, as does any comprehensive attempt to assess the potential of the country's private sector. Similarly, the absence of pre-project investigations has often led NGOs to ignore or bypass local institutions in favour of launching their own organizational blueprints whose sustainability is not always assured.

The external environment was clearly influential in all the case-studies, but was of particular importance to project impact in two of them: the WACU workshop in northern Uganda has been extremely vulnerable to both political upheaval and the slow pace of infrastructural rehabilitation, while both the Workshop's and the UWFCT's activities have been especially affected by the difficulties experienced by Uganda at the macroeconomic level. The case-studies also highlight the importance of state–NGO relationships, revealing their different, and changing, nature, sometimes positive and sometimes negative. Of importance, too, some of the case-studies suggest a certain blindness to the world outside the project, even to the world outside the approaches used by NGOs in other circumstances.

The Future for NGOs in Uganda

These conclusions do appear to have implications for future NGO involvement in Uganda. Overall impact has been hampered by the poor level of communication with government, particularly the limited involvement of NGOs in policy matters, while insufficient attention has been paid to the strengthening of existing (or the creation of new) institutions. It thus seems clear that NGO effectiveness, in its broadest sense, would benefit from closer co-ordination (in some instances even to the extent of integration of particular programmes) with government initiatives. The fact that NGOs have, at least in part, thrived because of the state's retreat, underlines the point that they are particularly well placed to contribute to a strengthening of public institutions, rather than developing their own separate systems for programme delivery.

Depending on precise modalities, the participation of NGOs in district-level planning mechanisms might provide an appropriate opportunity for increased collaboration, for a greater degree of much-needed NGO accountability, and for enhanced popular confidence in the state's legitimacy. The decentralization of official structures is, however, no panacea; it may well entail a closer control over the population. But here again, NGOs would be well placed to articulate the necessary countervailing power. Provided they can develop their own accountability mechanisms both internally and towards their target-groups, NGOs have a crucial role to play in strengthening the establishment of a civil society with diverse and effective pressure-groups able to sustain and reinforce mechanisms of democratic control, which are themselves increasingly seen as a pre-condition for genuine progress. Similarly, NGOs have an important role to play with regard to Resistance Committees, especially in developing their planning capacities and in providing a voice for the less articulate.

Should this role be extended to participation in national policy development? While NGOs may well feel that in so doing they might be seen to share responsibility for something over which they will have little subsequent authority, the lack of dialogue has clearly restricted their effectiveness. Their accumulated experience and their relative proximity to socio-economic groups with limited skills to articulate their interests would seem to provide them with a role in, at least, the formulation of future official poverty-alleviation programmes. Similarly, NGOs would seem to have a special task, indeed responsibility, in promoting a global strategy to tackle the country's North–South divide—possibly the main cause of instability in Uganda.

Clearly, NGO efforts will benefit from better co-ordination and collaboration (among themselves as well as with government) and making their experiences more widely known. In Uganda, the general public is not well informed about NGO programmes and, as a result, sometimes suspects their motives. Sharing project results will be all the more effective if it embraces national policy questions and the choice of target-groups as well as immediate programme issues.

In spite (but also because) of their rapid growth, some local NGOs remain weak and dependent on foreign funding, bureaucratically top-heavy (in contradiction to their message of self-reliance!) and without a clearly defined societal role. They still need to develop their corporate identity rather than trying to be an image of northern NGOs. Likewise, northern NGOs increasingly need to examine the dimensions of a new division of labour with their Ugandan counterparts, especially the role of local NGOs in fostering the development of grass-roots groups.

Finally, NGO effectiveness might well be enhanced through a move away from what is at present largely a reactive attitude to development problems towards a renewed attempt at imaginative programming. While a better understanding of social processes at work in the country will lead to a more precise definition of target-groups, involvement in infrastructural projects, in disaster prevention and preparedness (including institution-building), in tackling marketing constraints, in further strengthening the dynamism of the private sector, and in considering broader responses to conflict situations, all provide potential new avenues for effective and innovative NGO work in Uganda.

NOTES

1. Originally established in liberated areas as a mechanism to organize popular resistance, their role now embraces the settlement of disputes and other law-and-order functions, the provision of services and the formulation of development plans, and generally acting as a communication link between government and people.
2. The ODA disburses about one-seventh of its Uganda budget through a dozen UK NGOs.
3. This Poverty and Social Costs of Adjustment (PAPSCA) project was launched by the World Bank in 1990.
4. This case-study was undertaken with the assistance of Mary Nannono, Women in Development focal-point officer of the Ministry of Industry, Kampala.
5. The old Ugandan shilling (USh.) was officially valued at 1,450 to US$1 in 1986. Following the introduction of a new shilling in 1987 at a parity of USh.60 to the $, there has been a succession of devaluations, some very substantial, and the rate had dropped to USh.223 in 1989, and USh.440 by July 1990. By early 1995 the rate had declined even further to USh.918.

6. 'Allocation' was the standard (and *ad hoc*) administrative procedure used throughout the Amin years to transfer the use of 'Departed Asians' Properties' to Ugandan individuals or corporate bodies.

7. ACORD estimated in 1984 that 12,000 out of 50,000 households in Gulu and 33,000 out of 56,000 households in Kitgum used ploughs.

8. At the time of the study, IFAD was selling imported ploughs at USh.6,000 in a neighbouring district (approximately $7.50 at the open market rate), compared with USh.48,000 for a WACU plough.

9. This case-study was undertaken with the assistance of Mary Nannono, Women in Development focal-point officer of the Ministry of Industry, Kampala.

10. This case-study was undertaken with the assistance of Sam Kayabwe from the Makerere Institute of Social Research, Kampala.

11. It would be wrong, however, to make sweeping generalizations. An expensive NGO programme such as the WACU workshop, which has entailed a total investment of £500,000, still only represents less than £1 per head of population in the programme area.

12. This conclusion has been confirmed for a recent study of the impact of Finnish NGOs in Uganda (Bebbington, 1994).

10

Zimbabwe

In relation to a number of key development indicators, Zimbabwe's record during the 1980s was impressive. The economy grew at an average rate of 3.9 per cent a year, school enrolments rose from 1.3 million in 1980 to 2.9 million in 1989, including a ninefold increase in secondary-school places, while small-scale, largely peasant, agriculture flourished, with marketed output from the communal areas expanding twentyfold and rising from 4 to 20 per cent of national marketed output. Clearly, however, all is not well. In 1990 the government announced the inauguration of a structural adjustment programme approved by both the World Bank and the International Monetary Fund, aimed at raising and sustaining higher medium- and long-term growth and reducing poverty. Comparatively high average per capita income ($570 in 1992), a highly skewed income and wealth distribution, extensive lush and leafy urban suburbs, and a well-functioning transport system all disguise the extent and depth of poverty and malnutrition which also characterize contemporary Zimbabwe. At the start of the 1990s, over 25 per cent of the labour-force was unemployed, while the majority of formal-sector workers were probably in receipt of sub-poverty wages. In the rural areas, containing 70 per cent of the total population of 10 million, it is estimated that at least 55 per cent of households live in poverty: in many years between 25 and 60 per cent of farming families fail to produce sufficient food to cover their own basic requirements. This is the context in which NGOs operate in Zimbabwe today.

Following Independence in 1980, there was an explosion of NGO activity, with dozens of new foreign NGOs joining the few already present in the country, as well as a steady growth of both nation-wide and more locally-based indigenous NGOs. Following a brief overview of the present role of NGOs in Zimbabwe, this chapter summarizes the reports of in-depth evaluations of four NGO projects, and ends by drawing some more general conclusions based on their insights.

The choice of Zimbabwe as one of the four countries analysed in this study is of wider interest for three reasons. First, the post-Independence period has witnessed a notable shift in emphasis in NGO activities, from a prime focus on welfare and relief activities to more development-oriented forms of intervention, usually aimed, directly or indirectly, at poverty alleviation. In contrast to the experience of Uganda described in the previous chapter, most NGOs are able to concentrate on promoting development interventions without fear that this work will be continually disrupted. Secondly, Zimbabwe's comparatively well-developed infrastructure, its fairly efficient public administrative system, and its generally benign attitude to NGOs provide one

This chapter was substantially written by Ann Muir, based on her longer primary research report produced as a technical working paper of the Overseas Development Institute (Muir with Riddell, 1992).

of the most supportive contexts for NGO work in Africa today. Thus if NGOs have difficulty in achieving their objectives of poverty alleviation in this relatively support- ive institutional setting, their task is likely to be even more difficult in most other countries of Africa. Finally, the fourth case-study—the Campfire project in the Zam- bezi valley—reports on an innovative approach to poverty alleviation with potential applicability beyond the borders of Zimbabwe.

AN OVERVIEW

Numbers and Characteristics

Little is known about the overall impact of NGOs in Zimbabwe, either within gov- ernment circles or within the NGO world itself. There is no formal (or effective informal) mechanism for obtaining comprehensive information which would enable a sound assessment to be made. While foreign NGOs are required to be registered with the government prior to their involvement in the country, there is no uniform system of registration; some, but not all, are required to re-register after operating for two or three years, but there is no particular information requirement for this. The National Planning Agency (with overall responsibility for the national development plan) makes no mention of the role of NGOs in its published planning documents.

There is probably even greater ignorance about NGOs within official aid agencies (both bilateral and multilateral). What bilateral agencies tend to know best are details of the projects executed by NGOs from their own countries, as well as the projects or programmes of some of the larger NGOs involved in particular sectoral programmes, notably in the health and sanitation field. They tend to know least about smaller indigenous NGOs who, in growing numbers, knock on their doors to ask for funding, though a number of donors often know little about the projects of local NGOs even if these are funded by NGOs from their own country. Also surprising is the degree of ignorance among those working themselves for other NGOs: the over-publicity of the few conceals the paucity of information of the majority. NGOs tend to know about other NGOs working in the same locality and of the larger ones working in the same field or sectoral activity, but there is often a high level of ignorance especially of the different approaches or techniques used by other NGOs (see Riddell *et al.*, 1995).

What is striking, however, is that the further from the centre of government or the aid world one moves, the more (and the more detailed) is the information which different government officers have of the activities of NGOs in the areas covered by their respective jobs.[1] This is especially true of particular line ministries, especially agriculture, while, in contrast to the national level, some NGOs, or at least some of their projects, do appear in provincial planning documents. There is usually a great willingness on the part of NGOs working at these levels to provide information to officials with whom the NGO comes into contact.

How many NGOs are there? There are certainly thousands of non-governmental or private organizations in some way involved in promoting or initiating development projects or programmes in Zimbabwe. NGOs involved in development activities provide direct employment for thousands of Zimbabweans, they are found in both urban and rural localities throughout the country working across a range of activities, and they are a major source of foreign exchange to the national exchequer. In 1989 the Ministry of Labour, Manpower Planning and Social Welfare had a record of some 800 organizations registered with it (Hifab, 1989: 226), although many of these would be welfare rather than developmentally oriented. According to the umbrella organization, the National Association of Non-Governmental Organizations (NANGO), (previously VOICE, Voluntary Organizations in Community Enterprise), in 1988 there were over fifty international NGOs operating in the country. If size is a criterion, then there are certainly well over fifty NGOs, local and foreign-based, which employ significant numbers of people (over twenty each including field staff) and whose financial turnover exceeds Z$200,000. One of the fastest growing groups of NGOs in terms of finance and influence are the politically linked Zimbabwean organizations, operating in more than one locality. These would include the President's Fund, Child Survival (originally under the patronage of the President's late wife), and the Zimbabwe Development Trust (under the tutelage of Vice President Joshua Nkomo); the latter's total income for 1990 was well in excess of Z$1million.

There are no reliable estimates of either the total income and expenditure of NGOs operating in Zimbabwe or of the foreign-exchange inflows to the country resulting from their activity. However, in 1990 total spending by NGOs was probably approaching Z$150m., in quantitative terms amounting to between 15 and 20 per cent of the total value of official aid to Zimbabwe. To this needs to be added the substantial inflow of funds to foreign NGOs. Thus, the Dutch Embassy in Harare judged that $8m. came to Zimbabwe in 1989 solely from Dutch NGOs (de Graaf *et al.*, 1991: 8). 1995 estimates suggest that total inflows of funds to NGOs and NGO projects in Zimbabwe had risen to between Z$300m. and Z$500m. (Riddell *et al.*, 1995: 13).

Other trends are also visible. Thus, indigenous and independent NGOs have increasingly wanted to formulate an identity distinct both from foreign NGOs and from NGOs with affiliations or close associations with the ruling party, ZANU (PF). What is more, it would appear that the establishment of networks and information exchanges among particular groups of NGOs—often set up in response to feelings of isolation—has itself tended to have the effect of accentuating or perpetuating other divisions within the NGO movement as a whole.[2]

NGOs working in Zimbabwe can be classified into at least seven groupings:[3] foreign-based but locally-registered (international) NGOs; independent Zimbabwean organizations, operating in more than one, and in only one, locality; church-based Zimbabwean organizations, operating in more than one, and in only one, locality; and politically linked Zimbabwean organizations, operating in more than one, and in only one, locality.

A distinction can also be made between those organizations which see their role in terms of development and development promotion and those which see themselves— or which are seen by others—as more welfare-oriented in the work they do. Historically, almost all the larger NGOs were involved in some form of welfare work, especially during the UDI years when emergency relief was of such importance. Within the development category, one can also distinguish between those for whom self-management membership is of central importance and those for whom helping in a more paternalistic way is more the norm. The bulk of NGO activity takes place in the two Mashonaland provinces, the least in the two provinces of Matabeleland.

In the development sphere, most NGO intervention is concentrated around three broad areas of activity:

- designing and executing concrete projects for (and hopefully with) particular targeted groups;
- imparting particular skills, usually on an individual basis; and
- organizing, enhancing, or more generally empowering local groups, in particular to increase their ability to take responsibility and thereby to achieve more immediate requirements.

NGOs and Poverty Alleviation

The greatest concentration of NGO work is in the communal areas (formerly the 'tribal trust lands'), where early post-Independence interventions consisted of executing concrete projects among groups and/or encouraging more general group animation. However, these initiatives also embraced a wide range of technical assistance or skills training, both in the formal educational system and outside it; numerous foreign volunteers, some only high-school graduates, flew in to service new and re-opened schools and emergent centres of learning. The early 1980s also saw the beginnings of efforts to improve the health status of rural people in particular, a form of NGO intervention which was to expand rapidly as the decade progressed.

In the early 1980s, new NGO activities in the communal areas tended to occur in the more isolated areas which had been all but neglected by the colonial government in terms of economic and social services: Binga, for instance, was popular with some foreign NGOs. At the same time, the new government's emphasis on collective and co-operative (especially rurally based) enterprise and its desire to promote land resettlement through collective efforts appealed to a range of NGOs, leading to intensive efforts in co-operative development, including, importantly, work with ex-combatants. These continue to this day. More recently, however, the fashion of promoting collective co-operatives has waned, although some larger NGOs still work in this field, and new ones, like the Collective Self-Finance Scheme (CSFS) started in the post-1986 period. The communal areas as a whole then became areas of more intensive activity on the part of the still-growing numbers of development-oriented NGOs. Indeed, by the end of the 1980s, some specific localities had been all but divided off as exclusive areas where only one NGO was allowed to operate, not unlike the practice of the major missionary societies at the turn of the century. In addition, however, as the government clarified its own plans in the fields of water, health, and sanitation in particular, the growth of NGO involvement in these areas accelerated in the second half of the decade.

In relation to their mode of insertion into the communal areas, the word most commonly used by NGOs is grass-roots, without much unpackaging of the term: at its simplest it implies not the rich or richer stratum of communal area society. Discussions with NGOs suggest that until recently little consideration was given to the question of more precisely who within the communal areas were to be the targets of their approach; for a number of foreign-based NGOs in particular the issue is still not widely addressed.[4] Where the intervention is more concerned with the provision of tangible assets, such as wells, water-pumps, dams, and sanitation, coverage is usually of a geographically defined area.

For almost all other types of NGO communal area intervention, the approach is to work with and through groups. In general, it has not been common practice for NGOs to form groups with whom to work in these areas; rather they tend to work with groups which are already in existence. Yet the available evidence (though far from comprehensive) would tend to suggest that the poorest households tend disproportionately to be excluded from existing groups in the communal areas. This generalization would also appear to hold true for women's groups: those already in existence tend to draw their members from the most active and dynamic within particular localities. The outcome is that the poorest households, including those headed by single, widowed, or divorced women and those without access to income from formal-sector migrancy sources, tend disproportionately (though by no means totally) to be excluded from NGO interventions in the communal areas.

Poverty areas and issues other than in the communal areas have featured in the work of only a minority of NGOs. Thus, although there have been some exceptions (such as the British-based Save the Children Fund), NGOs have tended to be only minimally involved among the poor households of workers in the commercial farming sector, which contains at least one million poor people. Similarly, with few exceptions, there has been very little NGO activity among other low-paid formal sector employees in the urban areas, such as the 100,000 strong domestic workers and their families. There has also been next to no NGO developmental activity among poor urban communities, geared for instance to promoting self-employment opportunities among the unemployed, even though the urban churches in particular have for many years helped with relief and welfare efforts.

NGO–Government Relations

An increasingly important issue for NGOs active in development is their relationship with the government. In practice, the most common form of NGO intervention would appear to be complementary to that of government. Most projects or programmes could be termed 'gap-filling' with NGOs providing services and/or resources to groups or communities not supplied by the government and often not much different from those which government would like to provide, if it had the resources to do so.

The most explicit gap-filling role is providing services and resources delivered as part of a broad national or provincial plan. This covers, for instance, health-delivery services, and the provision of clean water and sanitation facilities, including the building of small dams, wells, etc. It would also include the provision of technical assistance and advisory skills, most common in the agricultural, education, and health sectors but, in the case of some NGOs, covering areas like building skills, process engineering, and advice on alternative energy sources. Most of the NGOs involved in these activities have been the larger foreign-based and foreign-funded NGOs.

Within the agricultural sector, NGO intervention in the communal areas is usually focused on one or more of a series of activities aimed at raising income levels. These include: the provision of credit, help with savings initiatives, technical advice on inputs and diversifying the range of crops produced, assistance with ploughing, the supply of inputs, and help with marketing. Only recently, and only then in particular localities, have systematic attempts been made by NGOs to co-ordinate their activities with those of the government in promoting agricultural development.

Two other types of gap-filling NGO interventions in the area of rural development have been assistance to co-operatives (mostly collective co-operatives) and the promotion of income-generating projects (IGPs), which became popular with NGOs in the early 1980s and were at their height in the 1984–6 period. The projects promoted were in general small-scale, and the approach used by NGOs was very similar to government-sponsored activities in this area, promoted especially among women's groups. Overall, both government and NGO efforts appear largely to have failed, as evidenced by a 1985 evaluation of NGO projects which concluded 'that the IGP activities of NGOs in Zimbabwe have had little impact on income generation and virtually no impact on employment generation' (Else, 1987: 6). According to the study, this has been because the NGOs promoting the IGPs simply lacked the range of skills necessary to execute such ventures—weaknesses, surprisingly, acknowledged by the NGOs actually promoting the projects! For many people involved in rural development in Zimbabwe, the term income-generation is now loaded with negative connotations, equated with income loss and seen more as a method of avoiding rather than addressing the factors perpetuating rural poverty. In contrast, progressive NGOs, such as the Organization of Rural Associations for Progress (ORAP), are now placing emphasis on what they term 'income-saving'.

The view that NGO activity is predominantly gap-filling needs some refinement. While, in their different interventions, the objectives of both the government and the NGOs may have been similar, there have often been differences in approach. What tends to distinguish many NGOs in rural development activities is the emphasis they place on co-operation, community participation, and group action as the basis upon which their projects and programmes are built. Even this point needs to be made carefully, however, for it would be equally wrong to argue that the government ignores group factors and promotes agriculture exclusively through emphasis on service delivery to and through individuals. Indeed, one of the principles of government action is its own emphasis on groups, and co-operatives. The difference is more that government interventions tend in practice to have more of a technical and impersonal touch, and be characterized by the sluggishness intrinsic to a large bureaucracy. Many

NGOs in Zimbabwe have more flexibility than the government: they have the ability to change course and to respond to the changing needs of the groups being assisted.

NGO innovation has by no means been restricted to rural development projects. Some NGOs such as the British-based Intermediate Technology Development Group (ITDG), as well as specialized departments or parts of the local institutions of Silveira House, the Glen Forest Training Centre, and the Manicaland Development Association, function principally as promoters of new ideas. Increasingly the ideas promoted—such as the use of bio-gas and solar ovens as substitutes for wood-fuel—are being adopted by peasant farmers, which is at least one indicator of success in this field.

Finally, NGOs in Zimbabwe have tended not to enter the stage of national public policy advocacy, to lobby for either improvement in group interests or changes in national or indeed provincial policies which might lead to a greater allocation of resources to the poor or a strengthening of their power to act for themselves. Even in the sphere of communal area development, in which they have been most heavily involved, very few NGOs have been active individually or in groups in attempting to influence the formulation of or alterations to agricultural and rural development policies. This is doubly strange because of the stress laid by so many NGOs working among the rural poor in the resettlement and communal areas on the concept of empowerment and the benefits obtained from group action. Group work has been dominated by trying to maximize the gains that groups could obtain within the wider context, rather than in trying to alter that environment or engage in debate to initiate change. It is therefore of more than passing interest to note that among the objectives of NANGO are 'to promote and facilitate the interaction . . . among local NGOs and relevant institutions, including Government, and to promote the linking up of the local organisations with national, regional and international bodies for the purposes of furthering (its overall) objectives' (NANGO, 1991: 4–6).

SILVEIRA HOUSE FARMER GROUP CREDIT PROJECT[5]

One of the oldest NGOs in Zimbabwe, Silveira House is a training and development centre run by the Society of Jesus (Jesuits) in the Roman Catholic Archdiocese of Harare. Its major activities cover agriculture, youth work, trade unions, civics, nutrition, dressmaking, and typing, plus an appropriate technology department. Underpinning these activities is a twin approach of, first, awareness-raising and motivation courses, and secondly, the execution of projects aimed at achieving economic betterment to enable people to gain greater control over their lives. Today it is one of the largest NGOs in Zimbabwe, employing over 150 staff. Two European church agencies, Misereor and CEBEMO, are the principal core funders, while Oxfam met the capital and recurrent costs of the agricultural programme from its inception in 1971 until 1990, totalling £217,797. As Silveira House has initiated few fund-raising enterprises of its own, it is largely dependent on outside donors, a normal situation for Zimbabwean NGOs.

Agricultural development and extension work were the principal focus of its early work. By the late 1960s, many of Zimbabwe's communal areas had become net importers of food; Silveira House, through its Catholic Association branches, knew that many migrant labourers preferred to cultivate the land 'if only they could make a decent living from it' (McGarry, 1990: 1). To meet this need it began agricultural extension work in the communal lands in 1965, and out of this evolved the Silveira House Farmer Group Credit Project, one of the earliest NGO agricultural initiatives in the communal lands. It originated from requests from a group of farmers, who were members of the Catholic Association in Rota Chamachinda, Mangwende in Murewa District, for agricultural training courses and assistance with maize hybrid seed, fertilizers, and pesticides to enable them to establish maize as a cash-crop. Maize was chosen because it was the staple food crop with an already established market, and it was easy to grow.

The Silveira House credit scheme is historically important to NGO agricultural development work in two respects. First, Silveira House was a major promoter of credit which, after Independence, was to become a standard government (through the Agricultural Finance Corporation) and NGO strategy for making capital available to small farmers to enable them adopt a scientific package, thereby increasing production and raising rural incomes. Secondly, the scheme actively promoted co-operative group work, a theme consistent with the socialist orientated climate of the liberation struggle, and one which was to dominate post-Independence government and NGO policy. It was also consistent with the particular Christian approach adopted by Silveira House.

Origins and Project Description

The Silveira House scheme consisted of a package of four complementary initiatives. First, it provided extension services and training in the scientific principles of agriculture using hybrid seed, fertilizer, and improved methods of crop husbandry. Courses were held at Silveira House and field training days were run locally in the villages. Secondly, it made available to groups of farmers short-term seasonal loans in the form of maize seed, fertilizers, and pesticides for three years—the Pump-Priming Revolving Loan Fund (PPRLF). Farmers had to meet almost 50 per cent of the cost themselves. Loans were made in the form of productive capital (seed and fertilizer) rather than cash, to ensure that the inputs actually reached the farmers (the loans included the cost of transport). Repayment was made in kind—the maize marketed—and deducted directly at the end of the season by means of a stop-order, a normal occurrence in Zimbabwe. Thirdly, the scheme was administered through groups of farmers, thus promoting co-operative organization. Critical to the scheme was the stipulation that all members marketed through the one Grain Marketing Board (GMB) card, and not individually to store-keepers, schools, and neighbours. Finally, a micro-project fund was included for lorries, maize storage sheds, and implements to ease marketing and supply problems.

The scheme had two main objectives: to overcome input shortages by providing groups of farmers with interest-free credit for three years, and to reduce labour costs through a co-operative policy of sharing labour, thereby achieving economies of scale in input supply and marketing. Credit was to be made available to strong cohesive groups considered creditworthy by Silveira House and, via the groups, to individual members who were judged creditworthy by group leaders on the evidence of their farming practices. If an individual defaulted, pressure was expected to be applied by other group members, since if the total loan was not repaid at the end of the season, credit was withheld from the group the following year.

The scheme also included group tasks: members worked together on their one-acre plots. Thus, 'everyone was the eyes of the group'. However the members worked together as an organized group for credit purposes on the one-acre plots of the PPRLF scheme; the rest of each member's farm remained his or her own personal responsibility and on this larger acreage they worked individually, or in traditional family and neighbour-based reciprocal work-groups.

The initial capital for the revolving loan fund of Z$2,000 in 1971–2 was applied to the first six groups covering 139 members. By the end of the 1970s, more than fifty groups embracing about 620 farmers were serviced with PPRLF funds, although in total over 170 groups, covering over 3,000 farmers, were being assisted by the centre, most consisting of those who had been weaned from the PPRLF but who were still dependent upon Silveira House for particular services. Thus, the administrative workload for the project included not only groups in receipt of PPRLF but also post-PPRLF older groups still using the Silveira House GMB card. By the end of the 1970s the PPRLF stood at Z$14,000. Up to 1980, one member of the Silveira House staff worked on the administration of the PPRLF loans for an equivalent of three months in the year, at a salary cost representing 12 per cent of the total loan fund. This excluded the cost of group formation and extension work. Throughout the 1970s, the PPRLF was unable to keep up with the farmers' demand for credit.

In 1978 the Agricultural Finance Corporation set up a small farm credit scheme which was reorganized and expanded after Independence in 1980, with financial assistance from the International Development Association of the World Bank. With its new mandate to deliver loans to communal land farmers, this government agency agreed to provide seasonal credit to the value of Z$755,202 to 123 Silveira House groups (covering 2,603 farmers) which had previously been in receipt of PPRLF for a period of two or three years. Under the AFC scheme, each farmer was entitled to a 100 per cent loan for 2–4 acres, an average of Z$290 per farmer and a tenfold increase on what had been available through the PPRLF (Reid, 1982: 2) One of the serious constraints of the PPRLF for farmers had been the limited scale of credit— for only half an acre. With the AFC scheme, the dramatic increase in credit was a powerful incentive to increase production.

Independence in 1980 saw major developments in the Silveira House credit scheme. First, there was an expansion in the PPRLF, which, after deducting loans not repaid, more than trebled to Z$63,000, providing assistance to over 1,700 farmers. Secondly, after the three-year period in the PPRLF scheme, groups were transferred to government credit provided through the AFC. PPRLF credit continued to be administered by Silveira House on an interest-free basis until 1983, the final year of the scheme, when a nominal rate of 5 per cent was introduced in order to familiarize groups with credit before transfer to the AFC.

The first two seasons were both good seasons with high levels of small farm productivity. Loan repayment to the AFC in 1980–1 was 95 per cent, falling slightly to 85–90 per cent in 1981–2. However, these figures disguise a problem of intra-group indebtedness. During the subsequent drought year, the rate of repayment fell to 40–45 per cent in 1982–3 before rising to 62 per cent in 1983–4. The actual seasonal repayments were considerably lower, since these figures included late repayments made over several seasons. In comparison, PPRLF repayment rates were 78 per cent in 1980–1, 80 per cent in 1981–2, and 50 per cent in the last year of the scheme, 1982–3. Interestingly, the repayment rate in the PPRLF had dropped relative to the high rate achieved in good seasons before the war intensified. During the drought years, however, PPRLF repayment was slightly higher than AFC repayment, probably because the loan was considerably smaller. Silveira House provided a rescue fund of Z$30,000 from a Silveira House trust fund (not from donors) to keep the scheme going until it was phased out in 1983. The revolving capacity of the fund was severely depleted as a consequence of defaulting, and the balance was used in the agricultural programme.

Intra-group indebtedness affected over one-quarter of the AFC groups in 1980–1. Over the years, it became more extensive and more complicated to calculate because of accumulating interest and the rise in interest rates from 7.5 to 13 per cent. Widespread non-repayment during the drought years further complicated the situation: the AFC permitted a more flexible schedule whereby farmers were able to repay over several seasons. At the time of our evaluation, however, there were only two to five groups per region still using the AFC scheme. The vast majority of the groups had collapsed, mainly but not solely because of indebtedness.

Approximately five Silveira House groups out of over 100 in Mashonaland East were still in receipt of AFC loans in 1989–90. These included two groups which were selected in 1990 for the newly introduced AFC group credit scheme which, ironically, is very similar to that proposed by Silveira House and rejected by the AFC at the beginning of the 1980s. Under it groups borrow from the AFC at 10 per cent interest and lend-on to credit-worthy members at 13 per cent, retaining the 3 per cent to meet administration costs.

Three Groups in Mangwende

Rota Chamachinda, Chaza, and Kwaedza are three Silveira House groups located in Mangwende communal land some 50 miles east of Harare, Rota and Chaza being amongst the first to be established some 20 years ago. Rota was the first Catholic Association agricultural group, set up at the initiative of Rota church members in the mid-1960s after discussion on the impact of declining soil fertility on yields. The agricultural assistance given to the group over the next few years had a demonstration effect and by 1970–1 there were six groups in Mangwende, five of them directly formed from Rota during the 1970s, with one established after Independence in 1980.

Underpinning the groups was a strong social and religious belief in *mushandirapamwe* or working together, based not only on the traditional system of shared labour, *nhimbe*, but on 'pulling together' to 'better ourselves'. From the beginning, the group set out to protect their efforts for economic betterment: members prided themselves on being hard-working Christians. A strong perception held by all group members was that farmers are poor because, barring illness, death, or similar misfortune, they are lazy: hard work was associated with being economically better-off, a common perception throughout Zimbabwe.

Group membership was village-based and characterized by clusters of two or three *kraal* groups (lineage-based family groups) from the village. Traditionally, the *kraal* is the most basic unit of social and political organization, and reflects the kinship basis of local life. The project had no intended gender focus but, by the nature of the socio-economic situation, women predominated as credit recipients. However, the groups refused to accommodate members who did not fulfil their labour obligations, and therefore put the group loan repayment at risk. Although the groups were able to utilize the labour advantages of economies of scale, these did not compensate for the disadvantage experienced by households with a shortage of labour—a characteristic of poorer households. This discriminated, for example, against a female head of household without children in Rota who had to leave due to sickness after the group had carried her for two seasons because she had no children to replace her labour contribution. Over the lifetime of the Rota group, approximately half the members were women. Women were frequently group secretaries and treasurers, but not usually chairmen, with the exception of Kwaedza, although here the group was dominated by a powerful male patron, who was also a member of the Silveira House advisory board.

Maize yields on the 1-acre scheme plots in Rota increased dramatically, from a modal class of 0–5 (91 kg.) bags per acre before the PPRLF scheme to a modal range of 16–20 bags during the scheme. This was attributed by the groups to the package of seed and fertilizer, improved methods of husbandry, and group discipline and commitment. In the three seasons of PPRLF credit up to 1972–3, loan repayment was 100 per cent and members were able to cover for one another as required. Thereafter, members continued to make group orders for inputs through Silveira House as this was more economical and logistically easier than ordering individually. Yields and sales from the group continued to increase, reaching 34 bags/acre in 1974–5.

In 1980 the Rota group was informed by Silveira House of the opportunity to register for the newly available AFC credit. The AFC scheme differed from the PPRLF in two fundamental respects. First, interest had to be paid on the loan: for the first two years this was pegged at 7.5 per cent to facilitate the transfer from an interest-free situation, but by 1983 it had reached the ordinary commercial rate of 13 per cent Secondly, in contrast to the PPRLF scheme, where loans were made and accounted for on an individual basis within the group, responsibility and repayment in the AFC scheme were tied to the group and members not in debt were liable for the debt of those who failed to repay: voluntary joint liability became mandatory joint liability. Like the PPRLF, the AFC scheme used the stop-order system of the GMB. However, unlike the Silveira House scheme, statements of account gave no details of individual grain payments; an individual could therefore be paying in more than his or her own loan and covering for a group member who had not marketed enough to repay his or her loan.

Thirty members of the Rota group registered for the AFC group credit and received their first loans for the 1980–1 season. By 1981–2 the number in receipt of loans had decreased to eighteen. Some had transferred to individual GMB cards now available through the newly established Agritex farmer extension groups, and others had left to set up new groups.

Ironically for Rota the first blow to *mushandirapamwe* came with Independence. The new government announced that fertilizer would be available through AFC loans for the communal lands, but only farmers with access to a GMB marketing card would be eligible. As only Silveira House groups had GMB cards, the groups were obliged to open up to new members. On the one hand, the groups welcomed the new credit, which had long been denied to farmers in the communal lands. On the other hand, it prevented the groups from selecting their members. Based on their PPRLF experience, the Rota members judged that they could risk a 100 per cent loan for 2 acres. Two members, however, took out loans for 4 acres. During the first two years, although the group repaid the total loan to the AFC, intra-group indebtedness set in, the biggest defaulters in Rota being those with the 4-acre loans. In Chaza and Kwaedza, too, the bigger borrowers were relatively more likely to default.

It was clearly impossible for the group to share labour on fields of 2–4 acres per member, and to supervise the use of loans. It was thus in the position of being collectively responsible, and individually liable, for the loan without effective collective responsibility over production. Those who failed to repay were asked to leave the group, leaving a debt behind. Intra-group indebtedness covered the loan for these first two years. But from the 1982–3 season, the first drought year under the scheme and when the interest rate was raised to 13 per cent, the group fell into debt with the AFC. In view of the special (drought) circumstances, the AFC allowed members to take on loans for the following year and spread repayment over several seasons. With no alternative but to try to produce enough to pay off accumulating debts, members took out further loans. But the drought continued for another two seasons and the debt situation worsened. To compound the difficulties, in 1983 the AFC delivered inputs to the group on a hectarage rather than an acreage basis, and some members carried loans for the equivalent of 8 acres.

Discipline and group cohesion broke down. The members attributed this to the lack of a common enemy (the Rhodesian regime), individualism, and an attitude based on the view that with Independence people could do as they want. New members who received fertilizer did not participate in group work, and the suspicion spread that working someone else's land would make that person richer. All these were local manifestations of the transition from the solidarity of the liberation struggle to newly found individual freedom at Independence. Ironically, solidarity had flourished during the capitalist pre-Independence regime but failed in the post-Independence period.

At the start of the drought years, honest members met the debts of defaulters, but black marketing spread rapidly. People who still considered themselves members in

1990 blamed a few members for starting the black-marketing of grain and avoiding the group card. Eventually, most of the honest members took the view that the debt was not their individual debt; they therefore paid what they considered they owed to the AFC and marketed the rest of their crop through an individual card—usually belonging to someone else. Silveira House estimated that 75 per cent of members were black-marketing.

In mid-1990 money was still owed to the AFC. On the one hand, members had made no move to repay the group debt, and during our evaluation there was no hint of any intention to do so; on the other hand, however, there was concern about reports of the AFC starting to confiscate property, notably ox-carts. None of the Silveira House groups had been visited by the bailiffs at the time of the evaluation, but many members in Rota and Chaza continue to look to the paternal role Silveira House played in the past to resolve their present difficulties.

Today, the groups are no longer functioning, though a hard core of largely original members still identify with the groups and are actively committed to the co-operative at Chamachinda. Shared labour continues but on the *nhimbe* basis, independent of the credit group. For many members, Silveira House has failed in what they perceive as its responsibility to assist the groups in resolving the debt problem. This is a view shared by our evaluation. When widespread defaulting and intra-group indebtedness set in for both the PPRLF and the AFC schemes in 1983, Silveira House dropped the PPRLF and turned its attention to the other more sustainable options of marketing and supply co-operatives based on the cash purchase of inputs, and credit unions.

Although the original AFC scheme is no longer functioning, the marketing and supply elements of the project, together with the maize shed, developed into the establishment of a co-operative at Chamachinda in 1984 (with 256 members drawn from the surrounding fifteen farmer credit groups), which sells fertilizer, seed, and implements, and provides maize storage facilities. The essential difference between the co-operative and the group scheme is that the co-operative deals only in cash and allows individual control of production to co-exist with co-operative supply and marketing services. It provides a service which is available to members and non-members, thus making the transport and service advantages of the group credit scheme available to those who cannot afford credit.

Interestingly, the co-operative suffers a similar problem of suspicion to that experienced by the credit groups. People have a sense that the co-operative is itself benefiting from bank interest when payment to an individual is delayed. As a result, members not only use the co-operative card but also individual cards and private merchants. Farmers prefer to work with what they know and understand, and if this appears exploitative to outsiders and something that needs to be changed, for farmers it represents financial control.

Impact, Sustainability, and Replicability

There is no doubt that the Silveira House scheme produced dramatically improved crop yields and that group members were well satisfied with the scheme while it was in operation. All members considered themselves better-off as a result of the scheme, although for several the loss of a spouse or of property during the war had wiped out the tangible benefits. In 1971 Rota group yields (sales equivalent) were 2.02 t/ha., compared with yields for the whole of Mangwende communal land of 0.36 t/ha. By 1978 the overall yield was 1.40 t/ha., and the sales equivalent for all Silveira House Mangwende groups was 9.22 t/ha. Thus the Silveira House PPRLF sales figures were 5.6 and 6.6 times greater than the overall average. Yields increased throughout Mangwende, but faster in the Silveira House groups, reflecting an increasing use of fertilizer amongst farmers in the scheme throughout the 1970s. However, post-scheme yields have dropped relative to project levels, although they are still higher than before the project. There is no current information on average yields in Mangwende but members thought their yields were now similar to those of non-members. The fall in post-scheme yields was attributed to declining soil fertility, lack of manure, and insufficient application of fertilizer.

In the early years, loan recovery rates never fell below 94 per cent, an achievement attributable to group cohesiveness, small interest-free loans, and reasonable harvests. When the war reached Mutoko in 1976–7 the repayment rate dropped to 96 per cent and, as the fighting intensified, to 43 per cent in 1979. With peace in 1980, the repayment rate rose again, to 82 per cent, and a number of loans outstanding from 1977–8 were repaid. Other benefits from the PPRLF included agricultural extension advice to group members who were not in receipt of credit, and to non-group members via extension days and agricultural shows. Silveira House was the only agency in the project areas actively promoting winter ploughing and the use of hybrid maize and fertilizer, and the project had a considerable knock-on effect.

The social impact of the credit scheme was greatest in the development of local institutional capacity, particularly in the establishment of a co-operative at Chamachinda. The original group members had a strong perception of what was required for working together—based on common interests—and this was translated into the development of a local supply and marketing infrastructure. Even given their disappointment with the group credit scheme after Independence and an episode of financial mismanagement at the co-operative (membership fell from 256 to 85 as a consequence), many of the original members are still actively committed to the co-operative.

While the project had no specific gender focus, the groups were none the less a major forum of local development activity for women. The credit scheme and its accompanying agricultural extension service brought women into a mainstream development project, which enhanced their economic productive power within the household, even if decision-making positions in the groups remained male-dominated. It was noteworthy, too, that all the Area Field Promoters, regional co-ordinators, and Silveira House-based staff were men, thus reflecting a social male bias.

Since the PPRLF did not charge an economic rate of interest, it was clearly not sustainable without regular topping-up by donors: it was subsidized to make it accessible to poorer farmers. For political reasons the AFC also subsidizes credit to small farmers (with government or donor funds), but it provides bigger loans and reaches more farmers. Both Silveira House and the AFC shared a similar problem of high administrative overheads for small loans, reduced somewhat through the system of working with farmer groups. But the AFC enjoys the advantage of organizational economies of scale. PPRLF groups had to be transferred to the AFC because Silveira House did not have the necessary capacity to administer a scheme which was growing rapidly. The question of sustainability is also one of group preparation and training to enable a successful transfer to commercial credit. The Silveira House scheme was weak in this respect: training which would have facilitated group credit management was neglected.

The sustainability of the group credit scheme was, in the first instance, dependent on the cohesiveness of the groups and the confidence of members in the organization of borrowing and repayment. The changing socio-political climate brought in its wake new members into old groups and the rapid establishment of new groups for the sole purpose of obtaining credit. Thus, the social basis underpinning the groups had changed, necessitating a new approach to, and training for, group dynamics and credit organization, if the scheme was to continue to function.

Silveira House developed, through its experience with the PPRLF, a model of group credit which was to become, in the absence of other group lending experiences, a blueprint which was then applied to a changing socio-political situation in other parts of the country. In the post-Independence development of the project there is also a strong impression of a preoccupation with the AFC which blinded the organization to the changing realities of the groups. This contrasted with the approach adopted before Independence, which had been characterized by regular contact, and a strong personal rather than an institutional relationship with the groups.

The PPRLF scheme did not, and before Independence could not, discriminate in favour of poorer farmers. Indeed, only the creditworthy were able to participate as members: farmers were selected on the basis of their creditworthiness. However, the central issue is whether poorer farmers can sustain seasonal credit. This question needs to be examined thoroughly before one would recommend embarking upon another credit project aimed at poor farmers. Relatedly, the AFC model, with the inflexibility of its mandatory joint liability and productive capital loans for the groups, has implications for the medium and longer term. When the AFC scheme was originally introduced, confidence was temporarily maintained because two good seasons disguised the potential problems.

Another important issue is the way in which interest is perceived by the groups. Members associate it negatively with profit: the AFC is widely perceived as exploiting the small farmer. In turn, Silveira House, by providing interest-free credit and failing to expose farmers to the actual costs of the credit which it was bearing, contributed to a misconception that interest-free credit could revolve without being depleted. Members understood their PPRLF loan commitments, but lacked the financial knowledge to understand how commercial credit operated.

The high costs of the project were justified in terms of the massive increase in yields achieved and the new farming practices adopted, in the absence of access to commercial credit for communal area farmers before Independence. However, the project failed to prove that seasonal credit is a workable means of providing farmers with access to additional funds. The PPRLF scheme is replicable but it is expensive to administer and in the final analysis is not sustainable. Two fundamental and wider issues therefore arise from the evaluation. The first is whether farmers can sustain a seasonal credit scheme which demands annual repayment out of annual production. The second is whether seasonal credit is the most efficient means for NGOs to raise rural incomes.

CHRISTIAN CARE MZARABANI FARMER CREDIT PROJECT[6]

Origin and Context

Christian Care was established in 1967 as the service division of the Christian Council of Rhodesia (now the Zimbabwe Christian Council). Like Silveira House, it is one of the oldest NGOs in Zimbabwe. The post-Independence period marked the beginning of its transition from being a relief-only organization to one which includes development projects. Christian Care's Operation Joseph (OJ) programme, implemented from 1985, was central to this reorientation. Within a longer-term approach to improving household food security, the immediate aim was to reach fifty communities or 2,500 families a year for three years from 1985 with a wide range of water, agricultural, and livestock development projects in communal lands throughout the country. Today, Christian Care projects are executed by its five regional offices in Harare, Mutare, Masvingo, Gweru, and Bulawayo. Altogether there are sixty-one members of staff. Most of the project staff are trained agriculturalists or social workers.

OJ has reached a large number of families throughout Zimbabwe (each of the five regional offices is responsible for a number of projects within the programme) and has brought Christian Care widespread recognition. Donors to this part of its work have included Christian Aid, the World Council of Churches, and the Interchurch Fund for International Development. Christian Care raises very little money locally, and is thus dependent on international donors for all its substantive projects.

The Mzarabani farmer credit group project is one of its early development projects, within the wider OJ programme. It is located in the Zambezi Valley part of the Centenary District in Mashonaland Central Province, about 250 km. north of Harare. It was established after the drought of 1982–5 as a relief project to assist eight farmers' groups with tractor tillage, cotton and maize inputs, and oxen, on the basis of interest-free credit. Unlike the Silveira House project, interest-free credit was delivered to farmers individually in the groups: there was no joint liability and no specific strategy for promoting co-operative organization.

In 1985, after the drought, a group of farmers from the Machaya ward in Mzarabani approached Christian Care for assistance with tillage and agricultural inputs. They knew the organization from its relief efforts in the area during the war years. Three groups were initially formed with a total of 141 members. Three other groups, each with thirty-two members, joined in 1987, and the last two groups, with thirty-two and fifty-seven members, joined in 1989, giving a total project membership of 326. All these groups were offshoots of government agricultural extension service groups which had been formed after Independence to provide agricultural training and access to AFC credit for inputs. The groups had no church basis.

During the liberation war, most farmers in the area were forcibly moved into 'protected villages': only those lucky enough to have homes near these 'keeps' were able to retain their personal property. On returning to their farms after the war most had to re-establish themselves completely, since they had also lost their cattle as the tsetse-fly control programme had been interrupted by the war. Three years later agricultural income was further hit by the drought of 1982–5.

At its broadest, therefore, the aim of the project was to establish self-reliance amongst the farmers. Underpinning it was the view of both the farmers and Christian Care that the major constraint on agricultural production was the lack of tillage and draught power. Apart from the objective of assisting farmers with tractor tillage, oxen, and inputs on interest-free credit, there was no clearly defined plan of implementation. The intended target-group was farmers without cattle but who were able to produce something. In practice, group members included both cattle-owners and those with no cattle. The farmers who approached Christian Care were mostly middle-income farmers. The original members joined for access to tillage, credit, and transport for fertilizer. Their primary interest was in cotton cultivation, with the intention of increasing its acreage, and thus increasing their incomes.

Christian Care provided credit to group members to enable them to have 2 acres of land tractor-ploughed, and to obtain necessary inputs, on the assumption that these were not readily accessible without credit and that the farmers would repay their loans. Under the project, Christian Care hires tractors, usually from nearby government facilities, and occasionally from nearby commercial farmers, at commercial rates which in turn it charges project members. Some members in each group had previously been in receipt of AFC loans; no screening-out of AFC borrowers was demanded by the project. In the view of both the farmers and Christian Care, the critical difference between the two schemes was that Christian Care credit was interest-free and with more flexible repayment terms.

It was the intention to establish a revolving loan fund (RLF) for each group. However, in practice Christian Care has administered the credit and repayments, but without adopting agreed auditing procedures. What is more, in 1989, four years after the project started, its National Council decided against any change in policy, thus preventing the organization from handling funds on behalf of project beneficiaries. By the early 1990s, in a move that took the project back to square one, outstanding credit was to be returned to the groups, with the intention that they would manage RLFs themselves.

Initial Assessment

The story of input delivery to the Mzarabani groups is a complex tale of changes and frequent failure to deliver on time. For instance, the original three groups asked

Christian Care for a tractor and inputs for each village in 1985. Instead, Christian Care offered 2 acres of tractor ploughing on credit, and inputs for maize and sorghum. As the request had been received late in the season, it was possible for only eighty-five out of 141 members to have their fields ploughed. More recently, Makomborero and Ngatishingei, the last two groups to join the project in 1989–90, had still not received their oxen by the time of the evaluation. No land was prepared for Makomborero, but credit was given for cotton inputs for 3 acres. Ngatishingei members had 3 acres ploughed and received inputs for 2 acres of cotton and one of maize, but some members took credit for only 2 acres. Seed arrived late in January: no fertilizer was delivered and the top-dressing did not arrive until February or March. At the time of the evaluation neither group knew what it owed Christian Care.

In theory, each group has a file in which Christian Care records individual credit provided and repayments made. However, these records are incomplete and the system used by the Harare office does not always differentiate between groups. None the less, there is little doubt that repayment rates have been extremely low. Overall Christian Care estimates the rate to have been only 15 per cent, but it has clearly varied dramatically from group to group. What is more, in the eyes of the first groups, though repayments did revolve they only provided additional funds for new groups: they saw Christian Care as assisting new groups with their money. This attitude was not strictly true, as Christian Care was bringing in new funds. It clearly reflects disappointment among the original groups about the limited credit available for oxen: 'Things changed at Christian Care . . . we had to be abandoned so that other groups could be helped.' It also reflects time constraints and a level of confusion in the timing and execution of the project.

The belief that their money had gone elsewhere was symptomatic of the patron–client relationship which the groups expected of Christian Care. Project members viewed Christian Care more as a parent who was expected to take care of its own group members and to educate them. Moreover, Christian Care reinforced this image to the extent that it never institutionalized the RLF, and managed the project unilaterally. It did not promote self-management or establish a committee to represent the groups: it relied heavily on personal relationships between staff and the groups. On the plus side, the project allowed repayments to be made over several seasons, and it was thus more flexible than AFC credit which charges 13 per cent interest on seasonal loans, which are repayable in kind each year. Nor did it enforce repayment in kind in the same season through the CMB stop-order system.

There are four main reasons for the low levels of repayment achieved. First, the maize yields were too low and losses on maize were not met by cotton income. Secondly, farming efficiency was reduced because of bureaucratic inefficiencies such as late tractor ploughing and the late delivery of fertilizer. Thirdly, poor weather conditions adversely affected crop production. Finally, repayment rates have been artificially low, in large part because the pace and amount of the repayments were not clearly set out: some members thought they had to repay input credit within three years and others according to their ability to do so. Moreover, project experience suggests that most farmers who received, for instance, Z$304 worth of credit (1988–9 costings) for 2 acres of cotton were able to repay only Z$150–Z$200—and that was from a reasonable harvest.

During the evaluation meetings, members referred to themselves as poor and powerless, but the evaluation did not find them powerless or necessarily dependent on Christian Care. However, in keeping with a system of local and political patronage, they astutely present themselves as such in order to maximize their access to aid funds, whether from the government or from an NGO. While the project has not created unnecessary dependence, neither has it empowered people in the sense of decision-making responsibility and local institution-building.

The problem for Christian Care was that, as an NGO, it could not enforce individual liability. It had established the principle of individual responsibility for repayment, but this meant that it had to carry increased debts from the uneconomic loans it had made, which depleted the project's overall revolving loan find. Furthermore, in the absence of policy to allow it to manage a proper RLF, debts in effect became outright grants.

But there was also considerable confusion. For instance, its repayment records make no distinction between oxen, tractor ploughing, and input repayments, and the scheme was operated on the basis of individual liability. Members are now adjusting to a completely new system of joint liability. But whatever system Christian Care adopts in future, it will need to top up repayments to the necessary credit level in order to cover debts and inflation. In particular, group leaders are worried about the impact of financial responsibility on ill-prepared groups. There is a fear among the groups that Christian Care will transfer funds to the groups too rapidly, and pass the buck.

There have also been problems with the overall management of the project. Originally, it was under the supervision of the national office in Harare; it was then handed over to the local regional office where it has experienced a fairly high staff turnover which has added to the problems. At the time of the evaluation, the regional office had been short of two project staff for the previous 20 months, with current staff carrying a very high project load. As a result, far less time is spent on each project than would be deemed necessary for efficient management. Staff vacancies have arisen principally because of difficulties in recruiting suitably qualified staff at Christian Care salary rates: international NGOs offer higher salaries than local NGOs can afford, and poach staff. Employment in local NGOs tends to be seen as a stepping-stone to an international NGO position.

One effect of these problems has been that staff have spent too little time with project members: in Mzarabani, some leaders were very critical of the short monthly visits—'half-hour meetings'. But this problem was also attributed to the 'Christian Care style of operating' which they knew in the 'keeps'. In the view of the evaluation many management weaknesses could have been resolved had members actively participated in, and owned the project, instead of being made passive recipients. In particular, the project had made it clear that, in the context of a long-term plan, credit for oxen would revolve until all members were assisted, and the group could itself have monitored repayment and followed up bad debts. Without confidence in assured oxen credit for every member, there was insufficient incentive for the groups to establish control.

Impact, Sustainability, Internal Constraints, and the Future

It is no easy task to assess the overall economic impact of this project, or indeed of many agricultural projects where base-line and monitoring data have not been collected during the project's development. What is more, it was not possible to collect data from non-project farmers as this would have been construed as an AFC exercise associated with the confiscation of property for bad debts. None the less, some broad trends would appear to permit certain generalizations.

Yields from project fields appeared no better, and in some instances worse, than those achieved by non-project farmers. Project farmers were thus considered by the local government extension officer to be of a similar technical standard and producing yields no higher than those of non-project farmers. For cotton, estimated project yields were 2 bales an acre—a typical yield in the locality. Yet yields were often lower than this because of failure to plough to the proper depth, poor weed control, incorrect spacing of plants, inadequate pest control, and late thinning. Christian Care provided no specific crop husbandry training to the groups. Similarly for maize, both the local extension officers and Christian Care estimate 2–3 bags of maize per acre to be a typical yield for project farmers, compared with the control production of 3.3 bags/ acre. These figures were also consistent with members reporting slightly reduced annual maize deficits. Using these average yields, for the 1987–8 season, a typical project farmer would have had a net return of Z$118.10 for the production of 2 bales of cotton, but would have lost Z$45.48 for 3.3 bags of maize.

Clearly a major factor has been reduced project impact because members did not have sufficient draught power and therefore control over their own land preparation. Tractor ploughing was not merely a short-term solution; it was clearly an inefficient option as government tractor facilities are unable to meet demand and late ploughing is therefore commonplace. It is instructive, too, to compare the money actually spent on tractor ploughing with the alternative of using it for ox-based tillage. To take the case of the Zongosa group as an illustration: if, in 1988–9, all the money put into tractor preparation and inputs had been used for oxen instead, an additional fourteen members could have benefited. Alternatively, this money could have purchased 14.6 span of oxen, bringing the total number of oxen recipients to twenty-four out of a total of thirty-two.

Some members joined the project in order to increase their cotton acreage. But they have not been able to achieve this to the extent anticipated, largely because Christian Care hired tractors for ploughing rather than concentrating on oxen provision, and land was frequently prepared late. In the view of those interviewed, the area under cultivation and production has been maintained at the previous level rather than increased.

In terms of its social impact, the project in practice discriminated against poorer farmers in three ways. First, poorer farmers tend to be those who cannot afford and who are less willing to risk taking out seasonal credit and credit for oxen, and so they automatically exclude themselves. Secondly, group members were selected on the basis of their creditworthiness. And thirdly, working with small groups which were already in existence meant working largely with the favoured few, who tend to include, and be dominated by, the more innovative and the better-off.

Another weakness of the project has been its lack of gender perspective. Women not only represented a minority of group members, but nowhere took the lead. Until mid-1990 all staff responsible for the project have been men. The project has had no specific impact on women, it has only benefited them indirectly through the men. A strategic effort needs to be made to give women a real say, for example by focusing on their specific responsibilities in the home and on the farm via water sources and gardens. The District Council has been looking at potential water sites for Christian Care, and this initiative could provide an opportunity to work with women on an equal basis.

The overall impact of the project was limited because it concentrated solely on the supply of tillage and crop inputs, without taking into consideration the marketing constraints facing farmers. Transport is one of the biggest constraints to development in Mzarabani, and delays in marketing cotton not only result in farmers losing money, but also create cash-flow problems, both by delaying debt repayments and by limiting the possibility of winter ploughing. Overall, therefore, the project's potential was blocked because of Christian Care's failure to move from a relief style of operation to designing and implementing projects to be managed by the groups themselves, in accordance with their own priorities and an assessment of all the constraints inhibiting agricultural development.

Part of the reason for this lay in management weaknesses. Underpinning the style of implementation was a welfare approach to development: organizing inputs and tillage and administrating credit for the farmers, rather than training the groups to do this themselves. Not enough staff time has been spent in the field consulting with the groups, and until recently group training in credit management and input supply has been completely neglected. The project was clearly under-resourced in terms of staff time and group training to achieve sustainability, and to this extent it has been under-funded.

Part of this problem lay in the project's origins. As there was no project plan for Mzarabani within the overall Operation Joseph programme, funding was not separate from OJ funding, and Mzarabani was never considered as a project in its own right. Furthermore, if the groups had been allocated an RLF budget at the outset, this would have encouraged a sense of ownership of the project among the beneficiaries.

The way in which groups and individuals interact in the Mzarabani project also gives grounds for doubt about its long-term sustainability. Originally the groups were established at the request of Christian Care in order to channel credit to individuals. Farmers joined for individual loans, and members were individually responsible for production and individually liable for debts. Apart from the common interest in a loan to purchase oxen and inputs, there was no social or economic justification for the group behaving as a group. When RLFs are established, joint liability will be dependent on members exerting social pressure on those who fail to repay, and without any institutional capacity in the RLF to absorb inflation and debt this situation will test group cohesion. This cohesion will be maintained in so far as each member is confident of receiving a loan, but should the RLF run out before every member has received his or her share of oxen in particular, it will inevitably be threatened. Some group leaders were already anticipating this potential difficulty, as the price of a span of oxen had risen from Z$500 to Z$830 in two years.

Clearly, serious questions also remain with regard to the viability of repaying seasonal credit for cotton inputs at the end of every season, whether a poor or a good one. To be viable in the longer term, the RLFs need to have sufficient reserves to absorb low rates of repayment in poor seasons while continuing to lend for the following season. Silveira House and Zimbabwe Trust had already encountered difficulties in credit schemes and RLFs which were implemented before Christian Care started the Mzarabani project: clearly, therefore, the project did not present the collective experience of NGO group credit schemes. These questions are all the more serious as the project continues to be replicated for other groups in Mzarabani.

The vast majority of group members feel that they cannot afford seasonal credit from the AFC both because the loans are too inflexible, especially in the event of a poor harvest such as occurs roughly every four or five years, and because the AFC demands immediate repayment in kind. But, given the low and poor repayment of the Christian Care scheme, the critical question is not who provides the credit—NGO or government—but whether seasonal credit is viable for farmers or not, and under what conditions. Providing seasonal credit may be an easy solution of what to do for NGOs wishing to help farmers in communal lands. But it is not an attractive long-term solution for the majority of farmers.

THE SIMUKAI COLLECTIVE FARMING CO-OPERATIVE[7]

Origins and Context

The Simukai Collective Farming Co-operative (SCFC) grew out of the formation in August 1987 of a group of guerrilla ex-combatants, and was formally registered a year later. Today the co-operative has some sixty members and operates a capital-intensive large-scale farm some 40 km. south of Harare, which it purchased with an AFC loan in 1983. The SCFC was selected for evaluation because it is one of the more successful collectives in contemporary Zimbabwe, and appeared to have achieved economic viability. It is thus atypical of the country's general collective experience, and the case-study should be read in this light. Yet explaining how it has achieved this success helps one understand some of the reasons why so many collective enterprises fail. These have included the immediate problems of lack of capital, inadequate skills training, and inadequate managerial capacity.

The basic data for the evaluation were obtained from fieldwork undertaken at Simukai in June 1990, supplemented by discussions held with some of the main NGO groups involved in funding and promoting collective co-operatives. These included the Collective Self-Financing Scheme (CSFS) and the Zimbabwe Project, which have both had direct involvement with Simukai, the Organisation for Collective Co-operatives in Zimbabwe (OCCZIM), the government's Department of Co-operatives, and two international NGOs, HIVOS, and NOVIB.[8]

Born in the liberation struggle, collective and producer co-operatives (henceforth referred to as collectives) have established themselves on the political and economic agenda of Zimbabwe since Independence: today there are estimated to be about 800 active collectives with a membership of over 25,000, including 7,000 ex-combatants. Most of them are industrial, others include trading, service, mining, fishing, and transport collectives. Only one-fifth are agricultural. Many of these are found in the commercial farming areas where they are usually part of official resettlement schemes. Only a handful have firmly established themselves, and Simukai is one of these. However it differs from resettlement-scheme collectives in that the members put their money together to buy the land for an agricultural collective.[9] Many ex-combatants had learnt the theory and practice of collective co-operatives while in training camps in Zambia, Mozambique, and Tanzania, and a few had been as far afield as the German Democratic Republic. They were encouraged by the government to invest their demobilization money in producer collectives which would create employment and income and become self-reliant. Because of their role in generating employment, collectives are promoted as a means of achieving economic power, eliminating exploitation and poverty, and increasing skills capacity (Government of Zimbabwe, 1983: 2). They represent the final degree 'of a transitory stage which facilitates the transformation from capitalism to socialism as part of the historical process of revolutionary development' (Government of Zimbabwe, 1983: 6).

In the case of Simukai, the original group of ex-combatants pooled their demobilization money to form the co-operative. They first tried to run a butchery, but even then intended to buy a working commercial farm. The early days were hard: the butchery failed and most of their initial capital was lost. Like the many hundreds of collective co-operatives established in Zimbabwe since Independence, Simukai needed additional funds, skills, and management training. But neither the government nor commercial financial institutions were willing or able to satisfy their requirements. Hence, like other collectives, SCFC turned to the NGO sector for help in 1983. Since then, it has had a particularly close relationship with the Zimbabwe Project and through it with a range of international, including British, funding agencies.

Originally a group of seventeen ex-combatants in their mid-twenties awaiting demobilization, by December 1981 Simukai's membership had risen to 150. Establishing a collective was in the first instance a means of providing employment, but it was also seen as a means of putting into practice the objectives of the socialist political and economic ideology which underpinned their struggle for liberation. Two initial problems confronted the collective. First, there was the lack of capital. Secondly, in the early days the collective was composed only of ex-combatants from Nkomo's ZAPU party.

It was not until 1982 that comrades from Mugabe's ZANU (PF) party started to join. A lack of both start-up and running capital and wider political problems constrained the co-operative's development for the next five or six years. To overcome the political problems, new members have deliberately been drawn from all over the country. To address the problem of lack of capital, further demobilization entitlements were added to the initial fund in 1983; since that date each member has contributed nearly Z$3,000.

After the failure of the butchery venture, a farm was leased—Eyerstone Farm just outside Harare. In January 1982 the collective was finally registered as Simukai Collective Farming Co-operative, and together with the lease on Eyerstone farm this marked the beginning of serious agricultural production and the implementation of ideas on collective production. However, half the members left during this early period, and for a time things were not to get any easier. Because of its ZAPU links, Simukai was suspected of hiding arms: the army occupied the farm for three months in 1982 and problems persisted throughout 1983.

In May 1983 a new injection of demobilization pay came through, giving a capital boost of Z$90,600. This enabled the collective to buy a farm, and to realize its aim of collective ownership. Negotiations began in June 1983 for Harlech farm, 40 km. south of Harare. It was secured by auction for Z$120,000, partly met by a Z$60,000 loan from the AFC to be repaid over twenty years. The AFC, which had organized the auction, had unexpectedly added in two neighbouring farms, and the total farm area more than doubled to 1,760 hectares. Simukai was the first self-financed collective to receive an AFC long-term loan; other loans were government-sponsored. As with Eyerstone, however, the purchase left Simukai with no working capital, but the new farms had far greater potential for becoming a viable enterprise, with irrigation for wheat, tobacco barns, and 1,000 hectares of arable land.

Again, Simukai was fortunate in the assistance it obtained from a range of NGOs. In these early years they provided grants: for two borehole engines and a welding machine (Zimbabwe Project), for fertilizer (World Lutheran Foundation), for poultry development (Belgium Socialist Solidarity), for piggery development (FEPA), for irrigated wheat (Zimbabwe Project), for water supply (various churches), and for nursery development (HIVOS). Later, in 1986, the Netherlands Reformed Church Commission for Interchurch Aid gave grants towards electricity and cropping costs, while between 1984 and 1988, HIVOS, the Zimbabwe Project, NOVIB, the World Reformed Christian Council, and Oxfam gave non-specific grants. In the first year, yields were low, but from 1984 production steadily increased, with a concentration on wheat, maize, soya beans, groundnuts, and vegetables on the cropping side, and, on the livestock side, beef cattle, pigs, and chickens. A local store was established, and later in the year a grinding-mill was installed both to prepare livestock feed and to serve the needs of the local population. In 1986 a pre-school nursery was built. The money for these developments came both from farm income and from specific NGO grants. Overall, NGO grants to Simukai have totalled approximately Z$550,000.

By 1990 some 45 per cent of the farm land was under productive use—arable land accounting for approximately 300 hectares and cattle for approximately 500 hectares.

Principal crops grown were irrigated winter wheat, flue-cured tobacco and maize, with smaller hectarages of soya bean and potatoes. Winter wheat and tobacco are the most profitable crops. Livestock consisted of 629 export quality cattle, 227 pigs, and 105 sheep.

In that year, the (always fluctuating) membership totalled thirty-six working members, most in their thirties, fourteen of whom were women. There were twenty-three families with thirty-seven children, and of these eight had both husband and wife as working members. A traditional gender division of labour prevails on the farm, in that women predominate in the departments associated with traditional female domestic and office work. Only one of the six production management positions, that of business department manager, is held by a woman, and there are no women office-bearers in the management committee. None the less, the domestic workload of Simukai women is far better than in most industrial, commercial, agricultural, or domestic enterprises, with pre-school facilities, communal food preparation, and 90-day maternity leave provisions.

When the collective started, none of the members had any experience of managing a commercial enterprise and the organization of production relied on 'persuasion to understand'. In the early years, social and cohesive characteristics were stressed: clearly, without these Simukai would not have survived. Thereafter, however, increasing emphasis was laid on skills development, and a more streamlined and specialized organization of production tasks was developed. The focus was on improving the level of education and skills of members, while the importance of management was explicitly acknowledged. By 1989 the production and political decision-making processes had been separated, to make them more efficient and to prevent the more skilled and better educated from dominating the political structure.

The Zimbabwe Project has played the most important external role both in organizing training courses and in meeting costs. Training has also been provided by the Tobacco Training Institute and the School of Engineering, while the CSFS has assisted with accounting and more broadly based managerial training. Member collectives of the CSFS are graded one to five on the basis of their financial management and planning skills, productivity, cohesiveness, and member involvement in decision-making. Simukai has a maximum grading of five, as compared with the majority grading of four. A profile obtained through the assessment of every collective is the basis for drawing up a business strategy for each. This includes a three-year development plan with specific aims and a detailed annual activity plan, with defined objectives and targets which set the basis for monitoring carried out by the management committee of the collective and CSFS technical staff, and specified projects on how to achieve them. A projected cash-flow profile is also drawn up to indicate financial requirements, and this is assessed by the development credit committee.

A basic principle of CSFS strategy is that finance is provided only after the collective applying for a loan has been given training in technical aspects of financial management, and in social aspects, including promoting positive discrimination towards women and children, and health and education needs. The CSFS extends credit provision to member collectives by enabling them to have access to commercial credit for which they would otherwise not be in a position to apply. The transfer to commercial credit is complete when commercial credit institutions accept the collateral of the collectives themselves, and when the role of CSFS simply consists of making a broad range of such sources available.

Simukai is not merely a system of production: it is also a way of life which strives to meet family and social welfare needs. Twenty-three families plus five single people live on the farm in three settler-style farmhouse complexes, which are somewhat run-down but have electricity and at least one running water tap each. A new purpose-built kitchen and dining-room were due to be built in late 1990, enabling the present kitchen and dining-room to return to their original use as a tobacco barn. The collective contributes to the cost of education on a sliding scale of 25 per cent for the first child, 20 per cent for the second, 15 per cent for the third and 12.5 per cent for the fourth at primary school, and 75, 50, 25, and 12.5 per cent for secondary school. The children also undertake collective tasks: each child is assigned to a department, the boys to livestock and the girls to administration and office work.

In general, donors have not been willing to donate funds specifically for social projects, but only for economic projects. However, in the context of rising farm income, extensive donor funding of Simukai has led inevitably to the fungibility of funds. In 1986 the collective financed the building of a crèche so that the women would not have to carry children on their backs to the fields. One member was sent for pre-school training, but then had to be transferred to the store. Toys and books have been obtained through small donations. A full seven-grade primary school consisting of two blocks and two classrooms was built in 1987, without external assistance. Once built, the government supplied teachers, but it is uncertain whether it will expand this assistance if the school expands. Secondary-school pupils attend a school in the neighbouring communal land.

Impact and Assessment

Simukai has developed into one of the most successful collectives (winning first prize in the Trade Fair agricultural co-operative section in 1990), and is perhaps the best-known agricultural collective in the country. It has received national and international media coverage, and is recognized by the government and the NGOs as a flagship of the collective movement. With respect to the government praise, however, this is somewhat ironic, since Simukai has developed without the assistance of any government funding. Critics argue that Simukai has succeeded in spite of government policy.

But how does one judge success? Certainly there can be no comparison between the impact of NGO assistance on Simukai and a collective farm which has not received assistance, for no agricultural collective has been able to survive without government or NGO finance, of which grants are a significant component. Significantly too, the history of Zimbabwe suggests that few private commercial farms established in the settler-colonial period would have survived without substantial support from the

Rhodesian Government, including large subsidies to enable them to become established, and extension advice (Hanlon, 1986: 12).

That said, the funds provided to Simukai by the agencies have been considerable: loans and grants from the NGOs amounted to some Z$750,000 over a five year period to 1989. On the basis of the 1989 membership, grants alone were equivalent to Z$8,815 per member per year over a six-year period, or Z$13,561 per working member. Grants provided were equivalent to 79.9 per cent of the project's asset value of Z$661,893 in 1989, and represented 89.5 per cent of total net deficits from 1984 to 1989. Equally, however, it is necessary to set this outlay in the context of the type of enterprise being assisted. Simukai is operating as, and was set up to be, a large-scale commercial farm. Moreover, the funding appears to have paid off, for the collective is about to become economically viable, paying its way exclusively through the use of commercial funding for current expenditure and future capital projects. In 1988–9 it made a profit on its farming operations for the first time, although overall it still had a net deficit.

The movement towards improved economic and financial performance is charted in the chronological account of the monthly allowances made to members. Thus in 1982 none were paid; in 1983 they were fixed at Z$30.00, but paid only twice that year. By 1989 they had been raised to Z$70 per month, and it was hoped to increase this to Z$120 in 1990. The allowances paid exclude the hidden benefits of free housing, food, and crèche facilities.

Overall, two particular characteristics of NGO funding limited the extent to which Simukai's funders were able effectively to assist collective co-operatives. First, funds were clearly limited, especially in relation to potential commercial sources of funds: even these comparatively wealthy NGOs had limited funds as well as other funding commitments. Secondly, the staff of a number of donor agencies have had little or no experience of working in collectives or commercial enterprise; nevertheless this has not prevented them from giving advice and basing the outlay of funds largely on their own judgement.

What the Zimbabwe Project could and did provide was the initial higher-risk funding in the form of grants and soft loans from its revolving loan fund, until such time as the collective was in a position to apply to the AFC and other commercial financial institutions for capital and running costs. Supporting Simukai to the extent that it did was certainly a risk for the Zimbabwe Project, since the project was only the first non-government-assisted agricultural collective to receive a loan from the AFC.

A final issue raised by the evaluation is the fact that, because NGO money is often provided in the form of grants, a strong sense is created in the minds of recipients that this is not subject to the same accountability procedures as are demanded in connection with either an NGO loan or, more significantly, a commercial loan. To the extent that this sense persists, it tends to work against the long-term sustainability of projects and their economic viability. Looking back on its history and drawing on the experience of other collectives, the Simukai leadership, while clearly grateful for the money it has received from the NGOs, is critical of the welfarist-type attitude that donor grants in particular impose on collectives. Such funding, it is argued, does not sharpen initiative. In contrast, the AFC mortgage 'woke us up'. It is difficult to break down the charity approach once it has invaded people's minds, but nobody wants to squander an overdraft.

NGO support proved critical in the early years, but two other factors were also important. One was the speed with which the collective managed to progress economically, enabling it to address a range of the membership's social needs: solidarity, economic progress, and social benefits reinforced each other. Another was flexibility in the way it operated. Simukai has been capable of changing its operational practices in relation to changing needs and demands, both internal and external. Critical, too, were the role and personality of its chairman. His entrepreneurial qualities and his ability to attract donor funding have played a very significant role not only in developing Simukai, but in establishing the CSFS.

Wider Issues

Silveira House and Christian Care have attempted to reach and improve the lives of a defined group of poorer farmers. In tackling the collective issue, the Zimbabwe Project, the CSFS, OCCZIM, and their NGO funders have adopted a more universal approach aimed not at a specific socio-economic group (although collectives do attract poor farmers) but at creating institutions, employment, and economic growth, and thereby alleviating poverty. One of the attractions of the collective co-operative movement for NGOs is that the members tend to come from the poorest groups of people: most young people attracted to the collectives have no money, but they tend to have a level of education which provides the potential for operating and running them.

Since the mid-1980s, the policy of most international NGOs and bilateral aid agencies has changed from supporting collectives individually, to channelling funds through local intermediate non-governmental institutions, such as the Zimbabwe Project, OCCZIM, and the CSFS. In addition, there has been a trend away from funding specific projects within a collective, to the more flexible approach of directing funds into the general budget. These changes came about because agencies were generally unable to provide enough start-up capital for any one collective and some preferred to spread their risks across several. Funding was therefore streamlined through those organizations with a special mandate for collectives.

However, the start-up grants of, for example, the Zimbabwe Project, Christian Care, and Oxfam have been of fundamental importance to collectives, for without them few, if any, would have been in a position even to apply for more substantial funding and eventually to obtain access to commercial funding. Not surprisingly, therefore, the collectives which are still struggling to become established voice few criticisms of NGOs and their donors. However, as they become more established, their political acumen becomes sharper and they tend to be much more critical of the limitations of welfare-orientated NGOs. As one member commented: 'There is a danger of NGOs undermining co-operatives. Sustaining them is not enough—we need to move forward.' There is clearly a view increasingly articulated among these people that too great a dependence on grants and NGO hand-outs conflicts with the objectives being promoted, by stifling initiative, eroding work discipline, and even frustrating the very process of empowerment by creating an unthinking and un-questioning dependence on welfare providers. For the members of Simukai, their success lay not in the extent to which NGOs had helped them but in their sound management and working practices, and their group cohesion.

If such a view raises questions about NGO support for the movement, other questions arise in relation to broader issues of equity. Equity in the context of the land issue places commercial agricultural collectives in a somewhat ambivalent situation. Simukai's farm covers 1,760 hectares worked by some thirty-six members, averaging approximately 49 hectares each. This is far more land than the labour-intensive individual farms in the resettlement areas of 4 to 4.8 hectares per family. The difference lies, of course, in farming methods, between capital-intensive and labour-intensive operations. Much capital-intensive agriculture in Zimbabwe is characterized by under-utilization of land whether by private commercial or resettlement schemes, while labour-intensive farming is characterized by a land squeeze and increasing soil deg-radation. As noted above, less than 45 per cent of Simukai's farming land is currently being utilized—and it is the success story.

Clearly the optimum size of a collective cannot be estimated in the abstract: it will depend on land quality, available capital, equipment, labour, skills, production costs, and crop and livestock prices. In a study of the employment-generation potential of co-operatives conducted for the Ministry of Community and Co-operative Development and Womens' Affairs in the mid-1980s, Tandon concluded that collectives are both under-capitalized and over-capitalized. They are over-capitalized in that a commer-cial mode of operation has been imposed on randomly selected groups of resettled communal land farmers who lack cohesiveness and the know-how to farm commer-cially. Capital obtained from NGOs is 'quickly wasted away leaving behind skeleton tractors' and capital from the AFC becomes a 'debt which neither the co-operative can pay nor the AFC forget' (1988: 101). In terms of generating employment, agri-cultural collectives are characterized by under-settlement and under-employment, and membership is well below land carrying capacity (1988: 70). Given both these types of problems and the shortage of land for resettlement, questions about the appropriateness of NGOs funding capital-intensive and land-extensive resettlement urgently need to be raised. At the same time, funding constraints have meant that most collectives are substantially under-capitalized and are struggling to survive at above-subsistence levels. In 1990 the Zimbabwe Project estimated that Z$10,000 was the minimum capital grant required per working member to establish a viable collective enterprise.

Here the role and function of the state needs to be highlighted. The success of Simukai contrasts sharply with the experience of most other collectives in post-Independence Zimbabwe. Their failure rate is high: indeed struggling collectives are the norm, and successful collectives relatively rare. The government has been vocal in its support of the collective co-operative movement but it has not provided the financial assistance required to create the extensive collective movement it has sought to establish. In the view of OCCZIM, even when everything is working according to plan something like five years are required for agricultural collectives to achieve viability on former commercial farms.

The Department of Co-operatives has been able to make only twenty establishment grants a year ranging from Z$250,000 to Z$300,000, and in 1990 only ninety-two resettlement agricultural co-operatives were operating. The amounts provided for the fortunate few are therefore far lower than the start-up capital available to Simukai. What is more, like all areas of government, the Department has been under increasing budget constraints, and with the start of the structural adjustment programme in 1990, the amount of funds available in the future was going to shrink further.[10] Furthermore, by the beginning of the 1990s, government officials were divided over the key issue of whether collective co-operatives should continue to be 'vigorously promoted'; there were increasing doubts about the economic and financial viability of collective production.

Commercial lending institutions are not willing to fund such risky ventures, especially given the record of failure, and NGOs simply do not have the money to bridge the gap between need and financial provision, although they have clearly played the most important role in financing the collective co-operative movement. Hanlon (1986: 46) judges that NGO funds have exceeded government spending in agricultural collectives, and argues that collectives were launched without funds on the assumption that NGOs would help. One of the reasons for both the gap in funding and the continuing dominance of NGOs is that the NGOs have failed to develop a lobbying role, a task which is within the mandate of OCCZIM.

Further problems remain to be faced. On the financing side, if emergent agricultural collectives do manage to scrape together funds to buy a commercial farm, they disqualify themselves from eligibility for a government establishment grant. They are thus doubly disadvantaged, because they have to buy the land and capitalize it themselves. There is also the question of skills. While experience, in Simukai and elsewhere, points to the fact that success is critically related to the level of skills among members, it also reveals that members who acquire skills and qualifications are the ones most likely to leave the collective.

The story of Simukai therefore raises a number of questions, both for NGO funding of collectives and for the type of large-scale commercial enterprise which has been funded. First, it is evident that Simukai has been a very expensive venture to fund: total NGO funding up to 1989 came to Z$13,561 per member, a considerably higher figure than the Z$10,000 estimated by the Zimbabwe Project. Secondly, NGOs are not able to base their funding of ventures such as Simukai on either equity or need, because the overall availability of funds is limited. Since Independence, government policy has strongly promoted the co-operative movement, but has failed to provide the necessary finance. In practice, NGOs have substituted for absent state funding. Thirdly, there is the question of whether mechanized capital-intensive, and therefore very high cost, methods of farming are an appropriate type of venture for NGOs to continue to fund in a country where unemployment is an increasingly important social and economic problem.

THE CAMPFIRE INITIATIVE AND ITS OPERATION IN DANDE COMMUNAL LAND[11]

In Zimbabwe an innovative approach to wildlife management is being introduced under the name of Campfire—Communal Areas Management Programme for Indigenous Resources. Campfire represents a radically new approach to rural development by combining the conservation and management of natural resources by the local communities themselves with employment and income generation in the poorest and most agriculturally marginalized and poor areas of the country. Conventional thinking tends to view agriculture and conservation as mutually exclusive interests, whereas Campfire, with its emphasis on natural-resource utilization which includes agriculture, regards non-agricultural natural-resource utilization as a diversification of agricultural production. By promoting the local management of natural resources Campfire is attempting to change long-established colonial perceptions under which wildlife became the property of the state and many of the former hunting grounds of communities were designated as wildlife areas.

The aim of Campfire is to enable local communities in the communal lands to manage their natural-resource base and to benefit directly from any profitable exploitation of that base. Three specific objectives are: first, to demonstrate in agriculturally marginal areas that natural-resource utilization options are profitable and environmentally more sustainable in the long term than cropping and livestock; second, to enable wards to benefit directly from natural-resource utilization, the revenue from which will at least supplement agricultural and other income sources; and, finally, to use natural-resource utilization as an instrument to develop local management capacity (for example, ward committees to construct water points, to record revenue earned, etc.) to ensure the maintenance of the natural-resource base.

Campfire combines a technical approach with one seeking economic empowerment. Its implementation encompasses a unique multi-disciplinary and multi-institutional approach. On the one hand, it includes ecologists, sociologists, and economists; on the other, it brings together two NGOs (the Zimbabwe Trust and the Worldwide Fund for Nature (WWF))[12], the Centre of Applied Social Science (CASS) at the University of Zimbabwe, and the Government, through the Department of National Parks and Wildlife Management (DNPWLM). Its major funders are official donors and not NGOs: the NGOs are mainly involved in implementation. The NGO with whom this evaluation was primarily concerned was the Zimbabwe Trust, which has received co-funding from the UK Overseas Development Administration for its part in Campfire programmes.

The case-study for the evaluation was Kanyurira ward in the Dande communal land, located in the Zambezi valley in the north-west of the country. Fieldwork for the evaluation was undertaken in mid-1990. Socio-economic data were obtained from an unpublished CASS baseline study, while more qualitative information was derived largely from focused discussion groups and individual interviews within the ward and with officials of Guruve District, the central government, and NGO personnel.

Unlike the Silveira House and Christian Care projects, which aimed to fill a resource gap, Campfire member wards are not perceived as resource-poor but rather as resource-rich. A positive attitude to rural poverty underpins the project's empowerment thrust: wildlife which was once a liability destroying crops and killing people is now perceived as an economic asset to be maintained and protected from illegal hunters.

Campfire has come to international prominence because it has been used by the government to promote Zimbabwe's opposition, along with other southern African countries, to the Convention on International Trade in Endangered Species of October 1989 (CITES), which banned the trading and selling of ivory. The Zimbabwe Trust has been in the forefront of a campaign to try to sell the Campfire conservation approach to other countries. Zambia has adopted a similar approach and Tanzania, Kenya, Namibia, and Botswana are actively considering a Campfire approach to conservation and rural development.

Origins and Objectives

Campfire has its legal origins in the 1975 Parks and Wild Life Act, which granted ownership of wildlife to private commercial farm and ranch landowners who were delegated the 'appropriate authority' (AA) for wildlife management. From 1980 the government permitted revenues from trophy fees of animals hunted and problem animals shot in the communal lands to be passed from the Ministry of Finance to the district councils where the revenue originated. A 1982 amendment to the 1975 Act allowed district councils to apply for AA status, but this was not implemented until 1986 when the DNPWLM introduced the Campfire programme.[13] Campfire can be implemented only by district councils with AA status, and this ensures that they hand down revenue derived from natural resources to the local communities—the wards— and assist local communities to manage their natural resources. The attraction is that safaris can be an important source of revenue for district councils: in 1990 Guruve District Council received Z$50,000 from the European concession operator. Safari operators employ professional hunters who have a loyal following of clients drawn mainly from the USA, Europe, and South Africa. It is an expensive industry: the safari operator puts up the capital required, approximately Z$500,000–Z$1m. and provides all back-up and logistical and administrative support.

Guidelines devised by the DNPWLM and the Ministry of Local Government in 1990 recommend that 50–55 per cent of the revenue from trophy fees be handed down to the different local wards in the communal areas, and that the district councils retain the concession fees and not more than 15 per cent of the revenue as a levy. The use of the money passed down to the ward is meant to be decided by the ward itself.

Three areas of potential conflict relate to the revenue derived from the scheme. The first concerns relations between the district council and the central government: revenue which once went direct to the Ministry of Finance is now meant to be retained locally at the district level. It is a radical approach to rural development, which promises economic benefits which will give more power to marginal rural communities. In some government quarters, the concept is regarded as subversive, working against the centralized economic and administrative structures established by the former Rhodesian regime, which remain relatively intact.

The second area of potential conflict lies between the district council and the wards. District councils are under-resourced to fulfil the development needs of their constituents, and for some time there has been pressure on them to generate their own income. There is thus a risk that they may wish to retain revenue rather than pass it on to the wards, as happened in Nyaminyami, for example, where the district council at first refused to pass the revenue on to the wards, declaring that the money was required for district council investments. A more likely scenario would be for a district council to make use of some, or all, of the ward revenue which is deposited in the district council's bank account, in order to ease its cash-flow problems, before the revenue is used for a ward project.

The third source of potential tension is at the national level, and is a subject already being debated in academic and political circles. It is argued, contra the Campfire approach, that if the state is the legal owner of the communal land and its natural resources, other citizens should also benefit. This view sits uncomfortably close to the possible argument of district councils that it should be their decision whether or not to allow wards to decide how the game revenue is used, and whether or not to hand down revenue to the wards under their jurisdiction.

Campfire in Dande Communal Land

Under Campfire, the local community at the ward level is responsible for maintaining its wildlife herds in order to ensure that the hunting and safari operations which are promoted are profitable. In return, the ward receives a share of the net hunting revenue obtained, the net proceeds being shared out among members of the local community in the form of both social services and household dividends. In practice, things are not quite so simple. Ward revenues are thus dependent on the quality and efficiency of safari operation management: there is no legal protection in the event of a loss of income from a badly managed operation. In turn, failure by the ward to earn sufficient income could lead to the neglect of wildlife, undermining the very aim of Campfire. Moreover, the revenues obtained are not received directly by the wards, but are channelled to them by way of the relevant district council (which in turn takes a percentage of the total revenue), links between the district council and the ward being formalized by means of ward wildlife committees (WWCs).

Dande communal land in the Zambezi Valley lies approximately 200 km. north of Harare within the jurisdiction of the Guruve District Council. It consists of eight wards, of which only three in the west—Kanyurira, Chapoto, and Chisungo—have large game for hunting. Campfire has been promoted most extensively in Kanyurira ward; it has still to be effectively established in Chapoto.

The mid-1980s master development plan for the region, the Mid-Zambezi Land Use Plan, proposed a Campfire component for the area, but excluded the three western wards which were outside its jurisdiction. However, the DNPWLM proposed establishing Campfire in these wards and called in CASS to evaluate the proposal.

WWCs had already been set up by the DNPWLM to deal with problems of animal control and compensation for crop damage, and CASS began its preparation work with these. Since 1986 CASS and WWF have been very closely involved in Kanyurira ward, CASS in attitudinal surveys, standard socio-economic baseline data collection, monitoring, and conscientization work.

An initial CASS survey in Kanyurira in 1987 revealed opposition to wildlife and a positive attitude to in-migration, the rationale being that, with more people in the ward, its bargaining position with the district council would be enhanced, so enabling it to attract more council resources. A year later things had changed, largely because in the intervening period a primary school had been built with wildlife-derived income—tangible evidence of Campfire's potential to fund ward development projects. Support was also facilitated by the proposal from WWF to erect an 18 km. solar-powered low-voltage electric fence around the village to protect the crops from marauding animals. The fence which cost Z$80,000 was funded by the mining group, Consolidated Goldfields, and was completed in August 1990.

The Zimbabwe Trust's involvement in Dande began in late 1988 with a request from the DNPWLM to make a soft loan to establish the district council safari operation (DCSO), replacing the absentee safari operator.[14] Under the arrangement worked out by the Zimbabwe Trust, the DCSO hunts in the concession area in the southern part of Dande including Kanyurira ward, while a private long-established operator continues to lease from the district council the concession area mainly in the Dande Safari Area and Chapoto ward in the north. The Trust's primary objective was to promote the capacity of local communities to manage their natural resources; however it took almost two years to convince Guruve District Council of the need for activities at the sub-district level, and it was only towards the end of 1990 that work was able to start at ward level.

Establishing and running a profitable DCSO in Dande required substantial funds and organizational skills. The Zimbabwe Trust had expected to assist the district council develop its own capacity to manage the operation, but by the end of 1989 it was becoming evident that the council did not have the capacity to do so. The Trust had to assume the role of safari operator, and this involved logistical, administrative, and accounting support for the district council. Although, in 1990, safari revenues covered costs, long-term viability is dependent both on the management capacity of the district council and on continued access to foreign exchange to replace imported equipment.

The Kanyurira WWC is a key part of the Campfire project, providing the interface between the district council and the local community. It is made up of nine members, all men. The chairman and councillor both represent the WWC on the Guruve District Council Wildlife Committee (GDCWC). WWC duties include supervising Campfire, electric-fence maintenance, organizing anti-poaching patrols, drawing up the ward land-use plan jointly with the village development committee, and siting water points to encourage wildlife to remain in the ward. In practice, relations between the district council and the ward are described by the WWC variously as 'distant' and 'weak'. Clearly, the ward tries to strengthen its bargaining position particularly as it believes the district council to be interested in the ward only because of its newly realized resources: 'Long back we had a distant relationship with Guruve District Council. Now we have a close one because we have money in our pockets . . . Everybody is after money.'

District councils are clearly powerful forces in the whole Campfire programme. They act as Campfire administrative agents for the wards where the programme operates, handling the ward account and effectively determining when the ward will have access to its revenue, apart from the household dividend. As the district council is effectively in control of the ward's money, the key issue is how to improve the latter's own administrative capability in order for it to obtain its due more quickly. During the evaluation, Kanyurira ward expressed disappointment that the NGOs— it is not clear to the WWC which agencies are responsible for the different elements of Campfire—had not yet delivered training in financial control and record-keeping, to increase its effectiveness in dealing with the council. Overall, the impression gained from the WWC of its relationship with the district council was one of uncertainty, and therefore of a certain degree of mistrust. The three members of the committee interviewed talked about taking over the management of the safari operation from the district council, within five years according to two, fifteen years according to the third.

Impact and Assessment

Campfire had only been operational for 18 months at the time of the fieldwork. It would therefore be premature to draw firm conclusions about whether it has achieved its aims of enabling local communities to manage their natural-resource base, and creating a positive economic outcome. The development of local resource-management capacity is still in its infancy, and the project's only economic impact on the ward and on individual households has been the revenue from the 1989 hunting operation. It is also too early to assess project impact on the longer-term ecological objective of maintaining the wildlife resource-base, and to judge the capacity of the district council to manage a safari operation after only its second year. Its management capacity is still evolving and developing.

None the less, the impact of Campfire on Kanyurira has already been considerable: where game animals were once a nuisance, destroying crops and human life, they are now perceived as an asset from which the ward can benefit financially. There is sufficient land for agriculture and wildlife to coexist, and ward residents perceive Campfire-derived revenue as a supplement to the agricultural economy: there is no conflict over the use of the natural resources.

On the financial side the results have already been noteworthy. For the 1989 financial year, Kanyurira received some Z\$47,000 from the operation, Z\$15,000 of which was allocated to a clinic, and Z\$7,000 for school furniture. The remainder was distributed as Z\$200 household dividends to 102 ward households. This dividend alone was equivalent to an additional 56 per cent of annual gross household income from selling cotton, the main source of cash income in the ward—even higher for the quarter of households which do not grow cotton. Dividends were used to buy household utensils and food, while the cotton farmers used the money for pesticides and tractor hire. With only one exception, the farmers talked about using the dividend to purchase cattle when the restrictions are lifted. Women, in particular, wanted to invest in oxen to reduce weeding. There have also been wider employment gains from the project: 22 per cent of ward households already have, or expect to have, some additional employment income from Campfire.

As for the future, over a five-year period to 1993–4, the Dande project is budgeted to cost approximately £837,000. Thereafter the district councils and wards are expected to become financially self-sufficient and self-managing. It is still too early to judge whether this will occur, but already the prospects are looking good: by the end of 1990, with help from the Zimbabwe Trust, the (expensive) safari operation had covered its costs. However, a range of additional costs are expected, such as fence maintenance and anti-poaching patrols. On the basis of 1989 revenue, these further costs represent 23.7 per cent of ward income from the DCSO, and 18.75 per cent of total income, that is, including the private safari operation.

Already, however, there have been problems. For instance, there was considerable confusion surrounding who decided how the 1989 revenue should be allocated, indicating substantial lack of communication between the ward and the district council. There was also a problem with the distribution of the dividends paid by the ward to households, as a few extra households were included and a number of widows failed to qualify as household heads. Also women have only benefited indirectly from Campfire as dividends were made to heads of household. Is it right to blame the Zimbabwe Trust, or CASS, or the WWF for allowing this confusion to arise? It is certainly true that they took no part in this section of the decision-making process. But that is part of their operating style: allowing the community to pursue its own learning experience and thereby learn from its mistakes. If they had intervened and disputes had arisen, they could well have been labelled as paternalists.

The WWC is confident that it has the ability to manage its revenue, the ward's wildlife resource base and the upkeep of fences, etc., and it is impatient for training to begin to enable it to do this. However, participation by individuals in Campfire is very variable, ranging from the massive commitment in time and effort made available to Campfire activities and discussion by WWC members and some of the younger male members of the community, to the limited participation of women and older men.

On the issue of equity and reaching down to the poor, Campfire scores well in at least three different ways. First, because it targets wards and not discrete self-selected groups of people, all members of the ward, including the poorest, are specific gainers from the project both as receivers of dividends and as users of the social facilities set up or improved. Secondly, there is a regional gain: because the concession areas define the economic communities, and because these tend to have restricted agricultural potential, they are biased towards poorer communities. Thirdly, in practice Campfire has tended to help poorer and more marginalized women to assert their rights. The only challenge to the traditional social and political environment has come from the conscientization effect of the dividend distribution on some widows. Precisely because Campfire has no specific gender focus, it could be that the process precipitated by the dividend distribution will be all the more powerful because of that. Instead of Campfire making a special case for women as part of the programme, women are themselves demanding an equal right to the dividend, and generating their own place in Campfire. Nevertheless, women are culturally marginalized in Campfire as the project has been applied only to wildlife (hunting is culturally a male domain), and not to the whole natural-resource base including agriculture.

In general, people perceive the dividend as supplementing rewards from agriculture, not replacing them. They therefore understand the critical importance of the balance between agriculture and wildlife. The two are not necessarily mutually exclusive: according to the ward land-use plan, land inside the fence is reserved for cultivation and livestock, and the game are outside. However, it is of interest to note that, with the exception of leading members of the WWC, many people wanted part of the 1989 revenue to help purchase a tractor for the ward for tillage and to transport cotton out for marketing. Cotton is clearly seen as an important source of income for the future, and is the principal driving-force behind demands for increased tillage.

There are certainly grounds for supporting the view that the future lies in agriculture, for the long-term prospects for game are by no means assured. Tsetse fly and restrictions on cattle have prevented widespread resettlement in the ward and restricted agricultural development in what many experts consider to be a fragile environment in one of the few remaining wildernesses of Africa, the Zambezi Valley. Where there is tsetse fly there is wildlife, and the wild eco-system is more likely to be preserved. Although farmers in Kanyurira and other wards have not kept cattle since the beginning of the century, they have not lost their socio-economic or cultural significance. Farmers want cattle for ploughing, weeding, transport, milk, and bride-wealth. In the long run, if and when the cattle restrictions are lifted with the eradication of the tsetse fly, some farmers are expecting to invest in cattle.

The issue of crop damage highlights the tension between individual and communal property. On the issue of compensation for crop damage by wildlife, one member of the WWC explained: 'There should be no compensation. Who is going to compensate, someone, because by virtue of his living in the village—the animal belongs to him!'. Compensation is seen as a contradiction of ownership, and this view has prevailed although another member of the WWC thought there should be compensation because of the fence. To date, no compensation has been paid in Kanyurira. Although one advantage of the fence is that people feel safer walking about at night, every year a life is lost because of animals. At present the dividend is perceived as a form of compensation. The extent to which this view is sustained will prove an interesting indicator of opinion in the ward about the merits of wildlife as compared with agriculture.

Finally, it should be noted that Kanyurira WWC is not only participating in Campfire but it is also endeavouring to push Campfire forward as much as possible on its own terms—a clear indication of the realization of economic empowerment and of the will needed to assert the local interests of the ward. And Campfire is already being replicated in another ten district councils, while a further nine have applied for AA status.

Wider Issues

Campfire deliberately sets out to achieve the participation of local communities in the management of their natural-resource base. It is built on the assumption that if communities can be given an economic interest in their natural-resource base, this will prove a sufficient incentive to ensure their participation in protecting that base, and their engagement in rural enterprises based on natural-resource utilization. In practice, however, Campfire has so far been largely conservation-driven. At present safari hunting dominates the rural enterprises associated with Campfire, but other land-use options include live wildlife sales, crocodile ranching, tourism, and photo safaris.

Social and institutional sustainability will clearly depend on whether the project is able to continue to generate sufficient income from wildlife and natural resources to make it worth while for the ward to continue participating in Campfire. It will also depend on whether district councils will hand down all the revenue which the local population perceives as rightly theirs. As district councils are under-funded by central government, there is a risk that they might withhold funds. In addition, sustainability is dependent on the economic relationship between agriculture and human population and wildlife, as discussed above.

Ultimately, the sustainability of Campfire is dependent upon whether the enterprise is profitable. At a managerial level it will depend on whether there is sufficient support for it in the wards, and on how each ward organizes itself to incorporate the project into daily life. In this regard, the evaluation was able to assess the relatively favourable context of Kanyurira ward as compared with Chapoto to the north, where Campfire has not yet taken root. Neither the district council nor the NGOs have actively promoted Campfire there, but militating against effective communal property management are both social conflicts and disputes over the use of natural resources. This clearly shows that what works in one socio-political and economic environment will not necessarily work even in another one that appears on the surface to be quite similar.

Kanyurira is characterized by a relatively small and homogeneous population, while Chapoto is far more heterogeneous. Kanyurira has a strong social base, and has developed its own mechanisms for dealing with internal conflict, whereas Chapoto is characterized by internal social conflict. Population size in relation to the income-generating potential of the natural-resource base has also been a critical factor. Hasler (1990: 1) observes that Chapoto ward covers 300 sq. km. and has a population of over 1,300, compared with Kanyurira's population of 482 extending over 400 sq. km. Thus in Chapoto more people will have to share less wildlife-derived income compared with Kanyurira. The basic issue is whether the level of wildlife-derived income ward members can expect from wildlife will be sufficient to maintain ward participation in the maintenance of the natural-resource base, or more precisely, whether farmers will benefit sufficiently from the dividend, community projects and/or the creation of sufficient additional local employment. Population or group size is also critical to cohesion and community decision-making: consensus is more easily reached in small communities where people have long established and trusted relations with each other. In addition, the DCSO is based in Kanyurira, and CASS and WWF have had considerably more contact with Kanyurira, while preparing it for Campfire. At the time of the evaluation, Chapoto and Chisungo did not receive the same attention.

There is a danger, especially in view of the speed and enthusiasm with which Campfire is being picked up in other districts by district councils (rather than being initiated by the wards concerned), that implementers will assume a preconceived idea of how wards should co-operate. The project's success clearly depends upon the co-operation and participation of the local community, particularly in game management. In this regard, there is obviously a critical relationship between the ward's population size and the income-generating potential of the natural-resource base. Increases in population would have three adverse effects: they could lower the unit dividend, increase the pressure for alternative (farming) land use, and would almost certainly reduce the level of popular participation in the project.

Communal property management is an extremely complex technical task, shaped by the political nature of community life and relations between people and their natural-resource base. The ecological viability of natural-resource utilization demands a planned approach to maintaining the balance in wildlife numbers (neither too few nor too many) including the protection of natural vegetation; constructing water sources; counting game and protecting it from illegal hunters—the importance of which is clearly understood by the WWC.

Since January 1989, ward management has been divided between the preparation stage of CASS and that of training in wildlife management, and developing its capacity. What needs to be asked is the extent to which CASS's role precluded an earlier intervention by the Zimbabwe Trust: the respective areas of responsibility in Campfire have become blurred in Kanyurira. This is not to suggest that little has been happening inside the ward. On the contrary, there has been a great deal of land-use planning activity culminating in erecting the electric fence around the village. CASS and WWF mapped out and wrote down in draft form the planning strategies proposed by ward residents. These were reviewed before they were finally presented to the district authorities in Guruve. In itself, the fence represents a concrete land-use management tool, and is the single most important development whether physical or psychological: it has made the wildlife option more feasible.

It is too early to draw conclusions about the ward's capacity to deal with technical and maintenance problems, but Kanyurira will be a test-case for other wards considering building an electric fence. The WWC had organized four people (including one woman) to work on keeping the fence clear of undergrowth, but in January 1991 new undergrowth had not been cleared and the fence short-circuited. Employment in fence maintenance and training had not yet been provided but was expected to start during the year. In the long term, fence maintenance and plans for sustainable land-use options will be a test of local management capacity.

The relationship between agriculture and common property management is further complicated by the distinction between individual control over the means of production in agriculture and collective control over the means of production in common property management. How the ward will address the cattle option represents a big unknown for Campfire in Kanyurira. But it also highlights a problem in common resource management when some people become 'more equal than others' and disproportionately reduce the grazing and natural-resource base potential for others, so widening the gap between the better-off and the poorer farmers. The relationship between agriculture and wildlife is ultimately determined by human-to-land ratios, and a serious threat to this would be official or even spontaneous resettlement. The game fence runs through the middle of the ward on an east–west axis; in the south cattle are permitted, but not to the north, where Masoka village is situated. Kanyurira is one of the first wards to the north of the mid-Zambezi resettlement area. To land-hungry people, and politicians with promises to fulfil, a sparsely populated ward like Kanyurira represents agricultural opportunity, and even more so if tsetse is eradicated.

Two final striking characteristics of the present status of the project in Kanyurira should be noted. The first is the enthusiasm and determination of the ward, and the second concerns the sustainability of rural enterprise based on natural-resource utilization. The ward is acutely aware of these large issues, and the overriding impression is one of Kanyurira trying to establish its own agenda. Campfire has succeeded in showing Kanyurira that it is in fact resource-rich.

CONCLUSIONS

These four evaluations examine only a corner of the overall picture of NGO project experience in Zimbabwe: it is thus not possible to use them in order to comment on the overall impact of NGO assistance. Nevertheless, as a number of the themes highlighted in the case-studies are common to many NGO strategies and interventions in Zimbabwe, some generalizations can be made.

One of the most widespread assumptions about NGO interventions is that they are directed at the poor. However, in the Silveira House and Christian Care projects (where credit played an important role in determining project membership), it appears that the worst-off and most disadvantaged were excluded. In practice, membership was dominated by those in a position to repay, especially households with cattle and with access to income from migrant labour. It should be added, however, that while the projects did not reach the poorest farmers, even the better-off farmers can be described as poor.

In contrast, the Simukai collective and Campfire approaches to the poor target them far more precisely. The Zimbabwe Project has built up a reputation as one of the first NGOs which struggling collectives approach for assistance, although because the CSFS collectives are those on their way to achieving economic viability, they are no longer the poorest collectives. For its part, the Campfire approach benefits the poorest in two ways. First, it targets whole wards, and thereby includes all the poorest in a given locality. Second, as the wards where Campfire is operating are in agriculturally marginal areas, the people assisted are among the poorest in rural Zimbabwe. The problem with both these types of approach is that, despite the large volume of financial resources applied, the number of the poor who are assisted has never been as great as in the less well targeted small-farmer programmes of Silveira House and Christian Care.

Compared with the government, NGOs both individually and as a whole clearly lack resources, and this limits their impact. However, their flexibility and their willingness to experiment and innovate are all strengths compared with government agencies. The Silveira House credit schemes before Independence, and Campfire today, are highly innovative interventions in rural development implemented and shaped by NGOs. The CSFS has also developed a new approach as a membership service agency for collectives.

The case-studies highlight a number of often interlinked problems: NGOs tend to over-stretch themselves, they often fail to provide the range of services required for viability, and there is a clear tendency for each NGO to work in isolation. Nevertheless, the Silveira House case shows that the project had a considerable knock-on effect, as knowledge of improved farming practices spread out from the groups to the broader community. Not that the ripple effects were all positive: in Rota after Independence there was considerable social conflict arising from what was now seen by outsiders as group exclusiveness once fertilizer became widely available. But this type of conflict did not arise in the Mzarabani villages. Instead there was strong demand to join the Christian Care groups, in the absence of other sources of credit (especially interest-free) to purchase oxen in particular.

Other problems concern exclusiveness and patronage. Exclusiveness comes both from the small-scale nature of many NGO projects, and from the benefits which the beneficiaries, over against the non-beneficiaries, are to receive. Exclusiveness lends itself to patronage, especially when farmers join groups in anticipation of material benefits and do not, at the same time, effectively engage in project management. But patronage problems also arise because NGO credit programmes offer higher attractive terms which no other agency, particularly government agency, is able to match.

In contemporary Zimbabwe, there is less sensitivity among NGOs to the role or importance of women's participation in their projects than in many other countries. The results are clear to see: women have not participated on an equal footing with men in the case-study projects, and in practice, there is a strong bias against women. In part this arises as a result of working through existing local structures, and is reinforced by the male cultural bias which characterizes many of the NGOs. If the Silveira House project proved to be an exception (more than 50 per cent of group members were women), this was more by default than design. Gender problems also arise because of a failure to define the specific needs of women and to ensure their active participation, although, in the case of Silveira House and Christian Care, this was symptomatic of a more general lack of targeting. In the Campfire case-study of Dande, because local structures of authority are male-dominated, women are excluded from the outset, even though widows have benefited from the conscientization effect of dividend distribution, which, in turn, posed something of a challenge to traditional social values.

Credit schemes clearly play a major role in NGO activity in rural Zimbabwe: they are very popular with NGOs, and the case-studies not only reveal successes but provide insights into the causes of success. In the case of Silveira House, credit was based on discrete groups, with potential members selected on the grounds of their credit-worthiness. Vetting for credit-worthiness and forming cohesive groups in which members felt accountable to one another were both critical factors contributing to the success of the joint liability schemes of the Silveira House project. When group control was lost, the scheme collapsed. A similar test is in store for the Christian Care groups which have been formed for the convenience of obtaining credit, which is provided without liability, individual or collective. It is questionable whether there is sufficient social cohesion within the groups for the project to succeed.

However the case-studies also raise a range of questions about the NGO approach to credit. One issue concerns the beneficiaries. While NGO (subsidized) credit probably reaches more poor farmers than does government (commercial) credit, it cannot reach the poorest because they are unable to afford it. Indeed, nationwide, credit probably reaches only a small minority of communal-land farmers, those confident enough to take the risk of borrowing, whether it be a soft NGO loan or a seasonal government loan at or near commercial interest rates. The vast majority of communal-land farmers finance crop production without loans from either the government or the NGOs. In addition, as noted above, providing credit at very attractive interest rates tends to breed exclusivity among the groups assisted.

A second set of issues concerns the longer-term impact of NGO credit programmes. There seems little doubt that providing subsidized credit to particular groups of farmers can have adverse effects: it can create the impression among those farmers that subsidized credit is normal, while also replicating such a view in the wider community. Certainly in the eyes of farmers, who broadly equate paying interest with sheer exploitation, the NGOs' approach was seen as fair. Clearly, however, it is simply not possible for NGOs to extend their credit schemes to more and more groups and, at the same time, to maintain a large subsidy element indefinitely. Thus, for the longer-term justification of such an approach, this benevolence needs to be accompanied by financial training to achieve business take-off and/or a transfer to the principles of commercial credit. What is equally worrying for Zimbabwe is evidence to suggest that not only is NGO credit not financially sustainable but nor is the government's AFC commercial credit: AFC repayment rates in the good years since Independence have been at the level of 72–5 per cent, but they have fallen to as low as 24 per cent in bad crop years, giving an average of 48 per cent for the whole period 1981–8.

The most fundamental question, however, concerns the assumptions underlying the whole NGO approach to credit. There is a real danger that too much time is spent on examining repayment rates when the bigger problem is probably not so much credit *per se*, but rather the inflexibility of seasonal loans. While repayment rates in NGO credit schemes have often been better than in the government's (AFC) scheme, in the (frequent) drought years, the rates have been low and have tended to fall. In practice, incorporating more and more farmers into credit schemes based on seasonal loans in the context of recurring drought is to expose them to greater risk.

Lack of title deeds in the communal lands to serve as security against loans necessitates the AFC having to use short-term seasonal loans, holding the crop-in-the-field as collateral. From the Silveira House case-study, however, it is evident that more flexible loans are also more accessible, and there is opportunity within the Christian Care project to experiment with more flexible credit. Unlike the AFC, Christian Care has the flexibility to risk its funds in order to innovate and design a more appropriate system which could enable farmers to diversify, and this is a valid role for NGOs. However, not even greater flexibility would ensure that credit reached the poorest farmers. They are marginalized by a range of other factors as well: rainfall; the quality of their resource base; the lack of manure, draught power, and implements; poor-quality roads; inadequate transport; and a poor supply and marketing infrastructure. With the exception of the Christian Care credit for oxen, none of the other projects directly addressed these constraints.

Finally, there is the question of the sort of groups to be supported with credit and the relative costs of different approaches. The case-studies suggest that the unit costs of providing credit might be improved by the provision of financial, technical, and managerial support, whether this comes in the form of training for communal-land farmers or for the capital-intensive co-operatives. Again, for the NGO, the per-farmer costs will be far higher for support given to capital-intensive collective projects than for communal-land farmer groups: ranging from a high of Z$10,000 for the former to Z$304 per farmer in the case of Christian Care credit inputs for the year 1988–9. If the prime concern of NGOs is to maximize the number of poor farmers assisted, they would reap a greater return by assisting communal-area farmers. However, if these communal-area farmers are to farm their land commercially and increase their share of total marketed production, then they will require assistance, and this will mean the provision of subsidies for some time yet. Thus, if the aim of the NGOs is to go beyond the marginal increase in incomes of the poor to addressing the question of the redistribution of income and wealth, higher project costs would be justified.

The case-studies also provide some important insights into improving local institutional capacity. The Silveira House project promoted co-operative activity in its groups, spawning new local supply and marketing co-operatives—new rural institutions—although lack of training in credit and financial management militated against greater impact. Thus, in every area the project met a fundamental need of all farmers, members and non-members, better-off and poor. There was also considerable networking among groups from different areas and provinces, and this has contributed to the strong sense of solidarity which remains among the original group members, almost ten years after the project effectively ended. Conversely, the Christian Care groups do not appear to share the cohesiveness of the Silveira House groups and the project as a whole, characterized as a top-down relief style of implementation, has failed to promote local institutional capacity.

While promoting local capacity is vital to rural development and collectives in Zimbabwe, scale is often a critical factor when looking at the capacity of NGOs to deliver technical, financial, and managerial assistance. One problem is that, when the need is great and NGOs have registered some success on a more limited scale, there is a great temptation to over-stretch themselves and extend the services they provide at the cost of impairing their efficiency. Thus the Silveira House credit project could not meet the demand for credit, and the Christian Care project was under-staffed and under-resourced. Scale is not only a matter of responding to need, but relates also to what the NGO can most efficiently deliver to meet the needs of its constituents, through cost-effective management.

The case-studies also raise the question of staffing. Particularly in the more welfare orientated NGOs, there is a lack of career development and staff training for project-level staff; as a result staff who are technically qualified in agriculture seldom exercise their technical skills. For example, Silveira House and Christian Care staff are supposed to help groups define problem areas and set priorities. But, with a large number of clients and in the absence of a structured and diagnostic approach, the result is a double loss to both the development of the NGO and to its projects, and one which reflects the welfare roots of both organizations. Their salaries and administration costs are lower than those of service agencies, but they exact a price from the projects when the staff leave for greener pastures.

NGO work in the collective co-operative movement highlights the tension between coverage and effectiveness. While both the Zimbabwe Project and the CSFS provide access to capital and play a critically important role in promoting institutional capacity in the collectives they assist, it is clearly impossible for the Zimbabwe Project to meet the full needs of the hundreds of collectives and co-operatives that it has on its books. In contrast, the CSFS, as a membership organization, has limited itself to meeting the needs of its few dozen member collectives, and is able to provide each with assistance on a regular basis.

While it is still early days for the Campfire project, there is ample evidence from Kanyurira ward of the importance of institutional factors, ranging from the need to strengthen the WWC and its links both within the ward and to the district council, and to the need to marry the sometimes potentially conflicting objectives of agriculture and conservation. Like the CSFS, the Zimbabwe Trust places a high priority on delivering this type of support to each of its clients, and it provides managerial support to small NGOs which are not necessarily in receipt of financial assistance.

Each of the four projects provided subsidies to create or promote rural enterprises, and to facilitate the integration of beneficiaries into the modern economy. Within this perspective, the case-studies confirm the findings of a 1987 survey of income-generating projects commissioned by the umbrella organization, the National Association of Non-Governmental Organisations (NANGO), previously VOICE. This suggested that the role and use of grants and soft loans are closely related to the attitudes of NGOs and project members towards project financial management and economic viability. Grants are usually perceived as gifts and the use to which the funds are put are not considered to be part of the costs of the enterprise. NGOs seldom inform groups and enterprises about the value of grants in kind, making it impossible to quantify these as costs. There is a tendency to throw grants at projects, almost in the hope that some of it will stick, without assessing the capacity of the collective, group, or institution to absorb and utilize them. NGOs which fall into this category and which tend not to provide effective business support with their grants and loans are sometimes referred to as welfare agencies by both their members and by other agencies. In the case-studies, the exceptions are the CSFS and the Zimbabwe Trust, which provide financial and managerial services to enable collectives and rural institutions respectively to utilize their capital efficiently.

NOTES

1. It is not being suggested that there is no interchange between some NGOs and some government officials or departments at the centre. Indeed in the case of CUSO, CIDA, and the Department of Co-operatives, there is a three-way relationship, covering the government, an NGO, and an official aid agency. What is more, there are very close links between NGOs and the Ministry of Education and Culture, especially in relation to the work of ZIMFEP, while in the field of social welfare, the government has even funded the work of some NGOs and promoted the creation and expansion of community and women's groups (see de Graaf *et al.*, 1991: 28 ff.).

2. One complaint frequently voiced is that when a major foreign donor sets up a network for indigenous NGOs in receipt of its funds, the effect is to isolate these NGOs from the wider movement.

3. See de Graaf *et al.* (1991: 15 ff.) for a different way of grouping NGOs.

4. As with so many generalizations about NGOs in Zimbabwe, there are notable exceptions. Thus the approach of the Belgium-based COOPIBO is both highly professional and acutely sensitive to the issue of rural differentiation.

5. This study was conducted with assistance from Mr Norman Musunhe of Silveira House and Mr Farai Maziwisa, with important inputs from members of Rota, Chaza, and Kwaedza groups, and the staff of Silveira House.

6. This evaluation was conducted with assistance from Mrs Tsitsi Kuuya of Christian Care and Mr Farai Maziwisa. Discussions were also held with members of all the groups in Mzarabani, the Museredza school, the DDF and ARDA, the Tsetse and Trypanosomiasis Control Branch in Harare, the Agritex officer for Machaya and Hoya, staff of the veterinary extension office, and staff members of Christian Care.

7. This evaluation was conducted with the assistance of Mr Farai Maziwisa, and the co-operation of members of Simukai, the CSFS, and the Zimbabwe Project.

8. The Zimbabwe Project has a mandate to support programmes assisting ex-combatants, large numbers of whom started collective enterprises. By 1990 it had assisted over 2,000 co-operatives including approximately 200 collectives. It sees its role as both a mediating agency between co-operatives, and a service agency, providing funding and training. Its major donors have been Oxfam, Christian Aid, and NOVIB, who jointly negotiate co-funding from the European Community. The CSFS, which grew out of OCCZIM (the representative body for collectives) and the Zimbabwe Project, was established in 1988 'to organise and strengthen viable co-operatives'. By 1990 it had a membership of thirty collectives, each of which pays an annual subscription of Z$100 plus minimum shares in

the scheme worth Z$200. Its principal donors are HIVOS, NOVIB, and FOS, with smaller grants from CAFOD and Christian Aid.

9. Many individual farmers in resettlement schemes form themselves into groups for the purpose of obtaining land, rather than through commitment to collective production, and many collective schemes are in fact composed of individual arable plots in addition to communal plots.

10. In 1989/90 the annual budget of the Department of Co-operatives was only Z$2.5m.

11. This evaluation was undertaken with Farai Maziwisa. Assistance was also given by Gift Chisunga, the WWC, and other members of Kanyurira ward in Dande, members of the Zimbabwe Trust, of CASS at the University of Zimbabwe, of the WWF, the DNPWLM, Guruve District Council, the Tsetse and Trypanosomiasis Control Branch in Harare, and Masoka school.

12. In 1990 the Zimbabwe Trust had thirty-one staff; fifteen of them are exclusively engaged in Campfire. Unlike most NGOs, it does not depend on public fund-raising, relying mostly on the blocked funds of UK companies in Zimbabwe and co-funding from ODA and some of the leading official aid donors. In 1989/90 its total income was Z$7m., and project expenditure was Z$3m., with management and administration accounting for approximately 20%. In 1989/90 expenditure on the Dande project was Z$695,492 or 23% of total project expenditure.

13. In the communal lands where land is owned by the state the district council is the representative of the state.

14. Safari hunting in Zimbabwe is organized on the basis of concessions (hunting areas) which are leased to safari operators for one to five years by either the DNPWLM or by district councils with AA status.

REFERENCES

ALLIBAND, T. (1983), *Catalysts of Development: Voluntary Agencies in India* (Hartford, Conn.: Kumarian Press).

ANNIS, S. (1987), 'Can Small-Scale Development be a Large-Scale Policy? The Case of Latin America', *World Development*, 15, suppl. (autumn), 129–34.

——HAKIN, P., and PEINNER, L. (1988), *Direct To The Poor* (Boulder, Colo. and London: Westview).

ARMSTRONG, G. A. and BRIDGER, G. A. (1986), *Cost Effectiveness: Appraising Projects with Non-Quantifiable Benefits* (London: Crown Agents).

AVINA, J. (1990), 'The Evolutionary Life Cycles of Non-Governmental Development Organizations', *Public Administration and Development*, 13/5: 453–76.

BALDWIN, D. (1988), *Non-government Organizations and African Development: An Inquiry* (Washington, DC: World Bank).

BARCLAY A. H., HOSKINS, M. W., NJENGA, W. K., and TRIPP, R. B. (1979), *The Development Impact of PVOs in Kenya and Niger*, Report prepared for USAID (Norwalk, Conn.: Development Alternatives Inc).

BEAUDOUX, E., CROMBRUGGHE, G. DE, DOUXCHAMPS, F., GUENEAU, M., and NEUWKERK, M. (1990), *Supporting Development Action at Community Level: A Methodological Guide* (Brussels: le Collectif d'Echanges pour la Technologie Appropriée (COTA)).

BEBBINGTON, A. (1994), *Strengthening the Partnership Evaluation of the Finnish NGO Support Programme: Country Case-Study Uganda* (Helsinki: Finnish International Development Agency).

——KOPP, A. (1995), *The Development Impact of Government Support to Swedish NGOs: Country Case-Study Bolivia* (Stockholm: Swedish International Development Authority).

BECKMANN, D. (1991), 'Recent Experience and Emerging Trends', in Paul and Israel.

BERG, R. J. (1987), *Non-Governmental Organizations: New Force in Third World Development and Politics* (Lancing, Mich.: Michigan State University, Center for Advanced Study of International Development).

BESLEY, T. and KANBUR, R. (1990), *The Principles of Targeting*, Working Paper WPS 385 (Washington, DC: World Bank).

BLACK, M. (1992), *A Cause for our Times: Oxfam the First 50 years* (Oxford: Oxfam and Oxford University Press).

BORTON, J. (1993), 'Recent Trends in the International Relief System', *Disasters: The Journal of Disaster Studies and Management*, 17/3: 187–201.

BOSE, A. and BURNELL, A. (1991) (eds.), *Britain's Overseas Aid since 1979: Between Idealism and Self-Interest* (Manchester: Manchester University Press).

BOWDEN, P. (1990), 'NGOs in Asia: Issues in Development', *Public Administration and Development*, 10: 141–52.

BOWMANN, M., BAANANTE, J., DICHTER, T., LONDNER, S., and REILING, P. (1989), *Measuring Our Impact: Determining Cost-Effectiveness of Non-Governmental Organization Development Projects* (Norwalk, Conn.: Technoserve).

BOWN, L. (1990), *Preparing the Future—Women, Literacy and Development*, ActionAid Development Report No. 4 (London: ActionAid).

BRATTON, M. (1990), 'Non-governmental Organizations in Africa: Can They Influence Public Policy?', *Development and Change*, 21/1: 87–118.

BRETT, E. A. (1989), 'Servicing Small Farmers under Duress: Institutional Crises and Reconstruction in Uganda' (Brighton: Institute of Development Studies; mimeo).

BRODHEAD, T. and HERBERT-COPLEY, B. (1988), *Bridges of Hope? Canadian Voluntary Agencies and the Third World* (Ottawa: North-South Institute).

BROWN, L. D. (1990), *Bridging Organizations and Sustainable Development*, Institute for Development Research, Paper No. A17 (Boston: IDR).

——and KORTEN, D. (1989), *Understanding Voluntary Organizations: Guidelines for Donors*, Working Paper WPS 258 (Washington, DC: World Bank).

BURBIDGE, J. (1988) (ed.), *Approaches That Work in Rural Development* (London, New York, and Paris: K. G. Munchen for the Institute of Cultural Affairs International, Brussels).

CAMERON, C. and COCKING, J. (1991), 'The Evaluation of NGO Activities, Organizations, Methodology and Results' (London: ODA, Evaluation Department; mimeo).

CAMPBELL, P. (1989), 'Institutional Development: Basic Principles and Strategies' (Geneva: International Council of Voluntary Agencies).

CANADIAN INTERNATIONAL DEVELOPMENT AGENCY (CIDA) (1986), *Corporate Evaluation of CIDA's Non-governmental Organizations Programme* (Ottawa: CIDA).

CARR, M., CROMBRUGGE, G. DE, and HOWES, M. (1984), *Assessing Rural Development Projects* (Brussels: le Collectif d'Echanges pour la Technologie Appropriée (COTA)).

CARROLL, T. (1992), *Intermediary NGOs: The Supporting Link in Grassroots Development* (Hartford, Conn.: The Kumarian Press).

CASSEN R. and ASSOCIATES (1986), *Does Aid Work?* (London: Oxford University Press).

CERNEA, M. M. (1983), *A Social Methodology for Community Participation in Local Investments: The Experience of Mexico's PIDER Project*, World Bank Staff Working Paper No. 598 (Washington, DC: World Bank).

——(1985) (ed.), *Putting People First: Sociological Variables in Rural Development* (New York: Oxford University Press for the World Bank).

——(1988), *Nongovernmental Organizations and Local Development*, Discussion Paper No. 40 (Washington, DC: World Bank).

CHALKER, L. (1989), 'The Role of NGOs in Today's World', Cecil Jackson Memorial Lecture delivered at the Commonwealth Institute, London, October (London: ODA; mimeo).

CHAMBERS, R. (1983), *Rural Development: Putting the Last First* (Harlow: Longman).

——(1985), 'Shortcut Methods of Gathering Social Information for Rural Development Projects', in Cernea, 399–415.

——(1994), 'The Origins and Practice of Participatory Rural Appraisal', *World Development*, 22/7: 953–69.

——PACEY, A., and THRUPP, L. A. (1989) (eds.), *Farmer First: Farmer Innovation and Agricultural Research* (London: Intermediate Technology).

CHENERY, H., AHLUWALIA, M. S., BELL, C. L. G., DULOY, J. H., and JOLLY, R. (1974), *Redistribution with Growth* (London: Oxford University Press).

CLARK, J. (1991), *Democratizing Development: The Role of Voluntary Organizations* (London: Earthscan Publications).

CLAYTON, A. (1994) (ed.), *Governance, Democracy and Conditionality: What Role for NGOs?*, INTRAC NGO Management and Policy Series, No. 2 (Oxford: INTRAC Publications).

COMMONWEALTH SECRETARIAT (1987), *Strategic Issues in Development Management: Learning from Successful Experiences*, 3 vols (London: Commonwealth Secretariat).

CONYERS, D. and KAUL, M. (1990), 'Strategic Issues in Development Management: Learning from Successful Experience', *Public Administration and Development*, 10: 127–40.

CORNEA, G. A., JOLLY, R., and STEWART, F. (1988) (eds.), *Adjustment with a Human Face*, ii. *Country Case Studies* (Oxford: Clarendon Press).

CROMBRUGGHE, G. DE, HOWES, M., and NIEUWKERK, R. (1985), *An Evaluation of EC Small Development Projects* (Brussels: le Collectif d'Echanges pour la Technologie Appropriée (COTA)).

The Courier (1987), No. 104, July–Aug.

DANIDA (1989), *Danish NGOs, Report No. 1, Synthesis* (Copenhagen: Ministry of Foreign Affairs, Department of International Development Cooperation).

DASGUPTA, B. (1977), 'India's Green Revolution', *Economic and Political Weekly*, 12, annual number.

DE CONINCK, J. with RIDDELL, R. C. (1992), *Evaluating the Impact of NGOs in Rural Poverty Alleviation: Uganda Country Study*, Working Paper No. 51 (London: Overseas Development Institute).

DE GRAAF, M., MOYO, S., and DIETZ, T. (1991), 'Non-Governmental Organizations in Zimbabwe: Report for the Impact Study Co-Financing Organisations' (Amsterdam: 3d Concept).

DICHTER, T. (1988), 'Insights into Cost Effectiveness From One PVO's Perspective' (Hartford, Conn.: Technoserve).

DRÈZE, J. and SEN, A. (1989), *Hunger and Public Action* (Oxford: Clarendon Press).

D'ROZARIO, A. (1989), 'NGOs Face Stricter Control from Bangladesh Government', *Asia Focus*, 14/3 (Oct.).

EDIRISINGHE, N. (1987), *The Food Stamp Scheme in Sri Lanka: Costs, Benefits and Options for Modification*, Research Report No. 58 (Washington, DC: Institute for Food Policy Research).

EDWARDS, M. (1989), 'Learning from Experience in Africa' (Oxford: Oxfam; mimeo).

——and HULME, D. (1992) (eds.), *Making a Difference: NGOs and Development in a Changing World* (London: Earthscan).

ELLIS, G. (1984), 'Making PVOs Count More: A Proposal' in Gorman, 201–4.

ELSE, J. (1987), *NGO Activities in Income-Generating Projects (IGPs) in Zimbabwe: Report of a Study Conducted under the Auspices of VOICE's Development Forum* (Harare: VOICE).

ESMAN, M. J. and UPHOFF, N. (1984), *Local Organizations: Intermediaries in Rural Development* (Ithaca, NY: Cornell University Press).

FARRINGTON, J. and MARTIN, A. (1988), *Farmer Participation in Agricultural Research: A Review of Concepts and Practices*, Agricultural Administration Unit Occasional Paper 9 (London: Overseas Development Institute).

——BEBBINGTON, A. J. and WELLARD, K. (1993), *Between the State and the Rural Poor: NGOs and Agricultural Development* (London: Routledge).

FEDERAL REPUBLIC OF GERMANY, FEDERAL MINISTRY FOR ECONOMIC COOPERATION (1986), *Learning From Mistakes: Findings and Conclusions* (Bonn: Der Bundesminister für Wirtschaftliche Zusammenarbeit).

FEUERSTEIN, M.-T. (1986), *Partners in Evaluation: Evaluating Development and Community Programmes with Participants* (London: Macmillan).

FINSTERBUSCH, K. and VAN WICKLIN, W. A. (1987), 'The Contribution of Beneficiary Participation to Development Project Effectiveness', *Public Administration and Development*, 7/1: 1–24.

FOWLER, A. (1988), *NGOs in Africa: Achieving Comparative Advantage in Relief and Micro-Development*, Discussion Paper No. 249 (Brighton: Institute of Development Studies).

——(1991), 'The Role of NGOs in Changing State-Society Relations: Perspectives from Eastern and Southern Africa', *Development Policy Review*, 9/1: 53–84.

GETUBIG, I. P. and LEDESMA, A. J. (1988) (eds.), *Voices from the Culture of Silence: The Most Disadvantaged Groups in Asian Agriculture* (Kuala Lumpur: Asia and Pacific Development Centre).

GILLESPIE, N. (1990), *Selected World Bank Poverty Studies: A Summary of Approaches, Coverage, and Findings*, Working Paper WPS 552 (Washington, DC: World Bank).

GOETZ, A. M. and SEN GUPTA, R. (1994), 'Who Takes the Credit? Gender, Power, and Control Over Loan Use in Rural Credit Programmes in Bangladesh', IDS Working Paper, No. 8 (Brighton: Institute of Development Studies).

GORMAN, R. F. (1984), *Private Voluntary Organizations as Agents of Development* (Boulder, Colo. and London: Westview).

GOVERNMENT OF ZIMBABWE (1983), *Government Policy of Cooperative Development* (Harare: Government Printer).

GRIFFIN, K. (1974), *The Political Economy of Agrarian Change: An Essay on the Green Revolution* (London: Macmillan).

GRIFFITHS, G. (1987), 'Missing the Poorest: Participant Identification by a Rural Development Agency', Discussion Paper No. 230 (Brighton: Institute of Development Studies).

HANLON, J. (1986), *Producer Cooperatives and the Government in Zimbabwe* (Harare: HIVOS).

——(1991), *Mozambique: Who Calls the Shots?* (London: James Currey).

HARRIS, M. and POULTON, R. (1988) (ed.), *Putting People First* (London: Macmillan).

HASLER, R. (1990), 'The Political and Cultural Dynamics of Resource Management: Campfire in Chapota' (Harare: CASS, University of Zimbabwe; mimeo).

HEIJDEN, H. VAN DER (1986), 'Development Impact and Effectiveness of Non-Governmental Organizations: The Record of Progress in Rural Development Co-operation'. (mimeo).

——(1988), 'The Role of the Private Voluntary Sector' in Burbidge.

HIFAB INTERNATIONAL and ZIMCONSULT (1989), *Zimbabwe Country Study and Norwegian Aid Review* (Oslo and Harare: Hifab and Zimconsult).

HOSSAIN, M. (1988), *Credit for Rural Poverty Alleviation: The Grameen Bank in Bangladesh*, Research Report 65 (Washington, DC: International Food Policy Research Institute and Bangladesh Institute of Development Studies).

HOWELL, J. (1990), 'Rural Poverty and External Aid', *Development Policy Review*, 8/3: 269–86.

HULME, D. (1990), 'Can the Grameen Bank be Replicated? Recent Experiments in Malaysia, Malawi and Sri Lanka', *Development Policy Review*, 8/3: 287–300.

HUNTER, G. (1981), *A Hard Look at Directing Benefits to the Rural Poor and 'Participation'*, Agricultural Administration Unit Discussion Paper No. 6 (London: Overseas Development Institute).

IMPACT STUDY CO-FINANCING PROGRAMME (1991), 'Significance of the Co-financing Programme: An Exploration', final report (Utrecht: ISCP).

JONES, S. and HOSSAIN, M. (1983), 'Production, Poverty and the Co-operative Ideal', in Lea and Chaudhuri.

JOSHI, P. C. (1974), 'Land Reform and Agrarian Change in India and Pakistan since 1947: II', *Journal of Peasant Studies*, 1/3: 326–62.

KAJESE, K. (1987), 'An Agenda of Future Tasks for International and Indigenous NGOs: Views from the South', *World Development*, 15, suppl. (Autumn), 79–86.

KORTEN, D. C. (1980), 'Community Organization and Rural Development: A Learning Process Approach', *Public Administration Review*, 40/5: 341–52.

——(1987), 'Third Generation NGO Strategies: A Key to People-Centered Development', *World Development*, 15, suppl. (Autumn), 145–60.

——(1990*a*), 'NGOs and Development: An Overview Paper', prepared for the World Bank (Boston: Institute for Development Research; mimeo).

——(1990*b*), *Getting to the 21st Century: Voluntary Development Action and the Global Agenda* (Hartford, Conn.: Kumarian Press).

KOTTACK, C. P. (1985), 'When People Don't Come First: Some Sociological Perspectives from Completed Projects', in Cernea, 325–56.

KRUEGER, A., MICHALOPOULOS, C., and RUTTAN, V. (1989), *Aid and Development* (Baltimore and London: Johns Hopkins University Press).

LAUNONEN, R. and OJANPERA, S. (1985), *Integrated Rural Development: An Approach Paper*, Report No. 10 (Helsinki: Institute of Development Studies, University of Helsinki).

LEA, D. A. M. and CHAUDHRI, D. P. (1983) (eds.), *Rural Development and the State: Contradictions and Dilemmas in Developing Countries* (London: Methuen).

LEMARASQUIER, T. (1987), 'Prospects for Development Education: Some Strategic Issues Facing European NGOs', *World Development*, 15, suppl. (Autumn), 189–200.

LIPTON, M. (1985), *The Poor and the Poorest: Some Interim Findings*, World Bank Discussion Paper No. 25 (Washington, DC: World Bank).

MACGARRY, B. (1990), 'Agricultural Technology Development by NGOs and the Scope for Closer Linkages with Formal Research Services' (Harare: Silveira House; mimeo).

MARSDEN, D. and OAKLEY, P. (1990) (eds.), *Evaluating Social Development Projects*, Development Guidelines No. 5 (Oxford: Oxfam).

————PRATT, B. (1994), *Measuring the Process: Guidelines for Evaluating Social Development*, INTRAC NGO Management Policy Series, No. 3 (Oxford: INTRAC Publications).

MUIR, A. with RIDDELL, R. C. (1992), *Evaluating the Impact of NGOs in Rural Poverty Alleviation: Zimbabwe Country Study*, Working Paper No. 52 (London: Overseas Development Institute).

MURTHY, N., HIRWAY, I., PANCHMUKHI, P. R., and SATIA, J. K. (1990), *How Well Do India's Social Service Programs Serve the Poor?*, Working Paper WPS 491 (Washington, DC: World Bank).

(NANGO) NATIONAL ASSOCIATION OF NON-GOVERNMENTAL ORGANIZATIONS (1991), *The NANGO Programme of Activities, 1991/92 to 1993/94* (Harare: NANGO).

NATH, N. C. B. (1989), *A Survey Report on the Voluntary Sector* (New Delhi: Foundation to Aid Industrial Recovery).

NG'ETHE, N., MITULLAH, W., and NGUNYI, M. (1990), 'Government—NGO Relationship in the Context of Alternative Development Strategies in Kenya', in *Critical Choices for the NGO Community: African Development in the 1990s*, Seminar Proceedings, No. 30 (Centre of African Studies, University of Edinburgh), 129–47.

OAKLEY, P. and WINDER, D. (1980), 'An Exploratory Review of Rural Social Development Projects and the Question of Their Evaluation', report produced for Oxfam (Oxford: Oxfam; mimeo).

——*et al.* (1991), *Projects with People: The Practice of Participation in Rural Development* (Geneva: International Labour Office).

O'CONNOR, A. (1991), *Poverty in Africa: A Geographical Approach* (London: Belhaven).

OECD (1988), *Voluntary Aid for Development: The Role of Non-Governmental Organizations* (Paris: OECD).

——(1990*a*), *Directory of Non-Governmental Development Organisations in OECD Member Countries* (Paris: OECD).

——(1990*b*), *Development Co-operation: Efforts and Policies of the Members of the Development Assistance Committee* (Paris: OECD).

——(1995), *Development Cooperation: Efforts and Policies of the Members of the Development Assistance Committee* (Paris: OECD).

OVERSEAS DEVELOPMENT INSTITUTE (1989), 'NGOs in Development', Briefing Paper (London: ODI).

PADRON, M. (1987), 'Non-Governmental Development Organizations: From Development Aid to Development Cooperation', *World Development*, 15, suppl. (Autumn), 69–78.

PALUMBO, D. J. and NACHMIAS, D. (1983), 'The Preconditions for Successful Evaluation: Is There an Ideal Paradigm?', *Policy Sciences*, 16: 67–9.

PAUL, S. and ISRAEL, A. (1991), *Nongovernmental Organizations and the World Bank: Cooperation for Development* (Washington, DC: World Bank).

PINTO-DUSCHINSKY, M. (1991), 'Foreign Political Aid: The German Political Foundations and Their US Counterparts', *International Affairs*, 67/1: 33–63.

PORTER, D. and CLARK, K. (1985), *Questioning Practice: NGOs and Evaluation*, NZCTD Pacific Aid Research Monograph No. 1 (Wellington: New Zealand Coalition for Trade and Development).

RAHMAN, M. A. (1990), 'Qualitative Indicators of Social Development Evaluation', in Marsden and Oakley, 40–50.

REID, J. (1982), 'A Review of the History and Role of Credit within Silveira House's Agricultural Scheme and Proposals Concerning its Future Development' (Harare: Silveira House; mimeo).

RENARD, R. and BERLAGE, L. (1990), 'The Rise and Fall of Cost-Benefit Analysis in Developing Countries', paper presented to the EADI Workshop on Approaches and Methods in the Evaluation of Aid (Oslo: European Association of Development Research and Training Institutes; mimeo).

RIDDELL, R. C. (1987), *Foreign Aid Reconsidered* (London and Baltimore: James Currey and Johns Hopkins University Press).

——(1990), *Judging Success: Evaluating NGO Approaches to Alleviating Poverty in Developing Countries*, Working Paper No. 37 (London: Overseas Development Institute).

——(1993), *Discerning The Way Together: Report on the Work of Brot für die Welt, Christian Aid, EZE and ICCO* (London: Christian Aid).

——and BEBBINGTON, A. J. (1995), *Developing Country NGOs and Donor Governments: Report to the Overseas Development Administration, London* (London and East Kilbride: Overseas Development Administration).

————and PECK, L. (1995), *Promoting Development by Proxy: The Development Impact of Government Support to Swedish NGOs* (Stockholm: Swedish International Development Authority).

——————SALAKOSKI, M., and VARIS, T. (1994), *Strengthening The Partnership: Evaluation of the Finnish NGO Support Programme* (Helsinki: Finnish International Development Agency).

——MATSVAI, S., and NCUBE, S. (1995), *The Development Impact of Government Support to Swedish NGOs: Country Case-Study Zimbabwe* (Stockholm: Swedish International Development Authority).

ROBERTS, H. (1985), 'Rural Development in Northern Uganda, a Review of ACORD's Rural Development Programme in Gulu and Kitgum Districts' (Norwich: Overseas Development Group, University of East Anglia).

ROBINSON, M. (1991a), *Evaluating the Impact of NGOs in Rural Poverty Alleviation: India Country Study*, Working Paper No. 49 (London: Overseas Development Institute).

——(1991b), 'Development NGOs in Europe and North America: A Statistical Profile', *Charity Trends*, 14th edn.

——(1991c), 'Participatory Impact Evaluation: Reflections from the Field', *Forum Valutazione*, No. 2 (Rome), 101–16.

——(1991d), 'An Uncertain Partnership: The Overseas Development Administration and the Voluntary Sector in the 1980s', in Bose and Burnell.

——(1992), 'Practical Issues in NGO Evaluation', paper prepared for the JFS–NGO Evaluation Workshop (Edinburgh, July).

——(forthcoming), 'Privatising the Voluntary Sector: NGOs as Public Service Contractors?', in D. HULME and M. EDWARDS (eds.), *Too Close for Comfort? NGOs, Donors and States*, International Political Economy Series (London: Macmillan).

ROHRBACH, D. D. (1989), *The Economics of Smallholder Maize Production in Zimbabwe: Implications for Food Security*, Michigan State University International Development Papers, No. 11 (East Lansing, Mich.: Department of Agricultural Economics).

SALMEN, L. F. and EAVES, A. P. (1991), 'Interactions between Nongovernmental Organizations, Governments and the World Bank: Evidence from Bank Projects', in Paul and Israel.

SANYAL, B. (1991), 'Antagonistic Co-operation: A Case Study of Non-Governmental Organizations, Government and Donors's Relationships in Income-Generating Projects in Bangladesh', *World Development*, 19/10: 1367–79.

SCHNEIDER, B. (1988), *The Barefoot Revolution: A Report to the Club of Rome* (London: Intermediate Technology).

SCOTT, W. (1985), *Concepts and Measurement of Poverty* (Geneva: UNRISD).

SEN, B. (1987), 'NGO Self-evaluation: Issues of Concern', *World Development*, 15, suppl., 161–7.

——(1990), 'Agriculture-Oriented Programmes for the Alleviation of Poverty', in *Evaluation of Poverty Alleviation Programmes*, i (Dhaka: Bangladesh Institute of Development Studies).

SMILLIE, I. and HELMICH, H. (1993), *Stakeholders in Development: Non-governmental Organizations and Development* (Paris: OECD).

SMITH, B. H. (1984), 'United States and Canadian PVOs as Transnational Development Institutions', in Gorman, 115–64.

——(1987), 'An Agenda of Future Tasks for International and Indigenous NGOs: Views from the North', *World Development*, 15, suppl. (Autumn), 87–94.

——(1990), *More than Altruism: The Politics of Private Foreign Aid* (Princeton, NJ: Princeton University Press).

SOMMER, J. G. (1977), *Beyond Charity: U.S. Voluntary Aid for a Changing Third World* (Washington, DC: Overseas Development Council).

STEPHEN, F. (1990), *NGOs—Hope of the Last Decade of this Century!* (Bangalore: SEARCH).

STEWART, F. (1985), *Planning to Meet Basic Needs* (London: Macmillan).

TANDON, Y. (1988), 'Employment Generation Potential of Cooperatives in Zimbabwe', report prepared for the Ministry of Community and Cooperative Development and Women's Affairs (Harare: Rescon; mimeo).

TENDLER, J. (1982), *Turning Private Voluntary Agencies into Development Agencies: Questions for Evaluation*, AID Program Evaluation Discussion Paper No. 12 (Washington, DC: US Agency for International Development).

——(1987), 'Whatever Happened To Poverty Alleviation?', Report for the Mid-Decade Review of the Ford Foundation's Programs on Livelihood, Employment and Income Generation, repr. in *World Development*, 17/1 (1987), 1033–44.

——(1988), 'What to Think about Cooperatives: A Guide from Bolivia', in Annis *et al.*

UNDP (1990), *Human Development Report 1990* (Oxford: Oxford University Press).

——(1991), *Human Development Report 1991* (Oxford: Oxford University Press).

UNDP (1992), *Human Development Report 1992* (Oxford: Oxford University Press).

——(1993), *Human Development Report 1993* (Oxford and New York: Oxford University Press).

—— (1994), *Human Development Report 1994* (Oxford and New York: Oxford University Press).

UNIA, P. (1991), 'Social Action Group Strategies in the Indian Sub-Continent', *Development in Practice*, 1/2.

UNIDO (1990), *Industrialization in the Least Developed Countries: The Potential Role of Development Projects in other Sectors*, PPD.R.37 (Vienna: UNIDO).

UPHOFF, N. (1985), 'Fitting Projects to People', in Cernea, 359–95.

——(1991), 'A Field Methodology for Participatory Self-Evaluation', *Community Development Journal*, 26/4: 271–85.

USAID (1985), *PVOs and the Promotion of Small-scale Enterprise*. AID Evaluation Study, No. 27 (Washington, DC: USAID).

—— (1986), *Development Effectiveness of PVOs* (Washington, DC: USAID).

——(1988), *The Effectiveness of PVOs*, Report of the Advisory Committee on Voluntary Foreign Aid, 1998 Report (Washington, DC: USAID).

VANSANT, J. (1989), 'Opportunities and Risks for Private Voluntary Organizations as Agents of LDC Policy Change', *World Development*, 17/11: 1723–32.

VERHAGEN, K. (1987), *Self-Help Promotion: A Challenge to the NGO Community* (Amsterdam: CEBEMO/Royal Tropical Institute).

WHITE, S. C. (1991), *Evaluating the Impact of NGOs in Rural Poverty Alleviation: Bangladesh Country Study*, Working Paper No. 50 (London: Overseas Development Institute).

WIDSTRAND, C. (1990), 'Evaluation and the Illusion of Knowledge', paper presented to the EADI Workshop on Approaches and Methods in the Evaluation of Aid (Oslo: European Association of Development Research and Training Institutes; mimeo).

WILLIAMS, A. (1990), 'A Growing Role for NGOs in Development', *Finance and Development*, 27/4 (Dec.), 31–3.

WOOD, G. D. (1994), 'Rural Development in Bangladesh: Whose Framework?', in *Bangladesh: Whose Ideas, Whose Interests?* (London: Intermediate Technology), 127–51.

WORLD BANK (1988), *Rural Development: World Bank Experience, 1965–86* (Washington, DC: World Bank, Operations Evaluation Department).

——(1989), *India: Poverty, Employment and Social Services* (Washington, DC: World Bank).

——(1990a), *World Development Report 1990* (Oxford: World Bank/Oxford University Press).

——(1990b), *Poverty and Public Expenditures: An Evaluation of the Impact of Selected Government Programmes* (Washington, DC: World Bank, Asia Country Department).

——(1990c), *Making Adjustment Work for the Poor* (Washington, DC: World Bank).

——(1991a), *World Development Report 1991* (Oxford: World Bank/Oxford University Press).

——(1991b), *Assistance Strategies to Reduce Poverty: A World Bank Policy Paper* (Washington, DC: World Bank).

——(1992), *Poverty Handbook, Discussion Draft* (Washington, DC: World Bank).

——(1994), *World Development Report 1994* (Oxford: World Bank/Oxford University Press).

——(1995), *World Debt Tables: External Finance for Developing Countries 1994–95*, i. *Analysis and Summary Tables* (Washington: The World Bank).

GLOSSARY

arrack locally brewed alcoholic drink
gram sabha village association
harijan former untouchables
kammas dominant rural caste
khas unused, government-held land
kraal kinship group
lanka river island
mahila mandalis women's association
mandal administrative division
mushandirapamwe working together
nhimbe shared labour
panchayat village council
samabaya samiti co-operative *samiti*
samiti co-operative group
sangam village association
upazila territorial sub-district
zamindar member of pre-Independence rural élite

INDEX